Research Methods f Interior Design

Interior design has shifted significantly in the past fifty years from a focus on home decoration within family and consumer sciences to a focus on the impact of health and safety within the interior environment. This shift has called for a deeper focus in evidence-based research for interior design education and practice.

Research Methods for Interior Design provides a broad range of qualitative and quantitative examples, each highlighted as a case of interior design research. Each chapter is supplemented with an in-depth introduction, additional questions, suggested exercises, and additional research references. The book's subtitle, *Applying Interiority*, identifies one reason why the field of interior design is expanding, namely, all people wish to achieve a subjective sense of well-being *within* built environments, even when those environments are not defined by walls. The chapters of this book exemplify different ways to comprehend interiority through clearly defined research methodologies.

This book is a significant resource for interior design students, educators, and researchers in providing them with an expanded vision of what interior design research can encompass.

Dana E. Vaux, PhD, is Associate Professor of Interior and Product Design at University of Nebraska Kearney. Her interdisciplinary scholarship investigates the connections between cultural-historical meanings and place.

David Wang, PhD, is Professor Emeritus of Architecture at Washington State University. He has published extensively on design research, most notably, with Linda Groat, *Architectural Research Methods*, 2nd edition, 2013.

Research Methods for Interior Design

Applying Interiority

Edited by Dana E. Vaux and David Wang

NEW YORK AND LONDON

First published 2021
by Routledge
52 Vanderbilt Avenue, New York, NY 10017

and by Routledge
2 Park Square, Milton Park, Abingdon, Oxon, OX14 4RN

Routledge is an imprint of the Taylor & Francis Group, an informa business

Library of Congress Cataloging-in-Publication Data
Names: Vaux, Dana E., editor. | Wang, David, 1954– editor.
Title: Research methods for interior design: applying interiority /
edited by Dana E. Vaux and David Wang.
Description: New York, NY: Routledge, 2020. | Includes bibliographical references and index.
Identifiers: LCCN 2020008943 (print) | LCCN 2020008944 (ebook) |
ISBN 9780367139445 (hardback) | ISBN 9780367139490 (paperback) |
ISBN 9780429029325 (ebook)
Subjects: LCSH: Interior decoration—Research—Methodology.
Classification: LCC NK2116.4 R47 2020 (print) | LCC NK2116.4 (ebook) |
DDC 729.072—dc23
LC record available at https://lccn.loc.gov/2020008943
LC ebook record available at https://lccn.loc.gov/2020008944

ISBN: 978-0-367-13944-5 (hbk)
ISBN: 978-0-367-13949-0 (pbk)
ISBN: 978-0-429-02932-5 (ebk)

Typeset in Univers
by codeMantra

Contents

Contributors

Erin Cunningham, PhD, is Assistant Professor in the Department of Interior Design at the University of Florida. Her research focuses on the history and preservation of 19th- and 20th-century interior spaces, including social settlement houses, vernacular architecture and public housing interiors.

Ozgur Gocer, PhD, is Lecturer at the University of Sydney in the Department of Architecture, Design and Planning. Her research expertise relates to GIS-based post-occupancy evaluation (POE) studies in outdoor and indoor environments, workspace design and climate responsive design.

Tasoulla Hadjiyanni, PhD, is Northrop Professor of Interior Design at the University of Minnesota. Hadjiyanni's driver is the belief that design can be leveraged for innovation and change to create culturally enriched, healthy and connected communities in which everyone can thrive.

Saleh Kalantari, PhD EDAC, is Assistant Professor in Cornell University's Department of Design and Environmental Analysis. He is the director of the Design and Augmented Intelligence Lab (DAIL) at Cornell, where his research group investigates the effects and opportunities of human–technology interactions in design and fabrication.

Ebru Ergoz Karahan, PhD, is Associate Professor of Architecture at Ozyegin University, Istanbul. Sustainable housing, occupant/user behavior, housing demand and project management are among her research interests. She is the founder and one of the coordinators of a working group at European Network for Housing Research.

Andrew Kudless is the Bill Kendall Memorial Endowed Professor in the College of Architecture and Design at the University of Houston. His creative work explores the emergent relationships between architecture, engineering, biology and computation.

Michael R. Langlais, PhD, is Assistant Professor in the Department of Educational Psychology at the University of North Texas. His research focuses on promoting healthy romantic relationship development, particularly the role that technology plays within those processes.

Bryan D. Orthel, PhD, is Associate Professor in the Eskenazi School of Art, Architecture + Design at Indiana University Bloomington. His scholarship focuses on perceptions and use of history and preservation, as well as the scholarship of teaching and learning for design.

Isil Oygur, PhD, is Assistant Professor of Industrial Design at Ozyegin University, Turkey. Her research interests focus on design anthropology, digital interactions, user-centered design and the scholarship of teaching and learning.

Jill Pable, PhD, is Professor and Chair of the Interior Architecture & Design Department at Florida State University. Her research focuses on the design of environments for disadvantaged people and especially places that help people exit homelessness effectively. She facilitates *Design Resources for Homelessness*, a non-profit knowledge resource.

Alana Pulay, PhD, is Assistant Professor in the School of Design + Construction at Washington State University. Her research and professional practice center around learning environments and include over sixteen years' involvement with architecture and engineering firms specializing in the design of sustainable K-12 schools.

Lisa Tucker, PhD, is Professor and Chair for Interior Design at Virginia Tech and teaches courses on sustainable design and upper-level design studios. She is a LEED BD + C and WELL accredited professional. Dr. Tucker is a registered architect and certified interior designer.

Dana E. Vaux, PhD, is Associate Professor of Interior & Product Design at University of Nebraska Kearney. Her interdisciplinary scholarship investigates connections between cultural-historical meanings and place.

David Wang, PhD, is Professor Emeritus of Architecture at Washington State University. He has published extensively on design research, most notably, with Linda Groat, *Architectural Research Methods*, 2nd edition, 2013.

Acknowledgments

Dana E. Vaux:

This book developed out of a need in my own classroom for a research methods book specific to interiors. How to inspire our next generation of designers—many of whom will enter the profession after earning a bachelor's degree—to understand the importance of research-informed design and, even more importantly, how to conduct research with the potential to inform design? Many excellent research methods books exist; however, I found it unwieldy to adapt them to a semester course at a "first look" level. Five years later, the results are many student projects based on primary research—and this book.

The subtitle to this book, "Applying Interiority," is a response to a long-standing call in interior design literature to consider the context of "interior." As we note in the Introduction, an interior does not exist apart from something else. The interconnectedness of interiors with broader social, cultural and physical contexts highlights the importance of this term for interior designers.

First and foremost, I want to thank David Wang. I continue to learn from him and am grateful for the opportunity to work with him on this project. His experience and expertise have made all the difference. I am thankful for his steadfastness and encouragement from the first idea to the final period. Many thanks to our contributing authors for their collegiality, scholarship and diligence in meeting deadlines as well as patience with numerous revisions. I also want to thank my colleagues Sylvia Asay and Mickey Langlais for contributing their expertise with invaluable feedback at opportune moments. Thanks also to Sarah Urquhart and Teegan Nordhues for reading and editing content when we needed an objective eye. Most of all, I must thank my husband Jim for his unwavering support. Finally, I want to thank my students who continually inspire me with their creativity and fresh perspectives. The heart of this book developed out of our work together.

David Wang:

Thanks first goes to my colleague Dana Vaux for putting this book together. Producing a book is an academic's version of running a marathon, with ups and downs along the way. Dana's dedication was unwavering throughout, keeping us on pace, and always well hydrated with good humor and collegiality. I greatly appreciated working with her. And this being an edited volume, we had company along the way. Thanks to all the contributors who worked hard to make this book possible. The domain of design research continues to grow, and each contributor should be proud for playing a part in this effort. Lastly, for me, whenever I publish works on research methods, I am grateful to Linda Groat at the University of Michigan. She first mentored me to see that design research applies to much larger concerns than physical buildings. All of our life experiences take place *in* built settings. In this sense, design research by its very nature concerns itself with interior realities.

Introduction

Dana E. Vaux and David Wang

Interior designers often work with allied disciplines and integrate knowledge from other fields of study. Indeed, the interdisciplinary nature of what a designer needs to know is inherent in all the design professions. A team of prominent interior design researchers recently made this point:

> As the design of interior spaces becomes more complex, the role of conducting and understanding original research is becoming an increasingly essential part of the design process. The 2014 CIDA Future Vision Report called designers to: "Guide design decisions through an understanding of research methods and findings". Yet, with the increased demand for higher standards and more skills, students in undergraduate interior design programs often lack time and opportunity to generate original research, understand its nuances, and apply findings to design solutions.[1]

The aim of this book is to provide, at least in part, an answer to this need. The interior design profession is indeed growing in complexity. Advancements in the healthcare, commercial, retail, hospitality, education and entertainment industries—to mention just a few—all challenge designers to rethink spatial planning. Innovations in virtual reality and computational design are revolutionizing design thinking itself. These developments underline the need for interior designers to stay current with increasing amounts of *generalizable* design knowledge. One challenge designers have in learning about research methods is we are trained to produce one-of-a-kind creative solutions. But an ability to generate knowledge applicable across many projects is what experience with research methodologies can provide. This book introduces readers and students to a sampling of the diverse kinds of generalizable knowledge interior design researchers are generating. As the citation above suggests, "understanding research methods and findings" can inform better creative design solutions, ones that meet the complex and diverse needs of today's clients.

Of course, efforts at integrating design and research have been ongoing. Nigel Cross's lifelong project of clarifying "designerly ways of knowing"[2] is based in rigorous research methods. The journal *Design Studies*, largely through Cross' efforts, continue to be a rich source of examples of design research. The journal *Design Issues* also echo this approach. But we can look closer to home: The *Journal of Interior Design* offers a steady stream of design research fitting comfortably with research protocols all researchers recognize. In *Architectural Research Methods*, also used in the academy for interior design, Linda Groat and David Wang's position is that a deeper grasp of research strategies and tactics across an interdisciplinary array of fields enables better design thinking on the part of designers.[3]

To introduce this book, we first survey standard features common to all research projects, drawing from examples in the chapters to follow. We then clarify what we mean by the subtitle of this book, *applying interiority*. Here, we recount how each chapter touches on a different facet of this rich term—and also how each chapter features the study of this term methodologically. Following this, we describe the organization of this edited volume. In brief, our approach is to "sandwich" each chapter with an Introduction that highlights the chapter's methodological aspect and, at the conclusion of each chapter, provide discussion questions, exercises and suggestions for further reading.

Standard Features of Research

A Research Topic

Identifying a clear topic is the fundamental requirement for any research project. This might seem obvious, but it is often a difficult problem, for two common reasons. First, research topics need to be precise, targeted to answer particular questions. But the tendency for design research students is to state a broad topic—for example: "I want to research sustainable design." This is a domain rather than a topic. Research topics within the domain of sustainable design are endless. A broad statement such as, "I want to research sustainable design" is a non-starter as a research topic. Consider in contrast the title of Chapter 3, by Erin Cunningham: "Narratives of Healing: The Records of the Visiting Nurse Service of New York in the Era of the Great Depression." The exact description of a topic is the reason why titles of research projects are often long. In Cunningham's title, we are told of a certain methodological focus: *narratives* of healing. We are given a particular period of time, and the work of a particular agency as recorded in archival records. The researcher still has to define what she means by narratives of healing; but the title tells us clearly what to expect.

Literature

It is probably impossible to identify a research topic, and then to know how to develop it through to generalizable findings, without literature. At surface level, literature simply denotes the many sources of information already on offer in the domain within which the researcher's topic resides, and within which the outcomes of the research project, if successful, *will* reside. In other words: research topics come out of familiarity with literature, and research results contribute to literature. But *how* does "the literature" help identify a research topic and provide information on how to develop it?

First, the literature helps the researcher familiarize him- or herself with the domain of knowledge related to her research topic: its general scope, its history, its key ideas, how those key ideas have changed either due to new knowledge within the domain, who the leading idea-shapers are and so on. The *primary* literature is the material contributed by leading thinkers who gave shape to the overall domain, and the *secondary* literature come from those who comment on, or add to, the primary ideas in some way. For example, in Chapter 5, Bryan Orthel recalls Martin Heidegger's theory of what "a thing" is. He also cites Ian Hodder's expansion of this notion of "thing." In this case, Heidegger is the primary source, and Hodder is a secondary source.

Second, the literature helps the researcher to group complementary and/or competing schools of thought within the domain. As well, the literature allows the researcher to see where gaps exist in this domain, gaps that his or her research can target. Consider an example from Chapter 2, "Understanding User Experience within Flexible Workplaces: An Ethnographic Approach." Here, Isil Oygur and her colleagues identify a theme in the literature, a "three-dimensional" classification (instrumental, aesthetic and symbolic) in how employees respond to artifacts in their work environments. Oygur's team noticed the opportunity to expand this theory by analyzing workers' *overall* perceptions of their office venues in general. This research represents an addition to the literature, because it addresses a question that was unanswered prior to their study. (But notice how the topic came out of familiarity with the existing literature.)

Indeed, to help students familiarize themselves with the chapters of this book, a warm-up exercise might be to survey each chapter and identify the literature that informed the chapter: What domain does the literature come from? Does the chapter integrate literature from several domains (which is common for interdisciplinary research topics)? Who are some of the primary sources? What kinds of secondary sources are cited?

Most beginning researchers think that "the literature" is something that is only relevant at the beginning of a research project. This is not true at all.[4] Information from "the literature" speaks to all stages of a research project as it is in process. As noted above, it gives shape to the topic. But specific literature is needed for particular facets of a project, some related to the topic itself, some related to neighboring domains. For instance, refer to Chapter 8, which features Jill Pable's sustained research into environments for the homeless. Without drawing from the *psychology* literature, she would not be able to conduct her inquiry and derive design guidelines for future facilities. Also, some literature is related not so much to a particular research topic *but to the research methods that fit that particular topic*. This book, for example, can easily fall into this category of literature for design researchers.

Additionally, researchers often use the terms "literature review" or "annotated bibliography." These terms are closely related. Some research papers have a "literature review" section, in which the author summarizes the pertinent literature related to his research topic, specifically how his topic emerged out of that literature. Now, the process that enables a researcher to report a literature review comes from an *annotated bibliography*. Nobody ever publishes annotated bibliographies as part of their research report because they are a specific research tool that helps the researcher think through his many literature sources. An entry in an annotated bibliography usually consists of: (a) the complete reference of the source, in either APA or Chicago format; (b) a paragraph summarizing the key points of the reference; and (c) a paragraph in which the researcher explains to himself how this particular reference helps him in formulating his research topic. We revisit annotated bibliography in the "Discussion and Exercises" sections of Chapters 8 and 12.

Methodology and Data: The Engine of a Research Project

So far, we have a research topic; we need to know the relevant literature; and we know that our research outcomes must be generalizable. But how do we get from the topic to the outcomes? Think of getting to your destination (i.e., getting your research outcomes) by driving a beautiful automobile. You are all packed and ready to go (i.e., you have a topic; you have relevant literature; you even know about generalizability)—only to find that your car has no engine. You can perhaps imagine what your destination looks like, but you never actually get there. The simple problem is that your car has no engine, which is to say that your research thinking is missing a methodology.

What do we need methodological engines for? We need them to generate *data*. Generally, data is what literature will *not* give us.[5] This is because data is original raw material a research project produces. It is this data that is in turn analyzed by the researcher to produce the research outcomes. This is why research outcomes are usually considered *new* knowledge, because it came out of original data the researcher produced and then analyzed by using the proper research engine (read: the relevant research method).

There are different kinds of research method engines. For example, *experiment* is the most widely respected research engine; almost all of the physical and engineering sciences use experimental research. Saleh Kalantari's research (Chapter 11) uses experimental tactics in simulating occupant responses to classroom settings; the Introduction to that chapter explains experimental research further. In the first of her series of studies reported in Chapter 8, Jill Pable also uses a tactic from experimental research (called a control group).

And then, there are many different kinds of *qualitative* research engines. Design research often uses qualitative research methods because this kind of engine helps us get data about human behavior in real-time social environments. In this book, Chapters 1, 2, 3, and 5 all *primarily* feature qualitative engines of varying kinds to generate data.

Between the experimental and qualitative varieties of research methods is *correlation*. This kind of engine generates statistically significant relationships between two variables. In Chapter 9 Alana Pulay seeks to correlate (a) classroom lighting with (b) teacher performance. Here, note that the goal is to isolate quantitative measures usually associated with experimental research, to understand qualitative elements of human behavior in real-time settings. Pulay's chapter demonstrates just how subtle (and challenging) this kind of research can be. Relatedly, Chapter 10 features Michael Langlais and Dana Vaux's research in correlating multiple factors as one step in creating a scale that measures whether or not virtual meeting places, such as Facebook, have the same "third place feel" of physical social venues like cafes.

In sum, this book provides readers with 12 samples of research methodologies as "engines to get there," that is, ways and means to obtain research outcomes: (1) interviews through focus groups, (2) design ethnography, (3) narrative inquiry, (4) adaptive reuse, (5) oral history, (6) philosophical method, (7) logical argumentation, (8) mixed methods, (9) correlation, (10) scale creation, (11) simulation and (12) creative scholarship. In each chapter, note the kinds of data being produced by the research method, and also how that data is then interpreted to attain the outcomes.

Generalizability

We mentioned this term in the opening paragraph. Suppose we are asked to design a classroom. We designers tend to begin with figural sketches, bubble diagrams and the like, on our way to answering the needs of the design program. There is nothing wrong with this, but note that solving design problems is action oriented. Design decisions often focus on answering *what-to-do* questions; that is, our design decisions are based on convictions of value about what *ought* to be done in designing a classroom. In contrast, research topics usually involve *what-is-the-case* questions. Given a classroom project, what are ten exemplars of classroom design in the literature that can yield guidelines for the design of *this* classroom? Note that we still must solve the design problem. But armed with answers from what-is-the-case research on those ten other classrooms, we have *generalizable* information that can apply to the design of this classroom. Now consider the title of Chapter 11, Saleh Kalantari's "Biometric Data and Virtual Response Testing in a Classroom Design." Note that Kalantari is not focused on designing this or that classroom. Armed with biometric and virtual response data from his study, we can design *any* classroom aided by his findings. This is the power of generalizability in research. This leads to the related theme of *validity*.

Internal and External Validity

In their book *The Designer's Guide to Doing Research*, Sally Augustin and Cindy Coleman define these terms as follows: "Internal validity describes the logical consistency of the reasoning within a study ... while external validity is the extent to which study findings can reasonably be applied in the real world. They are generalizable."[6] To give a well-used example, if a researcher discovers that "everyone who eats ice cream eventually dies," there is obviously some logical inconsistency in the internal workings of her methods. People who never eat ice cream also die. So, in turn, there is not really any applicability of this "finding" to other venues. In other words, the research has no external validity. As Augustin and Coleman properly note, it has no generalizability.

Some years ago, Edmund Morris wrote a history of U.S. President Ronald Reagan in which he, Morris, inserts himself into Reagan's life story as a fictional character.[7] By most standards of history research, this was quite controversial. It raises questions of internal and external validity. Internally, the logic of the account is muddled, because if we were to go back in time to those settings, we would not find Edmund Morris in them.[8] As well, we have little confidence to recommend this book to students learning about Reagan's presidency (at least it should not be the only book on the reading list). Why? Because of the lack of external validity of this biography, as attested to by the critics of this book.[9]

The English historian and philosopher R.G. Collingwood once made the point that any valid historical account must fit into "the one historical world."[10] This was his way of saying that historical narratives cannot be fictional ones; they must possess a logical coherence that can be verified by, among other tools, archival evidence. What the historian writes must, to the best of his or her ability, completely jibe with factors and events outside of that history but is nevertheless part of the world in which that history took place.

In sum, research protocols which cannot be replicated have little internal validity. And they also have little external validity because we cannot generalize (or apply) those findings with confidence to other similar settings.

Applying Interiority

Towards the end of the 20th century, a technical term increased in prominence in the interior design literature: *interiority*. Here is C.J. Hewlett, who wrote in 1985:

> Interiority, as a design solution, itemizes the tiers of awareness to which we respond, and these include our aspirations, functions, individualism, myths, place, structure, who, why and probably others.[11]

Hewlett's position was that the task of interior design is not simply to arrange objects in physical arrays for visual effect or human function, but rather embrace realities such as myths, aspirations and individualisms. These are not empirically measurable factors. This is the first distinction of interiority: it is not limited to *physical* interiors, meaning spaces enclosed by walls. Interior spaces demarked by walls are numerically measurable, whether by dimension, size, acoustical properties, flame spread rating and so on. But *interiority* as it is now commonly used in the literature transcends these physical constraints. Yes, measurable factors play a role in issues related to interiority; but if interiority includes aspirations, myths and individualisms, it necessarily embraces subjective human experience in an existential sense.

In 2011, Petra Perolini wrote, "There is a need for a transformation of what is taught in creating an understanding of interiority, inner minds, and inner dwellings, the working of consciousness and cultural difference."[12] Perolini goes on to define interiority as "a process *within* a person that reflects an individual's unique awareness of the world and a psychological relationship to the world that is meaningful" (italics added).[13] In this vein, writing in 1999, Cathy Ganoe's proposal for a narrative design method for interior design also cites Hewlett's call for interiority, which she simply defines as "internal values regarding social and personal awareness."[14] And Suzie Attiwill, writing in 2012, suggests, "Highlighting interior design as the *designing* of interiors focuses on ... potential new ways of thinking what is an interior, how is an interior, and when is an interior."[15]

Other examples in the recent literature concur. Jacqueline Power promotes "urban interiors" as an emerging area of research. Power examines villages of the indigenous Palawa peoples of Australia, arguing that the standard receptions of "interior" as spaces behind walls simply do not hold for this non-European culture. And so: "The concept of interiority has been proposed as a framework through which to expand the definition of interior ... (as) a means of engagement that is not necessarily attached to buildings."[16]

For our purposes, Chapter 1 of this book, in which Tasoulla Hadjiyanni examines the interiority experienced by residents in three Minneapolis neighborhoods, certainly echoes Power's understanding of "urban interiors." Interiority not only increases the scale of interior design toward landscapes; it also embraces the miniature. In explaining her Best of Show entry in the 2009 IDEC awards, Andrea Mina explains that her miniature constructions assert interiority because an encounter with her miniatures can bring about a sense of inhabitation.[17]

Our strategy for this book, then, is as follows. Editing a book "merely" on various research methodologies related to interior design can itself be too broad, on the one hand. On the other hand, the size limitations of this book suggested the need for a particular focus for the kinds of chapters we solicited—even though we wanted the types of research methodologies to be diverse. The solution was to focus on interiority as a thematic thread that weaves through the chapters. The result is an edited volume that adds to the discourse on interiority but in a way that provides readers with a variety of methodological approaches, all of which feature different facets of this technical term. Taken as a whole, the chapters provide an overall theoretical profile for what interiority entails but accessed methodologically. Here is a brief overview of the facets of interiority the contributors to this volume address:

Chapter 1 uncovers the interiority experienced by three minority cultural groups at the scale of their neighborhoods, with an emphasis on health. Tasoulla Hadjiyanni writes: "Reframing current discourses around neighborhoods and health from the perspective of interiority expands the types of questions that can be asked." The methodological tool here is the use of *focus groups*.

Chapter 2 is an example of how *ethnographic* research conducted in a large office environment allows us to see daily life through the users' eyes. Isil Oygur and her colleagues' term this "*felt* interiority." They write: "*in situ* participation builds rapport, which allows the participant observer to gain empathy with users and provide insights into the subjective details of their experiences. This is essential to gain insight into the felt interiority of Firma employees."

Chapter 3 contrasts with the previous two chapters which use on-the-ground methods in "real time." Here, Erin Cunningham accesses interiority from historical archives. Through *narrative inquiry* of visiting nurse documentation, Cunningham attempts to access Perolini's description of interiority (on the part of the tenement occupants) as workings of "inner minds, and inner dwellings, the working of consciousness and cultural difference."

Chapter 4 applies *historical research* methods for the purpose of an adaptive reuse project. The focus here is adapting a historic home dating from 1835 for use as a Bed & Breakfast. For Lisa Tucker, the key challenge for any adaptive reuse project is how to create the new while retaining the presence of the past in a continuous expression of the life of the structure. Interiority here has to do with maintaining this sense of historical continuity, so that designer and experiencer both reside within a "package of sense" that retains a phenomenological preservation of the past in the present.

Chapter 5 draws from Martin Heidegger's theory of "thingly-ness." Bryan Orthel weaves this philosophical principle with on-the-ground *oral history*. Through this, he argues his view that history—quite different from the common assumption that it is "fixed" like a museum display—is in fact "living and moving." This living and moving aspect of experiences of historical artifacts provides another facet of interiority at both the personal as well as communal levels.

Chapter 6 proposes that each cultural period has its own overall "Common Sense." David Wang suggests that it is *within* the cultural Common Sense that designers generate their creative productions, as they imbibe its values and transform those values into built environments. As the interiority of the Common Sense changes through time as cultures change through time, the designs of home interiors express these changes. This chapter features tactics of *philosophical* method: the search for first principles and how these principles in turn find expression in design.

Chapter 7 propounds the theory of Ethos-Intensive Objects (EIOs). Dana Vaux uses *logical argumentation* as a method to show that a locality's sense of place is profoundly linked to objects that are ethos intensive to that locale. EIOs, then, are not just physical objects; they are ethos intensive precisely because they unite the *internal* experiential gestalt of local residents with material objects, cultural practices and stories that together give a locale its distinctive cultural character. EIOs are a new way to appraise related theories of sense of place through the lens of interiority.

Chapter 8 answers this question: If interiority as defined in the previous chapter relates to a sense of belonging, how can design interventions help those for whom there are no EIOs to provide them with this larger sense of "home"? In a thematically linked series of studies over nine years, Jill Pable uses *mixed methods* to answer this question for an important demographic: the homeless. Within her mixed methods approach are statistical tactics, which the following two chapters foreground.

Chapter 9 uses *correlation* to discern if there is a significant relationship between classroom lighting and teachers' performance levels. Earlier we cited Perolini's view of interiority as having to do with "an individual's unique awareness of the world and a psychological relationship to the world that is meaningful." Alana Pulay uses statistical correlation to understand a teacher's subjective commitments to the task of teaching correlated to classroom lighting.

Chapter 10 also uses statistics. But here, Michael Langlais and Dana Vaux use this quantitative tool to *create a scale* and then apply it to measure the thirdplaceness of social networking sites. Social networking sites (SNS) have proliferated since Ray Oldenburg developed his theory of physical third places (cafes, barbershops, etc.) in the 1980s. Langlais and Vaux derived a scale of third place characteristics that updates Oldenburg's original framework. In this chapter they report how they tested this scale in analyzing four virtual SNS platforms: Facebook, Snapchat, Instagram and Twitter. Interiority here has to do with how people experience sense of belonging in virtual third places.

Chapter 11 also works with the virtual, in the form of augmented reality. Saleh Kalantari conducts *simulation* research to test-drive a "toolset" to measure occupant responses to classrooms before those physical settings are actually built. Kalantari envisions an online platform for this toolset that makes it available for simulating occupant responses to all sorts of environments during the design phase. What emerges is that, when it comes to the virtual, interiority takes on an added dimension in unifying subjective response to built environments prior to their construction.

Chapter 12 demonstrates how the *creative design* process can itself be a research method. This chapter features three creative design projects by Andrew Kudless. All three use computational design conjoined with traditional handcrafting or human participation to achieve organic expressions of form. By organic, Kudless means to create physical forms *from the inside* of the generative process, as natural processes would. In this sense the human maker is more of a participant than the cause of the generation. This is the concluding chapter of this curated collection because we think of it not as an ending, but rather a beginning, to the emerging reality of computational design—considered methodologically. As well, this chapter links the realms of design and research in general by searching for common ground.

The Structure of the Book: Chapter "Sandwiches"

The contributors to this book were asked to write on their areas of research, focusing on their topic and findings. In this context, a contributor may address elements of method, as is often the case with published research. *But the contributions are not themselves on methodology.* The methodological focus comes from the Introduction to each chapter, followed by a back section titled "Discussions and Exercises." These back sections are additionally divided into "Reflections about the Chapter You Just Read"; "Exercises/Suggestions for Further Study" and "Additional Connections and Information." (As a general note, for any exercises suggested in this book that involve interactions with humans please check with the appropriate Institutional Review Board (IRB).) In brief, the approach is to "sandwich" each contribution with front and back sections that focus on methodology. It is the 12 front and back sections of the chapters that serve as the methodological thread weaving this book together.

This also applies to interiority. While the contributors were aware of this theme as the *theoretical* thread weaving through the chapters, they were not asked to write about interiority specifically. Again, each author addresses his or her own research interest. For some, interiority is explicit. In others interiority is only implicitly present. Here again, it is the front and back sections of each chapter that highlight this theoretical theme.

Notes

1 Lisa Waxman, Amy Huber, Stephanie Clemons, and Lena McLane, "Research by Design: Linking Student Researchers with Industry Needs," 2016 *Interior Design Educators Council Annual Conference*, Portland, OR. www.idec.org/i4a/pages/index.cfm?pageID=4142. Accessed November 11, 2019.
2 Nigel Cross, *Designerly Ways of Knowing* (New York: Springer, 2006).
3 Linda Groat and David Wang, *Architectural Research Methods,* second edition (New York: John Wiley & Sons, 2013), 21–61.
4 For more on this point, see Groat and Wang, op. cit., 151–166.
5 Arguably, an exception might be meta-analysis of a large body of literature on a particular topic. But meta-analysis is itself a rigorous research protocol usually using statistical methods. So, the immediate collection of common themes in the literature still must be tactically arranged before the data emerges.
6 Sally Augusin and Cindy Coleman, *The Designer's Guide to Doing Research: Applying Knowledge to Inform Design* (New York: John Wiley & Sons, 2012), 27.
7 Edmund Morris, *Dutch: A Memoir of Ronald Reagan* (New York: Random House, 2000).
8 "Perhaps the book's salient characteristic … is Morris's insertion of himself into Reagan's life. Early in the book, for example, he places himself at the 1920 Chicago Aeronautical Exposition – an obvious fiction, since Morris was born in 1940." Linton Weeks, "In 'Dutch,' Biography With a Twist," *Washington Post*, September 22, 1999, p. A1; www.washingtonpost.com/wp-srv/style/features/daily/reagan092299.htm?noredirect=on. Accessed January 24, 2019.
9 See also John O'Sullivan, "Not the Authorized Biography," in *National Review Online*; www.nationalreview.com/2004/06/not-authorized-biography-john-osullivan/. Accessed February 14, 2019.
10 R.G. Collingwood, *The Idea of History* (Oxford: Oxford University Press, 1956), 246.
11 C. J. Hewlett, "The Future in Interior Design." *Journal of Interior Design* 11, no. 1 (1985): 11.
12 Petra Simona Perolini, "Interior Spaces and the Layers of Meaning," *Design Principles and Practices* 5, no. 6 (2011): 169.
13 Ibid., 170.
14 Cathy J. Ganoe, "Design as Narrative: A Theory of Inhabiting Interior Space," *Journal of Interior Design*, 25, no. 2 (1999): 1–15 (1).
15 Suzie Attiwill, "Practices of Interiorization: An Inter-Story," in *Meanings of Designed Spaces,* ed. Tiiu Vaikla-Poldma, 175-184. (New York: Fairchild Books, 2012), 175.
16 Ibid., 19.
17 Andrea Mina, "Intimate Immensities Miniatures, An Interior Architecture," *Journal of Interior Design* 35, no. 1 (2009): 33–35 (35).

Chapter 1

Focus Groups

Editors' Introduction by Dana E. Vaux and David Wang

In this chapter, Tasoulla Hadjiyanni seeks to understand the subjective outlooks of residents of three different cultural groups (Native Americans, African Americans and Somalis) as they live in their distinctive neighborhoods in the city of Minneapolis. Her primary research method is the use of focus groups. Interviews in focus groups allow design researchers to understand and gather data from the perspectives of the people they are designing for. Interviews provide the researcher with an opportunity to ask open-ended questions that may lead to information not related to the original question. Interviews allow the researcher to observe non-verbal cues, such as body language and tone of voice. However, a focus group interview is not simply a conversation or discussion. As a research method, a qualitative interview follows a specific, pre-developed plan for asking questions and recording answers.[1] Figure 1.1 "on page 12" shows Hadjiyanni's interview guide, which she developed prior to conducting her focus groups.

An interview can be with an individual or with a group of individuals. They can be informal or formal relative to the specific protocol of predetermined steps and questions, and the role of the researcher. John Creswell classifies interviews into four types: face-to-face, by telephone, by email, (these three types solicit individual answers to questions), and focus groups in which the researcher interviews participants in a group.[2] Each type of interview emphasizes a variety of techniques.

The research conducted in this chapter utilized *focus groups* to understand how individuals feel about their neighborhood in relationship to health. As an interview technique for gathering research data, the term "focus groups" evolved from a specific interview procedure developed by sociologists to inhibit the use of leading questions by interviewers/researchers. Merton, Kendall and Fiske further developed the semi-structured, qualitative process of focused interviews for social science research.[3] They also made a clear distinction between focused interviews, which they developed for the purpose of scientific inquiry, and focus groups, developed primarily for market research to understand public opinion of products, services and advertising methods.[4] They conducted the interviews primarily with groups; thus, the term "focus groups" eventually became associated with semi-directed group interviews conducted for research purposes based on the process they outline. This is apparent in the strong similarity between current focus group practices and Merton et al.'s original description.[5] While Merton intended to differentiate the term "focus interview" from the term "focus group," over time the two became synonymous and the term "focus group" became the widely accepted phrase.

Ideally, a focus group is 8–12 individuals and encompasses multiple groups for generalizability (three sessions is a good number). Krueger and King provide a list of characteristics to avoid in focus groups that include groups with erratic attendance—too many or too few people—groups with open invitations for the general public and groups that are perceived as threatening by participants.[6] If the group is too small, one voice may dominate; if the group is too large, this may also limit responses as some participants may be reluctant to speak out in a larger group. In a study on Facebook use among Mexican American adolescents, Rueda, Lindsay and Williams note that homogeneity across focus groups is preferable when the intention is to provide minority voices the opportunity to dialogue about sensitive topics among others of perceived similarity. We see the same method used in this chapter with the similar ethnicity among participants in each respective neighborhood.[7] Interview questions asked in focus groups need to be consistent across groups, and have consistent attendees. Also, demographics should be similarly maintained across groups (i.e., groups that are all one gender vs. mixed gender). The responses, which are considered "raw data," are sorted into themes that are then connected to established research findings or models to further define the research question. Are the findings similar or not? Do they further the model or provide evidence against it? Why and how?

The introductions to the chapters in this book will typically include some prompts for readers to note as they read. So, as you read this chapter:

1. Note how focus groups can provide rich, in-depth information that is not available through a survey.[8] A survey might be useful for gathering demographic information of focus group participants prior to the first meeting. In this way, it can generate both qualitative and quantitative data and provide prompts to the researcher for open-ended questions during a focus group.
2. Note also how a focus group setting itself can create a synergism among study participants as members of the group engage in an interplay of agreement and disagreement through conversation. However, the synergism can also result in wayward conversation that has nothing to do with the research questions. Therefore, it is important to manage focus groups without stifling the conversation and direction.
3. The researcher must come to a focus group well prepared. On the one hand, she must know what she is looking for when writing her questions. On the other hand, she must be careful not to *prod* her respondents to give answers that might not be their own "natural" views. In this chapter, note what preparation Hadjiyanni made prior to conducting her focus groups. She had a well-defined research topic: how residents in three culturally distinct neighborhoods feel about their locales in issues related to health. She also knew specific details about each neighborhood: its location, the quality of the location, population and demographic information, each neighborhood's history and so on. She then came to each focus group with what Ziesel calls an interview guide.[9] This is the preplanned set of questions, but preplanned in a way that would allow open-ended conversation between researcher and respondents. Hadjiyanni's interview guide for the Somali neighborhood is shown in Figure 1.1. Note how the research guide is written in a conversational manner.

Interview Guide used for this research for the Somali community (it is the same for the other two communities).
Permission by Tasoulla Hadjiyanni.

Name of cultural group: ____________________

Place: Time start: Time end: Date:__________

Welcome and thank you for taking the time to join us to talk about culturally sensitive housing and communities. My name is Tasoulla Hadjiyanni and assisting me is Karen James. We're both with the Interior Design program of the University of Minnesota.

We want to get some information from Somali community members about your community's needs. We want to know what you like in your housing and the city, what you don't like, and how these spaces might be improved. We are having discussions like this with several groups around the metro area.

You were invited because you are members of the Somali community and you all live in the metro area. Our discussion will last between 1 ½ - 2 hours. We will be recording the discussion because we don't want to miss any of your comments and we want to be sure that our recording is accurate. People often say very helpful things in these discussions and we can't write fast enough to get them all down. We will be on a first name basis tonight, but we won't use any names in our report. You may be assured of complete confidentiality. Our written report will inform the work of designers, affordable housing providers, and city planners to help them create spaces that meet diverse needs. The audio tape will be destroyed after our report is written.

Before we begin, I want to give a few guidelines.

1. We are looking for your honest thoughts and opinions. There are no wrong answers, only different points of view. Your opinions are important so don't worry if you are the only one who thinks a certain way. Just be sure to listen and respond respectfully as others share their views.
2. We ask that you turn off or silence your phones. If you must respond to a call, please step out and rejoin us as quickly as you can.
3. My role as moderator will be to guide the discussion. I will try to be sure that only one person is speaking at a time and, in order for us to cover all of the questions, I may need to interrupt at times to move the conversation along.
4. Finally, we ask that you do not discuss with others outside this room what others have shared tonight.

Before we begin, do you have any questions about the study or our background? Do you have any questions about the Consent Form?

Let us all take a few minutes and sign the Consent Forms.

Wait until all are signed and answer questions if needed.

Well, let's begin.

Turn on tape recorder.

We've placed name cards on the table in front of you to help us remember each other's names. Let's find out some more about each other by going around the table.

Today, we will be talking about health; by that we mean both physical and emotional health.

1. Tell us your name and one thing that a person can do to be healthy.

Summarize responses – make certain health is framed to range from eating healthy, exercising, having friends and family connections, having less stress, etc

Now, let's talk about the homes in which you live—we will focus on the inside of the home for now.

1. Tell us about one thing in the place where you live now that helps with your health—if there is such a thing.
2. Tell us about one thing in the place where you live now that you feel puts pressure on your health—if there is such a thing.

Now, we would like to talk with you about your neighborhood.

3. Tell us about one thing you like in your neighborhood because it helps with your health—if there is such a thing.
4. Tell us about one thing you do not like in your neighborhood because you feel puts pressure on your health—if there is such a thing.

Now, we would like to talk with you about spaces in the city—they could be anything from the library, to schools, mosques, stores, parks, buses, and even the airport.

5. Which is your favorite space in the city? And, what characteristics make it favorite?
6. Which is your least favorite space in the city? And, what characteristics make it least favorite?

Now, we would like to ask about the needs of others in your community.

7. What would make life in Minneapolis better for the health of Somali elders?
8. What would make life in Minneapolis better for the health of Somali children?

And one last question:

9. Suppose you had one minute to talk to the city planners on planning for housing and city spaces in the future. What would you say is the most important thing that they should plan for to meet the needs of the Somali community?

Before we end tonight, we want to summarize what we have heard to be sure that we understand your main thoughts.

Provide brief summary, using their words and main points.

Have we missed anything?

Thank you for your participation and for all of the comments you have shared with us today. Be sure to get your gift card before you leave.

Figure 1.1 Hadjiyanni's interview guide for the Somali community. (This is a template guide for all three communities.)

Interiority

A common theme throughout this book is that "interior design" is not limited to physically enclosed spaces at the scale of individual buildings. This book's Introduction explained how subjective experiences of "feeling inside" can take place at any scale, and we use the technical term *interiority* to denote this reality. As you read:

1. Consider how this chapter examines interiority at a neighborhood scale, and how this expands interior design's disciplinary reach beyond physical interiors.
2. Note how experiences of interiority can be either positive or negative. So, consider the ways an individual's internal sense of well-being relates to environmental arrangements in the neighborhoods in Hadjiyanni's study, either in a positive *or* negative sense.
3. Consider how traditional cultural ties inform *cross-generationally* with respect to positive or negative feelings of interiority.

The Interview Guide Hadjianni used for this research for the Somali community, which is the same for the other two communities is in Figure 1.1 above.

* * * *

Interiority at the Scale of Neighborhoods: Exploring the Health Experiences of Three Cultural Groups

Tasoulla Hadjiyanni

One challenge that has long limited the scholarship of interior design is the notion that interiors are defined by walls, physical boundaries that delineate a *here* and *there*, an *inside* and an *outside*, a *mine* and *yours*. In contrast, Petra Perolini[10] moves interior design inquiry beyond the material and the visible and encompasses instead the immaterial and the invisible. This expansion of interior design Perolini terms *interiority* and defines it as "a process *within* a person that reflects an individual's unique awareness of the world and a psychological relationship to the world that is meaningful...."[11] Such a conception of interiority allows this present chapter to assess residents' sense of well-being and belonging (or not) at the level of neighborhood scales, and still keep it within an expanded domain of *interior* design. At the neighborhood scale, often borders and barriers are invisible, and yet they can construct and produce difference and inequality. This chapter asks questions such as: How is Perolini's "awareness of the world" shaped at neighborhood scales? What role does spatiality play? And, what are the implications of this understanding for interior design scholars and practitioners?

If we maintain the conception of interiors as a space bounded by walls versus what lies outside those walls, studies at the neighborhood level (for example, relative to health, the concern of this chapter) might seem too far-fetched for interior design scholarship. Indeed, how groups of diverse cultural backgrounds interact with public space has long been the focus of fields such as urban design and policy, anthropology, sociology and geography.[12] As a result, the emphasis has been on what typically would be called "outside," such as streets and parks, corner coffee shops and sidewalks. Explorations of this nature leave much to be understood about the relationship of inside/

outside, that gray area where boundaries blend and dissipate as the private and public realms fuse into one another in human experience. Interior design scholarship can bring added value to this line of research. Reframing current discourses around neighborhoods and health from the perspective of interiority expands the types of questions that can be asked and allows for new methodologies that focus on unearthing the multiple ways by which inside/outside relationships are formed, enriching in the process conceptions of what constitutes interiors and why.

Exacerbating the disconnect between inside/outside is the fact that current studies of neighborhoods and health are primarily quantitative in nature, which does not allow for the nuances behind the multiplicity of factors that make up neighborhoods and notions of health to emerge. The focus is typically on isolating and testing for particular factors, such as walkability and accessibility, green spaces, crime and access to healthy foods.[13] Some aspects of life, however, are hard to quantify and measure, such as religious commitments, perceptions of safety support networks and the presence or lack of social capital.[14] Often, when these factors are accounted for at the neighborhood level, they are not examined with respect to how they fit within the continuum between health and environment. Adopting the perspective of interiority enables scholars to unearth how these factors intertwine and the ways by which they expand or limit a person's and a community's world awareness, revealing a holistic picture of the interiority of neighborhoods and what that entails.

This chapter's premise is that interiority is an experienced spatial construct produced at the intersections of environmental parameters with bodily, social, cultural, religious, historical, political and economic factors. As such, interiority is not a fixed spatial reality; instead, it is a malleable one, one that shrinks and expands, one that is constructed as often as it is deconstructed, one that shapes lives and well-beings in supportive or suppressing ways. It is the concept's relatability and adaptability that makes it suitable for an investigation of how neighborhoods and health inform one another. The personal experiences of a neighborhood's residents can unearth a communal sense of a shared experience, which can in turn inform the development of design interventions that support health and well-being. This chapter terms arriving upon this communal sense "the process of world awareness" and links it to Perolini's concept of interiority while also expanding upon it. Moving from interiority to "interiorities" builds on the concept's plural nature and the multiplicity behind interiority's many facets, giving interior designers more options for explorations and interventions.

The urgency behind such an inquiry is tied to studies that have linked one's ZIP code to that person's life expectancy. In the Twin Cities of Minnesota, for example, residents of the highest-income areas have been found to have an average life expectancy of 82 years, while residents of the lowest-income areas, which often overlap with high concentrations of people of color, have an average life expectancy of 74 years.[15] Projections show that by 2040, almost half of the state's population is expected to be people of color and much of the growth is expected to come from immigrants.[16] As the body of work on the minority/immigrant experience of neighborhoods and health is limited,[17] strengthening conversations around the impact of the built environment on health and well-being, particularly for diverse cultural groups, can inform the work of everyone from interior designers to city planners and public health officials.

This study uses insights from members of three cultural groups living in three different neighborhood types in the Twin Cities to expand discourses around the intersections of neighborhoods and health. The analysis explores how the "process of world awareness" unfolds in the lives of interviewees and the impact of the spatial parameters that intervene on their health and well-being. The study enlarges Perolini's understanding of interiority by adding diverse experiences and dialogues into explorations of the relationship between neighborhoods and health, problematizing the conception between inside/outside and public/private, and expanding the factors that designers need to be considering in their decision-making process.

Methods

This study uses the insights of members from three of the largest cultural groups in Minnesota: Native Americans, African Americans and Somalis. Examining the findings through the lens of interiority propelled us to delve deeper into the intricacies of the relationship between neighborhoods and health, and how a sense of world awareness intimately relates to the creation of *interior* worlds—at the neighborhood scale.

In order to capture the multiplicity of experiences within each of the groups, interviews in focus group settings were conducted in 2012 with community members: 15, 10 and 20 participants, respectively. The study was approved by the University of Minnesota's Institutional Review Board (IRB). All interviewees were over the age of 18 and were invited to join the conversation by community leaders and contacts with community organizations and institutions. The focus groups took place in community settings, making it easier for participants to attend. Food and monetary compensation were offered as incentives for participation.

Interview questions tackled three environmental scales—the home, the neighborhood and the city. The notion of health drew upon the World Health Organization's (WHO) definition of health as "a state of complete physical, social and mental well-being, and not merely the absence of disease or infirmity."[18] Participants were notified of this broad definition of health at the beginning of the focus group interviews and were asked to tell us what a person can do to be healthy; one thing in their home and their neighborhood that helped or put pressure on their health; their favorite and least favorite spaces in the city; what would make life in Minneapolis better for the health of their community's elders and children; and what would they say is the most important thing that a housing or city planner should be thinking about to meet the needs of their community. The qualitative data were transcribed and scanned to identify comments that related information on neighborhood aspects that impacted the health and well-being of those interviewed. A thematic analysis that used the lens of interiority organized findings according to the various parameters mentioned—from air quality to transportation options and community centers.

Discussion: Neighborhoods and Health

All across the board, when asked what a person can do to be healthy, interviewees mentioned activities such as eating healthy foods and exercising as well as feeling safe and having strong social relations. The analysis begins with brief backgrounds for each of the three groups and neighborhoods to help form the discussion's context. A common theme conforms to Perolini's definition of interiority, specifically, that residents' world awareness derives from invisible and immaterial dimensions of meaningfulness in relation to the built environment.

Little Earth Neighborhood—Native American Experiences

Little Earth is a planned urban housing development that includes apartments, townhomes and other amenities, located south of downtown Minneapolis in the East Phillips neighborhood. Little Earth was founded in 1973 to offer affordable housing for the city's Native American population. It is the only Native American preference project-based Section 8 rental assistance community in the United States—"Section 8" is a common name for the Housing Choice Voucher Program, funded by the U.S. Department of Housing and Urban Development. The program allows private landlords to rent apartments and homes at fair market rates to qualified low-income tenants. Currently, the complex has 212 housing units which house over 900 people, 98% of whom are Native Americans.[19] In the neighborhood surrounding Little Earth, 31% of the residents live below poverty compared to 21.3% in the city of Minneapolis.[20]

When asked what helped her to be healthy, a woman spoke of the sense of community that existed at Little Earth. The connections and pride in what constituted her community, and in turn the social aspects that created a sense of interiority, were shared through the story of a time when a little girl was missing, and everyone was looking for her:

> What makes me feel good is that I know everybody. And everybody knows me ... one time, I've seen her baby [another woman's] all the way by the basketball court and she lives all the way in the other cluster. Like probably 300 feet away. So I brought her baby home. Like "whatcha doin all over here by yourself girl?"

Participants credited Little Earth's community center, the setting of the focus group meeting, with its programs for youth and teens as well as adults for helping build those resident connections (Figure 1.2). Located at the entrance to the complex, the community center transformed into the "heart" and lifeline of the community, helping expand residents' awareness of who their neighbors were and where they lived, constructing interiority in a way that supported health and well-being.

A similar vision was noted for Little Earth's community garden. Participants felt that the garden was an opportunity to mingle and build connections across generations as well as to attain access

Figure 1.2 Little Earth's community center.

to healthy foods, strengthening the neighborhood's interior feeling. The women we interviewed held weekly meetings at the community center to plan the garden. Yet, their aspirations were overshadowed by concerns, partly due to the fear of toxins, which threatened to deconstruct Little Earth's sense of community by limiting social interactions and hence keeping people from expanding their world awareness: "Well, we have arsenic, and they say you can't dig so we've been doing a garden and don't dig." New soil had to be brought in and placed on top of the local soil so that the area residents could create the garden they cherished.

Visible threats to the women's efforts to build neighborhood connections were complemented by invisible ones. Watching their children play with dirt in the complex's playground elicited the same uneasy feelings to some moms who ended up choosing not to use the play areas (Figure 1.3). Lack of suitability of the play environments exacerbated these concerns and added to their limited use. As a woman said: "Our kids quit playing football, quit playing a lot of activities because there is no soft grass to fall on, they don't want to get all skunked up." Another woman talked about the needles, syringes and garbage being found in the playground areas. Even the playground equipment for children is unsafe according to this mother: "The swings broke off, it's just the metal." The lack of seating space for adults to watch their children while they play further prevented some mothers from partaking in health-promoting outdoor activities.

Little Earth's sense of interiority was further constructed by perceived "walls" and barriers that were grounded in safety concerns and apprehension about the area parks: "We got four parks!" one of the interviewees exclaimed, but crime concerns affected her ability to utilize parks and other nearby recreational spaces:

> [Violence] It's been pretty much every day. The people that do the crimes, they don't care if there's kids around or not.

Just like other interviewees, the fear of crime shrank this woman's world, instilling in Little Earth an interiority that suppressed her health by preventing her from using the bike paths available around the area to access other parts of the city, localizing her experience of place and impacting her options to engage in health-supporting activities.

Figure 1.3 Little Earth's playground raises safety and comfort concerns.

Figure 1.4 Crossing the bridge or the street can be uncomfortable and dangerous.

Immaterial dimensions of the environment added to these feelings. Along with what is in the ground, interviewees voiced uncertainty about the air quality of their neighborhood. Little Earth is located near a main highway and a commercial district that includes a large paint shop and an asphalt plant. "We breathe all that in," one resident exclaimed. Difficulty in breathing prompted another one to stay inside her home, isolating her and limiting the time she could spend outside, in the neighborhood: "The fumes, the pollution, there is an asphalt plant ... Foundry ... Smells like burnt grilled cheese all day ... it does smell like tar."

The well-being of community elders was another issue that preoccupied the discussion, which sheds light on how the needs of *all* community members, from children to adults, must be accounted in discussions around interiority. As an elder put it: "There is really nothing for us to do. We have one day a week on Tuesday morning where we have bingo and food and that's it." Elders have to leave Little Earth for activities that suit their needs, like the Wisdom Steps [walking club] down at the Indian center at Bloomington and Franklin. But crossing a busy street can be both cumbersome and dangerous for elders, and this kept them bounded and confined, speaking to interiority's bodily dimensions (Figure 1.4):

> You used to have, like 20 seconds to cross and they changed it to like 8 seconds and you gotta run to get across and it's not cool for the elders, because my dad got hit ... by a car ... they say, "oh well use the bridge" [there is a bridge that goes over the busy street]. Well for an elder, it's kind of hard for them to go up the stairs.

These Little Earth experiences point to interiority being a concept that is framed by bodily, social and environmental factors, each moderating how inside/outside intersect at both the home and neighborhood scales.

Rondo Neighborhood—African American Experiences

One of Saint Paul's most historic neighborhoods, the Rondo neighborhood, a thriving African American neighborhood, was severed in the 1950s due to the construction of Interstate 94. The homes of 433 households were demolished, 72% of which were of non-whites.[21] Many of the displaced residents

Figure 1.5 Fences spur feelings of lack of safety.

chose to stay in the neighborhood.[22] Currently, Rondo is part of the Summit-University Neighborhood and is home to approximately 18,707 residents, two-thirds of whom are renters. The median income as of 2016 was $49,485, and 28.7% of the residents are below poverty levels.[23]

A woman longed for the connection and sense of community she felt as a child and pointed to the number of renters as a threat to community togetherness. Who you know and for how long coupled with a feeling of stability and trust are crucial to the construction of interiority:

> [In the past] You couldn't go anywhere without somebody saying "Hey, I know your parents." But now, you don't want to say anything because you might be shot ... This used to be a homeowner area but now it's turning into a transient area because we have more renters in this area than homeowners. And we got the absentee landlords. The people that own the houses don't care; they aren't a part of the neighborhood.

Instability and high turnover of residents prevented neighbors from fostering connections, exacerbating feelings of lack of safety. The prevalence of fences in this area's neighborhoods is a physical testimony to how fear can translate into the built environment (Figure 1.5).

Part of the problem were visible signs that communicated "non-caring," such as lack of cleanliness, which further eroded the sense of interiority:

> Well it doesn't [feel safe]; they [renters] do things a lot more out of character. There was a time in St. Paul that you didn't see mattresses on the street; [now] they throw everything and anything out on the street.

Another participant elaborated on how outsiders prevented connections among neighbors from happening, and thus changed how residents could build community (Figure 1.6):

> We have a lot of noise, violence, the big cars running around with loud noise. We got kids who aren't controlled or controllable. They don't know how to treat people. Our elders are afraid to come out on their porches ... our elders are like prisoners in their own home.

Along with physical barriers, interiority is also shaped by what one sees and hears, the views and sounds that infuse private and public spaces, and inform and carve out experiences and

Figure 1.6 Typical Rondo houses.

understandings of the world. Many felt that limited opportunities to engage with elders were among the contributing factors that prevented youth from moving forward:

> How about if we have them engaging with the elders so that some of that heritage and background can grow to make them healthier and see what it is like and get some of that history? Now that is what we need, and we need to find a way.

The residents lamented about the lack of easy access to the community center that could serve as the ground for social interaction, one that builds interiority. At the same time, conceiving urban spaces such as front porches as intergenerational building blocks that help foster community connections and keep youth out of trouble speaks to a shift in paradigms on the part of designers and planners. Mediating public and private spatialities, front porches contribute to the experience of interiority in ways that fuse inside/outside relationships, expanding world awareness and nourishing the spirit of both young and old community members.

The experiences of Rondo residents highlight another potential oxymoron in design and planning decision-making—the benefits and challenges associated with proximity to major traffic arteries. When asked what prevented them from being healthy, residents raised three issues, all of which were interconnected: transportation, crime and poverty. The Rondo neighborhood, much like Little Earth, is near a highway and University Avenue, both major arterials that connect the cities of Minneapolis and St. Paul (Figure 1.7).

Residents, however, voiced similar concerns with air quality and noise: "People keep saying that their kids have asthma," one of the interviewees noted. This participant's insights demonstrate how proximity to a major highway does not necessarily facilitate access to transportation options, which was tied to lack of education and job opportunities, which were in turn tied to crime:

> Crime puts stress on you … there was a murder on my block … We got domestic assaults, we got theft, we got burglary … But it's because there is a lot of stress. All of it ties back to stress … and it doesn't help … that in Minnesota we have the highest achievement gap between African Americans and whites - the highest unemployment gap between African Americans and whites and the highest incarceration rate[24] … if you ain't going to educate us and you ain't giving us a job, that doesn't give us a lot of options. If you don't

Figure 1.7 University Ave is a major arterial that connects Minneapolis and Saint Paul.

> have living wage jobs in your area … you gotta go to other people's communities … and the buses, the buses don't come here to get them where the jobs are.

Another participant added that people standing at bus stops are vulnerable for getting robbed and threatened with guns. Some are even afraid of taking the bus to move around, further limiting their world awareness, health-supporting activities and socio-economic well-being.

In general, a feeling of abandonment and disregard was expressed throughout the interview, one that can be captured in this comment about parks in the area. Referring to the Jimmy Lee Park, the comments of one of the participants reveal the political ramifications of interiority:

> It was closed for 18 months because of contamination … You gotta put that dirt somewhere and usually they put it in communities of color … because they don't think that we are worth anything.

Rondo's interiority turns out to be constructed by both material and immaterial dimensions of space that conflate "worth" with environmental characteristics such as how clean and presentable a street is to what one hears and breathes.

Cedar Riverside Neighborhood—Somali Experiences

Thousands of Somalis came to Minnesota in the early 1990s to escape a devastating civil war, and the Twin Cities area currently has one of the largest concentrations of Somalis in the country—with over 50,000 Somalis; it even earns the title *SomaliLand.* The Somali interviewees were residents of Riverside Plaza, the city's largest affordable housing development complex located in Minneapolis' Cedar Riverside neighborhood (see Figure 1.8). Approximately 4,000 residents live there, 80% of whom are from East Africa.[25] In the overall neighborhood, Black residents make up 48% of the population and the median income in 2016 was $19,214, which places 45.7% of the residents below poverty.[26]

As new immigrants to the United States and the region, Somali participants pointed to the sheer numbers and prevalence of Somalis in the area as an element that helped foster their

Figure 1.8 The Riverside Plaza building.

health. This observation confirms studies that point to enclaves of like-minded people acting as sources of support[27]: the population is more dense, the Somali people. People may know each other and help each other and seeing your own kind [is important]. You speak the same language, stick together.

Interiority is thereby linked to who lives where, who is allowed "in" a neighborhood, who belongs and who does not. Living with others from a similar cultural background increases the shared sense of experienced interiority.

The Brian Coyle community center, across the street from Riverside Plaza, was also noted as aiding with their health—it was convenient and helped foster the community connections needed in displacement. The center provides services as well as space for formal and informal gatherings, including the focus group meeting for this study. After-school programs for children and teens as well as programs for elders and families are also held here. Adjacent to the center is a children's playground where mothers gathered to talk and have tea, forming close bonds with each other and with the places in which they lived. Further down is easy access to public transportation which enables residents to venture into other parts of the city (see Figure 1.9).

Figure 1.9 Access to amenities such as a children's playground and public transportation.

Figure 1.10 Shops in the area catering to East African residents.

Challenging their ability to lead healthy lives, some participants stated, were prescriptions dictated by their Muslim faith and the fact that many Somali women are veiled, which brings to the foreground interiority's spiritual connotations. Having an exercise room just for women would nudge more women to exercise as "most fitness centers are mixed, guys are there too." The fact that many women did not drive increased the need for gender-specific exercise facilities within walking distance.

Similar attention was paid to the needs of youth. Availability of after-school activities, as one participant said, keeps children "on track in school, and keeps them healthy." Intergenerational conflict is a particular concern for Somalis—"Americanized" youth want to move away from tradition while their parents struggle to keep them close to the family, the religion and the culture.[28] The influx of Somalis transformed the area physically as well as demographically, and now Somali grocery stores and restaurants as well as social services and mosques line the area streets (Figure 1.10).

But the prevalence of bars, including hookah bars in the neighborhood, added stress to parents:

> Safety is number one for us ... There are lots of bars and liquor stores in this neighborhood, also hookah places even though in Minnesota everything is smoke-free. Kids go there and get addicted; we are worried about the teenagers.

In family-centered neighborhoods, access to bars or adult-type entertainment can be a source of conflict and can rupture the fabric that holds families together and strengthens the area's sense of interiority.

Lastly, concern was raised for the well-being of the community's elders. Amenities such as space for social gatherings within the Riverside Plaza buildings would help ease some of the stress elders experience:

> it is important that [elders] come together socially and share news, chat, find out what is happening in the world, find support. Having a social gathering place would help.

The Somali malls in the area are places that elders frequent. Many run some of the small shops in the malls, and this makes them feel needed, enhancing their limited employment opportunities and impacting their economic well-being.

Religion is another cultural tradition that helps elders adapt to life in displacement. As Muslims, many Somalis pray multiple times a day:

> There is a mosque in this neighborhood. There are early morning prayers at 5:00am so elders have to walk to the mosque. Safety is an issue ... anything can happen. Need more lights on the street or surveillance cameras in the neighborhood.

Considering health's intersections with neighborhoods cannot be disassociated from cultural facets such as religious practices and beliefs as well as language and gender differences.

Implications

This study exposed the nuances behind Perolini's concept of interiority at the neighborhood level and reframed discourses around neighborhoods and health. Through the insights and experiences of members of the Native American, African American and Somali communities in Minnesota, the analysis shed light on the ways by which the shared experience of interiority by a neighborhood's residents and a person's world awareness, and in turn health, were restricted or expanded by environmental factors that ranged from air quality, noise and toxins in the ground to access to a community center, a community garden, upkeep of properties and perceptions of crime and safety. These environmental parameters endowed neighborhoods with an "interior" character that impacted health and well-being by intersecting with factors such as gender, age, race, background and language skills, along with social, cultural, religious, historical, political and economic factors.

The narratives shared by the interviewees pointed to world awareness being a process that looks to the past to inform the future; it is a personal process that also has a communal element and, as a result, takes on multiple forms and meanings. As expected, spatial characteristics of neighborhoods were implicated in many health-supporting processes and often acted as determinants of whether a person would adopt a healthy practice or not. Mediating the relationship between neighborhoods and health were *perceptions* of both how the neighborhood, in its holistic image, could be inhabited and used by residents and what health meant and for whom. Intriguing in the findings was the notion that what mattered most were not the individual environmental or social parameters themselves but their *intersections*—how each informed the other and everything in between. Perceptions of ground contamination in Little Earth, for example, impacted mothers' comfort and stress levels, which in turn impacted children's ability to use the playground, which impacted the creation of informal opportunities to build community connections, and thereby health and well-being. In communities of color, such perceptions also became narratives of social injustice that acted as powerful messages of race relations, marginalization and inequality.

The implications of the findings for interior designers can be summarized into three areas for consideration. First, interiority is not a fixed and visible spatial construct bounded by walls. Instead, interiority is firmly grounded in shared human experiences and, therefore, interior designers should complicate and broaden the spatial scales they work with and the factors considered in design and planning processes. Strong collaborations must be formed with community members whose insights and experiences will help guide the process and its outcomes.[29]

Second, interiority's relationship to health can be cultivated when access to health-supporting environmental factors is equally distributed across communities. For example, Minneapolis has over 180 parks within its boundaries and is ranked as one of the top biking cities in the country. But safety concerns, for both crime and contamination, prevented many of these members of immigrant and minority communities from using the parks, bike trails and playgrounds. Design interventions such as improved lighting, strategic placement of greenery and better maintenance can entice neighbors to use the parks and playgrounds, broadening their world awareness and strengthening the health of everyone from children to elders.

And third, interiority's plural nature points to the need for design discourses to stay away from the singular focus on individual factors, such as the walkability or air quality of a neighborhood. Monolithic/static understandings and design solutions are more likely to miss the diversity in experiences and contexts in which people lead their lives. Shifting paradigms from the singular "interiority" to plural "interiorities" provides a new lens through which to examine how different environmental parameters intersect with other parameters in ways that impact understandings of what interiorities at the neighborhood scale imply and their relationship to health.

The study's limitations are partly linked to the small sample sizes and subjects self-selecting to participate, both of which inherently carry the possibility of bias. The interviewees could have been saying what they thought researchers wanted to hear or only those who are dissatisfied with their living conditions could have chosen to attend the meetings. The food and monetary compensation the study's participants received could further be biasing the responses. Along these lines, the study relies on interviewees' perceptions and verbal narratives—it does not test actual health data for example. Future research can delve deeper into the question of neighborhoods and health by triangulating these findings with numerical data.

In closing, interior design research can contribute to understandings of interiorities at the neighborhood scale. Interior designers who are cognizant of the diversity of interior spaces and the impact of design decisions on health disparities can recognize the blurred boundaries of their work and develop ways to help overcome some of those barriers. Evaluating all design decisions for their health implications can be accomplished by inviting community members and public health officials to join the conversation.[30] With this knowledge, designers in partnership with planners and policy makers can envision new directions for the creation of inclusive neighborhoods and cities, ones that support the well-being of everyone and where all types of interiorities matter.

Acknowledgment: This research has been funded through the Agricultural Experiment Station of the University of Minnesota.

* * * *

Discussion and Exercises

Reflections about the Chapter You Just Read:

1. Please refer to the standard features of a research project explained in the Introduction. Then:
   a. In one sentence, identify the *research topic*. This sentence can be in the form of a question but does not have to be. In any case, write one grammatically correct sentence that captures the research topic of this chapter.

b. Identify the *literature* related to this research project.
c. Identify the *method* which the author used, and also the *data* which this method generated for analysis.
d. Explain how this approach is *generalizable* (or not).
e. Explain how you can have confidence (or not) of the *internal and external validity* of this author's overall approach.

2. Refer again to the Introduction to this chapter.
   a. Describe what a focus group is in your own words.
   b. Refer to Hadjiyanni's interview guide in Figure 1.1 on page 12.
      i. Imagine you are preparing to conduct a focus group in a diverse neighborhood. List the things you have to do to prepare your interview guide, based on Hadjiyanni's example.
      ii. List the interactive prompts Hadjiyanni planned in to her interview guide. What do these prompts do to create a conversational atmosphere in the focus group.
3. Divide into two groups, with one group the interviewers and the other group the interviewees. Practice role-playing through Hadjiyanni's interview guide. (For example, identify a "neighborhood" for your venue; it can be your school environment, town environment, etc.) John Zeisel provides the following "interview probes" to include in the planning of interview guides.[31] In your role-playing, list ways you can encourage the following (these are based on Zeisel):
   a. Strategies for *addition* and *flow*.
   b. Encouraging your interviewees to *reflect*.
   c. Defining but enlarging the *range* of the conversation: using cues, mutating themes to adjacent ones, etc.
   d. Capturing *emotion*.
4. Discuss the three neighborhoods in this chapter. In particular, consider the ways that the respondents' answers suggest the neighborhood as an interior or as having a "sense of insideness." Discuss how the focus group interview established the following:
   a. How are experiences of interiority the same and/or different for each neighborhood?
   b. How has each neighborhood created its own interiority?
   c. What role do physical factors and psychological perceptions play in the perceived interiority of each case study?
   d. How do social, cultural, religious, historical, political and economic factors impact a resident's sense of being "within" his or her neighborhood in environmental terms?
5. Consider how Hadjiyanni posits the definition of interior can expand to the neighborhood scale. She poses the following questions in regard to this:
   a. How is Perolini's "awareness of the world" shaped at neighborhood scales? What role does spatiality play?
   b. What are the implications of this understanding for interior design scholars and practitioners?
   c. Does Hadjiyanni sufficiently answer these questions? Why or why not? What additional research tactics can be used to further clarify answers to these questions?
6. Hadjiyanni specifically connects neighborhood interiority to health. Discuss this relationship. In what ways does interiority impact health positively or negatively in each neighborhood?

Exercises/Suggestions for Further Study

1. If you were asked to provide one design intervention for health for one of the neighborhoods in this study, what would it be? Select a neighborhood and explain your choice. Use Hadjiyanni's descriptions and findings for the community you select to explain your design intervention.
2. Hadjiyanni posits barriers and borders that may be invisible constructs that produce difference and inequality. Consider a neighborhood you are most familiar with, whether your current one or one from your past. Describe the neighborhood. Use Hadjiyanni's interview guide in Figure 1.1 on page 12. Respond to the interview prompts now for your selected neighborhood. What invisible borders or barriers of interiority, including physical factors and psychological perceptions, do your answers reveal?
3. Read the following study on physical and psychological factors of neighborhoods' sense of community: Kim, J., & Kaplan, R. (2004). "Physical and psychological factors in sense of community: New urbanist Kentlands and nearby Orchard Village," in *Environment and behavior, 36*(3), 313–340. Examine the interiority of the neighborhoods of Kentlands and Orchard Village as presented by Kim and Kaplan in this study. What do the findings tell you? What questions remained unanswered or unclear? Based on this analysis, create a list of interview questions (four minimum) for focus groups that would further develop the findings of this study.
4. Choose one of the neighborhoods in this chapter as the setting for a design studio project. Given the neighborhood's concept of interiority based on sense of wellness and belonging, write a design program for a community center utilizing Pena and Parshall's four categories of time, form, economy and function (see reference following). Discuss how findings from focus group interviews might specifically inform the program and influence a proposed design solution. (William Pena and Steven A. Parshall. *Problem Seeking: An Architectural Programming Primer*, 5th ed. New York: John Wiley & Sons.)

Additional Connections and Information

Generally, in qualitative research, group interviews are designated as focus groups, although the type and nature of group interview can vary.[32] Denzin and Lincoln define focus groups as "a situation in which the interviewer asks group members very specific questions about a topic after considerable research has been completed." Morgan provides two questions to evaluate whether interviews of individuals or focus groups are best suited for a research study: (1) whether information gained from an individual perspective is valuable enough to warrant the time it takes to interview participants one-by-one, and (2) if individual information would be lost or gained through discussion in a group interview.

As a research method, the focus group is part of the larger domain of *qualitative research*. This term embraces a broad variety of research tactics, and there are lengthy books devoted to the different ways to conduct qualitative research. So this chapter featuring one form of interviews—focus groups—is one snapshot of a much larger research domain. But across all of its varieties, qualitative research has the following common characteristics:

1. The research topic focuses on the human dynamics in a set of social parameters taking place in their "natural" setting. This means the qualitative researcher does not isolate her object of study in a laboratory or other artificially delimited setting. Instead, the researcher studies a real-time social setting—a community experiencing a crisis, a business organization (see, for example, Isil Oygur's ethnographic research in Chapter 2). In this chapter, Hadjiyanni seeks to understand the subjective outlooks of residents of three different cultural neighborhoods living in the city of Minneapolis.
2. The qualitative researcher therefore seeks to understand her human subjects from *their* perspective(s). In Chapter 3, Erin Cunningham uses qualitative tactics to see through the eyes of visiting nurses in impoverished neighborhoods in New York during the Great Depression. In Chapter 8, Jill Pable seeks to understand homelessness through the eyes of those undergoing this challenge. These chapters all use qualitative research tactics different from focus groups.
3. A qualitative research study typically uses many different research tactics to understand its research subject. Hadjiyanni's study uses interviews in focus groups as her main research tactic. But we have already noted her research on the formal, economic and demographic features of each neighborhood.

Notes

1 John Cresswell, *Research Design: Qualitative, Quantitative, and Mixed Methods Approaches*, 4th ed. (Los Angeles, CA: Sage Publications, Inc., 2014), 194.
2 Ibid, 191.
3 David L. Morgan, *The Focus Group Guidebook* (Thousand Oaks, CA: Sage Publications, Inc., 1997).
4 See Robert K. Merton, Marjorie Fiske, and Patricia L. Kendall, *The Focused Interview*, 2nd ed. (New York: Free Press: 1990); and Norman K. Denzin and Yvonna S. Lincoln, *Handbook of Qualitative Research* (Thousand Oaks, CA: Sage Publications, 1994), 364–365. Morton and colleagues were the first to develop the focus interview as a research tool. Denzin and Lincoln's book is the seminal source for qualitative research methods.
5 Morgan, op. cit.; Merton, op. cit.
6 R.A. Krueger and J.A. King, *Involving Community Members in Focus Groups* (Sage Publications, Inc., 1998), xv–xvi. They state, We're concerned about the misuse of the term *focus group*. Over the past two decades, this term has attracted lots of attention and has been badly abused. Indeed, some criticism of "focus groups" is justified, because what have been called "focus groups" are often no such thing.
7 See H. A. Rueda, M. Lindsay, and L. R Williams, "She Posted it on Facebook: Mexican American Adolescents Experiences with Technology and Romantic Relationship Conflict," *Journal of Adolescent Research* 30, no. 4 (2014): 419–445. These authors note the effectiveness of focus groups in encouraging in-depth conversation with those who share commonalities and also the importance of consistency with key questions between groups.
8 J. Fox, K.M. Warber, and D.C. Makstaller, The Role of Facebook in Romantic Relationship Development: An Exploration of Knapp's Relational Stage Model. *Journal of Social and Personal Relationships* 30, no. 6 (2013): 771–794.
9 Ibid., 228.
10 Petra S. Perolini, "Interior Spaces and the Layers of Meaning," *Design Principles and Practices* 5, no. 6 (2011): 163–174.
11 Ibid., 170.
12 Patricia Ehrkamp, "Risking Publicity: Masculinities and the Racialization of Public Neighborhood Space," *Social & Cultural Geography* 9, no. 2 (May 2008): 118–133. https://doi.org/10.1080/14649360701856060; Louisa Veronis, "Strategic Spatial Essentialism: Latin Americans' Real and Imagined Geographies of Belonging in Toronto," *Social & Cultural Geography* 8, no. 3 (June 2007): 455–473. https://doi.org/10.1080/14649360701488997.
13 Howard Frumkin, "Healthy Places: Exploring the Evidence," *American Journal of Public Health* 93, no. 9 (September 2003): 1451–1456.; Gina S. Lovasi et al., "Effect of Individual or Neighborhood Disadvantage on the Association Between Neighborhood Walkability and Body Mass Index," *American Journal of Public Health* 99, no. 2 (February 2009): 279–284. doi:10.2105/AJPH.2008.138230.; Wendy C. Perdue, Lesley A. Stone, and Lawrence O. Gostin, "The Built environment and its Relationship to the Public's Health: The Legal Framework," *American Journal of Public Health* 93, no. 9 (September 2003): 1390–1394.; Brian E. Saelens et al., "Neighborhood-Based Differences in Physical Activity: An Environment Scale Evaluation," *American Journal of Public Health* 93, no. 9 (September 2003): 1552–1558.; Jolanda Maas et al., "Green Space, Urbanity, and Health: How Strong is the Relation?" *Journal of Epidemiology and Community Health* 60, no. 7 (July 2006): 587–592. http://dx.doi.org/10.1136/jech.2005.0431; Douglas D. Perkins et al., "Participation and the Social and Physical Environment of Residential Blocks: Crime and Community Context,"

American Journal of Community Psychology 18 (1990): 83–115; Mai Stafford, Tarani Chandola, and Michael Marmot, "Association Between Fear of Crime and Mental Health and Physical Functioning," *American Journal of Public Health* 97 (November 2007): 2076–2081. doi:10.2105/AJPH.2006.097154; Simone A. French, Mary Story, and Robert W. Jeffery, "Environmental Influences on Eating and Physical Activity," *Annual Review Public Health* 22, no. 3 (2001): 9–35. doi:10.1146/annurev.publhealth.22.1.309; Carolyn C. Cannuscio, Eve E. Weiss, and David A. Asch, "The Contribution of Urban Foodways to Health Disparities," *Journal of Urban Health: Bulletin of the New York Academy of Medicine* 87, no. 3 (May 2010): 381–393. doi:10.1007/s11524-010-9441-9; Paula Jones and Rajiv Bhatia, "Supporting Equitable Food Systems Through Food Assistance at Farmers' Markets," *American Journal of Public Health* 101, no. 5 (May 2011): 781–783. doi:10.2105/AJPH.2010.300021.

14 Michal Mitrany and Sanjoy Mazumdar, "Neighborhood Design and Religion: Modern Orthodox Jews," *Journal of Architectural and Planning Research* 26, no. 1 (2009): 44–69. www.jstor.org/stable/43030852; Suk-Kyung Kim and Andrew D. Seidel, "Safe Communities for Urban Renters; Residents' Perceived Safety, Physical Territoriality and Social Ties in Urban Apartment Properties," *Journal of Architectural Planning Research* 29, no. 2 (Summer 2012): 133–148. www.jstor.org/stable/43030966; Andrea Altschuler, Carol P. Somkin, and Nancy E. Adler, "Local Services and Amenities, Neighborhood Social Capital, and Health," *Social Science & Medicine* 59 (September 2004): 1219–1229. doi:10.1016/j.socscimed.2004.01.008; Ann Forsyth and Katherine Crewe, "Finding Common Ground in the Metropolis: Do Planned Residential Enclaves Connect or Exclude? *Journal of Architecture and Planning Research* 28, no. 1 (May 2011): 58–75.; Emília M. Rebelo, "A Methodology to Assess Immigrant Land-Use Patterns in Concentrated and Sprawled Environments (the Case of the Porto Metropolitan Area)," *Journal of Architectural and Planning Research* 28, no. 2 (2011): 152–178. http://hdl.handle.net/10216/85672.

15 Craig Helmstetter, Susan Brower, and Andi Egbert. *The Unequal Distribution of Health in the Twin Cities* (Amherst, MA: H. Wilder Foundation, 2010).

16 Metropolitan Council, *Metro Stats – What Lies Ahead: Population, Household and Employment Forecasts to 2040* (2012).

17 Habib Chaudhury and Atiya Mahmood, "Introduction: Immigrants' Residential Experience – An Overlooked Area in Environmental Design Research," *Journal of Architectural and Planning Research* 25, no. 1 (2008): 1–5.

18 World Health Organization. Preamble to the Constitution of the World Health Organization as adopted by the International Health Conference, New York, 19–22 June, 1946; signed on 22 July 1946 by the representatives of 61 States (Official Records of the World Health Organization, no. 2, p. 100) and entered into force on 7 April 1948.

19 John Kunesh, "Little Earth Breaks Ground on New Affordable Housing Developments," *TC Daily Planet*, May 30, 2012.

20 Minnesota Compass (2011b, October). *Minneapolis neighborhood profile: Philips West.* www.mncompass.org/_pdfs/neighborhood-profiles/Minneapolis-PhillipsWest-102011.pdf. Accessed September 17, 2013.

21 F.J. Davis, *The Effects of a Freeway Displacement on Racial Housing Segregation in a Northern City* (Atlanta, GA: Atlanta University, 1965).

22 Joe Kimbal, "Sweet, Bitter Recalled in Rondo; An Oral History Effort Reflects the Power of Community in a St Paul Neighborhood," *Star Tribune*, January 17, 2005.

23 Minnesota Compass (2011c, October). *St. Paul neighborhood profile: Summit-University.* www.mncompass.org/_pdfs/neighborhood-profiles/StPaul-SummitUniversity-102011.pdf. Accessed September 17, 2013.

24 It should be noted that it is beyond the scope of this chapter to confirm or dispute interviewees' comments. Instead, the chapter purpose is to explore how these perceptions intersect with spatial parameters.

25 Issa A. Mansaray, "Riverside Plaza Renovation Disrupts Lives of Thousands," *The Twin Cities Daily Planet*, June 21, 2011.

26 Minnesota Compass (2011a, October). *Minneapolis neighborhood profile: Cedar Riverside.* www.mncompass.org/_pdfs/neighborhood-profiles/Minneapolis-CedarRiverside-102011.pdf. Accessed September 17, 2013

27 Ann Forsyth and Katherine Crewe, "Finding Common Ground in the Metropolis: Do Planned Residential Enclaves Connect or Exclude?" *Journal of Architecture and Planning Research* 28, no. 1 (May 2011): 58–75.

28 Rima B. McGown. *Muslims in the Diaspora: The Somali Communities of London and Toronto* (Toronto: University of Toronto Press, 1999).

29 Sara Kindon, Rachel Pain, and Mike Kesby (Eds.), *Participatory Action Research Approaches and Methods – Connecting People, Participation and Place* (New York: Routledge, 2007).

30 Shobha Srinivasan, Liam R. O'Fallon, and Allen Dearry, "Creating Healthy Communities, Healthy Homes, Healthy People: Initiating a Research Agenda on the Built Environment and Public Health," *American Journal of Public Health* 93 (September 2003): 1446–1450. PMC1447991.

31 Zeisel, op. cit., 239–245.

32 Denzin and Lincoln, op. cit., 1994; Cresswell, op. cit.

Chapter 2

Design Ethnography

Editors' Introduction by Dana E. Vaux and David Wang

Interior design often focuses on long-term user needs and behavior in the midst of spatial arrangements. Ethnographic research can greatly help in this process. In ethnographic research, the designer embeds herself in the client culture for which she is designing. With the agreement of her clients, she becomes as much of the daily operations of the culture as possible: a school, a hospital, a hospitality service such as a resort or hotel. This chapter is an ethnographic study of a flexible office workplace in a large international company.

As Isil Oygur and her colleagues make clear in this chapter, flexible office design is a major trend in office planning. One term these authors use to describe embedding themselves in the workings of their research venue (the office workplace) is *in situ*. The term means "in position within the original place." So, the aim of design ethnography is to see a user's world *through the user's eyes*. The authors' research findings, then, can provide insight into open office settings in general. Of course, understanding meaning from a user's perspective is the goal of all typologies of qualitative research. But the signature of ethnographic research is embedment *in situ* in the cultural environment under study. This *in situ* period is usually called doing *fieldwork*.

In this chapter, Oygur and her colleagues did their fieldwork in the offices of Firma, a pseudonym for a major international company based in downtown Istanbul, Turkey. Their ethnographic fieldwork lasted for ten days. The chapter also addresses the preparations before and the assessments after the fieldwork; so ethnographic research entails times of preparation that are in addition to the actual fieldwork. As the chapter notes, the ten-day fieldwork period is a standard length of time in ethnographic design research. In anthropology research (from which design ethnography is derived), fieldwork periods are usually much longer. If the resources and timeframe can accommodate it, fieldwork in design ethnography can take place over longer periods. Or it can be conducted in repeated segments of stays over a period of time. The advantage of several fieldwork periods is the possibility to triangulate findings from one session to the next.

This raises a major goal of ethnographic research, which is to generate *thick descriptions* of the life of the culture under study. The term was popularized by the anthropologist Clifford Geertz (1926–2006) in his *Interpretation of Cultures*. The authors of this chapter reference this work. Embodied cultural practices—even something as trivial as one person winking to another; to use Geertz's well-known example—necessarily involve multiple layers of meaning. The goal of thick description is to account for as many layers of meaning as possible in one holistic (= thick) description of a culture's practices. In this way, Geertz emphasized the *symbolic* depth of cultural practices. How and what does a culture take actions, figures of speech, dress, ways of operation, office layouts, and so on, to mean symbolically? For instance, in this chapter, higher-level employees of Firma tended to use meeting rooms open to everyone as their own offices by personalizing the spaces with personal markers such as photographs. One can see the tug-of-war between office (and design) policy, based on egalitarian ideals, versus individual practices and preferences. This tension can be understood at a symbolic level.

In short, to achieve thick description, ethnographic research makes use of many research tactics. Tactics are actions researchers *do* to procure their data. For example: the *idea* of conducting ethnographic research on this open office is a good one, but the idea alone is not sufficient to get the information Oygur and her colleagues need. Embedding themselves in the daily life of the office is something they had to do. But even just being there day after day is not sufficient. They need multiple tactics (things to do while *in situ*) in order to achieve their thick description. As you read:

1. Note the interviews, the journaling, the relational tactics, the observational techniques. As you come to the Methodology section of this chapter, keep a list of the research tactics used by the researchers. For the chapter overall, see if you can spot other tactics used to achieve thick description.
2. This research was done by a three-person research team. Note how they divide up their responsibilities. Keep in mind the necessary steps to assure owner collaboration at the outset and specific actions after the ten-day fieldwork period. For both pre and post, be sure to understand what the researchers did and why they had to do it. All of this illustrates research at the tactical level.

Some of the tactics used in this chapter are specific to ethnographic research. For example, the use of a journal for coding (Figure 2.3) is typical for research of this kind. This chapter falls into the large domain of *qualitative* research. Qualitative research seeks new knowledge about social-cultural relations in real time and in their "natural" settings. (In contrast, *quantitative* research often tends to isolate the factors under study, in a laboratory, or in a prescribed "unit of test." Later chapters will address research of a quantitative nature.) Qualitative research generally tries to see a setting through the eyes of someone living in that setting. Since interior design concerns people in real-time settings, varieties of qualitative research abound in this discipline, and this reality is reflected in several of the chapters in this book.

Interiority

As explained above, the authors of this chapter note that ethnography can provide holistic access to how users (in this case, Firma's employees) view their day-to-day spaces. They refer to it as *felt* interiority. How do employees *feel* about their spatially fluid workspaces, and in turn, how is this "felt interiority" manifested in their social-cultural behavior? As you read:

1. Note first the double-meaning of "interiority" in this chapter, namely: the researchers themselves embed *in* the open office environment so as to get an "interior" understanding of how the office workers themselves live *in* their workspaces.
2. As another example of using multiple tactics to achieve thick description, note how the authors organize their research (and hence their chapter) into aesthetic, instrumental and symbolic dimensions. Consider how this theoretical framework is itself a way to "get an inside view" of their subject matter.

One thing this book encourages readers to do is to compare similarities and differences in what "interiority" means from chapter to chapter. Prompts to consider relationships between chapters, not only with respect to methodology but also with respect to themes of interiority, will recur as these chapters unfold.

* * * *

Understanding User Experience within Flexible Workplaces: An Ethnographic Approach

Isil Oygur, Ozgur Gocer and Ebru Ergoz Karahan

The impact of workplace design on organizational success or failure has been recognized for several decades.[1] In order to assess this relationship, scholars often study employee satisfaction, productivity, creativity, motivation and well-being in relation to space planning.[2] These studies provide in-depth analyses of a single measurable phenomenon (e.g., satisfaction, productivity). But a person's experiences within a space are multidimensional.[3] Interior spaces stir emotional and intimate experiences through sensual modalities.[4] To get at the sense of *felt interiority* (see below) in a workplace calls for a broader approach. This challenge can be met by researching user experience through the emic and etic aspects of ethnography. Emic denotes understanding realities internal to the experienced context; while etic denotes external analytical aspects of emic conditions. In ethnographic research, the analyst uniquely understands the culture from an insider's perspective, while she is also able to view it from a removed, objective perspective.

We utilized this approach to assess a popular workplace design strategy: the flexible workplace. In the last decade, a growing number of firms have implemented flexible workplace designs. In these settings, employees, including higher-status workers, do not have private offices or allocated workstations. Studies show that flexible settings have both positive and negative impact on employees.[5] While flexible workplaces increase employee interaction and break down hierarchical structures, they can negatively impact employee motivation, well-being and satisfaction due to lack of personalization.[6] It is therefore important to study flexible workplaces from the user's point of view.

Flexible Workplace Design

Contemporary flexible workplaces are spatially designed to allow employees to decide when, where and how they want to work. Whether termed activity-based flexible offices, distributed workplaces, flexible offices, hot-desking, hoteling, networked offices or non-territorial offices, these types of workplaces all target the following goals: (a) increasing social interaction and collaboration, (b) increasing knowledge exchange, (c) fostering creativity and innovation, (d) breaking vertical hierarchy and (e) decreasing facility and rental costs by occupying smaller office square footage.[7]

Given that employees do not have assigned workstations, flexible workplace layouts offer such amenities as quiet concentration rooms, meeting rooms, break-out spaces, multimedia rooms and lounges.[8] The overall space is composed of an open office area(s) along with semi-enclosed and enclosed spaces for meetings and private consultations. Clean desk policies require each employee to clean his or her desk completely at the end of each workday to make it ready for its next user. And because of no fixed desks, employees are assigned lockers to store their documents and personal belongings.[9]

The benefits and pitfalls of flexible workplaces are still under discussion. Wohlers and Hertel's theoretical model is one such study.[10] According to their model, flexible offices raise issues of territoriality, autonomy, privacy, proximity and visibility. Open plan solutions are known to impede employee privacy.[11] Clean desk policies add to this shortcoming by making personalization difficult. An employee does not become attached to a workstation, resulting in territoriality issues which in turn lower organizational commitment and retention rates.[12]

People claim ownership at workplaces by decorating them and leaving physical markers. These markers communicate status, identity and distinctiveness.[13] Elsbach and Bechky observed that in the absence of personalization, employees first see a threat to their identity rather than to their status.[14] Barriers, enclosures and larger space allocations communicate status and rank.[15] Privacy through design elements is an indicator of hierarchy. In the absence of these hierarchical markers, employees must establish status, identity and distinctiveness by "marking a favorite workstation or always selecting the same workstation."[16] Gocer et al. coined the term "fixed-flexible working style" for open workplaces reflecting this reality.[17]

Other conditions such as site location and associations with nature (natural light, materials and colors) also impact employees' well-being, satisfaction, motivation and performance, and thus organizational success.[18] Consequently, "beyond simple notions of size and comfort, office design has gained attention for its ability to meet the emerging needs of employees who spend fewer, but perhaps more important, hours in the office."[19]

Methodology

The Three-dimensional Framework

Designing and framing the user experience within a space first require a deeper understanding of a user's affective responses. This relates to felt interiority as this term reflects one's *holistic* experience in a space,[20] and calls for studying physical as well as sensory interactions, perceptions, cognitions, values, emotions and meaning in relation to experience.[21] Thus, interiority is human-centric and multidimensional. Many scholars have attempted to frame this diversity in people's affective responses to design solutions.[22] They have proposed classification schemes to assess individuals' interactions with their environments and artifacts. These schemes mostly arise from industrial design; but they provide insights for evaluating an employee's experience in an office workplace.

In fact, several researchers have proposed a three-dimensional classification—instrumental, aesthetic and symbolic—to study employees' emotions and reactions to artifacts within offices.[23] This framework has been applied in different studies in various disciplines and also tested for its capacity to evaluate employees' perception of office space and workplace design features.[24] To our knowledge, it has not been used to analyze flexible workplaces.

For this study, we applied this three-dimensional framework to a flexible workplace in Istanbul. *Instrumentality* is the first dimension of the framework. This dimension assesses the workplace and its physical artifacts in terms of functionality and usability.[25] Ability to perform tasks, capacity to adapt to individual needs, anthropometric qualities, human factors issues, comfort, storage space and level of mobility are assessed under this dimension. *Aesthetics* is the second dimension. This relates to forms, shapes—their characteristics, properties and organization.[26] Beauty, attractiveness, ugliness and messiness are evaluated as aesthetic elements, as are color, materials, decoration, furniture and patterns of physical layout. *Symbolism*, the last dimension, has to do with associations, values and meaning.[27] Hierarchical symbols, prestige and representation of organizational values are part of the symbolic dimension of an office space.

In order to answer the research question "what is a user's experience in a flexible workplace?", we conducted an ethnographic study at a flexible workplace of a multinational company in Istanbul, Turkey. This workplace was one of the first companies in the world to implement a flexible workplace strategy. To protect the confidentiality of the firm, we chose not to include any information or photographs associated directly with the firm. We assigned the pseudonym "Firma" to this firm.

Firma's office occupies five floors, about 11,000 m^2 (approximately 9,000 m^2 usable floor space) in an intelligent building (it is a smart building) in one of the busiest high-rise business districts in downtown Istanbul. The lowest floor includes a reception area, meeting rooms, a cafeteria and service rooms such as those for copying and printing. Guests are mostly hosted on this floor. The rest of the four floors have almost identical functional and aesthetic planning for employees to conduct their everyday work. The design of the office was based on Firma's growth plan for 2020 and Firma's global flexible design guidelines. A local consultant architect and a building committee from Firma worked on the implementation of these guidelines for the Istanbul office in the mid-2010s.

The office consists of open plan office areas, more intimate workspaces, social areas and service zones (Figure 2.1). The intimate workspaces were designed using the room-in-a-room concept. These include four types of rooms: meeting rooms with fully glazed front wall and door; just-in-time rooms (single-person workspaces); wellness rooms and huddle rooms (small-sized rooms used for teamwork). These intimate workspaces are located near the core of the building, with the open workstations and social areas around the periphery. The architect explained that they "preferred this layout because it gives more employees access to daylight and windows and therefore, communicates that they are valued." There are four open office zones on each floor. Two of these zones are shorter, accommodating 30 workstations each; and two are longer, accommodating 60 workstations each.

All of the furniture is nationally and internationally well-known brands. There are three types of workstations in the open office areas (Figure 2.2). Each workstation includes desks for six people. Two of the workstations are in linear form. The third workstation is more triangular. This workstation

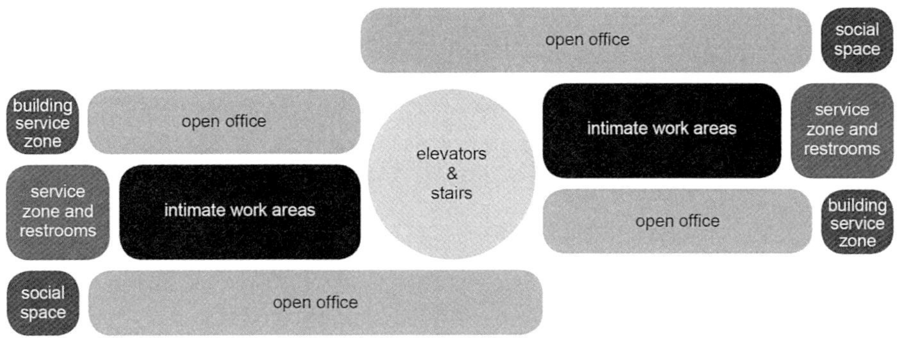

Figure 2.1 Blocking diagram of floor plan.

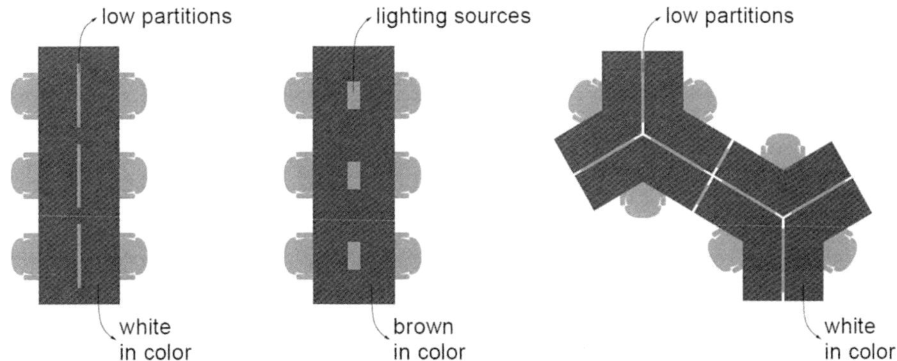

Figure 2.2 Types of desk patterns in furniture layout.

offers more desk space. It also gives an increased sense of privacy because of its form and the low partitions between adjacent desks.

Sixty-nine percent of employees surveyed were 29 years old or younger. The turnover rate tended to be high: 49.5% of survey respondents had less than two years' history with Firma. Females constituted 62.3% of the survey respondents; males were 37.7%. The employees are distributed into five departments classified by their category of their work. Each department has higher-status employee(s), managers, employees and assistants. Each department has an assigned zone in the space plan. Within these departmental zones, no one other than department assistants have assigned desks. Every employee has flexibility to work on the floor and at the desk he or she prefers. Because of the clean desk policy, employees are given lockers with nametags in which to store belongings, including laptops and work-related materials. These lockers are located in the hallways.

Data Collection and Analysis

We selected ethnography because of its ability to deeply capture user experience from both the emic (insider's) view and the etic (outsider's) view.[28] In order to gain insights into employees' experiences and triangulate them with the researchers', we used multiple data collection tools: (a) participant observation; (b) four semi-structured, contextual interviews; (c) 12 unstructured interviews; (d) daily conversations with employees; (e) a survey; (f) secondary research on the firm and its workplace; and (g) a post-fieldwork meeting to receive feedback for our findings. As well, prior to the study, we conducted meetings with firm representatives and tested the research protocol and data collection tools with a pilot study. Necessary updates to our protocol and tools were made based on this feedback.

Data collection took place one and a half years after Firma's move into their flexible office from an office with private rooms and/or personal desks. This time gap helped to minimize any "honeymoon effect" on employees' assessment of their new workplace.[29] In order to decrease the oddness of having an outsider hanging around in their office, the employees were informed about our study via an email prior to our first day in the field.

During the research, one of the researchers served as the participant observer. The other two researchers participated in the interview sessions and distributed the survey. All three performed data analysis. The participant observer spent ten business-days at Firma. While ten days are much shorter than typical ethnographic studies in anthropology, this length of time is common for applications of ethnography in design research.[30] It is not easy to study organizations *in situ* because of confidentiality issues and possible distractions an outside researcher can bring. Because of these factors, the ten-day period was decided upon in negotiations between the researchers and the organization.

During the ten-day fieldwork, the participant observer observed the employees while also studied alongside them, participating with them while they worked, rested, socialized and ate. Interactions also included informal conversations with employees. While some of these conversations were focused on employees' jobs and experiences within the flexible workspaces, others were everyday conversations. Because some employees worked after business hours, fieldwork took place both during and after business hours.

In situ involvement and data collection are necessary for two main reasons. First, "what people do is not always the same as what they say they do."[31] In a study looking into users' experiences, it is necessary to be with them real time. Second, *in situ* participation builds rapport, which allows the participant observer to gain empathy with users and provide insights into the subjective details of their experiences. This is essential to gain insight into the felt interiority of Firma's employees.

While *in situ*, the participant observer specifically looked for employees' routines, behaviors in space, uses of the spaces (from building to desk), workplace selections and workplace changes within the office. This observational data provided insight into users' unarticulated behaviors (i.e., behaviors that are not easy to verbalize).[32] Through conversations, the observer gained insights into users' ideas, expectations and attitudes. This verbal data was compared against observational data in order to render a better picture of actual situations.

All field notes were recorded within a journal during each *in situ* day (Figure 2.3). At the end of each day, the participant observer added reflections from the day to this journal. She also took photographs to document her observations reflecting users' experiences.

Prior to the ten-day *in situ* period, the researchers made visits to the site; they toured the workplace and held meetings with executives for approvals to conduct the study. After the fieldwork, they revisited the office one more time to reassess the validity of the findings.

During the ten-day fieldwork, the researchers conducted four semi-structured interviews with two higher-status employees, with one of the flexible workplace committee members (who became the key informant in the process) and with the project architect. The interview guidelines included questions regarding the design and development story of Firma's new workplace, the narratives

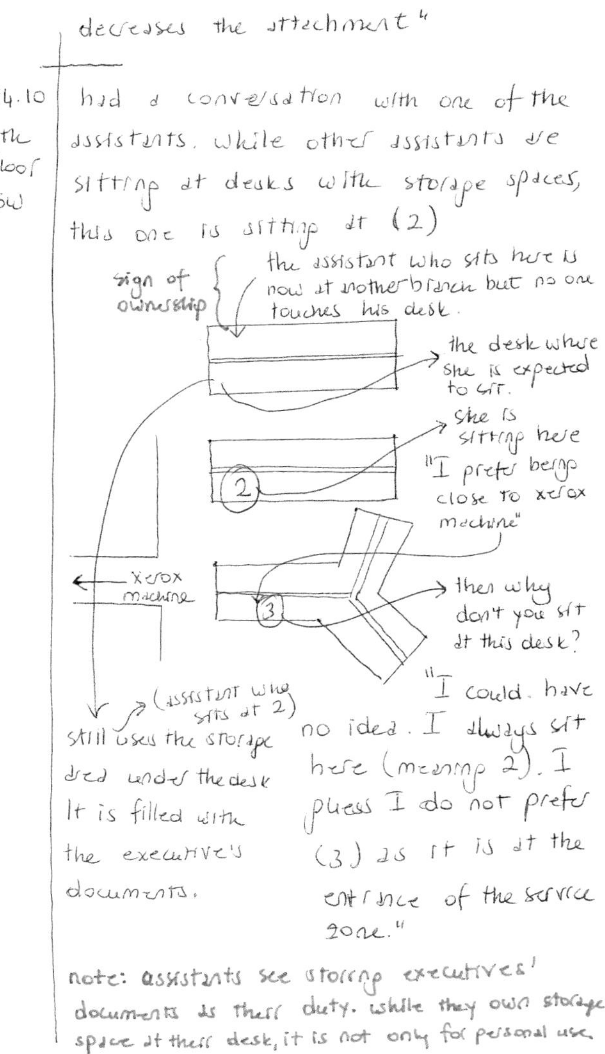

Figure 2.3 Journal page of field notes.

behind the decision-making processes in the shift to a flexible workplace strategy, the transition period from the old office to the new one and users' experiences at the new workplace from the interviewees' perspective. All four interviews took place on location during business hours and each lasted from 45 minutes to an hour.

As a requirement of their job, Firma employees spend most of their time working out of the office. Some people do not come to the office for days or even weeks at a time. Furthermore, more than 1,000 people work at Firma. This made it impossible to interact with every employee. In order to gain information from a wider group of employees and to triangulate observational and verbal data, the researchers distributed a survey. This survey was also the means to collect data on employee demographics. The survey was in two sections. The first section consisted of Likert-scale and multiple-choice questions to assess instrumental, aesthetic and symbolic dimensions of employees' perceptions. The second section consisted of open-ended and multiple-choice questions on demographics.

Our main data resources for analysis were the field notes, interview notes, written documents, photographs and survey results. The visual and verbal data collected through multiple tools were coded and grouped under different categories. After gathering all the data, a meeting was conducted with a selected group of Firma employees. In this meeting, we presented our findings and received additional data in the form of feedback.

Findings on Users' Experiences in Firma's Flexible Workplace

Because descriptive writing and thick description are distinctive characteristics of ethnographic studies, in what follows we describe Firma's employees' experiences within their flexible workspace under the aesthetic, instrumental and symbolic dimensions.[33] Again, what we are after is insight into the felt interiority of Firma's employees as they work daily in their flexible office space.

Aesthetic Dimension

Firma offers a holistic experience to its users in the aesthetic dimension. From its building to its interiors, from its furniture to its employees' dress code, from its website to its social zones, one feels a formal and "prestigious" corporate aesthetics. (Employees explicitly used this term to describe their workplace.) Perhaps in contrast to examples of playful flexible workplace design common around the world, at Firma, the flexible workplace emphasized formal and elegant aesthetic character. The dominant colors are white, tones of grey and orange, with orange being relatively less. Because of the dress code, employees mostly wear black-and-white business clothes in harmony with the colors of the office interiors. Two of the employees explicitly noted the change in their perception about the need to wear more formal attire upon coming to this workplace.

The unobstructed views without high partitions in office zones lent a feeling of spaciousness. There are no cubicles in the layout. Floor areas were not jammed with desks; in fact, space between desk rows was wider than expected. This is not surprising as the layout planning was based on the company's growth plan for 2020.

The furniture reflects the state of the art in office furniture design. The same applies for the seating units, coffee tables and lighting units in social zones. In reference to the furniture selection together with the interior colors and spacious layout, younger employees (between 25 and 35) particularly expressed positive views about "this prestigious design … complementing Firma's corporate image."

On the other hand, office tidiness and cleanliness change over the course of a day. Throughout the day, employees place personal belongings (e.g., laptops, documents, pens, snacks, water bottles) on desks. Trash and dirty mugs also pile up. Employees did not bother to take garbage to trash bins—there are no trash bins near desks—or take their mugs to the kitchenette when leaving the office. By the end of each day, several items, including packaging for snacks, sat on desks waiting to be discarded. Furthermore, there were piles of papers and pens on almost every desk. These papers and pens were not discarded by the cleaning team either; instead, they remained stacked on desks as piles.

Instrumental Dimension

While aesthetic impact might make first impressions, it became evident that the instrumental dimension played a central role in conversations and observations. Again, instrumentality has to do with physical artifacts and their function and use. In general, employees' comments on the instrumental dimension were in references to three aspects: desks, offices and flexibility.

On the desk level, employees reported locations of colleagues, distance to natural light and the service area, and noise level as reasons for selecting a desk location. A majority of the employees sit at the same desk every workday or check the availability of their favorite desk when they come to the office.

Another issue was the insufficient storage space at assistants' desks (as these are the only desks with filing cabinets). As one assistant explained, "Well, there is some more space under the desk, but it is impossible to reach because of its design. You need to get on your knees if you want to put something here." Not having enough storage space was also observed for the lockers provided for employees. This concern seems to be related to the clean desk policy as well. Because employees are not allowed to leave any physical markers or work-related items on desks overnight, they did not find the locker space sufficient for their belongings. They also complained about the hassle to store their items before leaving the office.

There were concerns regarding visual and auditory privacy. Audio privacy was especially relevant for the higher-status employees. During the field study, we observed that most of the meeting rooms were occupied by higher-status employees. Some rooms even contained their physical markers (e.g., plants, photo frames). When a higher-status employee is not there, other employees use these spaces. However, those physical markers convey symbolic meaning regarding the ownership of the meeting rooms.

Regarding the general office space, individuals in administrative services reported that they "had received several complaints in the first 3–4 months." This was the first intelligent building experience for many of the employees. They had difficulty using the controls to adjust for temperature, blinds and lights. Despite receiving emails explaining how to operate these controls, the majority were still not able to. Consequently, although we conducted the study in the wintertime, several windows were open to adjust for indoor air quality and temperature. As well, the automated lights tended to shut down an hour after the close of business hours, even if the floor was still full of employees. Employees got used to this problem: "If you wait for a few seconds and wave your hands and arms the lights would turn back on."

Some employees who spent more time in the office were bothered by the noise in the open office space. About one quarter of the employees indicated that they could not concentrate on their work due to noise. Several employees were observed listening to music with headphones to isolate themselves. Obviously, noise was more of a concern when the occupancy levels of the floors were higher.

The social spaces are marked with lounge chairs, sofas, book collections and coffee tables. These spaces are mostly located at the ends of open office zones. For this reason, they do not offer visual or audio privacy. They were empty for most of the day, with their most frequent use being after lunch.

All of this aside, employees were very positive about the flexibility to work at the floor and desk of their preference. Some even commented on increased interaction and friendship among employees as a result of the flexible workplace strategy. However, our observations showed that employees were not making full use of this flexibility. We observed that employees mostly preferred to sit near colleagues from their department in the zones assigned to that department. As a result, circulation across floors was limited.

Symbolic Dimension

While office aesthetics initially communicated symbolic aspects of Firma's workplace, we gained much deeper insights into the symbolic dimension of this workplace as we observed the behaviors of the employees and talked with them. While our findings on the mobility of employees among desks or across floors indicate that they were not making full use of the flexible approach, employees, especially younger ones (aged between 25 and 35), were positive about this design concept: "I enjoy having the flexibility to select my desk." They were proud of working at an office reflecting the state of the art in workplace design and strategy.

We already noted that, aesthetically, users found the office design prestigious and formal. When we asked the reasons for these associations, employees explained them in terms of the location of the office in Istanbul, or that they worked in an intelligent building, or that the office furniture was high quality, or the interior color scheme. The flexible workplace approach was also appreciated.

Symbolic prestige is also expressed in the employees' formal dress code and behaviors. The allowance of guests only on the first floor was also in line with Firma's formal and prestigious image. This allocation of space creates a separation between the employees and guests and further encourages the formal image of the organization.

But the formal design style and the clean desk policy brought a level of anonymity to the desks and the office space. We observed very few physical markers, such as frames including photographs of loved ones, either on desks or around the office. The desks with stable physical markers only belonged to assistants, who were few in number. As noted, only a few meeting rooms used regularly by higher-status employees displayed flowers and/or other personal touches.

Flexible workplace design seems to affect the hierarchical structure of the organization. The office design can encourage interaction. As one semi-structured interviewee and several unstructured interviewees noted, "Employees have better interaction with higher status employees and managers as they are more accessible because of the absence of private offices." But this absence of hierarchy was the biggest concern for managers and higher-status employees who are used to having private rooms. This is why these employees seemed to use meeting rooms to meet their need for value in symbolic ways.

Even though we saw them at different desks or zones, we observed the same groups of people sitting together every day. When employees come to work, the first thing they do is to leave their personal belongings (e.g., coats, laptops, bags) at a workstation to reserve that space for the day. Some employees also said they reserved a desk for their colleagues. This behavior, together with relocating based on the location of colleagues, indicates attachment to certain groups.

Discussion

Figure 2.4 summarizes all three theoretical dimensions in terms of users' positive and negative comments. This table underlines the fact that even though identified as three dimensions, the

	Positive Items	Negative Items
Aesthetic	• Spaciousness office design • Integrity in interior space and furniture design • Prestigious design of furniture	• Formal dress code among workers • Tidiness and cleanliness: Leaving cups and personal belongings etc around the place
Instrumental	• Flexible working • Increased interaction and friendship among employees	• Noise distraction • Insufficient storage space • Inadequate lockers • Lack of visual and auditory privacy • Lack of personal control to adjust the temperature, blinds, and lights
Symbolic	• Executive floor for guest • Location of the office in Istanbul • Working in an intelligent building • New ways of working: Flexible workplace approach	• Lack of belonging and self-attachment • Misuse of meeting rooms among managerial staff as private office

Figure 2.4 Positive and negative aspects of the aesthetic, instrumental and symbolic dimensions.

aesthetic, instrumental and symbolic elements work in tandem at the level of any one person's holistic engagement with his or her surroundings. Our earlier reference to felt interiority pertains to this holistic quality of experience. By the time an experience is felt, it is "my" experience, and that experience is within me even as I am within an environment.

The data from our ethnographic study shows that for the users, the most pleasant and satisfactory dimension is the aesthetic one. Positive comments on the aesthetics of Firma's workplace came especially from younger employees. For them, Firma's offices seemed to represent the state of the art in workplace design. This aesthetic quality in turn affects the symbolic dimension. Employees seemed to be proud to work at a place designed in keeping with the latest trends in workplace design. It motivated their attachment to the organization. Therefore, these findings support the significance of aesthetics on user experience, which is effective on employee satisfaction, productivity, motivation and well-being.[34]

As is the case for most flexible workplaces and open offices, users' comments on issues related to symbolic aspects were not always positive. Employees' preference for sitting at the same desk, a group's desire to sit in the same zone, higher-status employees' needs to use meeting rooms; these are all examples of concerns related to the symbolic dimension, perhaps in two ways. First, as pointed out in the literature, the absence of assigned desks raises concerns regarding status, identity, distinctiveness and attachment.[35] In order to regain these, employees create strategies such as defining a favorite spot and reserving it by leaving a coat there at the beginning of each day. We interpret the low rate of mobility as employees' desire to regain identity. This is in accord with Wohlers and Hertel's comments regarding the choice of a favorite desk and continuous use of it.[36]

Second, also supported by existing literature, the identity and status components of the symbolic dimension are not easily conveyed in this office as employees (including higher-status ones) do not have assigned offices/workstations.[37] And the clean desk policy does not allow employees to continuously mark workstations with personal belongings. Our observations indicate that having and being able to communicate, status and identity with physical markers (e.g., private office ownership) still appears to be significant. More frequent use of meeting rooms by higher-status employees and the reservation of desks using personal belongings can be interpreted as ways of communicating status and identity. Furthermore, leaving desks dirty might be related to employees' disgruntlement over a loss of sense of ownership and therefore of identity. Or similarly, because desks are not designated personal space, employees might just assume that custodial staff will clean up messes at the end of the day; this is also related to lack of ownership.

The need for privacy was a significant reaction to the open office plan. Employees cited the need for auditory privacy as the reason for their frequent use of headphones. Similarly, higher-status employees claimed to need more privacy, especially auditory privacy, because they held more confidential conversations. As a result, they used meeting rooms frequently as if they were their private offices. So, there is a tension between the claim that flexible workplaces reduce vertical hierarchy as a positive feature, versus the need for identity both functionally (instrumentally) and symbolically.[38]

The instrumentality (function and use) of the workplace was deemed least satisfactory of the three dimensions. Most of the concerns related to the instrumental dimension came from issues related to open office. But instrumental concerns might also be related to the intelligent building. For most employees, this was their first intelligent building experience. Consequently, they struggled to operate control devices and were often uncomfortable with the internal air quality, light and/or temperature.

Conclusion

Our analysis of a flexible workplace in Istanbul supports the idea of the interconnectedness between all three dimensions related to user experience.[39] As the most significant result of this interconnectedness, Firma's flexible workplace sacrifices aspects of the instrumental and symbolic dimensions for the sake of aesthetics. This conclusion raises concerns regarding the impact of the flexible workplace design strategy in user experience. At the level of felt interiority, it might illustrate a tension between corporate agendas for design and employee behavior (the actual practices at the employee level).

This study has theoretical and practical implications. Theoretically, it illustrates the value of applying the instrumental, aesthetic and symbolic classification scheme in tandem with ethnographic research tactics for the assessment of flexible workplace design based on user experience. We demonstrated and verified the possible transfer of the framework offered by Vilnai-Yavetz, Rafaeli and Yaacov to study flexible workplaces.[40] Practically, these findings remind designers, office planners and policy makers to assess these interrelated issues while making design decisions in relation to flexible workplaces. Furthermore, our findings indicate the significance of conducting ethnographically informed research in design practice for more in-depth analyses of the features related to user experience, which might otherwise be neglected.

We tested the three-dimensional framework only at a single workplace within a ten-day fieldwork period. It is necessary to repeat the same study at other flexible workplaces for stronger generalizability of our findings. It is also necessary to conduct studies of longer durations of time to better observe users' experiences. As well, findings reported in this chapter in conjunction with further studies on the topic from other geographic contexts will enable cross-cultural comparisons on the impact of flexibility on user experience in flexible office workplaces.

* * * *

Discussion and Exercises

Reflections about the Chapter You Just Read:

1. Please refer to the standard features of a research project explained in the Introduction. Then:
   a. In one sentence, identify the *research topic.* This sentence can be in the form of a question but does not have to be. In any case, write one grammatically correct sentence that captures the research topic of this chapter.
   b. Identify the *literature* related to this research project.
   c. Identify the *method* which the author used, and the *data* which this method generated for analysis.
   d. Explain how this approach is *generalizable* (or not).
   e. Explain how you can have confidence (or not) of the *internal and external validity* of this author's overall approach.
2. How do the authors define ethnographic research? In this context:
   a. What does *in situ* mean? Define and identify the benefit of *in situ* research.
   b. What does *fieldwork* mean? What went on during the fieldwork phase of this research, compared to what took place before and after it?
3. The authors' ethnographic methodology derives from a theory proposing aesthetic, instrumental and symbolic dimensions.
   a. Where did the authors get this idea? In what way do they justify its use as a framework for this study?
   b. Do you think the authors make enough of a distinction between these three categories?
   c. In what ways do these three categories run together? And how is this overlapping of the categories a problem in the way the authors presented their findings? Or: how is this overlapping the very nature of what they are after? Discuss.
4. The Introduction to this chapter asked you to consider ways in which "felt interiority," used in this chapter, relates to definitions of interiority in other chapters of this book. Here are more questions to consider:
   a. In what ways can Hadjiyanni's research in Chapter 1 be helped by an ethnographic component?
   b. How can Kalantari's virtual simulation research (Chapter 11) be a powerful tool for understanding employees' felt interiority in office plan designs of any variety?
   c. With reference to Kalantari's chapter, both he and the authors of this chapter refer to "thick description." In what ways does the use of this term in these two chapters differ, or the same? How do both get at "interiority"?
   d. Discuss the idea that Vaux's ethos-intensive objects (EIOs, Chapter 7) are themselves reflections of aesthetic, instrumental and symbolic traits of specific towns and communities. In other words, how can these three dimensions be used as a tool to analyze "sense of place" in general?

Exercises/Suggestions for Further Study

1. As a way to introduce students to design ethnography, read the section titled "The Table of Life" on pages 38–39 of *Design Ethnography* by Salvador, Bell, and Anderson (see the complete citation in the Additional Connections and Information section below). Similar to Oygur and

her colleagues, these authors gather both emic (insider's) views and etic (outsider's) views on cultural differences regarding food, family and social relationships in the United States compared to those in Italy based on the family meal.

a. Identify and list the emic (insider's) views the researchers were able to uncover.
b. Identify and list the etic (outsider's) views enumerated by the researchers.
c. Summarize how this data helped the researchers understand cultural differences between the two cultural settings.

2. In this chapter, notice how Oygur and her colleagues refer to the "triangulation" of data to ensure the validity of their findings. Now, conduct your own *in situ* observations during a site visit to a local coffee shop using physical documentation, behavior mapping, informal interviews and secondary research to triangulate findings. Work in teams to complete the following exercise as participant observers. (Please make sure you clear any protocols for research of this kind with your university's Institutional Research Board.) Your site visit should be at least one hour:
   a. Order a beverage and find a place to sit.
   b. *Physical documentation*: create a freehand sketch of the overall floor plan, estimating dimensions of the public spaces. Include counter and major furniture pieces, doors and windows. Take photographs (with the manager's permission) to document colors, materials, lighting. Note distinct areas or zones. Notice the sequence of those zones—the layout from entry to back, seating in relationship to electric lighting and windows, etc.
   c. *Behavior mapping*: on a second copy of the floor plan, observe and record the ways humans interact in the space from an etic view. Annotate the plan with noted behaviors of people in the space. How are people generally behaving in each of the zones you identified? How do the materials affect the behavior and why (i.e. behavior on upholstered vs. hard chairs, etc.)? Note circulation paths, where individuals and groups are sitting, and what they are doing.
   d. *Informal interviews:* To gain an emic view, engage in informal conversation with the employees, other patrons while waiting in line, or friendly patrons sitting nearby to understand their perceptions of this coffee shop.
   e. *Secondary research*: Search for additional information on the company through their website, written material available in the coffee shop, reviews on Yelp, etc.
   f. Write a summary of your findings, noting how each research tactic contributes to understanding the culture of the coffee shop and in particular how they *triangulate* to validate overall findings.
3. Conduct an ethnographic study of an open office environment using the framework applied by Oygur and her colleagues (again, check with your university's IRB).
   a. Arrange to visit a local business with an open office plan a minimum of three separate times for at least one hour.
   b. Before your first visit:
      i. conduct secondary research on the company
      ii. create a list of interview questions
      iii. conduct a preliminary site visit to document the physical layout of the office, including furniture, electric lighting, windows and doors
      iv. solicit information regarding office policies, such as the "clean desk" policy at Firma, and how desk assignments are handled
      v. conduct a survey of employees.

c. During the three on-site visits, use the following means of data collection:
    i. As in the chapter, specifically look for employee's routines, behaviors in space, uses of the spaces (from building to desk), workplace selections and workplace changes within the office. This observational data will provide insight into users' unarticulated behaviors (i.e., behaviors that are not easy to verbalize).
    ii. Engage in informal conversations to gain insights into users' ideas, expectations and attitudes.
    iii. Compare the verbal data with the observational data in order to *triangulate* the data and understand actual situations.
    iv. Record all the gathered field data for each *in situ* observation in a journal during the visit. At the end of each visit, add reflections to the field notes. Include photographs and sketches to document the observations.
d. After the site visits are complete, create a chart like the one on page 41 in the chapter, sorting the data into the framework categories aesthetic, instrumental and symbolic as positive items and negative items per category.
e. Analyze the categorical findings and resulting design implications/applications.

Additional Connections and Information

Ingold, Tim. "That's Enough about Ethnography!" *Hau: Journal of Ethnographic Theory* 4, no. 1 (2014): 383–395.

Murphy, Keith M. "Design and Anthropology." *Annual Review of Anthropology* 45 (2016): 433–449.

Otto, Ton, and Rachel Charlotte Smith. "Design Anthropology: A Distinct Style of Knowing." In *Design Anthropology: Theory and Practice*, edited by Wendy Gunn, Ton Otto and Rachel Charlotte Smith, 1–32. Bloomsbury Publishing, 2013.

Salvador, Tony, Genevieve Bell and Ken Anderson. "Design Ethnography." *Design Management Journal* 10, no. 4 (1999): 35–41.

Squires, Susan, and B Byrne, "Doing the Work: Customer Research in the Product Development and Design Industry." In *Creating Breakthrough Ideas: The Collaboration of Anthropologists and Designers in the Product Development Industry* (Westport, CT: Bergin & Garvey, 2002), 103–124.

Sunderland, Patricia L., and Rita M. Denny, "Framing Cultural Questions: What is Coffee in Benton Harbor or Bangkok?" In *Doing Anthropology in Consumer Research* (Walnut Creek, CA: Left Coast, 2007), 57–79.

Wasson, Christina. "Ethnography in the Field of Design." *Human Organization* 59(4) (Winter 2000): 377–388. https://www.annualreviews.org/action/doSearch?SeriesKey=anthro&AllField=10.1146%2Fannurev-anthro-102215-100224. Accessed June 12, 2019.

Notes

1 Sheila Danko, "Designing Emotional Connection into the Workplace: A Story of Authentic Leadership," in *The Handbook of Interior Design*, eds. Jo Ann Asher Thompson and Nancy H. Blossom (Chichester: Wiley Blackwell, 2015), 128–147; Kevin Kampschroer, Judith Heerwagen, and Kevin Powell, "Creating and Testing Workplace Strategy," *California Management Review* 49, no. 2 (2007): 119–137.

2 See Jungsoo Kim and Richard de Dear, "Workspace Satisfaction: The Privacy-Communication Trade-Off in Open-Plan Offices," *Journal of Environmental Psychology* 36 (2013): 18–26; Christina Wohlers and Guido Hertel, "Choosing

Where to Work at Work – Towards a Theoretical Model of Benefits and Risks of Activity-Based Flexible Offices," *Ergonomics* 60, no. 4 (2017): 467–486. Also Jungsoo Kim et al., "Desk Ownership in the Workplace: The Effect of Non-Territorial Working on Employee Workplace Satisfaction, Perceived Productivity and Health," *Building and Environment* 103 (J2016): 203–214; Jacqueline C. Vischer, "The Effects of the Physical Environment on Job Performance: Towards a Theoretical Model of Workspace Stress," *Stress and Health* 23, no. 3 (2007): 175–184; Jan Dul, Canan Ceylan, and Ferdinand Jaspers, "Knowledge Workers' Creativity and the Role of the Physical Work Environment," *Human Resource Management* 50, no. 6 (2011): 715–734; Janetta Mitchell McCoy and Gary W. Evans, "The Potential Role of the Physical Environment in Fostering Creativity," *Creativity Research Journal* 14, no. 3–4 (2002): 409–426; Rune Bjerke, Nicholas Ind, and Donatella De Paoli, "The Impact of Aesthetics on Employee Satisfaction and Motivation," *EuroMed Journal of Business* 2, no. 1 (2007): 57–73; Derek Clements-Croome, "Effects of the Built Environment on Health and Wellbeing," in *Creating the Productive Workplace: Places to Work Creatively*, ed. Derek Clements-Croome, 3rd ed. (London: Routledge, 2018), 3–40.

3 Briony Turner, Derek Clements-Croome, and Kay Pallaris, "The Multi-Sensory Experience in Buildings," in *Creating the Productive Workplace: Places to Work Creatively*, ed. Derek Clements-Croome, op. cit., 57–72.

4 Christine McCarthy, "Towards a Definition of Interiority," *Space and Culture* 8, no. 2 (2005): 112–125.

5 Andrew Harrison, Paul Wheeler, and Carolyn Whitehead, *The Distributed Workplace: Sustainable Work Environments* (London; New York: Spon Press, 2004); also Wohlers and Hertel, op. cit.

6 Rianne Appel-Meulenbroek, Peter Groenen, and Ingrid Janssen, "An End-user's Perspective on Activity-based Office Concepts," *Journal of Corporate Real Estate* 13, no. 2 (2011): 122–135; also Wohlers and Hertel, op. cit.

7 Wohlers and Hertel, op. cit.; Harrison, Wheeler, and Whitehead, *The Distributed Workplace*, op. cit.; Theo J. M. van der Voordt, "Productivity and Employee Satisfaction in Flexible Workplaces," *Journal of Corporate Real Estate* 6, no. 2 (2004): 133–148; Lynne J. Millward, S. Alexander Haslam, and Tom Postmes, "Putting Employees in Their Place: The Impact of Hot Desking on Organizational and Team Identification," *Organization Science* 18, no. 4 (2007): 547–559; Christine Barber, Andrew Garnar-Wortzel, and Trex G. Morris, "Workplace Mobility: Comparing Business Models of Early Adopters in Traditional Businesses vs. Consulting Firms," *Corporate Real Estate Journal* 1, no. 2 (2010): 168–180; Frank Duffy, *Work and the City* (London: Black Dog Architecture, 2008); Kimberly D. Elsbach, "Relating Physical Environment to Self-Categorizations: Identity Threat and Affirmation in a Non-Territorial Office Space," *Administrative Science Quarterly* 48, no. 4 (2003): 622–654; Kim et al., "Desk Ownership in the Workplace"; Sally Augustin, "Designing for Collaboration and Collaborating for Design," *Journal of Interior Design* 39, no. 1 (2014): ix–xviii; and Wohlers and Hertel, op. cit.

8 Harrison, Wheeler, and Whitehead, *The Distributed Workplace*, op. cit.; van der Voordt, "Productivity and Employee Satisfaction in Flexible Workplaces," op. cit.; and Wohlers and Hertel, op. cit.

9 P.M. Bosch-Sijtsema, V. Ruohomäki, and M. Vartaiainen, "Multi-locational Knowledge Workers in the Office: Navigation, Disturbances and Effectiveness," *New Technology, Work and Employment* 25, no. 3 (2010): 183–195.

10 Wohlers and Hertel, op. cit.

11 Kimberly D. Elsbach and Michael G. Pratt, "The Physical Environment in Organizations," *The Academy of Management Annals* 1, no. 1 (2007): 181–224; Jennifer Kaufmann-Buhler, "Progressive Partitions: The Promises and Problems of the American Open Plan Office," *Design and Culture* 8, no. 2 (2016): 205–233; James S. Russell, "Form Follows Fad: The Troubles Love Affair of Architectural Style and Management Ideal," in *On the Job: Design and the American Office*, eds. Donald Albrecht and Chrysanthe Broikos (New York: Princeton Architectural Press, 2000), 48–73.

12 Janice Barnes, "Situated Cognition in Flexible Work Arrangements" (Doctoral, University of Michigan, 2001); Goksenin Inalhan and Edward Finch, "Place Attachment and Sense of Belonging," *Facilities* 22, no. 5/6 (2004): 120–128; and Wohlers and Hertel, op. cit.

13 Elsbach, "Relating Physical Environment to Self-Categorizations," op. cit.; Kimberly D. Elsbach, "Interpreting Workplace Identities: The Role of Office Décor," *Journal of Organizational Behavior* 25, no. 1 (2004): 99–128; Samuel D. Gosling et al., "A Room with a Cue: Personality Judgments Based on Offices and Bedrooms," *Journal of Personality and Social Psychology* 82, no. 3 (2002): 379–398; Meredith Wells and Luke Thelen, "What Does Your Workspace Say about You?: The Influence of Personality, Status, and Workspace on Personalization," *Environment and Behavior* 34, no. 3 (2002): 300–321.

14 Kimberly Elsbach and Beth Bechky, "It's More than a Desk: Working Smarter through Leveraged Office Design," *California Management Review* 49, no. 2 (2007), 80–101 (81).

15 Elsbach and Pratt, "The Physical Environment in Organizations," op. cit.; Juriaan van van Meel, *The European Office* (Rotterdam: 010 Publishers, 2000).

16 Wohlers and Hertel, op. cit., 471.

17 Özgur Göçer, K. Göçer, Ebru Ergöz Karahan, Isil İlhan Oygür, "Exploring Mobility & Workplace Choice in a Flexible Office through Post-Occupancy Evaluation," *Ergonomics* 61, no. 2 (2018): 226–242.

18 Edward Finch, ed., *Facilities Change Management* (Chichester: Wiley-Blackwell, 2011); Mardelle Shepley et al., "Architectural Office Post-Occupancy Evaluation," *Journal of Interior Design* 34, no. 3 (2009): 17–29; Wohlers and Hertel, op. cit.

19 Elsbach and Bechky, "It's More than a Desk: Working Smarter through Leveraged Office Design," op. cit. 81.

20 Christine McCarthy, op. cit.

21 Paul Hekkert and Hendrik N.J. Schifferstein, "Introducing Product Experience," in *Product Experience*, 1st ed. (San Diego, CA: Elsevier, 2008), 1–8.

22 Richard Wener, "The Environmental Psychology of Service Encounters," in *The Service Encounter*, eds. J. Czepiel, M. Solomon, and C. Suaprenant (New York: Lexington Books, 1985), 101–112; Gerhard Heufler, *Design Basics: From Ideas to Products* (Zurich: Niggli Verlag, 2004); Cotzsh, "Product Talk," *The Design Journal* 9, no. 2 (2006): 16–24; P.M.A. Desmet and P. Hekkert, "Framework of Product Experience," *International Journal of Design* 1, no. 1 (2007): 57–66.

23 Iris Vilnai-Yavetz, Anat Rafaeli, and Caryn Schneider Yaacov, "Instrumentality, Aesthetics, and Symbolism of Office Design," *Environment and Behavior* 37, no. 4 (2005): 533–551. Also Kimberly D. Elsbach and Beth A. Bechky, "It's More than a Desk," op. cit., 80–101.

24 Noam Tractinsky and Dror Zmiri, "Exploring Attributes of Skins as Potential Antecedents of Emotion in HCI," in *Aesthetic Computing*, ed. Paul A. Fishwick (Cambridge, MA: MIT Press, 2006), 405–422; Cathy Mills and Larena Hoeber, "Using Photo-Elicitation to Examine Artefacts in a Sport Club: Logistical Considerations and Strategies throughout the Research Process," *Qualitative Research in Sport, Exercise and Health* 5, no. 1 (2013): 1–20; Manfred Thüring and Sascha Mahlke, "Usability, Aesthetics and Emotions in Human–Technology Interaction," *International Journal of Psychology* 42, no. 4 (2007): 253–264; Vilnai-Yavetz, Rafaeli, and Yaacov, "Instrumentality," op. cit.; Elsbach and Bechky, "It's More Than a Desk," op. cit.

25 Anat Rafaeli and Iris Vilnai-Yavetz, "Instrumentality, Aesthetics and Symbolism of Physical Artifacts as Triggers of Emotion," *Theoretical Issues in Ergonomics Science* 5, no. 1 (2004): 91–112.

26 Vilnai-Yavetz, Rafaeli, and Yaacov, "Instrumentality, Aesthetics, and Symbolism of Office Design," op. cit.

27 Iris Vilnai-Yavetz and Anat Rafaeli, "Managing Artifacts to Avoid Artifact Myopia," in *Artifacts and Organizations: Beyond Mere Symbolism*, eds. Anat Rafaeli and Michael G. Pratt (Mahwah, NJ: Lawrence Erlbaum Associates, 2006), 9–21.

28 Patricia L. Sunderland and Rita M. Denny, *Doing Anthropology in Consumer Research* (Walnut Creek, CA: Left Coast Press, 2007).

29 Shepley et al., "Architectural Office Post-Occupancy Evaluation," op. cit., 21.

30 Christina Wasson, "Ethnography in the Field of Design," *Human Organization* 59, no. 4 (2000): 377–388; Heather A. Horst, "New Media Technologies in Everyday Life," in *Digital Anthropology*, eds. Daniel Miller and Heather A. Horst (London; New York: Berg Publishers, 2012), 61–79; Sunderland and Denny, *Doing Anthropology in Consumer Research*, op. cit.

31 Diana E. Forsythe, "'It's Just a Matter of Common Sense': Ethnography as Invisible Work," *Computer Supported Cooperative Work: The Journal of Collaborative Computing* 8, no. 1/2 (1999): 128.

32 Elizabeth B.-N Sanders, "From User-Centered to Participatory Design Approaches," in *Design and the Social Sciences*, ed. Jorge Frascara (London; New York: Taylor & Francis, 2002), 1–8.

33 Michael J. Zickar and Nathan T. Carter, "Reconnecting with the Spirit of Workplace Ethnography: A Historical Review," *Organizational Research Methods* 13, no. 2 (2010): 304–319; Clifford Geertz, *The Interpretation of Cultures; Selected Essays* (New York: Basic Books, 1973).

34 Bjerke, Ind, and Paoli, "The Impact of Aesthetics," op. cit.

35 Elsbach, "Interpreting Workplace Identities," op. cit.; Elsbach and Pratt, "The Physical Environment in Organizations," op. cit.; Gosling et al., "A Room with a Cue," op. cit.; Inalhan and Finch, "Place Attachment and Sense of Belonging," op. cit.; Wells and Thelen, "What Does Your Workspace Say about You?," op. cit.; Elsbach, "Relating Physical Environment to Self-Categorizations," op. cit.

36 Wholers and Hertel, op. cit.

37 Elsbach and Bechky, "It's More than a Desk," op. cit.; Gosling et al., "A Room with a Cue," op. cit.; Wells and Thelen, "What Does Your Workspace Say about You?" op. cit.

38 Harrison, Wheeler, and Whitehead, *The Distributed Workplace*, op. cit.; van der Voordt, "Productivity and Employee Satisfaction in Flexible Workplaces," op. cit.

39 Rafaeli and Vilnai-Yavetz, "Instrumentality," op. cit.; Vilnai-Yavetz and Rafaeli, "Managing Artifacts," op. cit.

40 Vilnai-Yavetz, Rafaeli, and Yaacov, "Instrumentality," op. cit.

Chapter 3

Narrative Inquiry

Editors' Introduction by Dana E. Vaux and David Wang

Narrative inquiry is a qualitative method that provides a fluid, synthesized account. At its most basic level, narrative inquiry is the scholarship of stories. Narratives intertwine "real" stories based on "true-life" events and experiences in actual time and space with the narrator's voice and viewpoint from a later point in time.[1] Rather than simply reporting facts in chronological order, narratives place the reader "in" the context of events and places as they are described in the narrative. As Clandinin and Rosiek note, "Stories are one of the ways that we fill our world with meaning."[2] Uncovering those meanings through narrative provides understanding of human experiences. Clandinin and Huber describe narrative inquiry as "a way of thinking about, and studying, experience."[3] As such, it is closely related to some aspects of phenomenological research as a way to study experiences of individuals and inextricably linked with experiences in particular places.

Donald Polkinghorne divides narrative inquiry into two groups: analysis of narrative and narrative analysis. Analysis of narrative utilizes existing stories as its starting point. Narrative analysis utilizes raw data as its starting point. Out of this data the researcher attempts to construct a story that explains particular events or situations. Consequently, narrative inquiry can involve both the production of stories (the use of research data to construct new narratives) and the analysis of stories (the study of existing narratives).

In narrative analysis, stories are evidence that the researcher synthesizes into a focused account. The researcher disentangles threads of meaning in this collection of data, and the narrative provides a structure for reweaving them into a coherent discourse.[4] This can involve interviewing living participants who tell stories of their experiences as well as collecting "descriptions of events, happenings, and actions" to create a holistic picture of a setting or event from the viewpoint of human experience.[5] The accounts are "restoried by the researcher" into a narrative interpretation.[6] Vaux employs this narrative method in Chapter 7 to construct a new narrative illustrating how ethos-intensive objects contribute to place meaning.

Analysis of narrative collects stories and examines them for common themes and elements. Its basic function is to generate knowledge out of a "set of particular instances."[7] Existing storied accounts are collected as data, studied and examined to uncover embedded meanings. The researcher "analyzes the narrative ... for a close, interpretive reading of the subject at hand."[8] Similar to content analysis, he or she searches for categories and recurring themes to provide interpretive meaning.

The study in this chapter involves an examination of existing narratives utilizing the analysis of narrative method. Catherine Riessman's study *Narrative Methods for the Human Sciences* outlines four methods for narrative inquiry: thematic, structural, dialogical and visual.[9] Thematic analysis of narrative is content focused and concentrates on the meaning of a narrative rather than its form. This method closely parallels research methods used by historians and is often utilized when interpreting archival sources, such as "letters, diaries" and "auto/biographies."[10] When reviewing narratives from records in the archives of the Visiting Nurse Service, Cunningham conducts a thematic analysis to bring out hidden meanings in the text.

As you read this chapter, note how Cunningham utilizes narrative inquiry to foreground issues of race, class and gender and the following important points regarding narrative inquiry:

1. Narratives are dynamic. Their meanings often become more clear over time as social context changes. Notice how the nurses' records were at first utilitarian, both for professional documentation and fundraising, but subsequently they become important documents for raising social awareness.
2. The construction of a narrative is a shared voice of the source and the researcher. Note how Cunningham adds to the stories of the visiting nurses' accounts from her 21st-century lens, particularly regarding issues of race, class and gender.

Interiority

Cunningham writes explicitly from the lens of interiority in this chapter, illustrating how an interior encompasses more than what is contained within four walls. Accessing archival nursing narratives as data, she explores potential insights into experiences of interiority where boundaries are fluid with respect to physical attributes but contextual within social and cultural extents. In this way, she also explores the many scales of interiority, where "inside" elements of dwellings and "outside" elements of the street and city overlap with human experiences of poverty, acts of caring and issues of race, class and gender. Look for the following as you read:

1. Note how the nurses engage with varied scales of physical space mediated by social and relational realities.
2. Consider how Cunningham raises awareness of issues surrounding race, class and gender related to a sense of "insideness."
3. Cunningham states, "The interiors of the dwellings opened the door into an interiority that expanded beyond the physical walls of their inhabitant's dilapidated dwellings." Reflect on this and look for ways the recorded stories illustrate an interior "beyond the physical walls."

* * * *

Narratives of Healing: The Records of the Visiting Nurse Service of New York in the Era of the Great Depression

Erin Cunningham

Consider this story about Michael:

> After reaching the top floor, the nurse knocked many times before it was opened a tiny crack – just enough to enable a little boy to peer out…the boy [Michael] led her into the recesses of a dark room where the windows were closed and the shades drawn tight. In the far corner of the room … a woman lay hunched in bed, muttering to herself. The room was bleak and very cold, and only a few sticks of driftwood lay near a stove that had seen no coal for many a week.[11]

Stories like Michael's fill the records of the Visiting Nurse Service of New York, housed in Columbia University's Health Science Library. Archives such as this offer rich resources for narrative research—interviews, autobiographies, letters and accounts of nursing visits.[12] This chapter explores a series of visiting nurse practitioner narratives written in the 1930s, the era of the Great Depression, that documented their home visits—outlining the state of the homes, their treatment of illnesses, and the different organizations and institutions they employed in the treatment of the ill. Through a close reading of a selection of these stories, it explores how these archival sources can expand our understanding of the interior environment. It asks designers to consider how the design of interiors interacts with the "inner life" of its occupants, and how larger structural forces—like gender, race and class—also shape their interior world.[13]

The Visiting Nurse Service of New York provided a vital service. It developed at the turn of the 20th century in New York's Lower East Side to provide health care to mostly immigrant families living in tenements. By the 1930s, the community that the nurses served had grown from a small section of the Lower East Side, to over 100,000 patients across Manhattan, Queens, the Bronx and Harlem (see Figure 3.1).

The nurses no longer just served the impoverished of the Lower East Side but took on pay, and part-pay, alongside free patients. The patients they aided came from diverse backgrounds and ranged from mental health patients to maternity and tuberculosis patients. And, the spaces that the nurses entered included everything from the traditional tenement interiors, to migrant camps, and barges (see Figure 3.2). Although from disparate areas and backgrounds, the people that the nurses cared for were bound by a common set of experiences—depression, illness and isolation.

The broader purpose of this examination of archival nursing narratives is to explore their potential to provide insights into experiences of interiority. The definition of interiority is somewhat impressionistic. Scholars have described it as the "subjective feeling of space" or a feeling of inwardness, "interior-ness" or "inside-ness."[14] It invites a fluid approach to the interior environment—where the boundaries that define the interior are not necessarily marked by physical walls.[15] Instead, intangibles like the "inner life of the inhabitant" and larger "social and cultural contexts" can form the extents of interiority, and these move with us, dissolving the boundaries between building, street and city.[16] In short, interiority is inward, multi-scalar, relational and social, and it contains within it the promise to redefine the boundaries of the lived environment.

Historically, the concept of interiority underlies many urban reform initiatives—public health nursing included. For example, at the turn of the 20th century the Municipal Housekeeping Movement

Figure 3.1 Nurses with map of HSVNS Health Center Districts, 1948. Photo courtesy the Visiting Nurse Service of New York. See credits.

Figure 3.2 Visit to barge that is pulled up on piles, 1938. Photo courtesy the Visiting Nurse Service of New York. See credits.

catalogued its attention to the cleanliness and orderliness of the city as a natural extension of women's responsibility in the home.[17] It used this logic to bridge the divide between the private and public, interior and exterior, home and street. The street was construed as an extension of the home, and the act of caring for the streets affirmed this larger interiority. Public health nursing—which grew out of the same progressive reform fervor—used a similar logic. In her origins story, founder of the Visiting Nurse Service, Lillian Wald, recounts "reeking houses," "evil-smelling, uncovered garbage-cans," "overcrowded streets" and "slimy steps," which led her to the sick room and spurred her entry into public health nursing.[18] For Wald the streets of New York's Lower East Side were inseparable from the interiors of the homes; smell, dirt, disease and poverty forged an isolation that the nurses, through acts of healing, hoped to breach.

Turn-of-the-20th-century reformer Rheta Childe Dorr argued for a larger conception of home: "Home is not contained within the four walls of an individual home. Home is the community. The city full of people is the Family"[19] Her point is fundamentally about crossing scales. Our perception of "home" is not bound by walls.

By examining the cross-scalar implications of the visiting nurses' narratives, this chapter builds on the historic words of Dorr, and the current works of Petra Perolini, Christine McCarthy and Jacqueline Powers who leverage the concept of "interiority" to intersect the many scales of the built environment.[20] It also draws on the work of Lois Weinthal, who envisions the interior as a series of "concentric nested layers" that overlap and expand outward, from "the elements that are closest to the body" to "spaces where larger scales are accommodated."[21] Armed with an understanding of theories such as these, researchers can engage archives with new questions and find in them new answers.

In turn these narratives enrich our understanding of interiority. They move us beyond the physical characteristics of dwellings to capture the ordeals of the people who populate these spaces. And, by detailing how the nurses used these ordeals to connect and reconnect spaces, they allow us access to broader social and urban connections forged through the act of healing.

Narratives in the Visiting Nurses of NY Records

This study is historical in nature, involving the review of secondary sources and the textual analysis of primary accounts. Within this larger framework, however, it employs narrative methods to examine archival materials gathered from the Visiting Nurse Service of New York Records. The narrative approach applied to these archival stories is thematic, focusing on the content of the narratives rather than their structure. At its most basic, this approach involves examining narratives for reiterative themes and elements.[22] These themes emerge inductively, through a process of reading and rereading the narratives. Throughout this process, the thematic categories are contextualized with historical and theoretical readings that, in this case, examine the Great Depression and interiority.

The narratives examined as part of this project were written over the course of the 1930s. Nurses author the tales.[23] Their narratives allow us access into intimate spaces of healing where the treatment of patients took place in the home rather than in an institution. This care was personal, and it was collaborative, involving not only nurse practitioners but the patient, the immediate family and the broader community. Generally, the narratives were written after the nurse's treatment of the patient was concluded, or some kind of resolution was determined.

In their narratives the nurses provide case histories of the patients they visited, which were later used for publicity and fundraising reasons. The Great Depression, an economic collapse that began in 1929 and lasted until World War II, placed the nurses under immense fundraising strains. The narratives were used to raise awareness of the services the nurses offered, the plight of the people they served and the impact that they—and their patrons—had on the households that they entered. Consequently, the tales dramatize the nurse–patient interactions. And that is their appeal—they focus on human experience, both that of the nurses and the occupants of the homes they visit.[24] They are subjective; the nurse's analysis and viewpoint are transparent. And, the stories capture the emotionality of the site, humanizing the ordeals of the people the nurses treated.[25]

The basic tenet of the visiting nurses was to aid people who were sick at home. And, their stories offer an interesting glimpse into the interiors they visited (see Figure 3.3).

Figure 3.3 Nurse with elderly woman in shawl, Chinatown, 1936. Photo courtesy the Visiting Nurse Service of New York. See credits.

These were the homes of everyday people, who were struggling in the context of the Great Depression. The interiors they occupy are elusive spaces—they speak to a temporary, not a permanent, condition. Patients lived in old apartment houses, small railroad flats pushed up against the elevated street trains, hotel rooms, migrant camps and on barges. Some were "dark dreary rooms" with little access to light and air. Others were modest but "immaculate." Nurses told stories of people squatting in condemned and abandoned tenements, with "packing cases in place of furniture," no running water, and an "old coal stove" as the only source of heat.[26] They wrote of cramped apartments crowded with French and Italian antiques—the last vestiges of a wealthy past—"out of place in their present surroundings."[27] Nurses reported homes infested with cockroaches and rats "as big as cats."[28] Toilet facilities were often shared. In many cases, bills had gone unpaid and heat and electricity were shut off. Houses were often so dim from lack of lighting that the nurses "had to feel our way along the wall for the door of the apartment we were looking for."[29]

Nurses outlined the impact these interiors had on the health of the occupants. Many of the complaints the nurses tended to stemmed from the horrifying condition of dwellings: contagious diseases spreading as a result of overcrowding, and damp and dirty accommodations breeding pneumonia and infection. One nurse reported that a women had fallen down the stairs and broken her hip, because the landlord turned off the hallway lights; others reported children crowded into the same rooms and beds, transmitting communicable diseases like scarlet fever.[30] The nurses also told of children who developed colds in damp, leaking apartments: "when it rains they have to move the beds around so as not to be dripped on as the roof leaks in so many places" (Figure 3.4).[31]

In the old tenement houses, the toilets were often in the backyard. And, the trip to these toilets, down unlit corridors and rotten staircases, was hazardous to even the most able-bodied, and deadly to the elderly or those with disabilities. In one narrative, a nurse recounts the story of 80-year-old Mrs. Barry who had to use a "receptacle" in her apartment because she was unable to walk downstairs to use the facilities.[32]

Alongside charting the physical impact of the Great Depression on interiors and the physical health of its occupants, the nursing narratives also highlight its impact on more intangible aspects of the inhabitants' lives, such as their mental or psychological state. Essentially, the interiors of the dwellings opened the door into an interiority that expanded beyond the physical walls of their inhabitant's dilapidated dwellings and spoke to a shared experience of isolation—forged through poverty and pain.

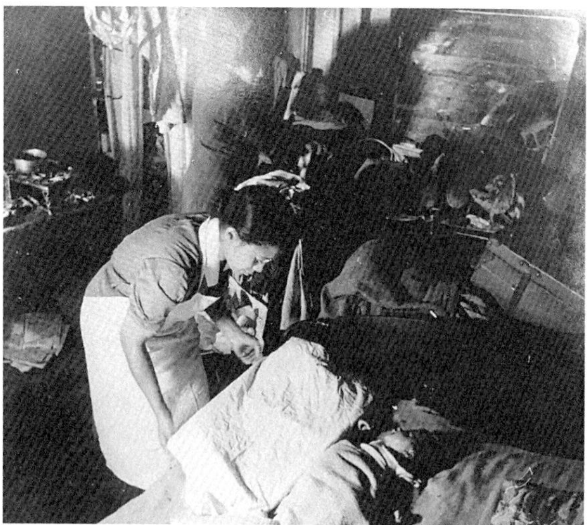

Figure 3.4 Nurse with infant and mother. Photo courtesy the Visiting Nurse Service of New York.

One nurse recounts the story of a Puerto Rican family living on relief:

> Caught up in the vise of a big city, they have been pressed into two tiny rooms. Outside, the elevated trains rumble by, the dust from the stampede below literally coats their window panes, yet strangely enough, they remain isolated and bewildered, sharing no part of the crowded life around them.[33]

A nurse from the Union Center wrote of a "small frail, 91 year old woman with a well-bread voice," living in a "small, bare but immaculately clean room." She had lived there "alone and uncared for" with failing eyesight and her body riddled with shingles for six months. The hospital had dismissed her as a "chronic invalid," and aside from a "kind soul" who brought her meals she had "little contact with the outside world and the hours were spent in reliving memories of an active, and heretofore

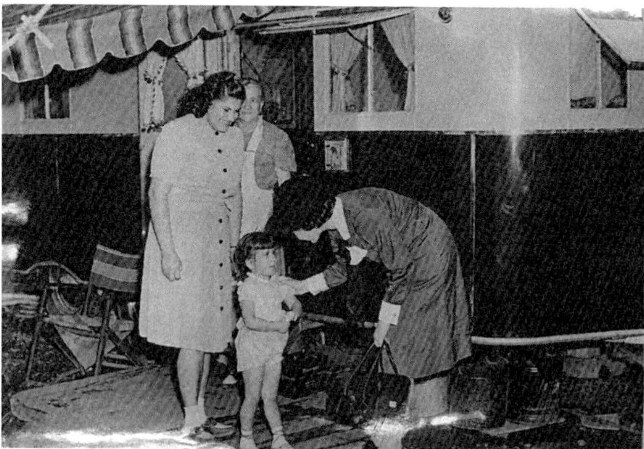

Figure 3.5 Nurse with child outside of caravan, 1938. Photo courtesy the Visiting Nurse Service of New York. See credits.

happy life, at the same time nourishing a growing resentment to the forgetfulness of a world for which she had done so much." [34]

Perolini states that we "experience interior spaces as relationships between exteriority and interiority – the contextual and physical experience of being in a space and the perceptions and feelings inside one's mind."[35] Narratives like the ones explored in this chapter help us to access this experience of interior spaces. They reveal the "complexities of the past," providing insight into everyday people, human experience and "shared meanings and values."[36] And, they are the focus of this study because they provide access to the personal, the relational and the intangible—all important components that make up interiority (Figure 3.5).

Narratives of Healing and Interiority

The Visiting Nurse Service of New York Records house dozens of these nursing stories. This chapter presents three of these narratives, focusing on distinct households in the Bronx, Manhattan and Queens in the 1930s.[37] The Great Depression frames these stories, which resulted in dramatic reversals of fortune for the residents. These narratives address the fallout from these changed circumstances: poverty, starvation, suicide, mental illness and delinquency. Filtered through the eyes of the nurses they provide detailed and, often, horrific glimpses into lives lived long ago. In each narrative, we don't know what happened to the families afterward; instead, they lock us into a moment, a time, a place.

All three stories involve a nurse entering the home to treat an illness. Each engages with physical space and scales as well as social relationships and practices. In these instances, interiority is not necessarily desirable. Poverty, bigotry and grief form the boundaries of this interiority. The case studies selected relate the conditions of families and households, and the forces that impact them, from hunger to pain, to isolation and destitution.

Themes of class, race and gender also emerge and may be understood spatially: for instance, the narratives point to the ways people were excluded from work based on race and gender. At the same time, the precarious nature of the interior environment marked concerns of downward class mobility and, possibly, the "physical collapse" of the home.[38] This relationship between conditions inside and outside the home exemplifies the interiority described here. In each of the three accounts we move beyond the walls that conceal private dwellings to explore the ways that healing brought nurses in and dwellers out to reveal the social, physical and even psychological forces that build our environments.

Narrative 1

The first narrative takes place in Morrisania—an area that is now known as South Bronx, New York. The nurse enters the home to treat a cold but is greeted with a much more dire situation.

> The Home Relief Bureau reported merely that one of the Harrison children had a cold. When the nurse got to the address on the call slip she thought there was some mistake. It was an empty tenement. She stepped cautiously inside the hall and heard people

> moving around in one of the flats. She knocked and the door was opened by a young woman. For a [*sic*] fraction of a second the nurse hesitated, then went quickly in. She thought she had become inured to extreme poverty but the scene confronting her was incredible. A young man was rekindling a fire in an old coal stove around which three children were huddled together. There were packing cases in place of furniture, a rickety iron bed with wretched looking covers and a couple of pans and some cracked dishes in the sink. The dampness of the room penetrated the nurse's heavy uniform coat. She was about to ask which was the patient – all the children looked ill – when there was a cry from the next room. What another? [*sic*] The mother said dully, It's Vallone, she's sick. The nurse went in, and in the dark unventilated room she saw a child about two years old, with a rash indicating measles, lying in a crib that was supported at one end by a box. She had a very high temperature. She was unwashed, her hair was slightly matted, and her tiny lips were cracked. It wasn't pleasant to see her tossing about on that uncomfortable bed. The nurse sent the father to telephone the supervisor and ask her to send for a diagnostician or ambulance, and wait for an answer.

With this passage, we are thrust into the action of the story. The nurse is responding to a report of an ill child. Following the address on a call slip, she confronts an "empty tenement." Inside she encounters extreme poverty, illness and desperation. This passage paints a vivid picture of the interiors that housed people during the Great Depression. We learn that her family is camping in an abandoned tenement—it is damp and fetid, furnished only with boxes and broken pieces of furniture.

> There was fortunately some warm water on the stove. She gave little Vallone a partial bath, alcohol sponge, mouth care, and brushed her hair with a towel. There were no linens for the bed so she smoothed it as well as she could and wrapped the child in a clean flannel nightgown provided by the mother. She lay still after that, soothed by the nurse's gentle care. The nurse then turned to the other children. Phil 6 1/2, Arnold 4 1/2 and Paul 3, had temperatures over 102 and bad coughs. She put them to bed, and with the help of the mother washed them. The father came back with a message that a doctor was coming immediately, so the nurse waited. He arrived shortly and after examining the children said they were all very sick and should be in a hospital, particularly Vallone. He marveled that she was still alive after being exposed to such conditions, and left with a promise to see that an ambulance was sent at once.

It is clear to the nurse that this is not a proper home environment. It is not a place of comfort or refuge, and its deficiencies are having a direct impact on the occupants' well-being; Vallone is deathly ill; the other children are failing as well. Although the family's time in the abandoned tenement is temporary, the consequences it threatened—the death of a child—are permanent. The nurse immediately sets to work, caring first for their physical health, and then expanding out to confront larger structural issues that are shaping the family's home environment.

> There was a look of such beaten indifference about the parents that the nurse postponed taking their history. She left them money for food and food order and said she would telephone the Home Relief and call again the next day. The Home Relief Bureau informed

> her that the family had applied for relief but they were not eligible for regular relief as they had been in the city only a few months.
>
> The next day Mr. H. told her they were both 26 years old. They were from a small community beyond North Tarrytown. When they lost their small business and could find no work they hitch-hiked to New York. There was no work here either. They did not know where to turn. Their only food for weeks was potatoes, spaghetti and tea given them by a Jewish greengrocer who was poor himself. The Center Committee supplied food until the nurse was able to make other arrangements. The family reported to the Resettlement Transportation Bureau and they agreed to send the family back to North Tarrytown, where they will be able to meet residence requirements, as soon as the children leave the hospital.[39]

The orientation comes at the end of the nurse's story. We find that joblessness, mobility, the search for work and sickness define this interior space. Issues of class, particularly "class insecurity" as a result of the Great Depression, are prevalent.[40] The parents, who had actively responded to joblessness through mobility, found themselves alone in the city without food, work or friends. Their mobility, rather than helping, exasperated the situation. They are completely isolated—"set adrift" in an "economic wasteland."[41] With the orientation comes the resolution.

We learn that the nurse, when she enters their makeshift home, breaks this isolation. She provides aid. She tends to Vallone, calls the doctors, provides money for food, telephones Home Relief and finally contacts the Resettlement Transportation Bureau, looking to ground the family again in home and community. Through her various engagements, she bridges scales and breaks Vallone's isolations, connecting the family to hospitals, food and transportation. The temporary community she constructs around Vallone's family redefines their interior space. In this sense, like a designer, the nurse is a creator of interiors. By altering the existing conditions, she works to forge better interiorities.

Narrative II

The second story comes from the Nursing Service's 79th Street Branch, which served upper East and West side Manhattan. In this story the nurse enters the home to treat the Father's severe asthma. Again circumstances are much more complex, expanding to encompass the family and broader social issues like racism and interracial relationships. The nurse begins with a brief orientation:

> Jack is a thirty-two year old Chinese, born in Shanghai and educated there. Though he comes from an old Chinese family he had attended a mission and became Christian. He was selected as one of twelve boys chosen throughout China, to come to the United States to study the organization of the Ford Plant so that they could then return to China to organize an overseas plant, modeled after the one in Detroit.
>
> A short time after they came to the United States conditions in China changed and these twelve young men were stranded here without funds or a means of livelihood. Jack, however, who was most intelligent, made the most of his opportunities while he was here and attended Columbia University, hoping that some work might turn up. But

> unfortunately, in spite of the fact that he is extremely well educated, and though he had been sent to the Philippines by China as a runner in an international contest, he has not been able to secure employment of any kind. Because of his color, the only jobs he would even be considered for, were as a cook or a chauffeur and even this he could not procure.

This narrative compares and contrasts with Vallone's family's story. The economic inequality of the Depression is an overarching structural issue; however, in this instance, so is racism. Jack is educated, comes from an "old Chinese family" and was selected for prestigious learning opportunities. Like Vallone's family, the nurse's narrative records changing circumstances; the Great Depression has resulted in downward class mobility. However, race compounds this issue. Jack's Chinese heritage, his interracial marriage (see below) and the mixed Chinese and Norwegian parentage of the children profoundly limit their opportunities. Widespread anti-Chinese sentiment marked this time period; between 1882 and 1943 federal law prohibited the immigration of all Chinese laborers.[42] Jack's intelligence and prestigious education from Columbia University neither overrides the racism he encounters, nor does it help him to obtain work for which he is vastly overqualified.

> The present situation in Jack's family is this. His wife, who is thirty-two years old, an American of Norwegian parentage, is in poor health herself. She tries very hard to keep their small apartment clean and to take care of the children, but conditions are becoming just a little bit too har[d] for her to bear. This is her second marriage and she came to it with a boy Robert, who is white and who had a definite mental attitude towards his yellow sisters and brothers and his "chink" father. The four children who are Chinese are not well, and particularly the little six year old girl is a great worry because her eyesight is bad.

With the next three passages the nurse outlines that this broader context of racial intolerance permeates the interior conditions of Jack's family: his children are underfed, his wife is worn out and his stepson is a bigot. The racism and illness that have caged him, and his family, in their home stress the point that interior conditions are more than physical.

> When we were first called into the home, it was to give care to Jack who suffers greatly from asthma and who has not had sleep for many weeks because as soon as he lies down, the asthmatic attacks come and he almost chokes to death. Our next problem was with Robert.
>
> After going into the home several times we were able to win him over and to get him to have a positive attitude toward his family, we have enlisted the help of the Big Brothers in keeping the boy away from the house and interested in recreation suitable for boys. He has now come to the point where he helps with the housework and takes care of his little brothers and sisters and even bathes them occasionally.
>
> There are many problems, however, in this family that have to be solved and which need the help of the nurses. Something must be done to help the father to get sleep and some degree of rest and relief from the terrific attacks which he gets. Something must be done to provide him with employment and to relieve his mental anguish for he is intelligent enough to recognize the symptoms of undernourishment which are so evident in his children and he wants them more than anything else, not to suffer because of the fact that there has been an alliance between himself and a white women. He is

> most happy with his wife and the two of them seem most concerned about keeping their home and their children intact. Yet the health of all of the children is bad for they are undernourished and live under distressing conditions because of this overcrowding.

In these passages the idea of "home" emerges, specifically the idea of an intact home. Illness, racism, bigotry and poverty threaten the home environment. However, the nurse suggests that with "the help of the nurses" this environment can be improved.

> We must try to watch these children's health, particularly since two of them showed suspicious reactions to T.B. tests.
>
> If the nurse is successful in having the gas and electricity turned on for the family, and if she can manage to get a job for the man through some channels, the health problem will not be so great, for at least their food will be available to help build up the weak little bodies. But here is a family where there are many implications and where tact and understanding are needed almost as much as material aid.
>
> It is to keep the nurses going into this home to provide what care they can to relieve this situation that we are using part of your gift.[43]

Like Vallone's story, there is the possibility of more severe consequences if Jack's dysfunctional home life is not addressed—TB, declining health, a splintered family. Again, we see the nurse acting as a design agent. Engaged in healing, the nurse looks to break the isolation that surrounds and encloses them as a result of interracial relations, poverty and illness, and create better interiors. She alters the physical interiors, working to have the gas and electricity turned on. And, she also looks to transform the boundaries of their interiority: she has the children tested for TB; she connects Robert, the stepson, with Big Brothers and looks to procure work for Jack. She cannot fix the larger structural issues such as the Depression and racism. However, the nurse brings healing by redefining the space in order to construct an interior that accommodates resolution. She acts with an urgency that appears to acknowledge that the "physical collapse" of the home is not unrelated to the collapse of the national economy.[44]

Narrative III

The third narrative is situated in Jamaica—a neighborhood in the borough of Queens. The nurse tells a tragic tale. She enters the home to examine a burned baby. The treatment of the baby is beyond her capabilities, and he is sent to the hospital where he dies the next day. She continues to visit the family, who struggle with the aftermath of a sequence of devastating events: the baby's death, the Father's suicide prior to the baby's death, and the mother's struggle with depression and subsequent attempt at suicide.

> The P. family was first known to the Henry Street nurse out in Jamaica in March 1934. At that time the family was on Home Relief and Mrs. P. was expecting her seventh child. Both father and mother were extremely worried about money. Mr. P. was a quiet, intelligent-looking man who at one time had owned quite a flourishing upholstering business, but he

> had lost this and been unable to find any sort of job. Eventually he became exceedingly depressed and moody, and then one day in February he kissed the baby, Raphael, good-bye, left the house and never returned. His body was found in the East River.
>
> After the death of the father, Mrs. P. turned all her affection to Raphael, the smallest boy, who was a cunning, talkative little chap. Ten months after her husband's death Mrs. P was preparing breakfast one morning when Raphael got in her way as he played around the gas stove. His mother stumble over him and a pot of boiling hot coffee that she was carrying to the table poured over his chest and abdomen. He died the next day at the hospital. Mrs. P. was almost demented. She was firmly convinced that her husband had called to little Raphael from the other world, and she recalled how when he went away from home he had kissed only the little Raphael good-bye. Mrs. P's attempt at suicide by gas was frustrated when the children came home from church one Sunday morning a little sooner than she had expected them.

In the first two passages of the narrative, the nurse furnishes the reader with background information. Like the other preceding narratives, class is a larger, structural issue. The P. family is experiencing downward class mobility—their prosperous lives made precarious by a crumbling national economy. But, in this case, the economic context is supplemented by a death, a suicide and an attempted suicide. As with the other cases, the nurse cannot change or fix this context; these events are permanent. The pain here is also different than Jack's asthma or Vallone's fever—it is emotional.

In the following passages, the nurse relates the inwardness of the P. family's story in her narrative. All the children are afraid to leave their suicidal mother alone. The mother sits on the couch and cries. The eldest sister, Julia, is placed in charge of the home; lacking suitable clothes, she is also bound to it. Her brother, Joe, escapes to the street in an attempt to distance himself from the grief of his home life.

> Home has been a very sad and depressing place for the other children in the family. Julia, the oldest daughter, decided to quit school last year, partly because she was afraid to leave her mother alone too much and partly because she had no suitable clothes and refused to go without stockings and always wearing the same poor dress. She has had to assume responsibilities suitable for an older person. She manages the family income of $75 received each month from the Department of Child Welfare, pays the bills, and does much of the housework. In addition she works five days a week caring for two little children, and thereby earns an extra five dollars to the family budget. She goes to continuation school once a week, and the nurse got her interested in a girls' club which meets once a week. The nurse has never seen Julia without an anxious look on her thin face.

The third passage connects back to the interior environment. There is something fundamentally wrong with the home. Rather than a refuge from the world, it is a "sad and depressing place" marked by gendered obligations. The mother, suffering from depression, cannot function in her traditional role as caregiver. Consequently, the eldest daughter is trapped in the domestic environment managing the family and taking on extra childcare duties.

> Mary, the fourteen year old, is very bright. She worked doing housework all last summer and saved the money so she could buy school clothes for herself this fall. She attends

> a vocational high school and is very anxious to complete her course. Dorothy is a pretty child, rather bold and forward and "lacking in respect", according to her mother. Marvel is a quiet, docile little girl who even at her tender age apparently knows she can never hope to take the place of little brother Raphael who died.
>
> Joe, the one remaining boy in the family, is thirteen. He is bright-looking and he used to do good work in school, but within the last few months he has said he hated school and he has stayed home for days at a time. Her refuses to go to church with the rest of the children. He was very fond of the little Raphael, and he tells his mother frankly that it was her fault the child burned. He fights with his sisters and teases them unmercifully. He has started "hanging around" with a crowd of rough older boys, and often he stays out very late at night. The nurse has been very much interested in Joe, for he has seemed to her to have excellent possibilities that were going to waste. She interviewed his teacher who said Joe was bright enough but he was inattentive and restless and that if he kept playing truant and hanging around with the gang he would soon be getting himself into trouble. When she talked to Joe about his plans and wishes and ambitions, Joe said the one thing he wanted more than anything in the world was "just a very little radio", and then there would be something at home that was cheerful. "How would you like to stay at home every night, nurse, with a bunch of girls and a mother who sits and cries and looks at pictures?"

Issues of gender, or at least the nurse's middle-class conception of gender, also arise in her description of Joe and her concerns regarding his possible slide into delinquency. In an era of Hoovervilles and massive unemployment, there were concerns of boys and men being lost to the streets.[45] Without the benefits of a nourishing, or "cheerful," home environment, and in a space that does not accommodate his gender, Joe is forced into the street and left susceptible to the various vices he might encounter there.

> The Henry Street nurse agrees with Joe that a radio would be a splendid thing for this family, and that all the family, not just the restless Joe, would be happier if they had one, "just a very little one". And so ten dollars has been obtained from a special fund, and in just a few days the P. family will be listening in while Joe tunes in on the nation-wide hook-ups.[46]

Throughout the narrative, the nurse acts to redefine the interior space; she looks to bring the women out of the home, and Joe off the street. She connects Julia with a girl's club and talks to Joe's teacher. Finally, the gift of a radio, providing "nation-wide hook-ups," promises transformation of the whole family's home life, redefining their interior world. With the radio the nurse is able to expand the boundaries of their home, without actually changing the physical parameters of their interior spaces. The radio—which draws Joe outside the home while placing him squarely within it—also helps to bridge binaries: male/female; public/private; street/home.

Conclusion

This chapter begins with the story of Michael, who shows up at his school pleading for help. There is more to his story. In response to his pleas, the school principal contacted a nurse. In a "rickety" riverside tenement known to "house shady characters," that nurse found the mother huddled under her blankets, feverish and delirious. Four months earlier, she had fled to this location to hide from an abusive husband. Although near death, she was fearful that seeking help would result in her discovery. Inside the house, the nurse lit the fire in the "bleak," "cold" room and then she called for a doctor, fuel, groceries and finally a housekeeper. She continued to visit the family—providing care and conversation. Finally, in response to the mother's heightened fears of discovery she sent the entire family to a convalescent home for a month to "regain their strength."[47] To "heal" the nurse had to address the spatial, physical and emotional needs of Michael and his mother. Narratives like Michael's, which number in the dozens in the Visiting Nurse Service Records, reveal that interiors are seldom contained by physical walls.

In fact, stories such as Michael's, Vallone's, Jack's and the P. family's broaden our understanding of the interior. In their narratives, the nurses drew the inside out, revealing an interiority of isolation, fear and depression bound by race, class and gender. This interiority was not divorced from materiality and the physical interior. Instead it was in dialogue with it; the inner lives of the inhabitants played out against the physical backdrop of these Depression-era interiors, and forces like economic dislocation and racial prejudice shaped that environment. Healing involved not only addressing physical and psychological needs, as well as acknowledging overarching structural issues, but transforming the material environment.

Narratives, like the ones examined in this chapter, invite designers to embrace a deeper understanding of human experience and the ways it shapes the built environment. Too often, we think about interior space as closed, or as separated, from the outer world when in reality it is not. Walls separate living rooms from the street, stoops from hallways, kitchens from alleyways. But in reality, these spaces are connected by us; we pass between them. This is interiority at its most basic: the connection between spaces—and conditions—thought to be separate. As the archival materials reveal, the ideas, the racisms, the sexisms, the enthusiasms and frustrations of the street and the home do not dissolve at the threshold; they travel with us, and, in those travels, they continue to shape our environments.

So, what does this mean for design application? In her discussion of the application of interiority to interior design, Perolini states, "What is designed is never simply an interior." She continues, "All interior design comes from an interiority, an experience of being in tangible physical space and from the experience of inside-ness, of constraint and containment within intangible social and psychological constructs."[48] To embrace this "complexity" creates reflective practice. This chapter suggests that one of the ways of accessing this complexity is through the narrative method. The nursing narratives explored here reveal the interplay between the spatial qualities of these Depression-era interiors, the inner-state of inhabitants and structural issues, like race, class and gender.

The Visiting Nurse Service narratives also highlight the potential of designers to interface with complexity. The nurses looked to define and shape interiors on multiple levels, and across scales, to facilitate healing, assistance and resolution; in doing so, they created not just healthier interiors but also healthier interiorities.[49] For them, healing meant communicating across different stakeholders and ways of knowing. The nurses were conversant in the different social organizations that existed, such as the Resettlement Transportation Bureau, Big Brothers and various girls' clubs. They were conversant in the needs, desires and agency of the people who dwelled in the interiors themselves. And finally, they were conversant in the structural forces like poverty and racism that shaped the interior conditions of their patients. As designers, we also need to think more comprehensively.

In their work, the nurses point to design's potential to alter the lived environment and invite us, as designers, to consider how we can broaden our understanding of "interior" to address the psychological and structural forces that are built into the spaces that we shape—in our studio, in our profession and in the community.

* * * *

Discussion and Exercises

Reflections about the Chapter You Just Read:

1. Please refer to the standard features of a research project explained in the Introduction. Then:
   a. In one sentence, identify the *research topic*. This sentence can be in the form of a question but does not have to be. In any case, write one grammatically correct sentence that captures the research topic of this chapter.
   b. Identify the *literature* related to this research project.
   c. Identify the *method* which the author used and the *data* which this method generated for analysis.
   d. Explain how this approach is *generalizable* (or not).
   e. Explain how you can have confidence (or not) of the *internal and external validity* of this author's overall approach.
2. Discuss the importance of history as a tool of analysis for interior designers as this chapter exemplifies. For example, how would awareness of historical knowledge gained from Cunningham's study inform the design of current housing trends, such as co-housing, micro-housing or subsidized housing?
3. This study involves the review of secondary sources and the textual analysis of primary accounts. How are these useful for understanding current issues and their relationship with interior design?
4. Cunningham makes the point that the Visiting Nurse narratives were "later used for fundraising." In fact, in the third narrative, a comment is written directly to a source who provided a "gift." Discuss how financial motivations might have impacted the tone of how these accounts were written.
5. In these stories, the nurse is a design agent; she works to create better interiors. However, this involves more than modifying the existing environment—she also has to confront larger structural issues that shape the built environment. Read Petra Perolini's article "Interior Spaces and the Layers of Meaning" and consider how the nurse's engagement with interiors speaks to "the agency interior design potentially has in the world" (see full citation in Additional Resources below). How can the idea of interiority help to reconceptualize our role as designers?
6. Note that Cunningham explains how race, class and gender are spatialized in these narratives.
   a. Although these narratives are from the 1930s, how do you think these factors continue to impact how we think about, and design, space today? Can you think of any examples?
   b. Vaux (Chapter 7), Pable (Chapter 8) and Cunningham all raise awareness of issues surrounding race, class and gender. How are these similar? Different?

Exercises/Suggestions for Further Study

1. A thematic analysis of narratives, which is similar to the method employed in this chapter, focuses on the content of narratives. In *Narrative Methods for the Human Sciences*, Catherine Riessman presents sociologist Maria Tamboukou's work as an excellent example of an academic study that applies thematic analysis to archival sources. Read Chapter 3 of Riessman's book and using Tamboukou's methods reexamine the narratives provided in this chapter. What other themes might be pulled out of these narratives? How would you go about validating these themes?
2. Although the concept of interiority takes us beyond the physical parameters of an interior space, it is not divorced from materiality. Reread the narratives provided and discuss how materiality and interiority intersect.
   a. How does Joe's experience of interiority differ from his sister Julia's experience?
   b. What other similarities and differences can you find within and between narratives?
   c. How does the experience of interiority for those living in tenements in Cunningham's examples differ from the interiority experience of homeless individuals explained by Pable in Chapter 8?
   d. Why does the radio matter? What are the implications for contemporary space?
3. Where might we gather stories from today? Find contemporary stories of spaces: Who authors these stories? What stories are they telling of interiors? What themes emerge? Can you identify interiority? Who are the design agents? And, how might these stories impact the design of this type of space?
4. The narratives presented in this chapter are stories of nurses' interventions. What connections are they creating? What stories are they telling of interiors? Read Edward Hollis' manuscript "Unreliable Guides: Introducing, Mapping, and Performing Interiors," (see reference below) which examines the stories people tell about interiors. Consider the following questions:
   a. In many ways the nurses are guides to these historic interiors. How are the nurses talking about interiors? What is their agenda? How does it impact the narratives, and the image of the interior that arises from these narratives? And, how does knowledge of the nurse's voice help us unpack these narratives?
   b. Despite the fact that nurses tell these tales, how is the construction of these historic interiors a "collaborative act" involving the researcher, the narrator and the inhabitants of the spaces?

Additional Information and Resources

Atmodiwirjo, Paramita and Yandi Andri Yatmo. "Interiority in Everyday Space: A Dialogue between Materiality and Occupation." *Interiority* 2, no. 1 (2018): 1–4.

Atmodiwirjo, Paramita and Yandi Andri Yatmo. Editorial: Interiority as Relations," *Interiority* 1, no. 2 (2018), 87–90.

Cunningham, Erin. "Bringing the Past In: Narrative Inquiry and the Preservation of Historic Interiors." In *The Handbook of Interior Design*, edited by Jo An Asher Thompson and Nancy Blossom, 70–94. New York: John Wiley & Sons, 2014.

Danko, Sheila. "Designing Emotional Connection into the Workplace: A Story of Authentic Leadership." In *Handbook for Interior Design*, edited by J. Thompson and N. Blossom (West Sussex: Wiley-Blackwell Publishing, Inc., 2015), 128–147

Hollis, Edward. "Unreliable Guides: Introducing, Mapping, and Performing Interiors." *Interiority* 1, no. 1 (2018): 21–35.

McCarthy, Christine. "Toward a Definition of Interiority," *Space and Culture* 8, no. 2 (2005): 112–125.

Morgan-Fleming, Barbara, Sandra Riegle, and Wesley Fryer. "Narrative Inquiry in Archival Work." In *Handbook of Narrative Inquiry: Mapping a Methodology*, edited by D. Jean Clandinin, 81–98. Thousand Oaks, CA: Sage Publications, 2007.

Perolini, Petra Simona. "Interior Spaces and the Layers of Meaning." *Design Principles and Practices: An International Journal* 5, no. 6 (2011): 163–174.

Power, Jacqueline. "The Australian Indigenous Sky Dome and its Potential to Reshape Interiority." *Interiors* 8, no. 3 (2018): 125–140.

Riessman, Catherine Kohler. *Narrative Methods for the Human Sciences*. Los Angeles, CA: Sage Publications, 2008.

Weinthal, Lois. "Introduction." In *Toward A New Interior: An Anthology of Interior Design Theory*, edited by Lois Weinthal, 11–19. New York: Princeton Architectural Press, 2011.

Notes

1 Groat and Wang, op. cit., 176, 180; Erin Cunningham, "Bringing the Past In: Narrative Inquiry and the Preservation of Historic Interiors," in *Handbook for Interior Design*, eds. J. Thompson and N. Blossom (West Sussex: Wiley-Blackwell Publishing, Inc., 2015), 70–94.

2 D. Jean Clandinin and Jerry Rosiek, "Mapping a Landscape of Narrative Inquiry: Borderland Spaces and Tensions," in *Handbook of Narrative Inquiry: Mapping a Methodology*, ed. D. Jean Clandinin (Thousand Oaks, CA: Sage, 2006), 35–75.

3 D. Jean Clandinin and Jerry Huber. "Narrative Inquiry," in *International Encyclopedia of Education*, 3rd ed., eds. B. McGaw, E. Baker, and P.P. Peterson (New York: Elsevier, 2010), 2. http://www.mofet.macam.ac.il/amitim/iun/CollaborativeResearch/Documents/NarrativeInquiry.pdf

4 Groat and Wang, op. cit., 173–185; William Cronon, "A Place for Stories: Nature, History, and Narrative," in *Journal of American History* 78, no. 4 (1 March 1992): 1347–1351; D.J. Clandinin and F.M. Connelly, *Narrative Inquiry: Experience and Story in Qualitative Research* (San Francisco, CA: Jossey-Bass, 2000), 63, 74; Margaret Portillo, "Narrative Inquiry," *Journal of Interior Design* 26, no. 2 (2000): iv; Part two of Chapter 7 is an example of this type of narrative method.

5 Donald Polkinghorne, "Narrative Configuration in Qualitative Analysis," in *Life History and Narrative*, eds. J. Amos Hatch and Richard Wisniewski (London: Routledge, 1995), 21; See Danko, op. cit., 128–147. Sheila Danko references this narrative method when she states, "Unlike case study reporting, which endeavors to provide a whole picture of the case with multiple issues and multiple voices, results presented using a story format intentionally focus on a particular issue in question and often a single voice."

6 John W. Creswell, *Research Design: Qualitative, Quantitative and Mixed Methods Approaches*, 4th ed. (Thousand Oaks, CA: Sage, 2014), 13–14.

7 Polkinghorne, op. cit., 14.

8 Norman K. Denzin and Yvonna S. Lincoln. *Handbook of Qualitative Research* (Thousand Oaks, CA: Sage Publications, 2000), 358.

9 Catherine Riessman, *Narrative Methods for the Human Sciences* (Thousand Oaks, CA: Sage Publications, 2008), 77.

10 Ibid., 63.

11 "Come Quick," 1930s, Visiting Nurse Service of New York Records, Box 203, Folder 10, Archives and Special Collections at the Augustus C. Long Health Sciences Library of Columbia University.

12 Barbara Morgan-Fleming, Sandra Riegle, and Wesley Fryer, "Narrative Inquiry in Archival Work," in *Handbook of Narrative Inquiry: Mapping a Methodology*, ed. D. Jean Clandinin (Thousand Oaks, CA: Sage Publications, 2007), 82.

13 We might understand a structural force as a social, political, legal, or economic condition that is beyond an individual's control, and is largely unalterable. See for instance: Paul Spicker, Sonia Alverez Leguizamon, and David Gordon, eds. *Poverty: An International Glossary* (London: Zed Books, 2007); Joel E. Black, *Structuring Poverty in the Windy City: Autonomy, Virtue, and Isolation in Post-Fire Chicago* (Lawrence: University Press of Kansas, 2019).

14 See Jacqueline Power, "The Australian Indigenous Sky Dome and its Potential to Reshape Interiority," *Interiors* 8, no. 3 (2017): 136; Petra Perolini, "Interior Environments: The Space of Interiority," *Zoontechnica: The Journal of Redirective Design* 3 (2014): 2.

15 Christine McCarthy, "Toward a Definition of Interiority," *Space and Culture* 8, no. 2 (May 2005): 112.

16 Paramita Atmodiwirjo and Yandi Andri Yatmo, "Interiority in Everyday Space: A Dialogue between Materiality and Occupation," *Interiority* 2, no. 1 (2018): 2; Paramita Atmodiwirjo and Yandi Andri Yatmo, "Editorial: Interiority as Relations," *Interiority* 1, no. 2 (2018): 88.

17 Daphne Spain, *How Women Saved the City* (Minneapolis: University of Minnesota Press), 9.
18 Lillian Wald, *The House on Henry Street* (New York: Henry Holt and Company, 1915), 5.
19 Rheta Louise Childe Dorr, *What Eight Million Women Want* (Boston, MA: Small, Maynard & Company, 1910), 327.
20 Petra Perolini, "Bringing Interiority to Interior Design," *Zoontechnica* 2 (2012): 1–11; Petra Perolini, "Interior Spaces and the Layers of Meaning," *Design Principles & Practices – An International Journal* 5, no. 2 (2011): 165–174; McCarthy, op. cit., 112–125; Jacqueline Power, "The Australian Indigenous Sky Dome and its Potential to Reshape Interiority," *Interiors* 8, no. 3 (2018): 125–140.
21 Lois Weinthal, *Toward A New Interior: An Anthology of Interior Design Theory*, ed. Lois Weinthal (New York: Princeton Architectural Press, 2011), 11–19.
22 This approach is often employed when addressing archival sources, such as "letters, diaries" and "auto/biographies." Donald Polkinghorne refers to this narrative approach as "narrative analysis." See: Polkinghorne, "Narrative Configuration in Qualitative Analysis," in *Life History and Narrative*, eds. J. Amos Hatch and Richard Wisniewski (London: Routledge, 1995), 14.
23 In this study I use the terms "narratives," "stories" and "tales" interchangeably.
24 D. Jean Clandinin and F. Michael Connelly, *Narrative Inquiry: Experience and Story in Qualitative Research* (San Francisco, CA: John Wiley & Sons, 2000), 20.
25 Although the stories are from the viewpoint of the nurse practitioner, often these stories include direct quotes from the patients—giving access to typically marginalized voices.
26 "Morrisania," 1930s, November 1935 Visiting Nurse Service of New York Records, Box 203, Folder 11, Archives and Special Collections at the Augustus C. Long Health Sciences Library of Columbia University.
27 Mrs. Kremer, letter to Mrs. Koenig, Visiting Nurse Service of New York Records, Box 203, Folder 22 Archives and Special Collections at the Augustus C. Long Health Sciences Library of Columbia University.
28 "Housing Stories," 16 December 1936, Visiting Nurse Service of New York Records, Box 203, Folder 30, Archives and Special Collections at the Augustus C. Long Health Sciences Library of Columbia University, 1.
29 "Housing Stories," 1.
30 "Housing Stories," 2.
31 "Housing Stories," 1.
32 "Housing Stories," 2.
33 "A Day with the Henry Street Nurse", November 1935 Visiting Nurse Service of New York Records, Box 203, Folder 26, Archives and Special Collections at the Augustus C. Long Health Sciences Library of Columbia University, 4.
34 "A small frail, 91 year old woman," 1930s, Visiting Nurse Service of New York Records, Box 203, Folder 22, Archives and Special Collections at the Augustus C. Long Health Sciences Library of Columbia University.
35 Perolini, "Bringing Interiority to Interior Design," 2.
36 Morgan-Fleming, Riegle, and Fryer, op. cit., 82; Margaret Portillo, "Narrative Inquiry," *Journal of Interior Design* 26 (May 2000): iv.
37 Because not all the narratives can be presented in this chapter, it was necessary to select representative and cogent accounts, thereby privileging some narratives over others.
38 For a discussion of the Great Depression, downward mobility and fears of "physical collapse," see Chapter nine of Nancy Isenberg's book: Nancy Isenberg, *White Trash: The 400-Year Untold History of Class in America* (New York: Viking, 2016).
39 "Morrisania," 1930s, November 1935 Visiting Nurse Service of New York Records, Box 203, Folder 11, Archives and Special Collections at the Augustus C. Long Health Sciences Library of Columbia University.
40 Isenberg, op. cit., 216.
41 Isenberg, op. cit., 211.
42 Lew-Williams Beth, *The Chinese Must Go: Violence, Exclusion, and the Making of the Alien in America* (Cambridge, MA: Harvard University Press, 2018).
43 "Jack is a thirty-two year old," 1930s, November 1935 Visiting Nurse Service of New York Records, Box 203, Folder 22, Archives and Special Collections at the Augustus C. Long Health Sciences Library of Columbia University.
44 Isenberg, op. cit., 211.
45 See: David Wolcott, "'The Cop Will Get You': The Police and Discretionary Juvenile Justice, 1890–1940," *Journal of Social History* 35, no. 2 (2001): 349; Eric C. Schneider, *Vampires, Dragons, and Egyptian Kings: Youth Gangs in Postwar New York* (Princeton, NJ: Princeton University Press, 1999).
46 "The P. Family," November 1935 Visiting Nurse Service of New York Records, Box 203, Folder 24, Archives and Special Collections at the Augustus C. Long Health Sciences Library of Columbia University.
47 "Come Quick," 1930s, Visiting Nurse Service of New York Records, Box 203, Folder 10, Archives and Special Collections at the Augustus C. Long Health Sciences Library of Columbia University.
48 Perolini, "Bringing Interiority to Interior Design," 9.
49 Petra Perolini, "Interior Spaces and the Layers of Meaning," 164.

Chapter 4

Applied Historic Preservation

Editors' Introduction by Dana E. Vaux and David Wang (with Lisa Tucker)

Historic preservation combines design and research and varies widely around the world. The original ideological divide surrounding preservation arose in the 19th century between John Ruskin (1819–1900) and Eugene Emmanuel Violett-Le-Duc (1814–1879). Ruskin, an architecture critic and social reformer, praised historic buildings as ruins that should not be improved. In fact, he argued that it was not possible to "restore" a building. But Violett-Le-Duc, an architect and theorist, sought to improve on history by providing for a building's completion whether it ever existed as such or not. An example is his proposal to correct the façade of Notre Dame by adding a second tower which he thought would have been built if the church had been completed.[1] Historic preservation in the United States lies somewhere between these two positions.

The preservation movement in the United States began as a grassroots movement led by local groups to save certain important properties; such as the efforts of the Mount Vernon Ladies Association, led by Pamela Cunningham, to preserve George Washington's house. But for many, historical awareness is not always an important matter. For example, Thomas Jefferson's descendants once used his Monticello home as a barn. Even today, not all appreciate the value of "saving" historic buildings. The example of using Monticello as a barn raises significant concerns over the *adaptive reuse* of historic buildings. This chapter by Lisa Tucker addresses one such example: the adaptive reuse of the Huffman House, a historic building in Craig County, Virginia, as a Bed & Breakfast.

Projects such as this highlight a tension between theory versus practice in this domain. In *practice*, the Secretary of the Interior's *Standards for Historic Buildings* codifies some of the grassroots practices of early efforts to preserve a historic property in language anyone can understand. The explanatory document accompanying the Standards is 252 pages long, with explanations about building materials, building features and systems, codes and interior spaces and finishes. A series of 50 Preservation Briefs further explain how to do the work successfully.[2] In order to retain National Register status, or to get on the National Register, or to receive federal (and in most cases state) tax credits, the standards must be followed and deemed in compliance by the local State Historic Preservation Office. The language in the Standards is what a designer is held to in practice. Interpreting these guidelines incorrectly could mean tax credits are not granted or a national register nomination revoked. This is one reason why preservation in the United States is often understood in largely technical terms.[3]

As for *theories* of adaptive reuse, Tucker's chapter looks to two important sources. First, she uses a theoretical framework proposed by Jules David Prown. Prown's attention focuses on historical analyses of material artifacts in general, within which he includes historic buildings. The framework is helpful because it guides the designer-researcher not only to understand the historic artifact as it is by *description* and *deduction* but also to properly *speculate* about its condition, which is particularly important for adaptive reuse.

Second, Tucker looks to Bie Plevoets and Koenraad van Cleempoel's "Adaptive Reuse as an Emerging Discipline: An Historic Survey."[4] These authors situate the work of adaptive reuse clearly in the domain of interior design, because adaptive reuse is very compatible with the "sensibilities of the 'interior thinker.'" Particularly in the case of adaptive reuse, they cite Radolfo Machado in noting that adaptive reuse projects should maintain a historical "package of sense." The new use for the building raises specific *theoretical* questions about what to do with artifacts. How to keep them operational and relevant? When is it appropriate to do so? When is it appropriate to *not* keep them? In some cases, a historic property should arguably be left alone because it is important as a record of its time. In other cases, an intervention might bring new life to a building—so this is the dichotomy of the Ruskin versus Le Duc argument. Tucker's chapter is informed by this discourse, being aware of Plevoets and van Cleempoel's argument that it is the interior designer who can bring a *poetic* sense by introducing "notions of empathy and generosity in our response to existing buildings and their adaptation to the needs and sensibilities of new users."[5] This relates directly to the theme that weaves throughout this book, *interiority*.[6]

This chapter weaves together three threads: the historical, the theoretical and the administrative in attempting a *holistic* approach to adaptive reuse. As you read:

1. Note the ways Tucker tries to balance participation *in* the "package of sense" associated with the historic Huffman Property, on the one hand, while also being acutely aware of the external codification of adaptive reuse as outlined in the Secretary of the Interior *Standards*, on the other.
2. Note how Tucker uses Jules David Prown's theoretical framework not only to maintain her participation in the history of the Huffman House but also to convey the historical presences of the Huffman House for others in continuing the use of the property as a "gathering place."

Interiority

Unlike new construction projects, a primary task for the designer in adaptive reuse is capturing Machado's "package of sense." He or she must participate in this package of sense in linking the "already written" past, through "each successive remodeling." Put another way, it is layers of past presences that give a historic building its authenticity, and the ability to participate in this sensibility is one that the designer cultivates within himself or herself. For our purposes, all of this is a complicated operation of interiority. It is precisely what distinguishes historic preservation work of any kind.

1. Note how Tucker works with this multilayered "package of sense" in maintaining historic integrity while using Prown's categories to realize the new use.
2. Also, be aware of how the chapter highlights how designers as well as crafts persons who work on historic buildings participate within a long tradition of (largely vernacular) life associated with the building by entering *into* that tradition and capturing it for others.

* * * *

A Local Meeting Place: The Adaptive Reuse of the Huffman House

Lisa Tucker

The practice of historic preservation is rich with a variety of methodological considerations. Indeed, its practice in the United States has been more methodological than theoretical. For purposes of enriching the theoretical context for a preservation project, this chapter overlays a material culture framework as proposed by Jules David Prown in "Mind in Matter: An Introduction to Material Culture Theory and Method" to the adaptive reuse of a historic building. Material culture includes the physical objects that a group of people use to define its culture, and Prown includes buildings in his methodological framework. The framework provides a context for decision making about the objects of material culture, in this case a complex of rural buildings with an accompanying local store associated with residential and social settlement patterns. The overall site is known as the Huffman Property, located in rural Craig County, Virginia. This chapter concerns the adaptive reuse of one of these buildings as a Bed & Breakfast business. The project illustrates the phases of adaptive reuse from the initial research through occupancy of the residential part of the property (Figure 4.1).

Figure 4.1 Huffman House Bed & Breakfast in Craig County, Virginia.

Historical Importance of the Huffman House

Located in rural Craig County, Virginia, the Huffman House (originally known as Creekside Farm) was first constructed ca. 1835 and is one of only four properties listed on the National Register in Craig County.[7] The Huffman Property lies along State Route 42, about halfway between New Castle and Newport. Because of its strategic location along a well-traveled rural road, the Huffman Property has always been a stopping place for travelers, both visitors to Craig County and locals.

Craig County lies along the Virginia/West Virginia state line in southwest Virginia and was formed from neighboring counties in 1851. The name of the county derives from "Craig's Camp: a frontier outpost in the colonies visited by then General George Washington in 1756. The first settlement, Newfincastle, was later renamed New Castle and is still the only incorporated town in the county"[8] (Figure 4.2).

The first owners of record for the property were John S. Easley and his wife Agnes C. (ca. 1833–1840).[9] John Easley was born in Pittsylvania County, Virginia, in 1790. He married Agnes who was the oldest daughter of John White. John White was a man of great wealth and influence during the Revolutionary War and relocated to Craig County (it was Giles County at the time).[10] John and Agnes were members of Sinking Creek Baptist Church of Christ (now called Level Green Church) located half a mile from the house.[11] It is not surprising that these prominent citizens in a small community were able to own and build on this property. The Huffman House is important to the history of the region as a rare surviving pre–Civil War house in rural SW Virginia. The barn also is a good example of pre–Civil War construction in good condition. Other reasons the entire property is significant came to light after a site visit and some archival research.

Dr. John B. Taylor purchased the property in 1860 and owned it until 1864. The 1860 Census for Craig County lists John B Taylor (41 years old) and his wife, Elizabeth (36 years old). During the Civil War, Taylor served with the First Regiment of the Virginia volunteers.[12] In 1864, Taylor deeded the property to George H. Williams. In turn, Williams sold the property to Marion L. Huffman in 1886.[13] In the *History of Virginia*-Volume 6 (1824), Marion L. Huffman is described as owning and operating a 375-acre farm, and as a Democrat who held positions in the local Disciples of Christ Church and the Masonic Fraternity.[14]

Figure 4.2 Site Plan.

Marion Huffman ran the store, referred to locally as the "Gathering Place." He also filled the role of the local postmaster,[15] because the store also served as the local post office from 1891 to 1907, according to receipts held by the Huffmans in their personal papers.[16] In addition to postal services, local telephone services were also routed through the Huffman store in the early 20th century. Mrs. Huffman relayed messages via a crank phone (this was sold as a part of the final store liquidation sale in 1977). Mrs. Huffman also claims to have filled orders for local inmates when local prison officials would bring orders to the store (although this could not be verified). The store sold a variety of wares including shoes, furs, local rabbits, ginseng, hams and other food items. Gas pumps located in front of the store provided locals with a convenient source of gasoline along Route 42. In addition to grain, groceries and services provided by the Huffman Store, some local residents stopped for a visit and for lunch. The charge for a meal was 50 cents and horses could be fed for an additional 25 cents.[17] As a convenient stop along Route 42, the Huffman store provides a good example of this type of facility in rural communities during the early 20th century. The sense we get from this record is of the store serving as an active hub for local social engagement.

Anah Estridge Huffman, Marion's son, owned the land after his father's death until he died in 1934. The land was then divided between Anah's wife Gillie and four children in 1938;[18] one of these children was Fulton Huffman. The current owners purchased the house from Fulton Huffman in 2003 and allowed him to continue to live there until his passing.[19] Fulton L. Huffman purchased his brother's, sister's and mother's interests in the property in 1946, once again consolidating the property under one owner.[20] He married Virginia Josephine Reynolds.[21] Ronald B. and Carol D. Baker purchased the property from Fulton in May 2003 and allowed Fulton and Virginia a lifetime estate.[22]

The current owners of the Huffman property, Ron and Carol Baker, wanted to determine if the property could be listed on the National Register without compromising the historic integrity of the property. Having established the historical significance of the property both architecturally and as a good example of a societal trends during the later 19th and early 20th centuries due to its location along a well-traveled route, a new use was identified for the building to continue its contributions to the local economy while respecting the rich history of the buildings and site. The Bakers sought to both live in the home and make it into a Bed & Breakfast serving Virginia Tech alumni during home football games, parents of Virginia Tech students for graduation and other events, and hikers on the nearby Appalachian Trail along with other tourists.

Adaptive Reuse: The Theory behind the Huffman House Project

Methods used for adaptive reuse of historic buildings closely ally with those of material culture. Prown defines material culture as "the study through artifacts of the beliefs-values, ideas, attitudes, and assumptions of a particular community or society at a given time."[23] Prown outlines a framework for object analysis using "artifacts as evidence ... an approach to material culture [in which] ... the evidence of the artifact itself has been plumbed as objectively as possible."[24] Prown's method involves three stages, which he argues should be undertaken in sequence: *description*—"recording the internal evidence of the object itself"; *deduction*—"interpreting the interaction between the object and the perceiver"; and *speculation*—"framing hypotheses and questions which lead out from the object to external evidence for testing and resolution."[25] Under these major headings, Prown delineates seven areas of consideration in analyzing an object of material culture. The framework provides both a theoretical and a methodological framework. Figure 4.3 captures this framework in a tabular form.

1	**Description**	Physical dimensions, the object itself	What does the building tell us?
	1(a) Substantial analysis		
	1(b): Content	analysis of style, motifs, decoration	What are the over representations?
	1(c): Formal analysis	Form or configuration	What is the object's visual, dimensional character?
2	**Deduction**	More of a phenomenological approach	What is the relationship between the building and those who use(d) it over time?
	2(a): Sensory Engagement	Textures and experiences of the senses	What does it look like, smell like, feel like and how can this be maintained over time?
	2(b): Intellectual Engagement	Testing intellectual knowledge against actual	How does what do we know intellectually compare to what is actually there?
	2(c): Emotional Response	Will vary from person to person	What is the subjective individual perception and experience?
3	**Speculation**	Our judgement	What is the preservation plan?
	3(a): Theories & Hypotheses	Proposal	How will we proceed?
	3(b): Program of research	Internal and external evidence as we move forward	

Figure 4.3 Jules David Prown's categories for analyzing objects of material culture.

The meaning of Prown's framework deepens in adaptive reuse projects. This is because, when applied to the artifact in this case, "a particular community or society at a given time" must necessarily be considered *through* time, to account not only for the originating culture but also for culture today. The point is that the designer must consider the marks of layers of time in adaptive reuse projects.

Bie Plevoets and Koenraad van Cleempoel's "Adaptive Reuse as an Emerging Discipline: An Historic Survey"[26] supplements Prown's framework in this regard. They cite Radolfo Machado's observation that adaptive reuse projects must capture a "package of sense":

> In the process of remodeling, the past takes on a greater significance because it, itself, is the material to be altered and reshaped. The past provides the already-written, the marked "canvas" on which each successive remodeling will find its own place. Thus, the past becomes a "package of sense," of built-up meaning to be accepted (maintained), transformed, or suppressed (refused).[27]

The stimulating challenge in adaptive reuse projects is that historic structures are not preserved to simply restore the past condition, as in museum displays of historical interior environments. And Plevoets and van Cleempoel argue explicitly that the interior designer is well equipped to achieve this "package of sense" in adaptive reuse projects. The designer of adaptive reuse projects must consider the fact that, while the past is present, the present is also active, resulting in an overlay of sensual experience. To this same point, Prown says this:

> Objects created in the past are the only historical occurrences that continue to exist in the present. They provide an opportunity by which "we encounter the past at first hand; we have direct sensory experience of surviving historical events." Artifacts may not be important historical events, but they are, to the extent that they can be experienced and interpreted as evidence, significant.[28]

In what follows, Prown's categories are overlaid with the design thinking involved in the adaptive reuse of the Huffman property, specifically repurposing it for a Bed & Breakfast to continue the tradition of the property as a local gathering place. The entire project was driven by the need to capture Machado's "package of sense" in the new use.

Stage I: Description

Prown defines description as "restricted to what can be observed in the object itself, that is, to internal evidence … the analyst must … continually guard against the intrusion of either subjective assumptions or conclusions derived from other experience."[29] By "internal evidence," Prown not only restricts analysis to the physical aspects of the object itself but also excludes any of the workings of "interiority" rooted in the analyst's own subjectivity. As designers, in this stage we seek to answer: What does the building tell us? This first stage of Prown's analytical framework comes closest to the regulatory aspect as adaptive reuse on any historic preservation work. In this case, the analysis was guided by the Preliminary Information Form (PIF) of the Virginia State Historic Preservation Office (SHPO). This document sorts information into two criteria. Criterion A assesses a property in terms of its significant contributions to the broad patterns of state history. Criterion C asks how the property embodies the distinctive characteristics of a type, period or method of construction; or how it represents the work of a master, or possesses high artistic values, or represents a significant and distinguishable entity whose components lack individual distinction. Results of the archival research findings, a complete assessment of all the buildings extant on the site and interview information from the former owners, revealed that the project exhibited significance for both criteria A and C.

For Criterion A, the Huffman property demonstrated a broad pattern of social history in rural Virginia. It was part of the frontier during the 18th century and has the potential to reveal archeological information from earlier periods. As noted above, the Huffman property is along a route connecting two towns, serving as a convenient stopping place for supplies, food, lodging and eventually mail. Over the years, there was a store added to the site that served as a post office and meeting spot. According to local lore, travelers stayed in the small room at the top of the stairs in the main house. While not uncommon during the 19th century, these facts demonstrate that the Huffman property is a surviving example of an important crossroad and exemplifies this broad pattern of social history.

Figure 4.4 Federal-style mantel.

For Criterion C, in 1835, the Huffman Property was on the edge of the frontier. There were few well-built houses in this part of the country. When originally constructed, the house featured Federal-era mantels and proportions, which would have been grand features in a house for the area at that time. Although it is a vernacular version of the Federal style, it is a good example for this type of architecture. This property is one of only four in Craig County listed on the National Register and is a rare surviving example of its type (Figure 4.4).

Prown further refines "internal evidence" by grouping it under the headings of *substantial evidence*: an account of the physical dimensions, materials and articulation of the object; *analysis of content*: reading of overt representations including decorative designs or motifs; and f*ormal analysis*: the object's form or configuration of its visual character. Following is a summary of these three subsets of "Description" for the Huffman Property:

1(a). Substantial Evidence

The Huffman property features six historic buildings including a farmhouse built ca. 1835, with an addition between 1907 and 1911; an early 19th-century barn; a corncrib; a wash house and garage; and an early 20th-century store.[30] The significance of the buildings can be divided into three basic varieties: the house for its architecture and early date; the farm buildings, most importantly the pre–Civil War barn, as an example of the operational farm complex; and the 20th-century store building, washhouse and garage as representative of the social patterns associated with the overall site in the early 20th century (Figure 4.5).

The store dates to 1901 and replaces an earlier one that had existed across the street. It features an open room in the front with a rear office and storage area. Original service counters and shelves date to the period when the store doubled as a post office. Original oak plank flooring six to eight inches wide remains, as do the original plaster walls.[31] Behind the store, a small frame building used by the store which might have been a garage, and a wash house date to the early 20th century and therefore contribute to the history of the site.

For the house proper, the vernacular Federal-era detailing of the primary dwelling supports the property owner's claim that the house was constructed ca. 1835. Six-over-six double hung sash windows with an attenuated muntin typical of the Federal period in Virginia and containing some original blown glass panes are protected by contemporary aluminum storm windows (ca. 1970). All four primary rooms contain vernacular Federal-style mantels. The mantels on the east side on both floors are more ornate than those on the west side. All feature attenuated engaged columns supporting an entablature of raised panels. The molding profiles are consistent with the Federal period in Virginia. All interior doors have vertical boards with horizontal cross bracing and early lock boxes. The baseboards are 12" in height, and random width heart pine flooring is found throughout the house. The trim is a simple architrave frame as seen throughout central Virginia during the Federal period.

In adapting the existing house for its new use as a Bed & Breakfast, an addition was added (Figure 4.6); the historic building informed the proportions of the addition. The wall-to-window ratios and the use of new materials strove to maintain the historic integrity of the lines of the existing house. The new addition was designed to both meet the Secretary of the Interior's *Standards for Historic Preservation* (see Additional Resources and Information section) and purposely complement, not compete, with the historic building. Internally, the majority of the new plumbing and mechanical requirements were placed in the new addition. An egress stair meeting current code requirements was also located in the addition. Care was taken to be formally seamless with the existing historic fabric of the house and to not damage historic materials.

Figure 4.5 Barn on the Huffman Property.

Figure 4.6 The Huffman House with addition.

1(b). Content

> The investigator is concerned simply with subject matter ... Content may include decorative designs or motifs, inscriptions, coats of arms, or diagrams, engraved or embossed in metal, carved or painted on wood or stone, woven in textiles, molded or etched in glass.[32]

Again, the house is a rare surviving example of the vernacular Federal style in rural SW Virginia. The Federal style emerged in the late 18th and early 19th centuries in the United States as the young nation sought to find balance between state- and national-level identities. Federal style is often coupled with the slightly earlier Georgian architectural style. Both styles reflect simple and symmetrically arranged rectilinear geometries with openings such as entries on a center axis and rows of dignified rectangular windows. The Huffman House reflects these sensibilities but also includes Victorian tracery décor over the front porch; this was part of the 1907–1911 alterations (Figure 4.7). In deference to its local character, it made sense to keep the tracery as its own unique regional expression, which might indicate an impact of southwest Virginia regional taste as opposed to the more formal Federalist buildings in the seats of political and economic power on the east side of the state; the Virginia State Capitol in Richmond or the Moses Myers House in Norfolk, comes to mind. The adaptive reuse sought to preserve this regionalist aspect of the Huffman House.

1(c). Formal Analysis

The house is two stories with a side-facing gable standing seam metal roof and exterior chimneys on each end. Exterior end chimneys are common in Virginia during this time period. The earliest section of the house (ca. 1835) sits atop a brick foundation. As was common in Virginia, the bricks were made from clay found and fired on the site for use in the foundation and chimneys. The bricks exhibit details

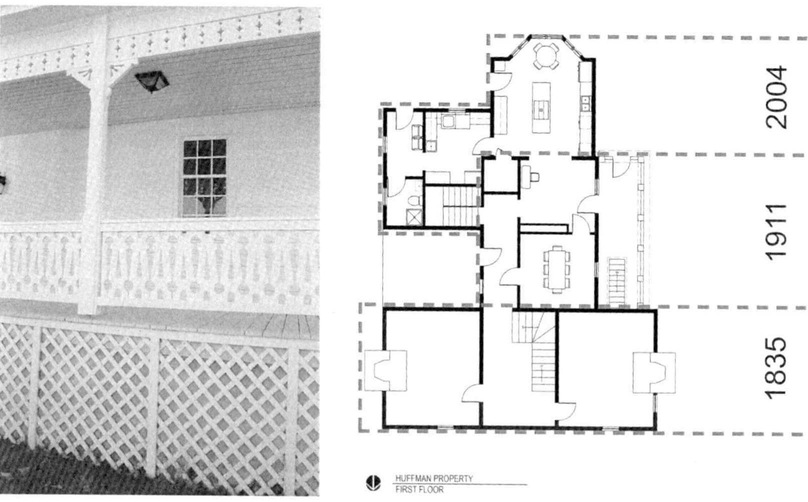

Figure 4.7 Plan of the Huffman House and Victorian tracery on the porch.

consistent with being hand formed and fired on the site including irregular surfaces, impressions from hand molding and variations in color related to the proximity to the wood fire.

In 1907–1911, a rear ell addition was made and the front porch was modified to include its current Victorian details (Figure 4.7). At a later time, the original German weatherboard siding was covered with vinyl. Concrete block was used to reinforce the porch, during this renovation period. Beginning in 2005, the most recent renovation included a large addition to the rear. The concrete block was parged, the vinyl siding removed and the wood siding repaired and painted.[33]

The interior of the house features a central hall plan with a narrow quarter-turn stair with winders in the original section. This plan type was very commonly used in Virginia in the early 19th century, although not so common in this part of the state. A central hall leads to the rear ell that contains the dining room and kitchen on the first floor and two additional bedrooms on the second floor. Built-in cupboards and trim in the ell are typical of the 1907–1911 period when the addition was constructed, and the interior doors of the rear ell are four panel doors with ceramic knobs.[34]

In dealing with the formal aspects of the adaptive reuse, the project included all approaches to historic preservation: stabilization (the outbuildings), restoration (the parlor with the removal of a 1970s bathroom), rehabilitation (the house) and preservation (the house, historic windows, doors, chimneys, mantels and other items). Interventions made in the 1970s were found to be non-contributing since they destroyed some of the character-defining spaces and were therefore removed. All extant material dating to ca. 1835 was retained and preserved. Only minimally invasive repairs took place including re-glazing of windows, reconsolidation of some wood frames on the windows, repair of existing plaster, waxing wood floors and applying paint to the walls and trim. Prior to applying new paint, the layers of existing paint were analyzed and recorded for future reference. The inside of the fireboxes was lined to allow them to be operational and safe. Some repointing of chimneys was required.

Stage II: Deduction

Prown:

> The second stage of analysis moves from the object itself to the relationship between the object and the perceiver. It involves the empathetic linking of the material (actual) or represented world of the object with the perceiver's world of existence and experience.[35]

The observer experiments physically with the object, injecting himself or herself into the investigation. At this stage, the object is only what it is at the moment of observation. "It is the analyst's task to find out what [the object] can tell, and perhaps, deduce what it can no longer tell."[36]

2(a). Sensory Engagement

Prown further states: "Where appropriate, consideration should be given to the physical adjustments a user would have to make to its size, weight, configuration, and texture. The experience of architecture or a townscape would involve sensory perceptions while moving through it."[37] In this project, the rural setting suggests that the property is similar experientially to what it might have been

Figure 4.8 The peacefulness of the site impacted the design thinking of the adaptive reuse.

100 years ago with the exception of paved roads and car traffic. Much of the landscaping remains, the approach to the house is the same and what a visitor sees as they get closer to the house remains the same. There is peacefulness to the site. One can hear birds and the creek beyond the house. It was important to retain this experience as a part of the rehabilitation (Figure 4.8).

2(b). Intellectual Engagement

For intellectual engagement, the designer asks: What do we know intellectually and what is actually there? This citation from James Marston Fitch, a preeminent scholar of historic preservation, can amplify the intellectual aspect of Prown's matrix for buildings.

> Such problems as these confront architects who aspire to work in historic preservation with the need for a new kind of theoretical apparatus. They must develop the capacity to work in modes of stylistic expression which are not their own; to learn to respect the aesthetic criteria of long-dead designers and craftspersons—criteria which might not be at all congruent with their own taste. They must have a willingness to investigate and then respect the historical development of the artifact in hand; an ability to subordinate their own preferences and prejudices to that record; and a readiness to collaborate with other specialists who will often have a more detailed understanding of the phylogenetic origins of the artifact in question. None of this implies that the field does not require designers of taste and creative ability. On the contrary, a very high degree of talent and imagination is called for: nevertheless, stricter and more objective restraints upon personal expressions are called for than in 'normal' architectural practice.[38]

Fitch touches upon an important point for designers in adaptive reuse work. There is not only a tension between theory and practice; the designer must also check his or her personal preferences in order to support the intellectual task of maintaining historical honesty in the artifacts. The underlying approach for this project was that all material from 1835 was significant. It represented the workmanship of

Figure 4.9 The new east bedroom.

the time, the materials that were available, and if it could be saved, it was. The indentations to wood over time and the imperfections reflect the history of the place and tell part of the story of the house over time (Figure 4.9).

2(c). Emotional Response

Here, the designer asks: What is the sensory component of the project? An aspect of historic preservation that is not often written about in the United States is the phenomenological aspect of adaptive reuse. But it is critical to maintain the *experience* of the historic artifact in order to be successful. How did someone originally approach this property? What was the experience of driving up the driveway? What did someone see in the 19th century? The early 20th century? And how can the designer help to maintain this experience as much as possible? The next section summarizes the solution for these questions.

Stage III: Speculation

In the speculation stage, the designer engages in as much creative imagining as possible while respecting the historical integrity so as not to create a false historical building.

3(a). Theories and Hypotheses

According to Prown, "This is the time of summing up what has been learned from the internal evidence of the object itself, turning those data over in one's mind, developing theories that might explain the various effects observed and felt."[39] For this adaptive reuse project, the question is: how does this inform design thinking and praxis?

As the history of the overall property indicates, the Huffman Property witnessed many different uses of the buildings. For instance, the store was the "Gathering Place," serving over the years as a post office, a phone center and a diner, aside from selling supplies. This is to say that this property was always a "working" property. Even though some of the owners were socially prominent, and hence were able to afford the property and its assemblage of buildings over the years, social status did not translate into "preserved" architecture. Prown makes the distinction between inherent and attached value. While the fabric or the materials of an object itself might be of inherent value, "more transient or variable are those values that have been attached by the people who originally made or used the object, by us today, or by people in any intervening moment."[40] Certainly the "gathering place" legacy of the property was an attached value that has accrued over the years, and this is something to which the adapted new use of the house as a Bed & Breakfast conforms.

The sensory experience of the new use must continue this vernacular feel, thus maintaining its identity as a gathering place for the local economy, even as the rich history of the buildings and site is also retained. The new owners, the Baker's, sought to both live in the home and make it into a Bed & Breakfast, a new gathering place that would serve (for instance) Virginia Tech alumni during home football games. It would also be a gathering place for parents of Virginia Tech students for graduation and other events, or for hikers on the nearby Appalachian Trail along with other tourists. All of this seems fitting for the renewed use of the property from a sensual point of view.

3(b). Program

Prown:

> The second step in the speculative stage is developing a program for validation, that is, a plan for scholarly investigation of questions posed by the material evidence ... Now the methodologies and techniques of various disciplines can be brought into play according to the nature of the questions raised and the skills and inclinations of the scholar.

For this adaptive reuse project, the question is: What is the preservation plan?

The specific challenges with this project were to meet the owners' needs functionally and aesthetically while also making sure the historic building was not compromised. Designing the new addition for living quarters for the Bakers required a careful analysis of the existing building with respect to the site and approach. Located to the southeast of the main house block, the new addition is not visible from the driveway approach to the house. This maintains what the house looked like from Route 42 and along the driveway throughout its history.

The 1907–1911 rear ell and porch additions contributed to the story of the property over time. Some elements of the porch had to be fabricated to replace missing balusters. The profile of the existing balusters was used and new balusters were documented in the construction drawings. As mentioned previously, the removal of vinyl siding exposed original weatherboard that was repaired and painted.

In addition to the barn the other contributing agricultural structure on the site is a corncrib. As often happens on a working farm, several buildings were demolished over time, including the original kitchen, the smoke house and any slave quarters. Also typical of an operational farm, a series of 20th-century agricultural buildings were constructed in the 1950s. Lacking any architectural significance to any period of importance to the property, these concrete block buildings were nevertheless left in place because their presence through recent years contributed to the history of the property and hence should be retained (Figure 4.10).[41]

Figure 4.10 Recently built agricultural structure on the Huffman Property.

Conclusion: Maintaining Historic Integrity

The project presented here includes several of the steps a designer might be involved with for an adaptive reuse project. It begins with identifying the historical significance of the building and getting it listed on the National Register of Historic Places and then extends to the preservation of the historic structure and the design of a compatible addition for which the owners received Historic Tax Credits. In this case, making the house into a Bed & Breakfast was what was financially viable given the existing house and location.

The new addition was designed to meet the Secretary of the Interior's *Standards for Historic Preservation* and to complement, and not compete, with the historic building. Several issues common to this type of historic preservation project arose during the process. The first related to research. It is very common with historic buildings to have rich oral histories, particularly when the building has been in the same family for many generations. Oftentimes, memories get distorted and stories get enhanced in the retelling. It is critical to find documentation to support year of construction and additions as well as to conduct a thorough on-site assessment using dating expertise in order to triangulate oral histories with physical evidence and archival documents.

A second common issue relates to concerns about energy efficiency. For example, there is always an urge to replace windows with energy-efficient solutions. This is in direct conflict with the Secretary's *Standards* and should be avoided. Oftentimes, there is a desire to insert foam insulation that can actually damage the historic materials over time. Frequently, owners will want to replace damaged materials with new ones—again violating the Secretary's *Standards*. As long as the designer communicates the importance of the historic materials as an important record of its time and the need to follow the Secretary's *Standards* in order to maintain National Register status and receive historic tax credits, all of these potential pitfalls can be avoided. Usually someone who has purchased or owns a historic property will appreciate this rationale.

The third area of potential problems relates to the contractor. It is much easier to remove and replace historic materials rather than repair and consolidate them. It takes a very special tradesperson to have the patience to work properly with a historic building. Fortunately, on this project the general contractor specialized in historic building rehabilitation and had several specialists on his staff to repair plaster, woodwork, windows, doors and other historic materials.

Historic projects are puzzles to be solved using a variety of sources—archives, interviews and the buildings themselves. It takes a unique type of designer who wants to do this type of work and is willing to set aside his or her own design preferences in service of preserving the past. Some designers dislike this type of work, feeling that following the Secretary's *Standards* limits the ability to be creative. This chapter argues the opposite—that designers need to be more creative to meet all the parameters and complexities in a preservation project, keeping in mind that it is important that the new work not simply mimics the old and thereby creates a false historical building.

* * * *

Discussion and Exercises

Reflections about the Chapter You Just Read:

1. Please refer to the standard features of a research project explained in the Introduction. Then:
   a. In one sentence, identify the *research topic*. This sentence can be in the form of a question but does not have to be. In any case, write one grammatically correct sentence that captures the research topic of this chapter.
   b. Identify the *literature* related to this research project.
   c. Identify the *method* which the author used and also the *data* which this method generated for analysis.
   d. Explain how this approach is *generalizable* (or not).
   e. Explain how you can have confidence (or not) of the *internal and external validity* of this author's overall approach.
2. Tucker organized her analysis based on Prown's categories of description, deduction and speculation.
   a. How do these stages move from objective information to informing Tucker's own subject response as a historic preservationist?.
   b. Were there overlaps in the three stages?
3. Reread the portion of the introduction and the chapter regarding a historic preservation project needing to achieve a "package of sense." Noting specifics, how does Tucker's intervention achieve this?
4. Discuss the ways Tucker uses Prown's framework as a guide to her analysis and as an engine to generate new data?

Exercises/Suggestions for Further Study

1. Search the National Register database to locate a historic building near you. Go to the National Park Gallery website, https://npgallery.nps.gov/, and search by state for a list of historic properties. Visit the site, touring the exterior and the interior if possible. (The interior of some sites may not be open to the public.) Answer these questions:
   a. What factors contribute to the building's value for historic significance?
   b. If it is preserved, which category of preservation best fits the type of historic preservation work conducted?

   c. If no preservation work has been done on the building, which of the four categories might be a reasonable approach?
   d. Explain your answer and document with photos.
2. Reread the section describing the historical significance of the Huffman Property (pp. 70–71). What other types of venues might be possible as an adaptive reuse for this property that is in keeping with its historical significance as a "local gathering place"?
3. Some preservationists make the argument that historic preservation is an avenue for sustainable design. Read Tucker's article on net-zero housing (see full citation in Additional Information and Resources section below) and consider how, in her article, Tucker argues that historic building practices can inform present sustainable solutions. How can the ten lessons Tucker articulates be further informed by Prown's framework? Create a table that summarizes your findings.

Additional Connections and Information

Preservation in the United States is guided by the Secretary of the Interior's *Standards for Rehabilitation, Preservation, Reconstruction* and *Stabilization* and has been largely technical in nature. These *Standards* state:

> *Preservation* is defined as the act or process of applying measures necessary to sustain the existing form, integrity, and materials of an historic property. Work, including preliminary measures to protect and stabilize the property, generally focuses upon the ongoing maintenance and repair of historic materials and features rather than extensive replacement and new construction. The limited and sensitive upgrading of mechanical, electrical, and plumbing systems and other code-required work to make properties functional is appropriate within a preservation project. However, new exterior additions are not within the scope of this treatment.
>
> The Standards for *Preservation* require retention of the greatest amount of historic fabric along with the building's historic form.
>
> *Rehabilitation* is defined as the act or process of making possible a compatible use for a property through repair, alterations, and additions while preserving those portions or features which convey its historical, cultural, or architectural values. The Rehabilitation Standards acknowledge the need to alter or add to a historic building to meet continuing or new uses while retaining the building's historic character.
>
> *Restoration* is defined as the act or process of accurately depicting the form, features, and character of a property as it appeared at a particular period of time by means of the removal of features from other periods in its history and reconstruction of missing features from the restoration period. The limited and sensitive upgrading of mechanical, electrical, and plumbing systems and other code-required work to make properties functional is appropriate within a restoration project.
>
> The *Restoration* Standards allow for the depiction of a building at a particular time in its history by preserving materials, features, finishes, and spaces from its period of significance and removing those from other periods.
>
> *Reconstruction* is defined as the act or process of depicting, by means of new construction, the form, features, and detailing of a non-surviving site, landscape, building,

structure, or object for the purpose of replicating its appearance at a specific period of time and in its historic location.

The *Reconstruction* Standards establish a limited framework for recreating a vanished or non-surviving building with new materials, primarily for interpretive purposes.[42]

The Huffman House Bed & Breakfast project illustrates all phases of an adaptive reuse from the initial research through occupancy of the residential part of the property. Beginning with a PIF and later a National Register Nomination, the project included a comprehensive Preservation Plan,

Standards for Rehabilitation

1. A property will be used as it was historically or be given a new use that requires minimal change to its distinctive materials, features, spaces, and spatial relationships. *As a single family residence and farm, adapting the property into a Bed & Breakfast while maintaining an operational farm required minimal changed to the materials, features, spaces or spatial relationships.*
2. The historic character of a property will be retained and preserved. The removal of distinctive materials or alteration of features, spaces, and spatial relationships that characterize a property will be avoided. *The historic character was both retained and preserved. Every effort was made to retain extant materials and features.*
3. Each property will be recognized as a physical record of its time, place, and use. Changes that create a false sense of historical development, such as adding conjectural features or elements from other historic properties, will not be undertaken. *The original section of the house (1835) and the later addition (1911) were retained. Later interventions such as the installation of a bathroom in the main parlor in the 1970s were removed since this intervention destroyed one of the most important spaces in the house. Nothing was added and no elements from other historic properties were introduced into either the historic house or the new addition.*
4. Changes to a property that have acquired historic significance in their own right will be retained and preserved. *All changes were retained that had acquired their own significance.*
5. Distinctive materials, features, finishes, and construction techniques or examples of craftsmanship that characterize a property will be preserved. *All historic fabric was retained and repaired in the historic house. The other historic structures on the property were stabilized and retained historic fabric.*
6. Deteriorated historic features will be repaired rather than replaced. Where the severity of deterioration requires replacement of a distinctive feature, the new feature will match the old in design, color, texture, and, where possible, materials. Replacement of missing features will be substantiated by documentary and physical evidence. *Deteriorated features such as windows were repaired and rebuilt using the historic material and wood consolidator (Abatron). Original glass was retained where present and new glass was provided where missing. All changes were carefully documented using written descriptions, construction documents, and extensive photography.*
7. Chemical or physical treatments, if appropriate, will be undertaken using the gentlest means possible. Treatments that cause damage to historic materials will not be used. *No chemical treatments were used and damage to historic materials was avoided.*
8. Archeological resources will be protected and preserved in place. If such resources must be disturbed, mitigation measures will be undertaken. *Areas of potential archeological importance were identified in the National Register nomination on the site plan. As an operational farm for nearly 200 years and the site of possible native American populations prior to that, the site was not disturbed beyond the new addition to allow for future archeological excavations. No archeological work was conducted and was outside the scope of this project.*
9. New additions, exterior alterations, or related new construction will not destroy historic materials, features, and spatial relationships that characterize the property. The new work will be differentiated from the old and will be compatible with the historic materials, features, size, scale and proportion, and massing to protect the integrity of the property and its environment. *The existing house informed the new addition in terms of materials, features, size, scale and proportion as well as massing.*
10. New additions and adjacent or related new construction will be undertaken in such a manner that, if removed in the future, the essential form and integrity of the historic property and its environment would be unimpaired. *The new addition is theoretically removable in the future and the original form and integrity of the historic property would be unimpaired. There is a clear separation between the old and the new.*

Figure 4.11 *Secretary's Standards for Historic Rehabilitation* met in the Huffman project. See credits.

construction drawings for an addition and rehabilitation, and ultimately the submittal of the project for Rehabilitation Tax Credits. Although not all projects include all of these elements, the Huffman project illustrates the many ways a designer might be involved throughout the process. Following in Figure 4.11 is the *Secretary's Standards for Historic Rehabilitation* and how each was addressed in the Huffman project.[43]

Additional Connections and Information

Ames, David and Richard Wagner. *Design and Historic Preservation*. Newark: University of Delaware Press, 2014.

Austin II, J. William and Rebecca H. R. Austin. *Related Families of Bottetourt County, VA*. Roanoke, VA: Clearfield, 2003.

Fitch, James Marston. *Historic Preservation*. Charlottesville: University of Virginia Press, 1990.

Grimmer, Anne E. *The Secretary of the Interior's Standards for the Treatment of Historic Properties with Guidelines for Preserving, Rehabilitating, Restoring and Reconstructing Historic Buildings*. Washington DC: US Department of the Interior National Park Service Technical Preservation Services: 1995 (revised 2017). https://www.nps.gov/tps/standards/treatment-guidelines-2017.pdf.

Kamin, Blair. "Historic Preservation and Green Architecture: Friends or Foes?" *Preservation* (Mar.-Apr. 2010): 28–33.

National Park Service. "Rehabilitation as a Treatment." Washington DC: NPS, https://www.nps.gov/tps/standards/four-treatments/treatment-rehabilitation.htm. Accessed 21 March 2018.

National Park Service. *Secretary's Standards for Historic Rehabilitation*. https://www.nps.gov/history/local-law/arch_stnds_8_2.html.

Plovoets, Bie and Koenraad Van Cleempoel, "Adaptive Reuse as a strategy towards conservation of cultural heritage: a literature review." *WIT Transaction on the Built Environmental* 118 (2011). doi:10.2495/STR110131

Prown, Jules David. "Mind in Matter: An Introduction to Material Culture Theory and Method." *Winterthur Portfolio*, (1982): 1–19.

Tucker, Lisa. "Huffman House, Peering Past the Present": IDEC South Regional Conference Proceedings. http://idecdev.i4adev.com/files/2007SouthProceedings.pdf

Tucker, Lisa. "Net Zero Housing: The Architects' Small House Service Bureau and Contemporary Sustainable Single-Family House Design Methods for the United States." *Journal of Interior Design* 37, no. 1 (2012): 1–15.

US Green Building Council. "Reference Guide for Interior Design and Construction LEED v. 4." Washington DC: USGBC (2013).

Notes

1 John Ruskin, "The Lamp of Memory," in *The Seven Lamps of Architecture* (New York: Thomas Crowell and Co., 1880): 232–261; Viollet-le-Duc, Eugène Emmanuel. "Restoration," in *The Foundations of Architecture: Selections from the Dictionnaire Raisonné*. Originally published in 1854. Translated by Kenneth D. Whitehead (New York: G. Braziller, 1990): 195–227.

2 Preservation Briefs, Washington, DC: US Department of the Interior National Park Service Technical Preservation Services. https://www.nps.gov/tps/how-to-preserve/briefs.htm. Accessed November 12, 2018.

3 Anne E. Grimmer, *The Secretary of the Interior's Standards for the Treatment of Historic Properties with Guidelines for Preserving, Rehabilitating, Restoring and Reconstructing Historic Buildings.* Washington, DC: US Department of the Interior National Park Service Technical Preservation Services: 1995 (revised 2017). https://www.nps.gov/tps/standards/treatment-guidelines-2017.pdf. Accessed November 12, 2018.

4 Bie Plovoets and Koenraad van Cleempoel, "Adaptive Reuse as an Emerging Discipline: An Historic Survey," in *Reinventing Architecture and Interiors: A Socio-political View on Building Adaptation*, ed. G. Cairns (London: Libri Publishers), 13–32. Their reference to Radolfo Machado is from his *Old Buildings as Palimpsest*. Radolfo Machado, "Old buildings as palimpsest: Toward a theory of remodeling." Progressive Architecture, vol 57, issue 11, pp. 46–49, 1976.

5 Ibid. (The version available to the editors have of this reference has no pagination, but is available at https://www.researchgate.net/publication/263124838_Adaptive_reuse_as_an_emerging_discipline_an_historic_survey. Accessed November 25, 2019.)

6 These theorists identify *typological* (by building type), *technical* (by guidebook), *programmatic* and *strategic* approaches. The last two categories impact the design thinking behind this present chapter as far as theory is concerned. For programmatic, the authors say: "This approach involves selecting as a starting point a specific function or program and then subsequently adapting the host building so as to accommodate it." Adapting the Huffman House into a Bed & Breakfast falls within this *programmatic* domain. In this approach, "the developers behind the projects often specifically look for historic buildings because of their 'authentic character'" .Editors' note: As for the *strategic*, Tucker makes clear her intention: to preserve the historic authenticity of the Huffman House even as a new use is introduced into it.

7 According to Land Tax Records for Craig County, significant property value increases occurred in 1866 (40% increase in building value) and 1911 (200% increase in building values). Although the land tax records could not help date the original house, the combination of deed records and the construction methods used in the physical building supported the ca. 1835 construction date.

8 "History of Craig County." Craig County. www.craigcountyva.gov/history-of-craig-county. Accessed November 7, 2018.

9 Historic Maps of Fincastle-Cumberland Gap Turnpike dates 1883. Consulted at the Newman Library, Virginia Tech, Blacksburg, VA.

10 T. Conduit and H. Maxwell, *West Virginia and its People*, Vol. 3 (New York: Lewis Historical Publishing Company, 1913), 1208.

11 *Church Book 20*, August 1836. Consulted at the Craig County Historical Society in New Castle, VA.

12 *Hard Times*, 1861–1865, a collection of Confederate letters and Lore Craig County, compiles by the Craig Country Historical Society.

13 Craig County, Virginia. Deed Books. Craig County Deed Book B, p. 6 and Deed Book D, page 444. Craig Country Courthouse.

14 *History of Virginia*, Vol. 6 (Chicago, IL and New York: American Historical Society, 1924).

15 Interview with Fulton and Virginia Huffman in March 2004.

16 Chataigne's *Virginia Gazeteer and Classified Business Directory of Craig County 1888–1889* lists Marion L. Huffman as the Postmaster.

17 Interview with Fulton and Virginia Huffman in March 2004.

18 Craig County, Virginia. Deed Books. Craig County Deed Book 4, p. 178. Craig Country Courthouse.

19 Interview with Carol Baker, 2004.

20 Craig County, Virginia. Deed Books. Craig Country Deed Book 8, p. 341.

21 J.W. Austin and R. Austin, *Related Families of Bottetourt County, VA* (Roanoke, VA: Clearfield, 2003).

22 Craig County, Virginia. Deed Books. Craig Country Deed Book 135, p. 553. Craig Country Courthouse.

23 Jules David Prown, "Mind in Matter: An Introduction to Material Culture Theory and Method," *Winterthur Portfolio* (1982): 1.

24 Ibid., 7.

25 Ibid.

26 Plovoets and Cleempoel, op. cit., 13–32.

27 Ibid., 4.

28 Prown, op. cit., 3. The citation in quotes is from an earlier article he wrote: Jules David Prown, "Style as Evidence," *Winterthur Portfolio* 15, no. 3 (Autumn 1980): 208.

29 Ibid., 7.

30 Lisa Tucker, National Register of Historic Places, Huffman House, Craig County, Virginia, National Register #4001546.

31 Ibid.

32 Prown, op. cit., 8.

33 Tucker, #4001546, op. cit.

34 Ibid.

35 Prown, op. cit., 8.

36 Ibid., 9.

37 Ibid., 9.

38 James Marston Fitch, *Historic Preservation* (Charlottesville: University of Virginia Press, 1990), 352.

39 Prown, op. cit., 10.

40 Ibid., 3.

41 Tucker, #4001546, op. cit.

42 Anne E. Grimmer, *The Secretary of the Interior's Standards for the Treatment of Historic Properties with Guidelines for Preserving, Rehabilitating, Restoring and Reconstructing Historic Buildings* (Washington, DC: US Department of the Interior National Park Service Technical Preservation Services, 1995 [revised 2017]). https://www.nps.gov/tps/standards/treatment-guidelines-2017.pdf. Accessed November 12, 2018.

43 National Park Service. *Secretary's Standards for Historic Rehabilitation*. https://www.nps.gov/history/local-law/arch_stnds_8_2.htm. Accessed October 17, 2018.

Chapter 5

Oral History

Editors' Introduction by Dana E. Vaux and David Wang

Oral history can mean researching what people in the past have said about a particular person, place or thing of historical importance. Or it can emphasize what *current* people say about that person, place or thing because of their prolonged experience with the topic over time. In the one case, the emphasis is on archives, specifically recordings of past oral statements. This has limitations for *oral* history because recordings from the past are often difficult to obtain, at least of sufficient amount for the historian to weave a historical narrative. This chapter takes oral history to mean the second option: which is exploring what a historic building in Frankfort, Kansas, means to current but longtime residents of the town. The research presented is an example of the vast domain of qualitative research.

From a research point of view, there are obvious overlaps between interviewing people regarding memories of the past and interviewing people in general about current circumstances. The primary difference between history research and qualitative research in general is indeed the focus on the *past* in history research. In this chapter, Bryan Orthel takes advantage of this overlap by substantively showing how past and present are not easily untangled. He thus argues that history is "living and moving." By this, Orthel points out that "history" is not a fixed reality. Even in histories of past events, various historians will narrate them differently. The fascinating question is to what extent a historian's narrative is so "living and moving" that the account becomes unreliable. This is the "sliding scale" of history research that comes ingrained in its nature. The back matter to this chapter suggests some additional readings in this regard.

An advantage in studying a building or artifact that endures through time is that the object "of the past" remains with us; and this opens up new possibilities for theorizing. In Chapter 4, for instance, Lisa Tucker looks to Jules David Prown's theory and methods in material culture research to inform her adaptive reuse of a historic building. In this present chapter, Orthel draws from Martin Heidegger's theory about the nature of *things*. For Heidegger *things* have materiality.[1] However, Heidegger maintains that a *thing* is not just the physical object itself but also an embodied web of meaning that includes space, time and the users of that object. The totality of "this *thing*," then, is a phenomenological interaction situated in cultural outlooks that change over time and what reveals the *thingly*-ness of an object. For Orthel, the "living and moving" aspect to the history of the Frankfort School is how the *thingly*-ness of the Frankfort School takes shape in the perceptions of current longtime residents of the town.

In order to uncover the *thingly* history of the schoolhouse in Frankfort, Kansas, Orthel and his design students engage history research tactics to understand the building from a historical perspective, then engage in a participatory design charette with local residents to help them uncover meanings of the building to individuals and resulting collective meanings.

This chapter fits into recent developments in history research that recognizes the *cultural turn*.[2] This term refers to the process historians developed to understand cultural events and the everyday experience of "ordinary people" from a historical vantage point. The cultural turn provided new methods for historians to uncover and understand meanings they were unable to address in socially privileged viewpoints of "top down" single narratives. Significantly influenced by Hayden White's view of constructed historical texts and Clifford Geertz's study of culture as interpretive thick description, historians began to understand the importance and impact of culture on historical accounts and looked to cultural anthropology, linguistics and semiotics for new modes of analysis.[3]

Making the cultural turn was beneficial for historians but is equally helpful for designers who wish to understand the impact of the past on the present, as is the case with Orthel's study of the Frankfort School in this chapter. Cultural history offers multiple stories and stories of "others" as an important part of history.[4] A diversification of approaches and an emphasis on interpretation of meaningful cultural and social relationships enable designers to understand the multiplicity of cultural meanings that cohere at different times and places.[5] As you read this chapter, look for the following research tactics. Some of these tactics are specific to history research and also suitable for design analysis, such as the community charette described in this chapter.

1. Note the types of data Orthel procures to capture the history of the Frankfort School as living and moving.
2. Place yourself in the shoes of Orthel's respondents to appreciate their perceptions.
3. Consider how applying history research as Orthel and his students do in this chapter might help designers in general work with local communities to identify uses and significance for historical buildings.

Interiority

The title of this chapter conveys a double meaning of "interior." It certainly can mean the physical interior of a building, such as the Frankfort School in this chapter. But via Heidegger's theory, the "*thingly*-ness" of the building changes in the *interiority* of a particular person's memories and subsequent perceptions of the building to become, in Heidegger's term, *this thing* for that person. In this chapter, "this *thing*" of the Frankfort School for one person might be quite a different "this *thing*" of the Frankfort School for another. The Discussion and Exercises at the back of this chapter suggests various applications for this formulation of history as living and moving. But as you read consider the following:

1. Note how the memories of individuals influence their ideas about "saving" the school.
2. In view of how Orthel defines *thingly* history, think about how this view changes the significance of the Frankfort School.

* * * *

Living and Moving, *Thingly* Interior History

Bryan D. Orthel

We are often tempted to reduce the focus of design history to the physical characteristics that can be seen, felt and otherwise sensed. In other words, design history overemphasizes the physical object itself. Because of this, historical interiors presented in house museums or carefully restored spaces are often cleansed of disharmonious elements and presented as complete, idealized views of past life. Visitors are asked to venerate a history that is static and fixed. In reality, the history of an interior space is a messy contradiction of incomplete information, heritage and material culture. The history of an interior requires comprehending complexities of how people understand and value the interior and its entanglements.[6] The historical interior is not static; instead, it is living and moving.

History that focuses on design as an object—an outcome, a physical result or a tangible entity—overlooks deeper historical and everyday meanings. Design history should help people understand each other as we were and are in the present day. This chapter examines how historical objects have traditionally been classified and interpreted, and then reframes them in a philosophical context to highlight history as a *living and moving* reality. The analysis draws from Martin Heidegger's essay "What Is a *Thing*?" and Ian Hodder's application of these ideas to material culture. Heidegger defines *thing* as "the existing bearer of many existing yet changeable properties."[7] Hodder demonstrated how *things* relate to "agency, meaning, phenomenology, self, and personhood."[8] The different experiences of a designed object result in distinct *thingly-ness* for each person because perception affects the "changeable properties." As Heidegger states, "The essential determination of the *thin*gness of the *thing* (is) to be *this* one."[9] For each personal encounter, the *thing* lives and moves a little differently.

Object-Centric History

Historical knowledge can be limited to factual information based on a record of sequential events (i.e., a chronology) or a listing of identifiable characteristics (e.g., place, designer, material). Such information provides data for analysis but does not tell us much alone. In fact, history's cultural turn challenged historians to examine "their subjects' representations of their world" rather than through the mediation of chronicles, institutions and systems.[10] Approaching design history requires a deeper interpretation of the data to understand what the information means in context of the past, current day and imagined future. The information only has value in what we determine it means for us in the present.

Architectural, interior design and design history have traditionally relied on object-centric approaches to determine historical meaning. This tendency probably derives from precedents in art history, archaeology and the design disciplines' own focus on physical outcomes. E. McClung Fleming outlined the basic methodology of this object-centric historiographic approach: identification, evaluation, analysis in relationship to originating culture and interpretation of significance to the present day.[11] Traditionally, historical knowledge entails reasoned, scientific thought and *a posteriori* analysis.[12] While there is scientific value in describing and cataloging for historical study, the object-centric approach privileges object and maker over user and experience. This perspective is neither living nor moving.

McClung's view is object-centric, and this approach privileges cultural or social preferences by highlighting design by some and denigrating design from others. Design historians must consider more deeply if their analyses unfairly judge or exclude.[13] Considering what is excellent, valued, meaningful and effective design requires critical analysis and diverse knowledge.[14] Object-based approaches to design history also presume a vast design literacy that is unfamiliar in the day-to-day lives of most people. Such approaches are inaccessible to the average person, the very individuals who are living in context with the design. This very idea—valuing the historical context of the average person—informed the "cultural turn" in history research.

Thinking about the Meaning of *Thing*s

Physical inputs and the experiencing person *together* become "*this thing*," in the words of Heidegger. Heidegger was one of several leading thinkers of the last century who broke away from the established scientific way of understanding human knowledge and experience. Descartes's *cogito, ergo sum* (I think, therefore I am) placed a divide between individual perception and the *thing* perceived. In contrast, Heidegger explored *things* in context of *existence*.[15] In his reasoning, a jug has physical materiality, but, more importantly, the human engagement with what the jug can do (e.g., hold, pour) is essential to the identity of that jug *as a thing*. This is what Heidegger means by *thing*ness. His idea extends the old High German usage, which understood the word *thing* as a social gathering to discuss items of importance.[16] An object's materiality, such as a physical jug, is a small aspect of how an object is actually understood and experienced in this *communal* sense.

More recently, the archaeologist Ian Hodder framed a related characterization of *thing*. Hodder emphasized *things*—regardless of scale and physicality—as moments of social interaction between people, not ideas. For Hodder, the ability of objects to convey meaning was useless unless the meaning was part of human identity and interactions. In this vein, *thing* entangles its object with changing, contested meanings linked to it over time.

For purposes of this chapter, *things*—and the history of *thing*s—matter primarily in relationship to humans' living experience. Hodder noted that "*things* create people as much as people create *things*."[17] It is therefore important to consider the difference between collecting objects in a place and developing understandings of what those objects and environments truly meant to those in the past and what they mean to those in the present. Hodder concluded, "Human experience is *thingly*, irreducibly so."[18] A *thing*'s sensorial and experiential characteristics are inseparable and largely phenomenological.[19] The *thingly* approach to design history supports design's fundamental outcomes (i.e., symbols, objects, actions and thoughts) as humanly-made, used and valued entities.[20]

Because *things* are fully defined according to how they are utilized in human living, understanding a *thing* leads us to interact historically with people (past or present) as they live(d). Interestingly, *things* mix concepts, material culture and built environments with the ways people value and use them. This is to say: material culture is innately *thingly* but not universally monolithic. Consider a tea set. Not only does it vary by culture (e.g., Britain or China) but it also changes according to social class and generation. In design theory, a *thing* should be recognized as participating in a cultural landscape, and hence is an intangible heritage and discourse.[21] What follows is an analysis of a living and moving, *thingly* history centered on the 1902 Frankfort School building in Frankfort, Kansas.

Frankfort School Building, Frankfort, Kansas

The "living and moving" history of the Frankfort School (Figure 5.1) was accessed and revealed through interactions with current residents of the community as they and students from Kansas State University explored what to do with the school building. Oral history interviews and participatory design processes were used to discover the values and ideas the residents shared and to encompass ideas about the past being actively used to shape the future.[22]

The community of Frankfort, Kansas (approximate population 710), is located in the northeastern quadrant of the state, approximately 20 miles south of the Nebraska border. The town remains a viable social and commercial place with a grocery store, gas stations, public school, several religious congregations and supporting commercial activities. The community's primary economic base derives from agriculture (wheat, corn and soybeans). The grain elevator near the railroad line adjacent to the town remains the area's major economic life stream. The community was platted in 1867 as a railroad community on the central branch of the planned transcontinental Union Pacific railroad line. Like many railroad towns, Frankfort was laid out as a grid of streets. The railroad line arcs around the southern and western edges of the town, separating the community from the adjacent creek watershed. The topography rises toward the northeast, with the top of the prominent rise occurring

Figure 5.1 The Frankfort School remains a prominent thing in the community. The building includes a day-lit basement, two floors of classrooms and a large attic space originally used for vocational training and sports.

about the intersection of Locust and Fourth streets. The town is also located along the Kansas White Way, a circa-1914 road from the Missouri River to Denver, Colorado, intended to boost commercial development. Two state highways intersect at the town's main and cross streets.

The northwestern corner of Locust and Fourth streets is occupied by a 1902, Renaissance Revival–inspired school building that is the tallest in the community (Figure 5.1), excepting the grain elevator. The future of this building has been uncertain since classes ended in 1997. In 2013, purchase of the building by a non-profit community organization spurred discussion and actions to preserve the building for an unknown future use.[23] In 2014, the Frankfort Development Trust, a non-profit organization advocating for the building's preservation, contacted Kansas State University for assistance. Over 18 months, students from the university's interior design program collaborated with Frankfort residents to explore viable future uses. The collaboration sought to define the problems the community could address rather than find a specific solution. The project's process resembled standard programming strategy: establish goals, collect and analyze facts, uncover concepts, determine needs, state the problems.[24] The community's understanding of the Frankfort School and its history was the starting point. Archival research and participatory design exercises were used to gather information and analyze the situation (Figures 5.2 and 5.3). Most importantly, oral history interviews helped students ground the building in the diverse meanings associated with it by residents.

The Frankfort School was revealed as a *thing* representing complex social, cultural and economic ideas. Residents understood the school as an essential part of their individual growth and the community's social life and core to their identities. The residents were unsure how reuse of the school could integrate the school's past and associated values and also be part of the community's future. A *thingly* approach to the building clarified the multiple meanings community residents valued or were widely assumed and left unsaid.

Figure 5.2 The interior of the school remains largely unchanged since the mid-1990s. Years of delayed maintenance resulted in damage to original features and structural systems.

Figure 5.3 Participatory community interaction involved mapping residents' values. Students led a day-long discussion with residents to elicit information about their values, concerns for the future and ideas for the reuse of the school building.

The contrast between the object-centric history and thingly history of the Frankfort School quickly emerges in how the school is described in archival documents and oral histories. The Frankfort School building was listed on the National Register of Historic Places in 1972. The National Register paperwork stated:

> The Frankfort School was erected in 1902–03 to replace an 1880 building, which had been struck by lightning on August 20, 1902, and burned beyond repair. Within weeks after the fire a local architect, A.W. Snodgrass, was hired to prepare plans and specifications for a new school building. On November 21 a picture of the proposed structure was printed in the Frankfort Review, along with an announcement that the contract for construction would be let soon. Shortly thereafter, two Frankfort men, Olaf Anderson and John C. Reipen, were awarded the contracts, respectively, for the stone work and the carpentry work. Evacuation of the basement was completed by mid-December, and the school house was finished in time for classes to begin October 19, 1903, although the opening date had been somewhat delayed. The final cost of the building was estimated to be $20,000.[25]

The report concluded, "The building is an excellent example of Renaissance influenced turn-of-the-century school architecture in Kansas."[26] The building's massing, construction materials and roof features were also described. Construction documents from 1908 detailed the addition of plumbing and heating systems to the building. The school served all grades until a dedicated high school was opened in 1923. These details describe the school building as an object.

The Frankfort School also fits into broader data about schools built in Kansas during the decades before and after 1900. While many communities continued to build and support one-room school houses, other communities opted for more elaborate buildings designed in academic styles.[27] The

Renaissance Revival appearance of the Frankfort School was not a signature of its architect. Schools in Wichita, Kansas City, Junction City and other Kansas communities were built with similar spatial organizations (four classrooms flanking a central corridor on multiple floors) and stylistic influences (drawing from Richardsonian Romanesque to Renaissance-influenced aesthetics). Limited availability of timber on the prairie shifted construction to masonry of locally quarried limestone or site-made brick. The Frankfort School was also not unusual in its ambition for the community size. Some small Kansas towns opted for smaller schools, but Frankfort and others matched the schools constructed in larger cities, like Kansas City or Wichita. There is no documentation for how the Frankfort School's pedagogy may have influenced its form.

While these facts are helpful to place the Frankfort school in place and time, none of them tells us what the school or building meant for the Frankfort community. In order to create a *thingly* history, the author and students collected stories and interviews from residents to discover the true meaning and purpose of the Frankfort School.

The Research Process

The research process occurred in three phases: (1) an initial phase of data collection designed to collect information valuable for both design research and research for design; (2) a student-led phase of data collection and analysis focused on collecting background information needed for a design process; and (3) a summative phase of analysis to determine what generalizable information emerged from the design history project. Multiple parts of the project involved participatory processes to engage members of the community in the design and history research. Students identified information beyond what is commonly considered in programming and contextualized their outcomes in broad ways. For many readers, the outcomes of these oral histories will not look like a typical design history. Yet, the process crafted deep historical knowledge in order to understand the residents, their community and the problems they ultimately needed to solve.

Data collection consisted of archival research (e.g., historic documents and drawings), formal interviews, informal conversations with community members, a participatory community design process and detailed observation of the extant building (Figure 5.3). Data collection strategies overlapped and occurred simultaneously. Strategies and tactics varied by the type of information: (1) Archival research recorded through copying of documents and development of researcher notes; (2) Formal interviews were recorded and transcribed, with interview participants having the opportunity to review the transcripts and edit the information; (3) Informal conversations were recorded through researcher notes; (4) Participatory community interactions were recorded through the created artifacts (idea maps and drawings), digital photography and researcher notes; and (5) Observations of the landscape were recorded through digital photography and written notes. The matrix in Figure 5.4 summarizes these tactics.

Information was shared between students through an online learning management and cloud-based storage systems. Five months of the projects were incorporated into an advanced design studio. Regular discussion of the information occurred in support of the design process. Data collection methods were reviewed by an institutional review board (IRB) for compliance with research regulations and ethical expectations.

The outcome of these efforts was a layered collection of information which, in turn, is important in understanding the *thingly* design history. For example, oral history interviews with local residents

Data collection	Types of data	Intended purpose
Archival research	• Historic building drawings and construction specifications; • Historic photographs; • School yearbooks and educational records; • Historic newspapers	• Identify information outside the realm of human memory
Oral history interviews (formal interviews)	• First-person memories and retelling of stories; • Statements of historical values based on lived experience within the community	• Identify ideas individuals value the most; • Gather information not available through other sources
Informal interviews	• First-person knowledge of the community and information sources; • Broad context for information (e.g., otherwise unstated linkages between people and/or places)	• Identify local sources of information (e.g., people, organizations, repositories); • Understand relationships between individuals and places that are not recorded (e.g., friendships, memories)
Participatory design process	• Group-based exchange of ideas; • Identification of group dynamics which may inform how / which ideas are expressed	• Prompt social interaction that connects ideas which any one individual or interview may not draw out; • Begin negotiation of ideas between multiple people to support communal decision making; • Identification of communal values separate from individual values
Observation of extant building and cultural landscape	• Photography of existing conditions; • Identification of conditions separate from their description in other data collection methods; • Recognition of unstated or ignored conditions (e.g., undesirable situations left out of the stories); • Information related to physical condition of buildings and landscapes	• Contextualization of information outside of the layered bias of other sources (recognizing the continued, inherent bias of the researchers); • Develop questions and lines of inquiry for interviews and community interaction • Support for the design process

Figure 5.4 Information sources. The research process for this case involved gathering data from multiple sources to contextualize inputs and ideas discovered through each source.

drew out multiple stories about the closure of schools in nearby towns. By themselves, these stories were interesting but not definitive. During participatory discussions and observation of the landscape, the significance of these stories was clarified. Residents shared a common belief that the school defined the existence of a community. A community would somehow cease to exist if it lost its school through closure or consolidation. Notably, several residents had adopted the Frankfort community when their own schools had closed. Even though the 1902 school building was no longer used, the residents projected their concerns of loss of community identity onto the loss of the school building. This layered mixture of information provides a strong example of a *thing*. Meanings, physicality and social negotiation mixed together.

A *thingly* design history, then, involves much more than any single building or moment in time. A *thingly* design history must align with current community sensibilities that embrace physical objects but is not limited to them.

Living and Moving History

Vibrant meanings in individual stories and shared heritage are part of the Frankfort School's *thingly* history. The residents of the Frankfort community share vibrant stories filled with history as they understand it. For them, Frankfort is a community comprising people who have supported each other. Fiona, a longtime resident, described the community:

> Well, I don't know a lot of early-early history. I know bits and pieces of things I think are interesting. Erm ... [Laughs] I told somebody once it's like *Mayberry R.F.D.* but with internet.[28]

Fiona's sentiments are one example of individual interest in the town's history expressing deep loyalty and support among residents which recurred across most interactions with Frankfort residents. Floyd, a retired lifelong resident, emphasized how "all of the people around here, if somebody gets sick, they come and help."[29] Other residents had similar refrains (e.g., "I've always been amazed that when there's a need, why, everybody comes together") and recounted the community's action when a tornado destroyed a dairy, the community fundraising to rebuild the park or the assistance people shared with neighbors during wintery weather.[30] Florence, a resident who regularly visited Frankfort in her childhood, said, "Part of what makes a small town [a] community ... is all those common experiences."[31] The *thingly* history of Frankfort began with how the community's residents shared their mutual experiences in this place.

The Frankfort School was built to replace a previous building destroyed by fire. The community's elementary school was located there from 1903 to 1997. Moving the school to newer buildings on the high school campus in 1997 was a significant turning point. At the time, the school district offered the 1902 building to the community, but the town leaders declined. The building was mostly vacant or used for storage for 17 years. In early 2013, the community learned the building was listed for sale via an online auction site. A group of concerned residents organized, held community meetings and purchased the building in September 2013. They felt the building was an "eyesore" representing community failure to do better.[32] Yet, they did not want it to be torn down. Interestingly, Francine, a lifelong resident, ascribed emotions to the building: "It's crying. It's sad and it wants to be fixed up."[33] For many residents, the building's condition indicated something sinister about the future. Felicity, a local business owner, explained, "I think everyone here is community-oriented, but I don't think a lot of people realize the value and the history of the community, and that's kind of what we're working with the grade school to save."[34] Saving the school building became an expression of community identity and claim for Frankfort's future.

As the *thingly* history unfolded, the school building served as a foil for residents to express their desires and values. The residents' actions drew the building, individuals' histories and complex value systems together. The *thingly* stories of the school came in two parts: individual expressions of history and statements of shared heritage.

Individual Histories

Frankfort residents told personal histories of memories that linked their own experiences with the school building. Felix, a former resident, spoke fondly of the hours he spent playing in the building after hours but also remembered the recesses he spent inside with his nose in a corner for "talking too much."[35] Francine, a lifelong resident, recalled the seductive draw the fire escape slides had for a small child.[36] She longed to climb the slides and rapidly descend but was thwarted by vigilant adults. Francine also remembered the school as "clean-smelling [and] friendly."[37] Fiona remembered all the students gathered into one classroom to watch the moon landing on a black-and-white television set.[38] Florence recalled visiting her grandmother, who worked in the school office.[39] Flora, a former teacher, remembered setting up the kindergarten classroom.[40] During tours of the building, residents recounted many additional stories inspired by specific spots inside. The space and individuals' memories required each other. This interiority is an inseparable part of personal experienced histories.

Flora's stories about teaching kindergarten connected her personal experience, specific physical space and key ideas about the *community* as an interiority. The Women's Civics Club approached the school district about starting a kindergarten in 1955. The district declined but offered space in the school if the women wanted to teach the class themselves. They did. A basement room near the cafeteria and boiler room was fixed up, repainted and housed the kindergarten for decades. The kindergarten was supported by the civics club and female volunteers. Flora's kindergarten stories were about the children—learning to teach little boys to behave and later tracking her students' accomplishments after they left her classroom in the early 1960s. She looked forward to seeing photos of her classes published in the newspaper ahead of the 50th anniversary of their kindergarten year. "I think that'll be a fond memory too, to share with all those little students," she said.[41] Almost every resident mentioned the kindergarten room as they talked about the school. The stories these people told formed a deep, shared understanding across generations. Their individual experiences linked together in the abstract, *thingly* existence of a place like the kindergarten room and conveyed their membership in the community as parents, siblings, neighbors and friends.

Most Frankfort residents explicitly disavowed any attempt to recount dates or sequences of events. The *formal* history of Frankfort or the Frankfort School was only tangential to the issues at play. Fred, a younger resident, acknowledged this disconnection:

BDO: What is the important history about Frankfort that I should know?

FRED: The important history about Frankfort—Oh gosh. Well, you know, it's a good question because I think I'm at a point in my life where the only *really* history that's relevant to me is the history that—that I have experienced.[42]

BDO: Do you know the specific history of the school?

FRED: Can I be honest?

BDO: You can be honest.

FRED: I know bits and pieces. I know that at one point it had a bell tower. I know that at one point the library was in the upstairs. I know the last kindergarten class was the [graduating] class of 2009... [pause]

BDO: And...

FRED: But that's the extent of the history. And I'll be honest, it—that part of it is not irrelevant but not important. Because I do think it's important in the scheme of things, but to me I don't have an interest in learning about it and I don't have an interest in how it plays out to the big picture.[43]

The building's social history was supported by elements of material culture. Faye, one of the community's recognized historians, gathered photographs and other memorabilia related to the school.[44] She was compiling a miniature archive that documented the people who worked at the school, the spaces as they were and the experiences of the children. She bemoaned that most school records were destroyed rather than moved to the new school. Even as she collected physical artifacts, Faye said the most important part of the project was "just simply the people" of Frankfort.[45] The individual aspects of *thingly* history come together through negotiation of shared heritage.

Negotiating a Shared Heritage

Heritage emerges as individuals recognize and develop their shared values, experiences and goals. Sense of belonging pulls people *into* community even when conflict emerges. Frankfort residents had mixed opinions about saving the school building. Regardless of their views, they sought the betterment of the community.

One group of residents saw the building as too far gone to be saved. The economic costs would outweigh the potential benefits. These views came with head-shaking, "I just don't see it" comments during community meetings about the building's future. Other residents understood the campaign to preserve the school building more idealistically. Felix described the school building as "a very enduring structure ... It represents—represents security or something permanent. Erm—I don't know. [Losing it would be] hard."[46] Many community members shared this conflicted duality: admiration for the building and the recognition their actions were driven by more abstract purposes.

Residents acknowledged their efforts to preserve the school building were about more than the physical structure. Fred said:

> First of all, I'm really passionate about the community ... And, so, I'll say first and foremost I [made an effort to preserve the school building] because I thought it was the right thing to do. Second of all, I think that across Kansas, across rural America we see this growing trend of ... old buildings and everyone wants to sit on their butts and not do anything so we just tear it down, because [it] is the easy solution—[pause] ... And I think restoring this grade school is the good thing to do for the community and I think it sets a message that, you know, we care not only about where we've been and what has been given to us—we care about what we're doing right now and we care about the future of Frankfort. And I think that's real important.[47]

For many residents, acting in the spirit of the Frankfort community was more important than any one aspect of the building. Other residents preferred pragmatic reasons for preserving the school building. Flora understood the building was architecturally "very dynamic looking" but emphasized its value as a space that "serves the rest of the community."[48] Her concerns included maintaining accessibility to upper levels of the building for older residents. Florence, a leader of the preservation efforts, described the building as:

> An opportunity for economic development for Frankfort, that, you know, maybe we can bring other businesses into Frankfort. By using the building maybe, we can encourage younger generations of people who grew up in Frankfort to come back, because we have cool loft apartments or because we have senior living now in the grade school.[49]

Residents also shared other reasons for supporting the preservation of the school indexed to their own views of the community. Faye wanted the school building to be repurposed because "I just want it to stay in the town. I don't want it to be replaced with some metal tin-shed building—[laughs]—or—I just want something the town can be proud of."[50] Felicity continued this idea:

> I think the grade school is the most beautiful building in town and that's the reason that it needs saved ... And I think it's just a beautiful building. It needs to be valued and it needs to be restored and kept livable.[51]

The architectural value of the school was frequently contrasted to prefabricated metal buildings, which are commonly used in the community by agricultural, industrial and religious entities. A metal building on the school grounds originally housed the gymnasium. It has since been sold and converted into a carpentry shop. Felicity explained the conflict:

> There's no building [in town] that is more spectacular than [the 1902 school] building. And part of what bothers me is the effort that it took to build it. And today we—like look around here—[metal] building there, [metal] building there, [metal] building there. And they're good buildings but they aren't the architecturally significant buildings that the grade school is and I just think we have to appreciate that and it has to be saved if at all possible.[52]

Florence was more direct: "I have some memories associated with the grade school. Could you build a metal building and make memories in it? Sure—for sure you could—it doesn't really matter."[53] Her voice implied a caveat: Somehow, not all memories are equal. The memories anchored in the school building are esteemed differently. For these residents, memories or experiences connected to a metal building lack connection to the past in the way the 1902 building may endorse memories as part of the continuum of Frankfort's history. Fiona noted,

> [The school is] a testament to a period of time when people didn't know what the future was going to hold. The town was maybe about 30 years into the incorporation [when the school was built] and [the school] was—it was an indication they wanted things to last.[54]

The heritage shared by Frankfort's residents emerged from exploring a *thingly* understanding of history, which represented a network of individual values and common experiences.

Things as historical records: Applications in teaching and learning

The Frankfort School history (or histories) recounted here is an active use of a *thing* to negotiate meaning. Valued, used, *thingly* history is alive and emotive and *moving*. Further, *interior* histories are about how people understand their places in time *at present*. If we wait until people are unable to express what they understand, then we (collectively) lose part of our social reality. The *thing* requires coming together to negotiate and entangle with each other. Recording this interaction is capturing design history. If we only focus on material culture as objects or moments far in the past for which we have limited evidence of meaning, we are crafting a design and interior history that is weakened by its incompleteness.

As this chapter highlights, "interior histories" are of *thing*s rather than objects. As *thing*s, objects and participants entangle in living and moving histories. The key to using *thingly* history starts with actively understanding how we—designers, instructors, students and stakeholders—define history. Activating *thingly* history requires context, a multilayered approach to gathering information and an openness to understanding the world from other peoples' viewpoints.

Doing *thingly* history calls for collaboration: designers, students, instructors and project stakeholders working together to establish the context for how they understand history. All participants begin with open dialogue about how history is defined and framed. Historical references in daily life are usually rooted in negotiated meanings, the values people attach to place and *thingly* conceptions of the world. By drawing out the ways people understand history, we develop an awareness of others and different ways others may use history to various ends. A simple series of questions can prompt reflection and exploration in this regard (Figure 5.5). These prompts encourage us to rethink our own knowledge in preparation for how other people may consider history.

So, a multilayered approach to collecting background information is essential to shaping a *thingly* understanding of the history in play. The multilayered approach involves actively searching for conflicting sources and views that have been excluded, or challenge hegemony. Figure 5.4 lists the multilayered sources of information used in the Frankfort project. The data collection requires additional preparation to consider how to include all views.[55]

As described above, the multilayered approach should be completed iteratively to allow for repeated gathering of data and analyses followed by additional, more informed interaction and analyses. Information from different sources develops a more complete image of the *thing* and the associated social negotiations. In the Frankfort example, residents included stories in the oral history interviews about the closure of schools in nearby towns. By themselves, these stories were interesting but not definitive. During participatory discussions and observation of the landscape, the significance of these stories was clarified. Working to understand a given *thingly* history will include individuals' perspectives, community-wide understandings, framings of the problem requiring a solution and the practical, tangible realities of place.

History discussion questions

1. What is history?
2. Where have you learned history? What have you learned (e.g., facts, dates, people, theories, themes, experiences)?
3. Where have you seen history used in pop culture? Provide a specific example. Describe how the history is used and why it is included.
4. Have you used history in the last week? Where / When / Why / How?
5. Does your personal history (e.g., region where you spent your childhood) affect how you live? Do you do something in your daily life (e.g., daily habits, social interactions) as a specific reflection of your own history?
6. Have you thought about your own history since starting this project? If so, in what context? Has recalling that experience affected how you have approached the project?
7. Is history important to you? Why?
8. How important is history to you?
9. What are the ways that you typically interact with history (e.g., documentaries, books, statues, historical plaques, stories, traditions)?

Figure 5.5 Contextualizing *thingly* history: The questions can be used to begin an open-ended discussionamongthestudents,instructorsandstakeholdersabouthowtheyunderstandand use history.

The meanings and values of history are inherently about how people in the present shape understanding of the past to define the future.[56] Understanding a *thing* from the perspective of other people is difficult. Any interpretation is limited by what can be known from the available data. In the Frankfort case, the students were able to speak directly with individuals (aged 80+ to early 20s) who had firsthand experience with the community and school building as students, teachers and parents. Of course, individuals' stories and retellings have been recrafted from their first experience into the story they want people to hear today. Researchers should therefore recognize how and why narratives are manipulated.[57] Taken as a whole, these stories actively come together as part of a *thing*, now *communally* understood.

Traditional history research tactics may be used as a researcher develops a *thingly* understanding. Approaches like archival retrieval or object observation support the researcher's understanding of what community members and stakeholders express. The archival data by itself is insufficient. To determine the *thingly*-ness of a historical artifact requires tactics qualitative researchers know well: formal interviews, informal conversations with community members and participatory community design processes. Triangulation between the kinds of data obtained, from archival to behavioral to informal conversation and observation, contributes to researchers', students' and stakeholders' understandings of the *thingly* character of their subject matter.

Conclusion

The history of the Frankfort School is living and moving. The stories—the history—told by community members were active, ongoing efforts to maintain a way of living in this small, Kansas town. The stories were full of emotion and vibrant meaning. They were shared and mixed with other individuals' experiences to form what the community recognized as the history of the school. This dynamic exchange centered around the *thingness* of a building and drove their efforts to protect and restore the 1902 Frankfort School. As a *thing*, the Frankfort School revealed how this physical environment is intricately linked with the uses, values and ideas of the people around it.

The individuals' storytelling and restoration work *protected* the community even as it sought to preserve the building. Fiona unwittingly explained:

> I felt that being that generation that had a chance to save [the school] for another 100 years—I wanted to be that generation that did, not the one that someone down the line said … "How come you didn't save that?"[58]

Fiona recognized an obligation in the vision Frankfort's earlier residents held. She, like other residents, believed future generations should have access to the community identity represented by earlier residents' ideals. That sense of belonging in the community mattered to Fiona:[59]

> I want [Frankfort] to be a place that my grandchildren can come back if they want to live there, because it would be sad if we lost real America … And this is one little piece of it.[60]

The residents maintained a desire to be a community that cares and acts, at least partially because that is a legacy they drew from their ancestors. While the physical form of the school provided the justification for their actions, the school was an incidental outcome, rather than the primary result, of their work.

While Frankfort residents have not determined what the future use of the school will be, they are moving forward with repairs to stabilize the building. The exact future of the school building remains unknown, but the interior history of the school has new life. This *thing*—the Frankfort School building, the communal memories and associated social actions—has its own history, one that is living and moving.

Acknowledgments

The on-the-ground efforts of the Kansas State University student team were extraordinary. I am most thankful for their work. I want to also thank the Frankfort Development Trust and residents of the community for the invitation to participate in the project. The conclusions and analysis of the situation presented in this chapter are mine alone and have not been endorsed by any other participant in this project.

* * * *

Discussion and Exercises

Reflections about the Chapter You Just Read:

1. Please refer to the standard features of a research project explained in the Introduction. Then:
   a. In one sentence, identify the *research topic*. This sentence can be in the form of a question but does not have to be. In any case, write one grammatically correct sentence that captures the research topic of this chapter.
   b. Identify the *literature* related to this research project.
   c. Identify the *method* which the author used and also the *data* which this method generated for analysis.
   d. Explain how this approach is *generalizable* (or not).
   e. Explain how you can have confidence (or not) of the *internal and external validity* of this author's overall approach.
2. In what way is history living and moving according to Orthel?
3. Compare the resulting interiority of the Frankfort community to the interiority of the HEW Village of Richland in Chapter 7.
4. Refer again to the Introduction of this chapter and Chapter 1: How do the interviews conducted by Orthel to understand individuals' memories of the past differ from the interviews conducted by Hadjiyanni in Chapter 1 to understand individuals' perceptions of current circumstances?
5. Discuss the participatory design aspect of the Frankfort School project. In what ways did interacting with the community help the student-designers, and in what ways did the interactions help the community in their process to save the schoolhouse?
6. What tactics did Orthel use to gather this information, and what benefits and potential disadvantages can come along with this method?

7. Consider how the experienced interiority is the same, or different from, the interiority of the individuals whose stories are related in Chapter 3.

Exercises/Suggestions for Further Study

1. The oral histories of this chapter record individuals' memories of the school. Read the article cited here. As you read, note the memories of childhood homes that individuals associated with their adult home. How might that information be useful in designing a new home for the individual? Marcus, Clare Cooper. "Environmental Memories." In *Place Attachment*, eds. Irwin Altman and Setha Low, 87–112. New York: Plenum Press, 1992.
2. Choose a historical event that occurred in the last 75 years. Read a summary of it from a historical source (textbook or encyclopedia). Interview three to five individuals who experienced the event and ask them to tell you about it. Compare the "oral histories" you collected from the interviews of individual accounts to the facts you collected from the historical source. What are the similarities and differences between the two sources? What did you learn from the personal accounts that added to the story of the event?
3. Review the "History discussion questions" provided by Orthel in Figure 5.5, recording notes for your responses to each one. In small groups of three to four, discuss your answers with your classmates. With your group, choose one question to elaborate on and then share your discussion points with the class.

Additional Connections and Information

The following literature is helpful in framing how to consider the tangible and intangible information encountered in *thingly* history:

Bennett, Milton J. *The Value of Cultural Diversity: Rhetoric and Reality*, keynote address to International Conference on Integration, Shared Identities in Diverse Communities, and the Role of Culture, Media, and Civil Society, Tallinn, Estonia [video, 30:29 minutes, 16 November 2017]. Retrieved from https://youtu.be/1rwQF0b2K4Q

Bennett, Milton J. "Towards Ethnorelativism: A Developmental Model of Intercultural Sensitivity," in *Education for the Intercultural Experience*, 2nd ed., ed. R.M. Paige (Yarmouth, ME: Intercultural Press, 1993), 21–71.

Cahill, Caitlin. "Including Excluded Perspectives in Participatory Action Research," *Design Studies* 28, no. 3 (2007), 325–340.

Crenshaw, Kimberle. "Demarginalizing the Intersection of Race and Sex: A Black Feminist Critique of Antidiscrimination Doctrine, Feminist Theory and Antiracist Politics," *University of Chicago Legal Forum* 1989, no. 1 (1989), article 8. Retrieved from https://chicagounbound.uchicago.edu/uclf/vol1989/iss1/8

Hayden, Dolores. *The Power of Place: Urban Landscapes as Public History*. Cambridge: MIT Press, 1995.

Hunt, Lynn, Ed. *The New Cultural History*. Berkeley: University of California Press, 1999.

Lewis, Pierce. "Axioms for Reading the Landscape: Some Guides to the American Scene," in *The Interpretation of Ordinary Landscape: Geographical Essays*, ed. Don Meinig (New York: Oxford University Press, 1979), 11–32.

Luck, Rachel. "Learning to Talk to Users in Participatory Design Situations," *Design Studies* 28, no. 3 (2007): 217–242.

Mitchell, Don. "New Axioms for Reading the Landscape: Paying Attention to Political Economy and Social Justice," in *Political Economies of Landscape Change* (The GeoJournal Library, vol. 89), eds. J.L. Wescoat and D.M. Johnston (Dordrecht, NL: Springer, 2008), 29–50. https://doi.org/10.1007/978-1-4020-5849-3_2

Notes

1 Martin Heidegger, "*What is a Thing?*" trans. W.B. Barton, Jr., and Vera Deutsch (Chicago, IL, 1967) 95 (1967), 4. Heidegger recognizes narrower and wider meanings of "thing." But his emphasis is on the thing as physical object. See also 6 A thing in the sense of being present-at-hand: a rock, a piece of wood, a pair of pliers, a watch, an apple, and a piece of bread. All inanimate and all animate things such as a rose, shrub, beech tree, spruce, lizard, and wasp. And 7: In asking "What is a thing?" we shall adhere to the first meaning" (meaning the definition cited from 6).

2 Lynn Hunt, "History, Culture, and Text," in *The New Cultural History*, ed. Lynn Hunt (Berkeley, CA: University of California Press, 1989), 1–22, 20.

3 Hayden White, *The Fiction of Narrative: Essays on History, Literature, and Theory, 1957–2007* (Baltimore, MD: Johns Hopkins University Press, 2010); Clifford Geertz, *The Interpretation of Cultures*, Vol. 5019 (Basic books, 1973).

4 G. Iggers Georg, "Historiography in the Twentieth Century," in *From Scientific Objectivity to the Postmodern Challenge* (Hanover, NH and London: Wesleyan University Press, 1997), 152.

5 See Dolores Hayden, *The Power of Place: Urban Landscapes as Public History* (Cambridge: MIT Press, 1995) for an understanding of how history and culture together provide a broader view of the cultural setting.

6 Erin Cunningham, "Navigating the Past: What Does History Offer the Discipline of Interior Design?" *Journal of Interior Design* 39, no. 3 (2014): v–xii.; Mary Anne Beecher, "Toward a Critical Approach to the History of Interiors," *Journal of Interior Design*, 24, no. 2 (1998): 4–11; Dana Vaux and David Wang, "Ethos-Intensive Objects: Toward a Methodological Framework for Identifying Complex Client Cultures," *Journal of Interior Design* 41, no. 4 (2016): 13–27; Lois Weinthal, "Preface," in *Toward a New Interior: An Anthology of Interior Design Theory* , ed. Lois Weinthal (New York: Princeton Architectural Press, 2011); Mark Hinchman, "Interior Design History: Some Reflections," *Journal of Interior Design* 38, no. 1 (2013): ix–xxi; Tiiu Poldma, "Interior Design at a Crossroads: Embracing Specificity Through Process, Research, and Knowledge," *Journal of Interior Design* 33, no. 3 (2008): vi–xvi.

7 Heidegger, op. cit., 34.

8 Ian Hodder, *Entangled: An Archaeology of the Relationship Between Humans and Things* (Malden, MA: Wiley-Blackwell, 2012), 139.

9 Ibid., 16. Italics added.

10 Lynn Hunt, "History, Culture, and Text," in *The New Cultural History*, ed. Lynn Hunt (Berkeley, CA: University of California Press, 1989), 1–22, 20.

11 E. McClung Fleming, "Artifact Study: A Proposed Model," *Winterthur Portfolio* 9 (1974): 153–173; See also: Susan M. Pearce, "Thinking about Things," in *Interpreting Objects and Collections*, ed. Susan M. Pearce (London: Routledge, 1994, original work published 1986); Doug Blandy and Paul E. Bolin, "Looking at, Engaging More: Approaches for Investigating Material Culture," *Art Education* 65, no. 4 (2012).

12 Fred N. Kerlinger and Howard B. Lee, *Foundations of Behavioral Research*, 4th ed. (New York: Harcourt College Publishing, 2000); Arthur C. Danto, *Narration and Knowledge* (New York: Columbia University Press, 1985, original work published 1964).

13 Smith explicitly challenges people working with history and heritage to acknowledge authorized heritage discourse Heritage discourse, in providing a sense of national community, must, by definition, ignore a diversity of sub-national cultural and social experiences ... The heritage discourse also explicitly promotes the experience and values of elite social classes. This works to alienate a range of other social and cultural experiences and it has been no accident that the heritage phenomena has been criticized for absenting women, a range of ethnic and other communities, Indigenous communities, and working class and labor history. Laurajane Smith, *Uses of Heritage* (New York: Routledge, 2006), 29.

14 Jack Travis, "Intersections: Black Culture + Design Culture" (keynote presentation, Interior Design Educators Council annual meeting, Boston, MA, March 2018).

15 Martin Heidegger, *Poetry, Language, Thought*, trans. Albert Hofstadler (New York: HarperPerennial, 1971).

16 Ibid., 172–175.
17 Hodder, op. cit., 32. Smith offers a distinct, but complementary, view. Heritage, not history, involves renewing memories and associations, sharing experiences...to cement present and future social and familial relationships. [It is not] just about material things ... heritage [is] a process of engagement, an act of communication and an act of making meaning in and for the present. (Smith, 2006, 1)
18 Hodder, op. cit., 38.
19 See, for example: Rachel Hurdley, "Dismantling Mantelpieces: Narrating Identities and Materializing Culture in the Home," *Sociology* 40, no. 4 (2006): 717–733.
20 All four are clearly inherent to interiority. Buchanan uses the word *things* to mean physical objects; in this essay, objects have been substituted to avoid confusion. Richard Buchanan, "Design Research and the New Learning," *Design Issues* 17, no. 4 (2001): 2–23.
21 See, for example: Dell Upton, "Architectural History or Landscape History?" *Journal of Architectural Education* 44, no. 4 (1991): 195–199; Peirce F. Lewis, "Axioms for Reading the Landscape: Some Guides to the American Scene," in *The Interpretation of Ordinary Landscapes: Geographical Essays*, ed. Donald W. Meinig (New York: Oxford University Press, 1979); Julie Riesenweber, "Reworking A Working Landscape: Architecture, Ideology and Material Conversations at the Senator John and Eliza Pope Villa, Lexington, Kentucky" (unpublished, 2001); Emma Waterton and Steve Watson, "A War Long Forgotten," *Angelaki* 20, no. 3 (2015): 89–103.
22 The research component of this project included nine formal interviews with residents of the Frankfort community. The participants varied in age from recent high school graduate to long-retired farmer. The interviews are part of a broader research project exploring how individuals understand and use history in their communities. As such, the interviews fit into a research methodology to generalize information across multiple places. Interviews were conducted in a location selected by the participant (e.g., private home, local restaurant, the school building). Some interviews were conducted by telephone. Data collection methods were reviewed by an institutional review board (IRB) for compliance with research regulations and ethical expectations.
23 Interestingly, the 1902 school building is not the first school building to be preserved in the town. The original school building from 1870 was relocated to the city park in 1995. It sits next to stone and metal memorial markers recognizing war veterans and early pioneers.
24 William Peña, Steven Parshall, and Kevin Kelly, *Problem Seeking: An Architectural Programming Primer*, 3rd ed. (Washington, DC: AIA Press, 1987).
25 Richard D. Pankratz and Charles L. Hall, *National Register of Historic Places Inventory – Nomination Form: Frankfort School* (Topeka: Kansas Historic Society, 1971), 3.
26 Ibid.
27 One-room schools in places like Phillips County (1899), Sumner County (separate schools in 1894 and 1904), and nearby Riley County (1903) remained common solutions for rural communities in Kansas. Communities near Frankfort, such as White Cloud (Doniphan County, 1871) or Kansas City (Wyandotte, 1898, 1905, and 1909), built schools of similar size and styling to Frankfort's 1902 school. Further away, Stillwater (Johnson County, 1910), Burlingame (Osage County, 1902) and Burns (Marion County, 1905) also built schools on par with the Frankfort example. Refer to the Kansas Historical Society resources inventory (www.khri.kansasgis.org) for complete records of documented historic buildings and landscapes.
28 Fiona, interview by the author, November 2014, transcript FKS04.195.
29 Floyd, interview by the author, December 2014, transcript FKS01.073.
30 Flora, interview by the author, November 2014, transcript FKS03.286.
31 Florence, interview by the author, June 2015, transcript FKS09.153.
32 Fred, interview by the author, May 2015, transcript FKS05.082.
33 Francine, interview by the author, May 2015, transcript FKS07.055.
34 Felicity, interview by the author, May 2015, transcript FKS08.046.
35 Felix, interview by the author, December 2014, transcript FKS02.061 and FKS02.230.
36 Francine, transcript FKS07.341.
37 Francine, transcript FKS07.193.
38 Fiona, transcript FKS04.373.
39 Florence, transcript FKS09.058.
40 Flora, transcript FKS03.079.
41 Flora, transcript FKS03.194.
42 Fred, transcript FKS05.187, emphasis in original.
43 Fred, transcript FKS05.235.
44 Faye, interview by the author, May 2015, transcript FKS06.521.
45 Faye, transcript FKS06.708.
46 Felix, transcript FKS02.158.
47 Fred, transcript FKS05.131.
48 Flora, transcript FKS03.116 and FKS03.134.
49 Florence, transcript FKS09.346.
50 Faye, transcript FKS06.198.
51 Felicity, transcript FKS08.071 and FKS08.106.
52 Felicity, interview by the author, May 2015, transcript FKS08.219.
53 Florence, transcript FKS09.152.
54 Fiona, transcript FKS04.077.

55 See the "Additional information and resources" section at the end of the chapter for a list of some useful, interdisciplinary resources.

56 Laurajane Smith, "The Discourse of Heritage," in *Use of Heritage* (New York: Routledge, 2006), 11–43.

57 Catherine Kohler Riessman and Lee Quinney, "Narrative in Social Work: A Critical Review," *Qualitative Social Work* 4, no. 4 (2005), 381–412; Edward W. Said, "Invention, Memory, and Place," in *Landscape and Power*, 2nd ed., ed. W.J.T. Mitchell (Chicago, IL: University of Chicago Press, 2002, original work published 1994), 241–259.

58 Fiona, transcript FKS04.077.

59 Fiona, transcript FKS04.413.

60 Fiona, transcript FKS04.125.

Chapter 6

Philosophical Method

Editors' Introduction by Dana E. Vaux and David Wang

What is philosophy, and what is philosophical method in the sense this chapter uses it? To begin, let's imagine the following. Suppose we are viewing the Mona Lisa at the Louvre in Paris. Our guide asks us, "What do you see in this work of art?" We might answer, "This is a portrait of a woman." Or we can be more technical and say, "This is an oil painting on canvas," or "This is a painting by Leonardo da Vinci." Suffice it to say that our guide's question would not stir answers of a philosophical nature. But after touring us through the Louvre for the entire day, suppose our guide asks us, "What *is* a work of art?" This is a question of a different nature altogether. It does not simply ask about what we can observe about a particular work of art. This question targets everything that can be included in "work of art." Armed with the answer to *this* question, we can exclude anything that does not belong in the category "work of art." This kind of question is a philosophical one.

Based on this example, we can say that *philosophy seeks to get to the first principles about a specific topic in order for that topic to be explained in a universally applicable way.* What are the first principles that help us recognize a work of art when we see one? The task for the philosopher of art, then, is to design a pair of philosophical eyeglasses that will help us recognize *any* work of art. Since Classical Greece, philosophers have attempted to answer this question to varying levels of success—which is to say that "doing philosophy" is not an easy thing.

In this chapter, David Wang highlights the philosophical first principles that shaped the interiors of the medieval home as well as the post–Industrial Revolution home beginning in the 1850s. Wang begins by referring to Witold Rybczynski's description of home interiors in medieval times. Rooms had multiple functions: people ate and bathed in the same room, furniture was movable to serve multiple purposes, and the idea of "privacy" was unknown. A historian might document examples of how privacy was not an important value in medieval times. A philosopher, however, would ask *why* privacy was unknown in those times. What first principles were active such that privacy in residential interiors was a non-issue in the medieval period—while it is such a *basic* value for us in our culture?

To answer this question, the chapter has an introductory section in which Wang introduces the idea of the *Common Sense* (which he at times abbreviates CS). Common Sense here means a communally shared set of outlooks that the bulk of a community takes for granted. Before we can understand how a culture defines a value like privacy, we must first understand how a culture defines any value, and this has to do with a culture's shared Common Sense. Eating and bathing in the same interior space in medieval times becomes more understandable because the first principles shaping the Common Sense of those times did not recognize a value termed "privacy." The philosophical task is to explain the first principles that shape that culture's Common Sense, so that privacy was not important during the medieval times Rybczynski describes.

The CS of a culture, therefore, significantly impacts the decisions people within that culture make. Wang cites Jon Lang's point that designers' decisions are value-laden, or *deontic*, ones. This means that a culture's overall Common Sense shapes design values, which in turn places a kind of implicit deontic mandate—an "ought to"—in how design decisions are made. It is important to note that when a designer makes a design decision, he or she may not be aware that the decision reflects values informed by the CS. The decision simply reflects what the larger cultural Common Sense regards as good or proper. For instance, in today's culture, a designer can make many design decisions in accord with sustainable practices without consciously deciding to do so. This is what Lang means by deontic design decisions.

For this reason, the title of this chapter, "Interior Design in the Common Sense," suggests that design comes *from within* the Common Sense of its cultural times. Wang compares and contrasts interior design in the Common Sense of two different cultural periods. As noted already, one is medieval home interiors that is the focus of Rybczynski's *Home: A Short History of an Idea.* The other period Wang considers comes from Adrian Forty's *Objects of Desire*, which analyzes four stages of residential interiors beginning around 1850, just after the beginning of the Industrial Revolution, to the mid-20th century. Wang suggests that a distinct difference between the medieval home interior and its post–Industrial Revolution counterparts is the emergence of an awareness of the individual, specifically the emergence of the importance of a private domain separated from the public realm. As you read this chapter:

1. Note how the first principles of a culture are established by reference to the historian Franklin Baumer's five basic questions all cultures must answer. These questions are: (1) Who is God? (2) What is human being? (3) What is nature? (4) What is society? (5) What is history? By comparing and contrasting how the medieval Common Sense answered these questions with how they were answered by the post–Industrial Revolution Common Sense, Wang not only identifies first principles but also uses the framework of these five questions to highlight differences between cultures.
2. Note also how broad ideological developments contribute to the "atmosphere" of a cultural Common Sense. To this end, the chapter references the Protestant Reformation, the beginnings of scientific thinking, the mass production of goods enabled by the Industrial Revolution and, in the conclusion, the impact of cyber technology.

Interiority

We all live *inside* the cultural outlook of our communal Common Sense. Even if we try to break free from the particular set of values of our Common Sense, this still requires an engagement with these values *from within*. Wang's chapter underlines how impactful this *philosophical* interiority can be as design finds expression in physical forms and environments.

1. Philosophical interiority is not a term Wang uses in his chapter. But we suggest this term captures the idea that all people live within the *ideological* space created as their culture answers Baumer's five questions. As you read, think about how the cultural Common Sense *you* live in would answer these questions, and how this impacts your design decisions. The conclusion of the chapter and the subsequent exercises will help your thinking along these lines.
2. Note Baumer's five questions and the answers each cultural Common Sense provides (see Figures 6.4 and 6.8). Think through how the answers contribute to shaping a lack of privacy in the medieval case, and an emphasis on a private realm in the post–Industrial Revolution examples.

* * * *

Interior Design in the Common Sense

David Wang

As designers, the projects we design and build do not happen in a vacuum. A complicated weave of cultural factors impacts our design thinking. These factors entail developments occurring in our culture, but even more importantly, they include our own ideological values as we live *in* our cultural settings. Jon Lang has pointed out that we design in certain ways and not in other ways because our values drive design decisions that are *deontological.*[1] This word simply means that we make design decisions because we think they *ought* to be made in certain ways and not in other ways. And cultural norms inform us about what ought to be done so that it becomes second nature to us.

Consider an example from imperial China. In that culture, women had their own designated interior areas within residential compounds.[2] In Chinese culture at that time, this practice was received as the social norm. But for us living in a contemporary Western culture, this practice is not welcome. In fact, the deontic position is to *reject* segregation by gender in the interior spaces we design. The important point here, however, is to realize that both views are *normative* in relation to the culture in question.

Consider also "sustainability" as a broadly shared value today. This commitment finds expression in many ways including smaller-sized automobiles with higher gas efficiency, straw bale and other forms of off-grid housing, and locally grown "slow foods" as compared to the packaged products of agribusiness. Values related to living sustainably, then, are now fairly normative in our current culture. Consequently, many designers understand the deontic "ought to" in designing with sustainable practices in mind.

When a practice or an outlook such as spatial separation by gender or sustainable design becomes widely accepted in a culture, it resides within the *Common Sense* of that culture. Common Sense (or CS) does not mean to bring an umbrella if the forecast is for rain. When capitalized, Common Sense means a culture's normatively shared sense of how things should be, and hence what should be done. To the extent that living sustainably has become a commonly accepted value in today's culture, to that extent it is within the CS of our culture.

Interior design happens within the Common Sense of its cultural times. Hence the title of this chapter is "Interior Design *in* the Common Sense." My aim is to explore the philosophical first principles upon which a culture's Common Sense is built. My focus will be upon the interior design of the domicile and how the interiors of homes in various cultural eras embody the CS of those cultures in physical ways. I take my examples from two readable accounts of domestic interiors from the literature: Witold Rybczynski's *Home: A Short History of an Idea* and Adrian Forty's *Objects of Desire,* specifically the chapter titled "The Home." For example, here is one of Rybczynski's descriptions of the medieval residential interior: "The medieval home was a public, not a private place. The hall was in constant use, for cooking, for eating, for entertaining guests, for transacting business, as well as nightly for sleeping."[3] Rybczynski also points to The Great Bed of Ware. This bed "was so large that 'Four couples might cozily lie side by side /And thus without touching each other abide.'"[4] Obviously, this was a different cultural Common Sense than ours. In this chapter, I am not interested in merely reporting what Rybczynski says about the medieval home; my aim is to highlight the philosophical *atmosphere* of a cultural time for which "privacy" was a non-issue. How was privacy not an issue? *Why* was this? Philosophy answers this question at a level Rybczynski's book perhaps does not address.

And here is an example from Adrian Forty; he is describing the home in the Victorian era (1837–1901):

> By the late nineteenth century, it was principally women whose moral character was revealed by the choice of furnishings. The pressures on women to take part in this bourgeois charade were considerable. So close had the identification between woman and house become that a woman who failed to express her personality in this way was in danger of being thought lacking in femininity.[5]

It is unfortunate that Forty uses the word "charade" because even though it is quite believable that women suffered under these social pressures, the values he describes were the norm within the communal Common Sense of those times. Victorian culture did not regard women's moral character reflected in the interior design of their homes a charade. When it comes to a culture's Common Sense, there is an important distinction between individual preferences (not to mention Forty's own cultural biases as he analyzes a past culture) in contrast to the communal commitments indigenous to a culture's CS. I address this further below.

What factors contribute to shaping the Common Sense of a culture? One way is to identify universal factors (or first principles) shared by all cultures in contrast to ideological traits peculiar to any one culture. Then one can determine how these universal factors are expressed in interior environments as individual cultures understand them. In order to explain cultural shifts in Europe from 1600 to 1950,[6] Franklin Baumer identifies five universal questions all cultures must answer: (1) Who or What is God? (2) Who or What is Human Being? (3) What is Nature? (4) What is Society? (5) What is History? Every culture answers these five questions each in its own way. I use these five universal questions to assess residential design in the Common Sense of the cultures in Rybczynski's and Forty's works. But before applying Baumer's five universal questions to the specifics of medieval and Victorian interiors, we need to consider the Common Sense itself in more detail.

The Percolations of the Common Sense

The three amoeba-like blobs in Figure 6.1 represent the Common Sense of three modern time periods. From left to right, the first blob is a light solid line labeled "CS at 1966" (the diagram does

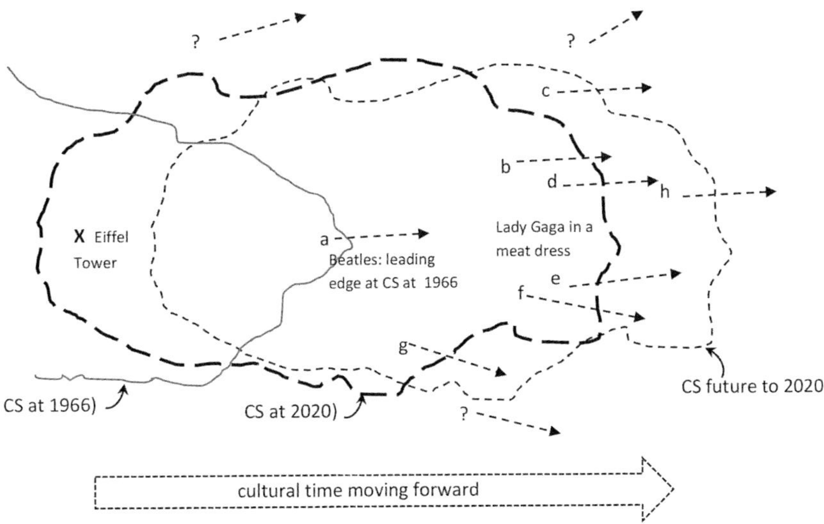

Figure 6.1 The Common Sense (CS) as it moves through cultural time.

not show this blob completely). The next blob is a bold dotted line labeled "CS at 2020." This blob represents our current cultural Common Sense. The third blob (to the right) is in a light dotted line, and this one is labeled "CS future to 2020."

We can now identify four general traits of the Common Sense from the diagram. The first trait of the CS is that it *moves* through time, as indicated by the large dotted arrow of time underneath the blobs. A well-known example from cultural history provides an explanation for this. When the Beatles debuted in the United States in the 1960s, young people loved them. But many of their parents were appalled—after all, they had "long hair." In the CS of 1966, the Beatles were at the cutting edge (see "a" in Figure 6.1). But by 2020, they are safely ensconced in the *center* of the Common Sense of 2020. In fact, many of the Beatles' songs are now considered "classics."

For an example more specific to interior design, Lang cites this from Frank Lloyd Wright: "To reduce the number of necessary parts of the house and the separate rooms to a minimum, ... (so that) light, air and vista permeate the whole with a sense of unity."[7] (Figure 6.2) In the early 20th century, Wright revolutionized residential interiors with fluid interior spaces offering extensive views to the outside. His *deontic* idea was at the cutting edge of the CS in which he lived. It went against the usual practice of the time, featuring floor plans divided into small enclosed rooms. But today, "open concept" residential interiors are safely ensconced within our cultural common sense. At least some of this is thanks to Wright's trailblazing ideas for flexible residential interiors. So again, the first trait to remember about the communal Common Sense is that it moves through time.

The second trait of any Common Sense is that artists in general tend to be among the kinds of people at the leading edge (or cutting edge) of a CS. Again, "a" in Figure 6.1 shows the Beatles at the leading edge of the 1966 Common Sense. Another example: some years ago, my students told me about Lady Gaga performing in a meat dress ("d" in Figure 6.1). For my generation, this seemed odd. But to my students, performing in a meat dress was generally accepted. The event was widely documented in popular media[8]—and even mentioned in scholarly analyses[9]—as an innovative expression of an important artist; this indicates that it is (or was) at the cutting edge of the CS at that

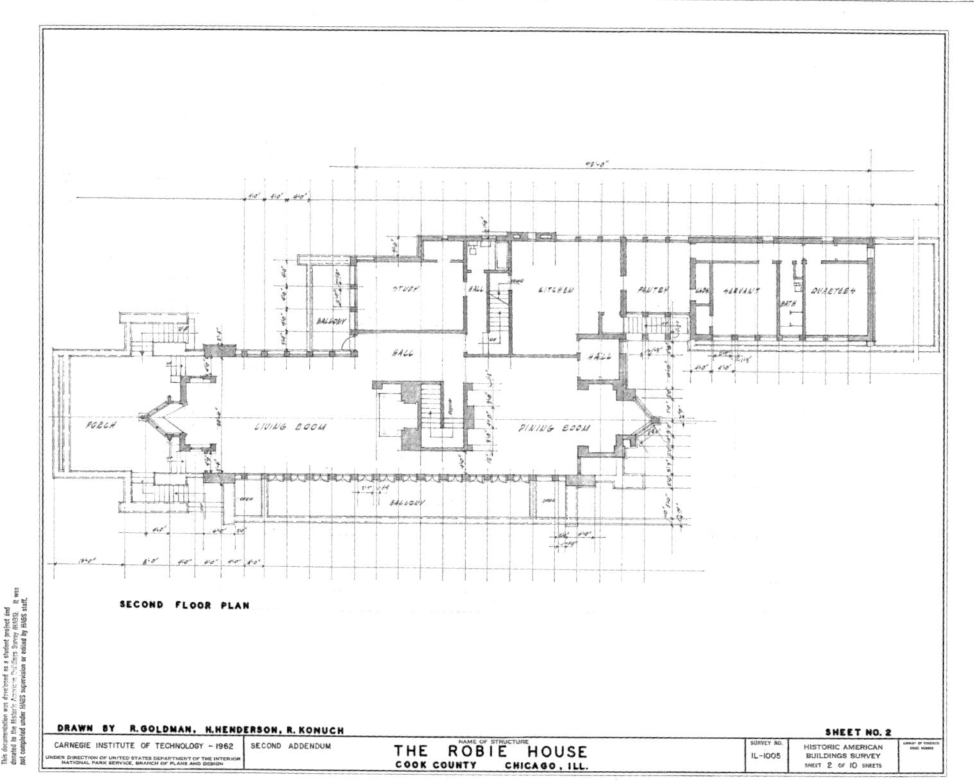

Figure 6.2 Floor plan of Frank Lloyd Wright's Robie House. The house dates from 1909 and is located in the Hyde Park section of Chicago. The open interior plan was revolutionary at that time. Historic American Buildings Survey (HABS); see credits.

time. Figure 6.1 indicates that dancing in a meat dress still remains somewhere at the vanguard of the 2020 CS.

Third, not all innovative ideas are received by the Common Sense. In fact, many are not. We will never know how many are not accepted by the CS since only their innovators thought their creations were innovative. These unknown attempts are denoted by the dotted arrows with question marks *outside* of the CS domains in Figure 6.1. The Common Sense, then, does a lot of filtering. Because the CS is a *bulk* communal reality, to a large extent it is blind to individual preferences.[10] So, on the one hand, designers at the leading edge of their CS might generate new creations never before seen in the CS. But on the other hand, there are no guarantees that the CS will accept what designers create. This highlights the problem creative people often face: their creations can impact culture greatly; but then, it is often the case that nobody ever hears about their efforts.

Fourth, no CS is "completely new" relative to its past iterations. Any Common Sense has within it the accrual of past versions of itself. We already noted that the Beatles' music was once *avant-garde*, but is now considered "classic." To put this point slightly differently, present-day popular music has within it the "genes" of the Beatles' innovations. Similarly, an "X" designates the Eiffel Tower in Figure 6.1. Parisians hated the new Tower when construction began in 1887. In fact, the author Guy de Maupassant, 37 years of age at the time, ate his lunches at the base of the Tower just to avoid looking

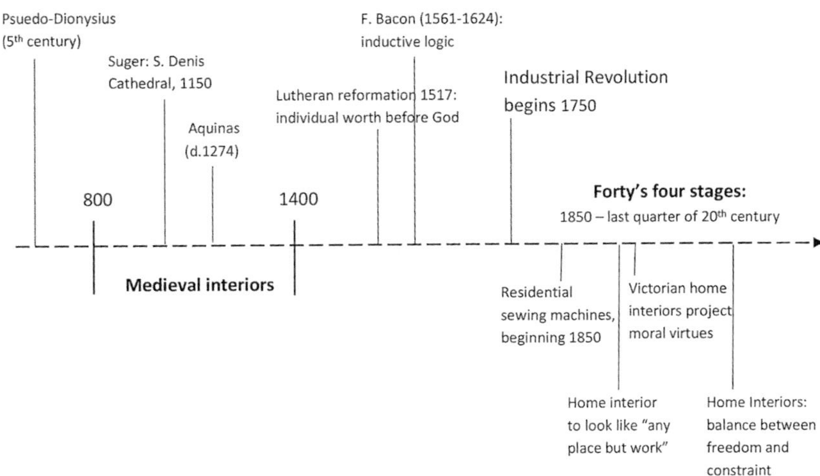

Figure 6.3 A timeline indicating the two periods, with key events, addressed in this chapter.

at it.[11] But today, removing the Eiffel Tower from Paris would be unconscionable. The Eiffel Tower is one example of how cutting-edge creations eventually become accepted and how that acceptance in turn informs current practices. In the case of the Eiffel Tower, its enormous height enabled by structural iron is now commonplace in skyscrapers built of structural steel.

The cultural memory of a Common Sense therefore has *depth*, as the outlooks of layers and layers of past cultures remain *within* it. This leads to all sorts of contemplations on the ability of history to teach us about current events; or about the attraction we have for antiques (i.e., for "retro" design); or even about the possibility that a past innovation may not be recognized as important until a *subsequent* Common Sense centuries later receives it for the significant development that it was.[12]

As we now look at the interiors of Rybczynski's and Forty's concerns, it is helpful to provide an overall timeline of the points in history that will be mentioned in the sections below (Figure 6.3).

The Residential Interior in the Medieval Common Sense

We begin with Rybczynski and the medieval period. We can think of the advent of Charlemagne in the late 8th century all the way to the early Renaissance in the late 14th and early 15th centuries as "medieval." This is a dauntingly long period of time to target conclusions about home interiors. However, the fact that we can even posit the idea of a "medieval interior" underlines just how unchanging some of the bulk characteristics of the medieval Common Sense were. The reason for this was the durability of the underlying philosophical structures woven throughout medieval society and how long the answers to Baumer's five universal questions (God, human being, nature, society, history; see Figure 6.4) remained largely the same.

The Canadian cultural philosopher Charles Taylor suggests that the medieval outlook produced a "porous" sense of human being-in-the-world, and this term is sufficient for us to see how Baumer's universal factors find expression in medieval concepts of the interior (italics added):

> By definition for the porous self, the source of its most powerful and important emotions are outside the "mind"; or better put, *the very notion that there is a clear boundary,*

1. What/who is God?	All powerful source of the cosmos as a divine creation
2. What/who is human being?	Fallen from grace but redeemable through the auspices of the Church by means of its sacraments and liturgical practices connecting the penitent to the Christ
3. What is Nature?	The cosmos filled with the presence of God and his work of salvation, expressed in all natural forms as symbols. Nature is *enchanted*. See Charles Taylor's decisive analysis of the medieval enchanted world in *A Secular Age* (Harvard University Press, 2007, 2018)
4. What Society?	Society and Church were generally indistinguishable. To be in good standing in medieval society was to be in the Church. Excommunication meant something tantamount to non-existence.
5. What is History?	For human life, a brief journey to heaven. The historian Barbara Tuchman notes that there was not a unified calendar during medieval times, suggesting that temporal time was not something to be coordinated and documented in chronological order. *A Distant Mirror: The Calamitous 14th Century* (Random House, 1978), 17.

Figure 6.4 Franklin Baumer's five questions any culture must answer, here applied to the medieval Common Sense.

> *allowing us to define an inner base area, grounded in which we can disengage from the rest, has no sense* … The porous self is vulnerable to spirits, demons, cosmic forces. And along with this go certain fears which can grip it in certain circumstances.[13]

In the medieval CS, the supernatural domain was one and the same with the empirical world of the senses. God and angels, demons and evil spirits were in the immediate spatial and physical world. The overwhelming medieval impetus was to be in the good graces of God as dictated by various institutional practices of the Church, so as to be in safe haven. In fact, for the medieval individual, all that was seen, heard, touched, smelled and tasted was united with cosmic forces, rendering the boundary between the *inner* sense of self and sense of place as fluid and somewhat indeterminate.

With respect to nature, then, this was an *enchanted* world.[14] Emile Male, in his *The Gothic Image*, describes it this way:

> The whole world is a symbol. The sun, the stars, the seasons, day and night, all speak in solemn accents… the material world is a constant image of the spiritual world … The juniper tree, the terebinth, and the snowy peaks of Lebanon are alike thoughts of God.[15]

Social practices were aligned with this symbolic reception of nature. Male further states:

> Spring, which gives news life to the world, is the symbol of baptism … Summer too is a type, for its burning heat and light are reminders of the light of another world and of the ardent love of the eternal life. Autumn, season of harvest and vintage, is the dread symbol of the last Judgment … Winter is a shadow of that death which awaits mankind and the universe.[16]

Taylor's insight of "the boundary between the self and other is fuzzy, porous"[17] helps to explain Rybczynski's observation that there was no clear divide between a public versus a private domain.

We can now better understand why it would be acceptable at that time for people to be dining at the table in the same room with someone taking a bath in a portable bathtub.[18] Privacy was "ill-defined" because it was the nature of the porous self to be open to a variety of "presences" in the human sphere but also in the supernatural sphere. Furthermore, Rybczynski cites the philosopher John Lukacs in noting that terms like "self-confidence," or "self-esteem," only emerged in common parlance several centuries after the medieval cultural world.[19] The point is the "self" as an individuated autonomous reality was yet in the future.

How does this porosity express itself spatially? Vertically and horizontally, space was experienced as an extended community. Even as medieval persons are never alone in their house because of the squeeze of people, they are never alone spiritually as well; they are beings in a chain of beings. This idea stems from a philosophy called Neo-Platonism that significantly informed the medieval Common Sense. Neo-Platonism posited that all of reality was an emanation of light from God, who is Light. A community of beings populate this emanation:

> Hierarchy causes its members to be images of God in all respects, to be clear and spotless mirrors reflecting the glow of primordial light and indeed of God himself. It ensures that when its members have received this full and divine splendor, they can then pass on this light generously and in accordance to God's will to beings further down the scale.[20]

This statement is from Pseudo-Dionysius (probably a 5th-century thinker); he had tremendous influence in medieval ideas. For instance, Dante's *Divine Comedy* was very much informed by Pseudo-Dionysius's Neo-Platonism[21] (see Figure 6.5).

Hence, the medieval person lives with a sense of participating in a tremendously extended vertical spatiality. The medievalist C.S. Lewis expands on this in his commentary on the medieval model of the cosmos:

Figure 6.5 An engraving by Gustave Doré (1832–1883) illustrating *Paradiso* by Dante Alighieri; WIKI public domain; see credits.

Figure 6.6 Looking upward at the ceiling of the nave of Notre Dame Cathedral. Photograph courtesy of Nicole Clements.

> To look up at the towering medieval universe is much more like looking at a great building … the spheres … present us with an object in which the mind can rest, overwhelming in its greatness but satisfying in its harmony.

This vertical spatiality, then, was *habitable*, and in light of its sublime immensity, the medieval porous self finds harmony. Consider Paris' historic cathedral, Notre Dame (Figure 6.6), destroyed by fire as this book was in process. Cathedrals such as Notre Dame brought heaven down to earth. The cathedrals were three dimensional creations of the Word of God, into which supplicants stepped, looked up at the ephemeral light, and found themselves at home. In this way, we understand why medieval royalty and upper classes interred themselves inside cathedrals so that their entrance into heaven would be assured.

Horizontally, medieval life was profoundly communal. And so, "just as one did not have a strongly developed self-consciousness, one did not have a room of one's own."[22] The walls that surrounded the cities defined "interior" more than any walls that demarked individual residential privacy. City walls brought all aspects of life inside the walls into a single, defined community. Fairs were held in piazzas; religious processions streamed through alleyways; and guilds knitted tradespeople together in economic linkages. In addition to these communal elements, the church with its varieties of priests, friars, monks, and lay confraternities spoke of community in heavenly terms. All of these factors worked together to render the town itself a larger *horizontal* interiority into which residential interiors were merely woven as a part (Figure 6.7).

Within this town-scale interiority, Rybczynski has us imagine a day in the life of a medieval scholar. After devotions in the cathedral, the scholar attends a public execution, after which he attends a celebration of some sort ("an astounding mixture of good and bad taste") where after washing his hands with perfumed water, he'd laugh as dwarfs jumped out of enormous baked pies.[23] The various events he experiences, whether in the open air or upon entering the hall for that celebration, were

Figure 6.7 The Piazza S. Marco, Venice. This famous square, elements of which date back to the 14th century, illustrates the horizontality of the medieval townscape.

"interior" in his sense of place. Given immense vertical spatiality, along with a horizontal communal spatiality, Rybczynski therefore notes the transitory aspect of the medieval residence as such. "In the Middle Ages people didn't so much live in their houses as camp in them."[24]

We can conclude this brief segment on medieval interiority by noting three points regarding medieval furniture, function and comfort. *Furniture* was movable, and whatever furniture there was (Rybczynski suggests chairs didn't even come into regular use until the 15th century) served multiple functions: chests for both seating and storage, tables were demountable trestles, and even beds were collapsible. The space itself served as business and residence. And so, rooms were multipurpose.[25] *Function* was not understood as one physical object for each discreet use and spaces followed suit: no space was designed for one single use. Finally, *comfort*, as a concept, was not a recognized value. The relationship between "self" and "comfort," then, emerges as a potent philosophical linkage—*which came later than the medieval period.* When self is porous, designing for individual comfort was not a priority.

When Rybczynski says the medieval home was more like a camp site, is he projecting a value judgment from our era onto that past era? Probably. On the one hand, his description certainly helps *us* understand what life in a medieval residence might have felt like. But on the other hand, someone living in the Middle Ages would not have been pining for the more settled home environment they *could* have if only they lived 500 years in the future. They wouldn't consider this camp-like setup as something they had to put up with. The point is this: to get at the *philosophical* grounding of the Common Sense of any cultural period, it helps to place ourselves *in* the context of the people of that CS. From this interior standpoint, there are *desirable* reasons why a point of view becomes normative within a cultural Common Sense. So, while medieval home interiors might seem like campsites to us, what might have been the positive elements in the medieval CS that made interiors the way they were? Perhaps it was a larger sense of belonging to a vast vertical space that included heaven and a larger horizontal sense of belonging that embraced the entire urban community as "home." In our day, when "sense of place" research is driven by a loss of constructs like heaven (again see Taylor) and communal life (see Robert Putnam's *Bowling Alone*),[26] it might be good to reconsider these values from the medieval Common Sense. After all, the traces of past cultural ideas are always still with us, still embedded somewhere in our own CS.

The Rise of *Individual*-Awareness

As we transition from Rybczynski's to Forty's analyses of home interiors, we need to note an idea that emerged between the Common Sense of medieval times and the Common Sense characterizing much of European and American culture after the Industrial Revolution. This is the notion of "the self." Rybczynski cites an observation from Nancy Mitford that links the rise of selfhood during the reign of Louis XV in the early 18th century:

> Formality was replaced by vivacity, grandiosity by intimacy, and magnificence by delicacy. "Versailles in the eighteenth century," wrote Nancy Mitford, "presented the unedifying but cheerful spectacle of several thousand people living for pleasure and very much enjoying themselves." ... it was precisely during this period, and mainly because of its hedonistic interests, that comfortable furniture first appeared.[27]

What happened in philosophical ideas between the medieval period and the Versailles of the early 18th century to stir such a change in social practice, not to mention in furniture design? For Rybczynski, Mitford's observation suggests it relates to the rise of individual enjoyment of the senses. We can consider two general ideological developments prior to the 18th century (but emerging out of the medieval centuries), both of which contributed to the elevation of the self over the communal whole. One was the Protestant Reformation, and the other was the emergence of inductive reasoning.

The Protestant Reformation, which began with Martin Luther (1483–1541), radically altered the belief system of the medieval CS by critiquing a corrupted Church and exposing the moral failings of its leadership. For the first time the Church was no longer infallible and authoritative, and the individual could now have access to salvation by the practice of his or her own faith in the Bible instead of through the Church's institutional structure. This shift in belief put more power on the shoulders of the individual and changed the fiber of how people lived and operated. For instance, Luther taught that it was not only the clergy who served God, but people in all walks of life can serve God by faithfully doing their jobs. This view elevated the value of the individual, and an individual's work. This new sense of self-importance came into competition with a sense of belonging to a whole. When Mitford made note of the CS of the French aristocracy of the 18th century engaging in "the ... cheerful spectacle of several thousand people living for pleasure and very much enjoying themselves," a *philosophical* analysis might need to take into account the rise of the value of the individual tracing back to the ideas of Luther.

The other development that elevated the individual self over the communal whole was the rise of scientific method. Francis Bacon (1561–1624) had an enormous influence in what was to become a scientific way of viewing nature. Just as Luther rejected the idea of salvation through the Church in favor of salvation through individual faith, Francis Bacon (1561–1624) rejected the Church's tendency to anchor all knowledge on the teachings of institutional Church authority. Bacon emphasized the importance of firsthand observation of nature and experimentation.[28] Church authority emphasized *deduction*: derive understanding for how to live based on what established authority teaches. In contrast, Bacon's emphasis on experimentation was *inductive*: based on what you see, devise *new* conclusions about how to live. This was the beginnings of scientific method, a technological outlook

1. What/who is God?	Bacon's era gravitated towards Deism, i.e., God is removed, and nature worked in accord with its own (God-given) laws.
2. What/who is human being?	Enlightenment humanism emphasized human autonomy, with increasing confidence that human reason (via scientific method) can explain all phenomena.
3. What is Nature?	Nature can be studied empirically, and armed with scientific knowledge, human reason can manipulate nature for human use.
4. What Society?	Society and Church increasingly separated; with the intelligentsia promoting human reason over divine revelation. This led to the view that society can be autonomously defined along humanist values of social contract (Rousseau); or the supremacy of the ruler/state (Hobbes).
5. What is History?	Inductive reason laid the philosophical groundwork for the idea of *progress*: Today is better than yesterday because of the powers of scientific reason. See J.B. Bury, *The Idea of Progress* (Dover, 1955).

Figure 6.8 Franklin Baumer's five questions any culture must answer, here applied to the Common Sense in Europe (and also generally the United States) from 1850 to the mid 20th century.

in which controlling nature to maximize human comfort prevailed as a rationale for learning. The proliferation of mechanical devices made possible by the Industrial Revolution some two centuries after Bacon was thanks to his ideas on experimentation. Recall that Mitford's observation concerns *individual* comforts and the pleasures informed by the idea that nature can be manipulated for human comfort. We have moved a long way from the communal nature of the medieval Common Sense, toward a Common Sense that unreflectively prizes *self*-awareness.

With these developments as a backdrop, Baumer's five universal questions took on different answers for the emerging industrial age as shown in Figure 6.8. Unlike the all-powerful God of the medieval CS, here, God is further removed, leaving nature's laws to speak for divine presence. Rather than a weak fallen creature needing God's grace administered through the Church, the human being emerges as a *reasoning* power that can explain all phenomena. Rather than an enchanted nature that participates in spiritual realities in the medieval CS, here human wellbeing depends to a large extent on how a manipulated nature can serve human ends. As for Society, the 17th and 18th centuries saw new theories of how human communities can prosper by social contract (Rousseau),[29] or under powerful sovereigns (Hobbes)[30]; the Church as a source of authority receded. Finally, history can be viewed as a continuous unfolding of improvement, thanks largely to human rational development.

Bacon's views helped spawn the Industrial Revolution and its proliferation of machines and mechanical devices. This resulted in a Common Sense that did not so much see societal life as regulated by divine authority but rather as a functioning kit of parts regulated by relational agreements: between natural forces, between the political sovereign and the subject; between factory owners and workers; between the genders; and so on. Underneath Forty's analyses of home interiors from 1850 to the latter half of the 20th century (the last home interior shown in Forty's chapter dates from 1954), the answers to Baumer's questions motivate expressions in design terms that reflect these alterations in the Common Sense. Specifically, we see the rise of the primacy of individual identity expressed in various designs of the home.

Forty's Four Themes of Home Interiors

Forty draws out four themes of home interiors during this period: (1) the home "as anyplace but work"; (2) the home as a sign of character; (3) the home in transition from beauty to efficiency and (4) home interiors as a balance between freedom and constraint in an economic sense. These four themes can roughly be tracked as stages through time from 1850 to the mid-20th century. Each of them emphasizes the home as a place for self-identity and comfort, while deemphasizing the communal whole.

Forty's first theme is about the home designed to be "any place but work." In the early days of the Industrial Revolution, places of work were congested and unhealthy. Thus the need arose for residential interiors to be refuges from places of work. New Common Sense values developed, such as the home as a place set apart from the public realm to affirm an individual's *true* identity. Forty cites this from the diary of a clerk named Mark Rutherford:

> I cut off my office life ... from my home life so completely that I was two selves, and my true self was not stained by contact from my other self. It was a comfort to me to think the moment the clock struck seven that my second self died ... I was a citizen walking London streets; I had my opinions upon human beings and books; I was on equal terms with my friends; I was Ellen's husband; I was, in short, a man.[31]

Attitudes such as this resulted in interior décor of residences emphasizing stark differences between life at home and life at work. The interior shown in Figure 6.9 is similar to ones Forty includes in his chapter to illustrate home interiors now designed as a haven far away from the industrialized city.

Aside from separating workplaces from the residence, Rutherford's diary notes another trend: distinct social constructions of gender. Indeed, the Industrial Revolution brought intense attention on the role of the woman of the house. For instance, in the early 19th century, "sewing" took place in factories, with industrial weaving machines. But new means of industrial manufacture brought about increasing opportunities for wealth production. The question was how to increase market share by

Figure 6.9 A Victorian living room similar to the one shown in Forty's chapter. This one is in the Victorian Village, Museum of Transport and Technology (MOTAT), Auckland, New Zealand. WIKI Creative Commons Share Alike 3.0; see credits.

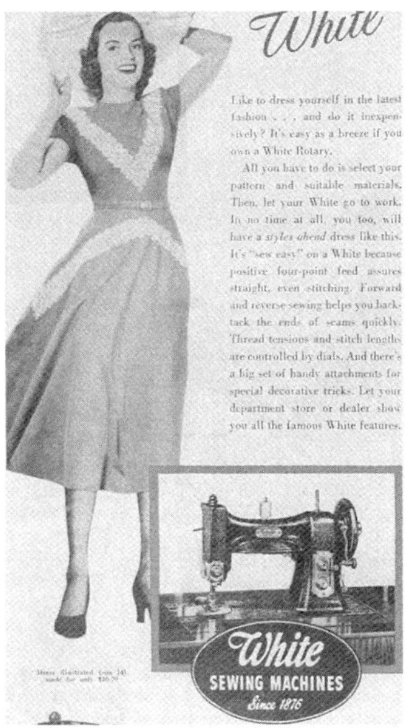

Figure 6.10 Advertisement for a sewing machine from an 1889 edition of *The Ladies Home Journal*. WIKI public domain; see credits.

appealing to the social construct of the housewife. Why not a residential sewing machine? Forty cites an advertisement by the Singer Company from this era:

> The great importance of the sewing machine is in its influence upon the home; in the countless hours it has added to women's leisure for rest and refinement; in the increase of opportunity for that early training of children ... in the numberless opportunities it has opened for women's employment; in the comforts it has brought within the reach of all, which could formerly be attained only by the wealthy few.[32]

Ads like this reflect economic motivations that spurred the innovation of domestic sewing machines: one designed to look like a squirrel; one housed in an embroidered box; another one perched on a floral stand. All of this to enable the woman of the house to have a better life (Figure 6.10).

This leads to the second of Forty's themes: The home as a sign of moral character. In a Common Sense shaped by the set of answers to Baumer's questions listed in Figure 6.8, what we see is a heightened projection of moral meaning onto physical objects. Forty's focus is on the woman of the house who embodies moral rectitude, as noted at the beginning of this chapter. Forty cites Elsie de Wolfe, an early American decorator important in the development of interior design as a profession:

> We take for granted that every woman is interested in houses ... And we take it for granted that this American home is always the woman's home: a man may build and decorate a beautiful house, but it remains for a woman to make a home of it for him.[33]

Figure 6.11 is a painting that appears also in Forty's chapter: it conveys the message that the man's dedication to work outside the home, and the financial success that he accrues, are reflected in the delicate furnishings of the home, and the elegant dress and comportment of the housewife.

Figure 6.11 The Awakening Conscience (1853). Painting by William Holman Hunt (1827–1910). This painting also appears in Forty's chapter. WIKI public domain; see credits.

The sociologist Thorstein Veblen (1857–1929) has noted that social stratification in the industrial age resulted in multiple distinctions of dress: uniforms and liveries for servants, for example. This is because industrial weaving machines mass-produced clothing that once only the wealthy can afford; so insisting on uniforms for the servants was a way of maintaining class distinctions.[34] Veblen also focuses attention on the woman of the house, and in the same terms as de Wolfe (italics added):

> It is by no means an uncommon spectacle to find a man applying himself to work with the utmost assiduity, in order that his wife may in due form render for him that degree of vicarious leisure *which the common sense of the time* demands.[35]

Forty's third theme notices the shift from beauty to efficiency in home interiors. The 19th century saw breakthroughs in the understanding of germs and other harmful microorganisms. It was at this time that Louis Pasteur (1822–1895) developed theories of vaccination and pasteurization in fighting disease. As a reflection of these developments, Forty notes that a subtle shift took place in which the home as a projection of moral values shifted to the home as a place of cleanliness and orderliness (read: hygiene). The clutter of Victorian interiors gave way to more sparsely furnished rooms with "art furniture." These were much lighter in weight and reflected honesty in their construction: "furniture which disguised the way they were made … was regarded as dishonest and therefore to be avoided." These simpler and honest interiors, notes Forty, "conformed to the Christian virtues that it was believed that domestic life should demonstrate."[36] Compare this with the blocky all-purpose medieval furniture mentioned earlier. In *that* cultural period, the idea that furniture—of all things—can

Figure 6.12 Second-floor bathroom of Chateau-sur-Mer, Bellevue Avenue, Newport, Newport County, RI. Source dated 1933. WIKI public domain; see credits.

be symbols of Christian virtue would have seemed quite strange in a cultural Common Sense that was itself nevertheless very "Christian" (Figure 6.12).

Forty's fourth theme is balance between freedom and constraint. Here, the accoutrements of the home interior became a visual barometer of the occupant (the self) as an economic construction. The contemporary home is "both a factory of private illusions and a catalogue of ready-made tastes, values and ideas."[37] By this Forty means freedom to choose from a vast variety of objects of décor for the home (all made possible by the Industrial Revolution), on the one hand; and economic constraints that hinder the resident from having all he or she wants in order to create a sense of home, on the other. The contemporary home interior, then, reflects an equipoise of this tension on a case-by-case basis.

Conclusion

Forty published *Objects of Desire* in 1986. Since then, much has transpired in the way of cultural ideas and values. Our contemporary Common Sense is not the same as the CS at the end of the 20th century. A topic for analysis is how *much* it has changed, and how those changes impact residential interiors. For instance, at the outset of this chapter we noted that sustainable design is now largely a normative value, a factor not mentioned in Forty's study. Even more significant is the impact of information technology. More people than ever are connected by electronic networks (see the social networking sites addressed in Chapter 10). How does cyber connectivity impact the design of residential interiors? Consider this: "Regular work-at-home, among the non-self-employed population, has grown by 173% since 2005, 11% faster than the rest of the workforce and nearly 47x faster than the self-employed population."[38] It is a fascinating return to the medieval reality of the residence as also the workplace—although of course with significant differences, not the least of which is convenience for the self. One at-home worker reports that her backyard office, designed as a retro airport lounge, is also a party room, where her "stand-up work bar" is adjacent to a wine bar. Another worker, a designer, described at-home workers as "trying to find ways to push work and living closer together … in a highly curated and designed environment."[39]

Electronic connectivity can turn entire neighborhoods into an "interior" of linked workspaces. Tony Hsieh, the CEO of Zappos, promoted this idea for his company. One of the designers

> participated in the development and analysis of coworking space inside Zappos headquarters and led a local coworking experiment that launched in early 2012 and eventually grew to include nearly 200 stakeholders, among them Zappos employees, area residents, start-ups, independent workers, and others. The spaces were improvised from a network of existing ones: a coffee shop, the courtyard of a Thai restaurant, an old church hall, the lobby of a casino, and an empty corporate apartment.[40]

That Hsieh's list of locales do not include the *home* office is itself revealing. A deeper analysis might discern that the entire network has become a kind of home environment, thus once again returning to more of the horizontal communal spatiality of medieval times. But this time around, the new horizontal spatiality celebrates a wall-less connectivity that blurs local and global.

This chapter connected philosophical currents active deep within the Common Sense of a culture to how that culture expresses itself in the interior design of the domicile. Interior design comes out of this Common Sense of a culture. For medieval culture, philosophies of heavenly presence on earth, life as a journey to eternity, communal life over any sense of a private life all led to, in Taylor's words, a "porous self" to which projections of self-identity upon home interiors and furnishings were foreign. In contrast, all of Forty's themes of home interiors between 1850 and the mid-20th century result from a highly developed sense of the individual self, and hence the privacy that self requires. As designers live in our contemporary Common Sense, what designs might come out of this interiority? And how can we understand current cultural trends so that *what* we design comes from *within* these developments? Hopefully, this chapter provides tools to answer these kinds of questions.

* * * *

Discussion and Exercises

Reflections about the Chapter You Just Read:

1. Please refer to the standard features of a research project explained in the Introduction. Then:
    a. In one sentence, identify the *research topic*. This sentence can be in the form of a question but does not have to be. In any case, write one grammatically correct sentence that captures the research topic of this chapter.
    b. Identify the *literature* related to this research project.
    c. Identify the *method* which the author used and also the *data* which this method generated for analysis.
    d. Explain how this approach is *generalizable* (or not).
    e. Explain how you can have confidence (or not) of the *internal and external validity* of this author's overall approach.
2. Define "Common Sense" as this chapter uses the term. How is it different from the colloquial use of this same term?

3. Refer to Figure 6.1
   a. Summarize the four characteristics of the communal Common Sense.
   b. Wang points out that designers and artists are often at the leading edge of their CS. Select some current designers and, taking examples of their work, suggest why these works are at the leading edge of the CS relative to them. Specifically, what cultural ideas are they trying to embody?
4. In your own words, describe the vertical and horizontal sense of space in medieval culture. How do these sensibilities impact the medieval home interior?
5. In what ways did the ideas of the Reformation and Francis Bacon encourage a more defined sense of self?
   a. How does each of Forty's four stages of residential interior design reflect the importance of self-identity?
   b. Discuss self-identity as a *philosophical* notion, and how this single notion is reflected in each of Forty's stages of residential interiors.

Exercises/Suggestions for Further Study

1. Refer to the charts in Figures 6.4 and 6.8. Take the same five questions and make a chart for how today's Common Sense (in your home culture or country) would answer these questions.
   a. Do this exercise individually, and then:
   b. Discuss the answers as a class and come up with a single chart that is a composite of the individual answers. How you think these five answers can be expressed in residential interior design? In the interior design of an office? In the interior design of a school? In the interior design of a museum?
2. Refer to the Code of Ethics of the International Interior Design Association (IIDA) here: https://www.iida.org/resources/content/6/3/6/0/documents/IIDA-Code-of-Ethics_Designer.pdf. Wang says that the unique position creative people find themselves in is that, at one extreme, their creations can impact culture greatly; but at the other extreme, it is possible that nobody ever hears about their efforts. But this might apply more to art and artists than to professional interior designers. Write a short essay on how the professional practice of interior design, as defined within the bounds of the IIDA Code of Ethics, represents an intermediate position between these two extremes.
3. In Chapter 10, Langlais and Vaux analyze social networking platforms like Facebook as new examples of "third places." Keeping in mind the thoughts in the conclusion of this chapter, itemize ways in which cyber connectivity can change the design of residential interiors.
4. Translate philosophical ideas into design solutions by taking a well-known segment from a philosopher's writings and then, with some background research on that philosopher, design a home for him or her that is your interpretation of that philosopher's outlook applied to today's cultural setting.
   a. A home for Plato based on his theory that knowledge can be likened to an ascent out of a dark cave. Republic VII. This segment is available online at http://faculty.tamuc.edu/jherndon/documents/plato.pdf.
   b. A home for Descartes based on his "I think, therefore I am" from his *Discourse on Method*, Part 4. This entire work is short and is available on line at https://www.earlymoderntexts.com/assets/pdfs/descartes1637.pdf.

c. A home for the Chinese philosopher Laozi based on his *Daodejing* (this also is a small book, and there are various online sources for it. This link provides the popular translation by D.C. Lau: https://www.centertao.org/essays/tao-te-ching/dc-lau/).

Additional Connections and Information

1. Two important sources of the theory that material culture reflects "the spirit of the times" are:
   a. G. W. F. Hegel. *Introductory Lectures on Aesthetics*, translated by Bernard Bosanquet (Penguin, 1993). For a summary of Hegel's stages of art history, see Jack Kaminsky, *Hegel on Art* (Albany: SUNY Press, 1962).
   b. Heinrich Wolfflin, *Renaissance and Baroque*, translated by Kathrin Simon (Cornell University Press), 1964.

   In addition, much of the early theories of the Modernist Movement draw from the vigor of Hegelian "spirit of the times" ideas. Among these are:

   c. Le Corbusier, *Towards a New Architecture* (Dover, 1985); and Sigfried Giedion, *Space, Time and Architecture: The Growth of a New Tradition* (Harvard University Press, 2009).
2. Pierre Bourdieu's technical term *habitus* is a good source to understanding how a cultural Common Sense embraces all that a person within the culture thinks, acts and adorns in ways that conform to the habitus of that culture. See his essay "Habitus" in *Habitus: A Sense of Place,* edited by Jean Hillier and Emma Rooksby (Ashgate, 2005), 43–49.
3. Two recent works connecting philosophy and design are:
   a. Jean Baudrillard, *The System of Objects* (Verso, 2006). This book has specific sections on interior design as a function of the social order of things.
   b. Georges Teyssot, *A Typology of Everyday Constellations* (MIT Press, 2013).
4. This book supplements Rybczynski's book: J. Huizinga, *The Waning of the Middle Ages: A Study of the Forms of Life, Thought and Art in France and the Netherlands in the XIVth and XVth Centuries* (Doubleday Anchor, 1954).
5. Some other references mentioned in this chapter:
   a. Charles Taylor, *A Secular Age* (Cambridge, MA: Belknap, Harvard University Press, 2007).
   b. A much more readable summary of Taylor's work is James K.A. Smith, *How (Not) to be Secular* (Grand Rapids, MI: Eerdmans, 2014).
   c. J.B. Bury, *The Idea of Progress: An Inquiry into its Origin and Growth* (Hardpress Publishing, 2018).

Notes

1 Jon Lang, *Creating Architectural Theory* (New York: Van Nostrand Reinhold, 1987), 210–232.

2 See Patricia Ebrey, *The Inner Quarters: Marriage and the Lives of Chinese Women in the Sung Period* (Berkeley: University of California Press, 1993).

3 Witold Rybczynski, *Home: A Short History of an Idea* (New York: Penguin Books, 1987), 26–27.

4 Ibid., 28. Rybczynski cites the medieval source only as a poem by Prince Ludwig of Anhalt-Kohten (1596), quoted in Gloag, *Social History*, 105.

5 Adrian Forty, *Objects of Desire: Design and Society Since 1750* (London: Thames and Hudson, 1986), 105–106.

6 Franklin Baumer, *Modern European Thought: Continuity and Change 1600–1950* (New York: MacMillan, 1977).

7 Cited in Jon Lang, *Creating Architectural Theory* (New York: Van Nostrand Reinhold, 1987), 219. The citation itself is from *Frank Lloyd Wright; Writings and Buildings*, eds. Edgar Kaufman and Ben Raeburn (New York: Horizon Press, 1960), n.p.

8 Many articles in popular media address the meat dress. For example: Jillian Mapes, "Lady Gaga Explains Her Meat Dress: 'It's No Disrespect'," *Billboard*, September 13, 2010. www.billboard.com/articles/news/956399/lady-gaga-explains-her-meat-dress-its-no-disrespect. Accessed November 6, 2019. Or: Maeve Keirans, "See What Lady Gaga's Meat Dress Looks Like Now – 5 Years Later," *MTV News*, August 28, 2015. www.mtv.com/news/2254239/lady-gaga-meat-dress-vmas/. Accessed November 6, 2019.

9 See Michael Broek, "Hawthorne, Madonna, and Lady Gaga: 'The Marble Faun's' Transgressive Miriam," *Journal of American Studies* 46, no. 3 (August 2012): 625–640.

10 In his analysis of history, G.W.F. Hegel (1770–1831) identifies "world-historical individuals" who change the direction of history. Many of these are easy to name: Caesar (Hegel's example), Constantine, Charlemagne, Luther, Marx, Hitler, so on. Of course these rise above the mass of anonymous individuals to whom the CS is blind. Now, my observation is that "world historical individuals" are not limited to political history. We can easily identify persons who also changed the course of design history. In interior design, Elsie de Wolfe and Dorothy Draper come to mind. See Hegel's *Philosophy of History*, III. Philosophical History, Sections 31–35. www.marxists.org/reference/archive/hegel/works/hi/history3.htm#032. Accessed May 13, 2019.

11 See Aleksandra Andonovska, "Guy de Maupassant ate lunch everyday at the base of The Eiffel Tower ..." *Vintage News*. www.thevintagenews.com/2016/09/20/priority-french-writer-ate-lunch-everyday-base-eiffel-tower-place-paris-not-see-2/. Accessed May 6, 2019.

12 For elaboration on this point, see Mihaly Czikszentmilayli's observations on "The Systems Model" of creativity in *Creativity: Flow and the Psychology of Discovery and Invention* (New York: HarperCollins, 1996). "According to the systems model, it makes perfect sense to say that Raphael was creative in the sixteenth and in the nineteenth centuries but not in between or afterward." 27–31 (30).

13 Charles Taylor, *A Secular* Age (Cambridge, MA: Belknap, Harvard University Press, 2007), 38.

14 Ibid., 25.

15 Emile Male, *The Gothic Image: Religious Art in France of the Thirteenth Century*, trans. Dora Nussey (New York: Harper & Row, 1958), 31–32.

16 Ibid., 31.

17 Ibid., 3.

18 Rybczynski, op. cit., 30.

19 For instance, "John Lukacs points out that words such as 'self-confidence,' 'self-esteem' ... appeared in English or French in their modern senses only two or three hundred years ago." Ibid., 35.

20 Pseudo-Dionysius, *The Celestial Hierarchy*, 165A-B, in *Pseudo-Dionysius the Complete Works*, trans. Colm Luibheid (New York: Paulist Press, 1987), 154.

21 See David Allison Orsbon, "The Universe as Book: Dante's 'Commedia' as an Image of the Divine Mind," in *Dante Studies, with the Annual Report of the Dante Society*, no. 132 (2014): 87–112 (96).

22 Rybczynski, op. cit., 35.

23 Ibid., 31–32.

24 Ibid., 26.

25 Ibid., 24–27.

26 Robert Putnam, *Bowling Alone: The Collapse and Revival of American Community* (New York: Simon & Schuster, 2001).

27 Rybczynski, op. cit., 83. The citation is from Nancy Mitford, *Madame de Pompadour* (New York: Harper & Row, 1968), 111.

28 Francis Bacon, "The Great Instauration," in *The New Organon and Related Writings*, ed. Fulton H. Anderson (Indianapolis, IN; and New York: Bobbs-Merrill Company, 1960). "The entire fabric of human reason which we employ in the inquisition of nature is badly put together" (p. 3). The "inquisition of nature" was a characteristic turn of phrase by Bacon—must be by empirically measurable facts ascertained piecemeal, to induce broader principles from those facts.

29 Jean-Jacques Rousseau: *The Social Contract*, in *The Social Contract and Discourses* (translated by G.D.H. Cole Everyman's Library, 1986).

30 Thomas Hobbes, *Leviathan* (Indianapolis: Hackett Publishing Company, 1994).

31 Forty, op. cit., 100.

32 Ibid., 98.

33 Ibid., 104.

34 Thorstein Veblen, *The Theory of the Leisure* Class (New York: Penguin, 1994), 74–81.

35 Ibid., 81.

36 Ibid., 111–112.

37 Ibid, 119.

38 "Telecommuting Trend Data (updated July, 2018)" from GlobalWorkplaceAnalytics.com. https://globalworkplaceanalytics.com/telecommuting-statistics. Accessed May 25, 2019.

39 For examples of integrating home and work, see Lana Bortolo, "4 Trends in Home-Office Design," *Entrepreneur*, August 3, 2015. www.entrepreneur.com/article/248061. Accessed May 20, 2019.

40 Ben Waber, Jennifer Magnolfi, Greg Lindsay, "Workspaces That Move People," *Harvard Business Review*. https://hbr.org/2014/10/workspaces-that-move-people. Accessed May 20, 2019.

Chapter 7

Logical Argumentation

Editors' Introduction by Dana E. Vaux and David Wang

Logical argument is not new to the design field. For example, although not formally identified as such, Christopher Alexander's *Pattern Language*, Kaplan and Kaplan's preference framework, and Oldenburg's third-place characteristics (see Chapter 10) are all logical frameworks.[1] For design research, logical argumentation entails developing a framework that brings together a seemingly disparate array of facts into a single explanatory system. Usually these frameworks are expressed by categories, or some sort of matrix in which the categories are related together.

The idea of an explanatory framework is very common. Think of a train schedule. It brings together (1) times of day, (2) station names, (3) the number or name of the train and (4) the number of the boarding platform, all in a single matrix. The "facts" already exist; the task of the schedule maker is to *illustrate* how these facts relate to each other in a logical way. With the schedule in hand, a passenger is given an overview of the entire train system in a logical format.

Logical argumentation in design research resembles making a train schedule but with an important difference. Even though the "facts" exist, the researcher is not a scheduler who begins his or her day knowing what arrival times relate to which train stations. In contrast, the researcher begins by having an *intuition* that some diverse set of facts just might relate to each other in such a way that can explain a particular topic of interest in a powerfully novel way if clearly brought together in a single logical framework. To illustrate, some years ago, Kevin Lynch devised five categories that make up our mental maps of cities: paths, nodes, districts, landmarks and edges. Regardless of which city, Lynch's logical framework explains mental mapping of cities with these five categories.[2]

More recently, Joseph Pine and James Gilmore developed a logical frame that captured the entire history of the US economy in four stages: the agrarian, industrial, service and experience economies. They recount how a family in each stage acquires a birthday cake: making it from scratch (agrarian), making it with cake mix from the store (industrial), buying a cake at the Baskin-Robbins (service) and holding the entire birthday party at Chuck-E-Cheese (experience).[3] Note that both these examples bring together diverse facts that, prior to the logical frame, seem unrelated to each other.

A characteristic of logical frameworks is their *novelty*. This is generally because the wide variety of facts the researcher draws from cuts across disciplinary domains, which is why logical frameworks in design research tend to be interdisciplinary.

Developing a logical argument is an intuitive process much like the iterative design process. For example, in this study, Dana Vaux began with the word *ethos*, which came up in a discussion of her research as an encompassing term to describe sense of place. Her interest piqued, she discovered *ethos* originated from ancient Greek. She then looked it up in a Greek–English lexicon and realized that the English word only accounts for one of three Greek meanings. Meanwhile, she was studying Lefebvre's theory of spatial production and began to make connections between Lefebvre's spatial triad and the origins of the Greek word. Comparing these two ideas resulted in the ethos of place matrix—dwelling, ritual, story—used in this chapter. So, she did not set out to create a logical framework; it was a process of discovery.

One of Vaux's students developed a logical framework through a similar process. The student was studying restorative theory and began to see patterns in her literature review between positive restorative outcomes and elements in the built environment. Vaux suggested the student look at Christopher Alexander et al.'s *Pattern Language* and compare it with the findings in the literature. She was able to link findings in the restorative theory literature with Alexander's patterns. The result was a matrix that highlighted built environment elements conducive to creating restorative environments, which the student used to inform the design of her senior project.

The value of logical argument for interior design is its ability to access data from a wide, interdisciplinary number of sources and then find points of convergence towards an interpretive consensus. Logical argument is therefore useful for organizing considerable amounts of information.[4] It allows designers to sort evidence into focused categories, structuring items from a broad set of facts into a measurable framework which can be operationalized for design.[5]

This chapter employs logical argument to develop a framework that helps designers uncover communal place meanings for application to design solutions. The process generated a new analytical tool to comprehend a communal sense of place: ethos-intensive objects (EIOs). EIOs are "things" (built structures, landmarks, slogans, events, etc.) in a community that contribute to its unique sense of place or ethos. By investigating the EIOs of a place, a person can discover place meanings inherently understood by locals.

Understanding place meaning is essential to the design process. As Vaux explains in the chapter,

> In order to do anything enduring as designers, we need to understand the context and constructs of a place. Otherwise we may fall prey to creating environments that do not resonate with communities, creating visual noise that conveys "somewhere else" to residents, rather than contributing to an existing sense of place that communicates "my city".

Vaux uses logical argument to sift through historical data and synthesize it as evidence into a coherent whole. The data for this chapter were collected and categorized by EIOs in order to identify relevant emerging themes. Vaux then further defines the EIO framework to establish its generalizability to any location. Finally, Vaux uses the EIO framework to investigate the historical place meaning of Richland, Washington. As you read, observe the following:

1. Consider the process Vaux uses to derive categories common to logical argumentation.
   a. Categories derived by merging Lefebvre's spatial triad and the Greek meaning of ethos, resulted in a theoretical framework—dwelling, ritual, story.
   b. Experiential categories obtained through a triangulation of data further define the dwelling, ritual and story of Richland through its landscape, vernacular objects, iconic objects and public performances.
2. Note how the these categories merge into a framework provides a template to explain the overarching narrative of place meaning for the city of Richland.
3. Consider also how the chapter is an example of qualitative research that utilizes multiple tactics to answer the research question.

Interiority

This chapter views "interior" at the scale of a city through the multiple layers of place meaning identified in EIOs. In this chapter, Vaux explicitly relates the term interiority to subjective dimensions of place identified through EIOs. These deeper meanings constitute the communal belongings that resonate with a sense of interiority inherent in places—an intangible spirit or character of a specific place that resonates with human experience and creates a sense of "insideness."

1. Look for ways that interiority is identified through EIOs.
2. Consider the connections between the multiple layers Vaux identifies in physical objects, human activities and stories or myths that together contribute to place meaning.
3. Note how Vaux's chapter identifies interiority at the scale of communities.

* * * *

Understanding Place Meaning through Ethos-Intensive Objects

Dana E. Vaux

As Dolores Hayden notes, *place* is one of the "trickiest words in the English language."[6] A focus of study for anthropologists, cultural geographers, urban planners and sociologists is understanding why humans attribute meaning to specific places and why certain places hold meaning for communities of people. Researchers agree that place differs from space. Space refers to a general environment, while place represents a specific context that has special meaning to an individual or a group of individuals. Place meaning is a social phenomenon that resonates with attributes ascribed by people as well as the intrinsic character of the setting.[7] Residents as well as visitors recognize when places have a strong, identifiable character. However, place meaning is not static. A place has an organic history, just as a person does. A *place* changes over time expressing itself as it matures through the objects of human attention that represent the way of life for a community. Anne-Marie Fortier refers to these objects as a "group's belongings" that create attachment to place through the "common history, experience or culture of a group."[8]

Ethos-intensive objects (EIOs) have been identified as one way to interpret these belongings.[9] This chapter proposes EIOs as a logical framework to analyze the corporate "belongings" of a community. EIOs are those things that represent the intrinsic character of a specific community. These EIO "things" include built objects, physical landmarks, festivals, art installations and anything that is identifiable and defining to a community. For example, world-famous EIOs would be the Eiffel Tower in Paris, Mt. Everest in Nepal and the Cherry Blossom Festival in Washington, D.C.

EIOs provide a generalizable way for comprehending the "insideness" of any communal place or the *interiority* of that place. Petra Perolini defines interiority as "a process within a person that reflects an individual's unique awareness of the world and a psychological relationship to the world that is meaningful."[10] The culture manifested in EIOs represents an *interior* specific to that place; the characteristic spirit, or atmosphere of a culture or community defined as its ethos.[11]

Most commonly, interior is defined in relationship to a physical building shell or "exterior." And yet, an interior is more than four walls enclosing defined space; it simultaneously represents multiple layers that define our significant places.[12] The Council for Interior Design Qualification identifies these layers as the "physical location," "social context" and the "culture of the occupants."[13] Similarly, EIOs identify the "material, social and imaginative" layers of an "interior" related to people's attachment to place.[14]

EIOs uncover the embedded meaning humans attribute to a place manifested in three theoretical categories: dwellings, rituals (or communal practices) and stories. These three categories are further comprehended through four experiential categories: landscape, vernacular, iconic and performance.[15] A logical matrix makes these categories actionable and embraces a sliding scale of communal experiences integral to understanding place meaning.

In this chapter, I first explain the theoretical derivation of the logical framework of EIOs resulting in the categories of dwelling, ritual and story. I then describe the experiential categories that activate the meanings of dwelling, ritual and story. Finally, I identify EIOs in a case study of Richland, Washington to demonstrate the generalizability of the theory and its use for designers.

Part One. EIO Framework: Theoretical and Experiential Derivations

To fully understand what an EIO is and how EIOs contribute to place meaning, it is important to understand the origination of the term *ethos* in its Greek roots as well as grasp how humans experience space. While the English translation of the term "ethos" utilizes only one of the Greek meanings, the Greek has three meanings for ethos:

ηΘOs (āthōs): customary abode or dwelling place. This is the single English use of the word.
εΘOs (ēthōs): customary practice
íΘOs (ēthŏs): morals or character

To create the logical frame for EIOs these Greek terms are overlaid with philosopher-sociologist Henri Lefebvre's three dimensions of space. Lefebvre's spatial triad is based in multidimensional human experience. For Lefebvre, humans construct places of meaning by associating physical space with meaningful practices as well as mental images and symbols associated with built forms. These are his three spatial categories:

Representations of space or physical space: artifacts and conceptions of physical space
Spatial practice or human activities in space: human activity that takes place in a space
Representational space or mental associations with space: stories and ideas that people mentally associate with a space

Combining the Greek notions of ethos with Lefebvre's layers of constructed space results in the logical framework for ethos-intensive objects, or EIOS, as shown in Figure 7.1.

As objects of shared meaning between members of a community, EIOs trace a deeper understanding of place sensibilities for a cultural community. A community's corporate sense of belonging is necessarily multilayered, incorporating human attachment to a place at a communal scale. This is one reason for looking to Lefebvre's analyses of spatial production in conjunction with early Greek meanings of ethos. Both embrace multilayered perceptions of lived experience. Intersecting Lefebvre's three categories of spatial production with the three definitions of early Greek meanings for ethos demonstrates the universality of spatial experience at the public level resulting in a locale-specific ethos. The result of the overlap is three categories of EIOs useful as an analytic tool for designers: dwelling, ritual and story. Figure 7.1 shows how the logical framework of dwelling, ritual and story defines EIOs from the intersection of Lefebvre's spatial triad and Greek definitions of ethos. It is important to note that Figure 7.1 demonstrates how "objects" of a place are defined by ideas *as well as* empirical things. EIOs therefore espouse layers of meaning that humans embrace as a corporate identity through the categories of dwelling, ritual and story.[16] Following is a further explanation of these categories.

EIO Logical Framework

EIO Category	Lefebvre +	Greek =	EIO Definition
Dwelling	Physical Space *Representations of space*	Dwelling Place *ηΘOs [āthōs]:*	Built forms that represent place
Ritual	Human Activity *Spatial Practice*	Customary Practice *εΘOs [ēthōs]:*	Communal practices, activities and rituals
Story	Mental Associations *Representational Space*	Morals, Character *íΘOs [ēthŏs]:*	Myths, stories, legends of everyday life

Figure 7.1 The logical framework of Dwelling, Ritual and Story defines EIOs from the intersection of Lefebvre's spatial triad and Greek definitions of *ethos*.

Theoretical Categories: Dwelling, Ritual, Story

Dwelling: Representations of space (Lefebvre) + Dwelling place (ηΘOs [āthōs]):

The category of *dwelling* includes objects of space and the ideologies connected with them. For example, city planners who want to boost commerce in a downtown area might create certain kinds of buildings, parking, traffic flow and gathering areas to accomplish that objective. In this category, *representations of space* is a conception of the language of planners, commerce and community.[17] These include physical objects with attached meanings, such as a gated community with perceived nuances of privacy and possibly social class.

Ritual: Human activity (Lefebvre) + Customary practice (εΘOs [ēthōs]):

The category of *ritual* encompasses everyday practices such as ordering a favorite drink at Starbucks (which seems to have become a communal ritual; see Figure 7.2); city-wide celebrations such as parades or community festivals. Even routines of work such as harvest and long commutes are *rituals*. On the communal scale, communities often look back to historical events to recognize or create the city's unique identity, real or imagined, through public performances. Rituals can also embody perceptions or myths derived from community values, which we understand through the third category, story.

Figure 7.2 Ritual: human activities such as ordering your favorite drink at a coffee shop.

Story: Representational spaces (Lefebvre) + Morals, character (ίΘOs [ēthŏs]):

The category *story* encompasses the images, symbols and mental states related to a collective lived experience which includes emotions, memories and sentiments related to place. Often, local distinctiveness is created through stories of the past and includes urban legends associated with specific places.[18] Sometimes the story becomes a legend that historical facts reveal as myth, aggrandized either over time or intentionally for commercial purposes. Some locales even invent story identities that may not represent actual historical realities.[19] For example, "downtown" idealizes an unequivocally public, democratic and inclusive story, often overlooking urban realities such as homelessness, racism and urban decay that are equally part of that story.[20] Dwelling, ritual and story are theoretically derived categories. In the next section, EIOs are discussed in relation to the human *experience* of a lived reality.

Experiential Categories

There are four experiential categories: the natural landscape, vernacular built forms, iconic objects and public performance. Unlike the *theoretical* derivations of dwelling, ritual, and story from Greek/ Lefebvre, these *experiential* categories were derived through first-person ethnographic engagement with several locales as part of a larger study.[21]

The Natural Landscape

EIOs in the *natural landscape* of a place contribute to the ethos and story of a community. Natural landscape attracts and deters settlement, shaping the people and industries that contribute to a community's personality as humans reshape and repurpose their natural surroundings. Human intervention changes the natural landscape over time, and in response, nature impacts human behavior. The importance of this connection is highlighted by historian William Cronon's statement that the use and adaptation of the natural world is a "fundamental narrative in all of history without which no understanding of the past could be complete."[22]

Vernacular Built Forms

Vernacular EIOs represent industry, commerce and everyday activities. These structures are the ordinary, commonplace buildings where people live, work and play. Vernacular objects embody the tales of everyday life and culture. The Vernacular Architecture Forum suggests that vernacular architecture and its settings shape everyday life and are "charged with dense cultural meanings that speak to both makers and users."[23] Because of their continued use over time, vernacular built forms communicate a great deal about a locale and its inhabitants as remnants of the past are brought forward to the present.

Iconic

Iconic EIOs are built forms that are readily associated with a place by local residents and visitors. They have deep historical roots in the community's earliest beginnings, often representing industry brought to the city for commerce and development and associated with persons of importance in the community's social and economic history. Iconic objects are ethos intensive precisely because they continue to define a community in some way *over time*, playing a role in its past and present, such as the Eiffel Tower noted earlier. These objects are often chosen for inclusion in representative logos.

Performance

Performance EIOs look back to the community's history, celebrating its roots as well as representing everyday practices. Fortier describes performative acts as "discourses and practices through which ... culture is produced." This includes festivals, public art installations and parades as well as civic protests. As EIOs, public performances often represent the construction, formation and reflection of a collective community identity.

Together, EIOs of the natural landscape, vernacular objects, iconic objects and performance contribute to a collective place experience.

The second part of this chapter takes a deeper look into the EIOs of Richland, Washington through first-hand ethnographic observations utilizing the framework of dwelling, ritual and story. Armed with these three theoretical categories, ethnographic engagement revealed Richland's EIOs of landscape, vernacular built forms, iconic built forms and performances (Figure 7.3). In turn, these EIOs reveal a community conflicted by its past and unsure about its present and future identity.

EIOs of Richland

	DWELLING Human constructions	RITUAL Communal practices	STORY Myths/Legends
LANDSCAPE *The Desert*	*Vast & empty space*	*Exploitable wasteland*	*Relocation and loss*
VERNACULAR BUILT FORM *The ABC houses*	*Building a city to build a bomb*	*One day of pay "for the war effort"*	*Patriotism vs "Downwinders*
ICONIC FORM *"B" Reactor*	*Historic Monument*	*Nuclear clean up*	*Secrecy and mission*
PERFORMANCE *Atomic Frontier Days*	*City planning and promotion*	*Celebrating atomic heritage*	*Changing personas*

Figure 7.3 Richland's EIOs: the desert, the Alphabet houses, the B Reactor and the Atomic Frontier Days.

Part Two—Richland: "The Atomic City"

Once known as "the Atomic City," Richland's history and ethos interlink with the nearby buildings of the Hanford Site.[24] Located in the desert of southeast Washington State, Richland functioned as a bedroom community for personnel at the nearby Hanford Site, a decommissioned nuclear production complex managed by the US Department of Energy (DOE), where plutonium was developed and manufactured for the atomic bomb dropped on Nagasaki, Japan in World War II (WWII). With connections to the nation's nuclear program, the atomic age dominates Richland's past and present story of place as a community involved in scientific development. That is the city's uncomplicated, most visible story. Its history is one of tension between national agendas and local efforts at creating place meaning. From its beginning, Richland's story is one of diverging priorities and ideologies represented in its landscape, vernacular, iconic and performance EIOs (Figure 7.3).

Natural Landscape EIO: The Desert

Richland's topography is unexpected in a state known for its evergreen trees and mountains.[25] The semiarid steppe of Washington's Columbia River Basin, with the soil consisting of large deposits of gravel, sand and silt geologically classifies the region as a desert.[26] With six inches of annual precipitation on average, sagebrush and desert grasses are the only naturally supported vegetation.[27] However, human appropriations from irrigation by early farmers to US government military operations redefined the region's geology and its history over the course of the 20th century.[28] The apparent visual barrenness of the landscape ultimately factored into the location's selection for a covert US military operation to produce plutonium for atomic bombs during WWII (Figure 7.4).[29]

When Colonel Franklin T. Matthias perused the western open landscapes of the United States in December of 1942 in search of an "isolated location"[30] for the WWII Manhattan Project's plutonium production, his goal was to find an area where "the population and the economy would not be disrupted."[31]

Figure 7.4 The desert of eastern Washington State. This is an experiential landscape EIO which gives expression to the theoretical categories of *Dwelling* as a vast and empty space; *Ritual* as exploitable wasteland; and *Story* as relocation and loss. WIKI Creative Commons; see credits.

His flight over the desert of Washington—with its proximity to electric power generated by the new Grand Coulee Dam, the Columbia River as a water source to cool nuclear reactors, and a sparse population—looked promising.[32] He noted that the site perfectly met the project criteria as "an area with almost no people, very undeveloped [with] gravel, deep gravel, for foundations."[33] Matthias's superior, General Leslie R. Groves, selected by the US Army Corps of Engineers to oversee the Manhattan Engineers District (MED) project in Washington State, agreed. Groves observed that "most of the farms did not appear to be of any great value" and the small population and the isolation of the site would enable the army to easily "evacuate the inhabitants by truck."[34] E.I. DuPont, the project's corporate contractor, concurred. From their east coast viewpoints, the barren landscape was "very undeveloped" and had a "relatively small amount of cultivated land."[35] However, documents and accounts of local farmers provide a different perspective.

Locals considered their "rich" land to be developed and growing. Plats of the early Richland settlement show utility, water and sewage infrastructure along with developed lots, streets and blocks.[36] Richland had a post office, school district, churches and enough businesses to sustain it. A 1939 census recorded the population of Richland at 247, and nearby communities of Hanford at 463, and White Bluffs at 501, not including approximately 1,000 more people in surrounding unincorporated areas.

Ultimately the early settlements of Richland, Hanford and White Bluffs were "purchased" by the US government for "very little" according to farmers who claimed most landowners "didn't get paid nearly enough to replace what they lost."[37] The number of people evacuated to make way for the Manhattan Project varies among non-government document sources, most falling in the range of 1,200–2,000. Some residents resisted and were eventually "loaded off on trucks"—as Groves had predicted—although most acquiesced with patriotic pressure to contribute "for the war effort."[38] Residents of the original communities sentimentally remember the early settlements as "lost to the desert sands and the restless winds."[39]

As an EIO, overlooked and ignored, the desert's inhospitable characteristics were first appropriated as crop lands through irrigation, and then its desolate demeanor contributed to its appeal for government acquisition. An EIO valued because of its perceived expendability,[40] the desert surrounding Richland became a disposable landscape for nuclear experiment and production.

Vernacular Built Form EIO: ABC Houses[41]

The early farming community of Richland was selected to house upper-level military personnel and DuPont employees working on the Manhattan Project. The farming community was evacuated by the US government to build the Hanford Engineer Works (HEW) Village. Thousands of houses built by the government comprised the new bedroom community that served "highly skilled operations personnel" working nearby at the Hanford site.[42] Referred to as the Alphabet (ABC) houses because of their alphabet nomenclature, the HEW Village replaced the vernacular farming structures of earlier settlements (Figure 7.5).[43]

The ABC houses allow us to view the HEW Village residents' everyday lives. As EIOs they also represent a behind-the-scenes story of place meaning evidenced in the city's historic role in WWII and the experiences of these "atomic pioneers" that continues to influence Richland today. Behind the quaint, simple house plans is a veiled story of secrecy, class stratification and ideological conflict.

Many factors influenced the decision of who would be "selected" to live in the village and who would be required to live elsewhere. One consideration was safety. Early planning determined a minimum required distance of ten miles up wind from the plant for a safe residential zone.[44] In order to save time and money in the construction process, the Army Corps and DuPont decided to

Figure 7.5 Richland HEW "Village," circa 1948: Aerial view from the river looking southeast, circa 1944. USGov-DOE public domain; see credits.

place the Village (planned for DuPont employees) on the old Richland town site, a safer distance from the plutonium production plant, but construct a laborers' camp on the old Hanford town site for the general workers. Neither the MED or DuPont wanted to risk having operations personnel too close to the Hanford Site to ensure safety in case of unexpected problems (or explosions).[45] HEW Village had full-service provisions but with qualifications that resulted in a community based on rank, race and education, demographics that continue to define Richland today.[46] The homes were allocated by salary, position, marital status (those without families housed in dormitories) and family size. DuPont executives appeared first on the list.[47] Responding to DuPont's expectations, the HEW Village architect modeled plans after east coast Four Square and Cape Cod style for single-family "better homes," which he placed with views along the river. The west coast Ranch style typified the "blue collar" duplex models.[48] (See Figure 7.6.)

The results of heightened security in HEW Village were many. Government provisions supplied everything from coal for the furnace and "pews in the churches, to the display cases and cash registers in the stores, to the chairs, beds and lawnmowers for the homes."[49] However, while the villagers enjoyed new homes for low rent and "a larger paycheck than ever before," these amenities came with government management and control.[50] During the planning process, the MED purposely limited the commercial facilities in an effort to keep better control. For example, they reduced the number of barbershops to one for an estimated 7,500 residents. In order to keep gossip and outside socialization to a minimum, Ganzel's Barber Shop was the only barbershop Hanford workers were allowed to patronize.[51] The telephone book was classified and the telephone lines were tapped.[52] Police reported no crime during those years, because of the security clearance necessary to qualify for HEW Village residency. A village police officer remembers a primary part of his job consisted of driving around town when a dust storm was brewing in order to warn the village housewives in time to get their clothes off the line.[53]

At the end of WWII, postwar expansion of the nuclear program brought thousands of new employees to Richland. Village newcomers, unaccustomed to government management, sought to establish free enterprise as the town transferred to a self-governed, modern, postwar American suburb complete with a shopping mall and a commute to work.[54]

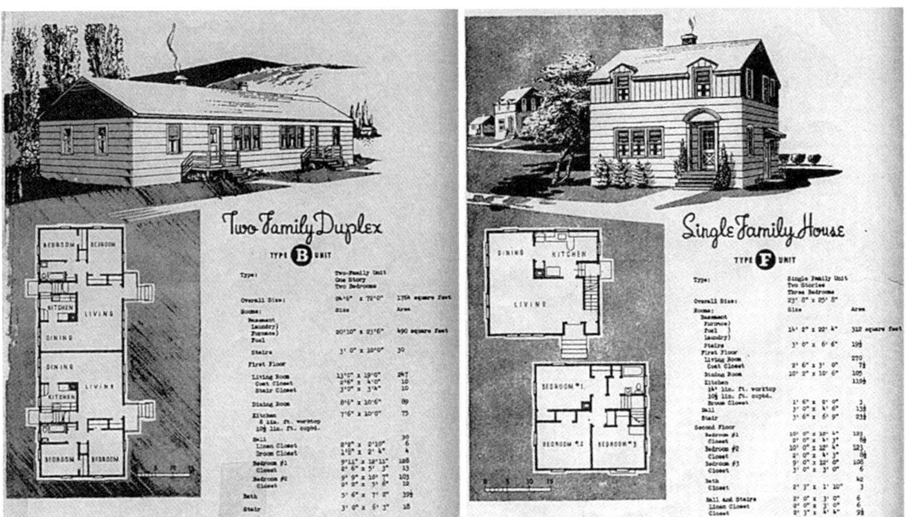

Figure 7.6 Ranch style "B" duplex plan for blue-collar staff; Cape Cod style "F" family home for executives. This is an experiential landscape EIO which gives expression to the theoretical categories of *Dwelling* as building a city to build a bomb; *Ritual* as one day of pay "for the war effort"; and *Story* as patriotism vs "downwinders. Scanned image courtesy of East Benton County Historical Society.

The ABC houses embody a struggle that continues today between government control and a corporate presence in Richland. "The Hanford Engineering Works Village was shaped by a peculiar mix of military austerity, business concerns, economic opportunism, and democratic and environmental ideals ... overlaid on a settlement landscape," notes historian David Harvey.[55] The "carefully selected" population of the HEW Village still represents the city's demographics with over 80% educated Caucasians.[56] Richland has the highest per capita doctoral degrees in the United States outside of California's Silicon Valley.[57] Over one-quarter of the population are engineers, managers and professionals with salaries to match.[58] However, while its toxic past and present are still a matter of contention in public discussion, it is a conversation most residents choose to ignore.[59]

As vernacular structures, the ABC houses remain connected to everyday life in Richland and serve as objects of collective remembrance, commemorating the birth of the atomic age played in the rebirth of the city's ethos. In many ways, the ABC houses were essential to establishing the city's commerce and its role in the nuclear energy industry, both of which continue to impact the local economy and its ethos. The early farming pioneers who first transformed the desert into crop lands had no idea another generation of pioneers would follow, reinventing the desert and the town, bringing the atomic age to Richland and the Hanford plutonium production site to the desert.

Iconic Built Form EIO: "B" Reactor

B Reactor is an original facility at the Hanford plant constructed in 1943 for plutonium production (see Figure 7.7) and is closely linked with the city of Richland's history and ethos. Now managed by the US Department of Energy (DOE), the Hanford Site produced plutonium for the atomic bomb

Figure 7.7 B Reactor at the Hanford site. The site was built for plutonium production in WWII and is the first nuclear reactor designated as a national historical landmark. This is an experiential landscape EIO which gives expression to the theoretical categories of *Dwelling* as historic monument; *Ritual* as nuclear clean up; and *Story* as secrecy and mission. WIKI public domain; see credits.

known as "Fat Man," which razed Nagasaki, Japan, on August 9, 1945. Although the site produced the plutonium, not the bomb itself, it is often credited for "the bomb that brought an end to WWII."[61]

B Reactor's role in WWII is significant but is equally significant to Richland's ethos of place. Workers at Hanford, whether scientist or laborer, likened their roles to pioneering, a perception heightened by the rustic living conditions along with the sense of mission. The secret "cloak and dagger" aspect of the government project led many Hanford Site workers to remember their experiences with a frontier nostalgia.[62]

As one of "three hidden cities" where work on the atomic bomb project was done by 100,000 workers,[63] the city was also a mystery to the workers. Secrecy from the Axis Powers (Germany, Italy and Japan) for the sake of the Allied Forces was paramount to the success of the Manhattan Project, and therefore, workers at the Hanford plant had limited scope of the project. Work was isolated so that no one would fully know what the outcome entailed.[64] As one worker recalled, "The Hanford workers had a saying: 'The only bad part about this job is that when our kids grow up and ask what we did in the war, we will have to answer, 'Damned if I know!'"[65]

They finally knew on August 6, 1945, when the first atomic bomb was dropped on Hiroshima, Japan.[66] Newspaper headlines stating, "IT'S ATOMIC BOMBS," shocked the world and the workers.[67] No one working at Hanford even imagined the possibility. After the dropping of the second bomb on Nagasaki, Japan on August 9, 1945 with plutonium manufactured at the Hanford Site, the Japanese surrendered. In celebration, the headline of August 14, 1945, in the Richland *Villager* read, "PEACE! OUR BOMB CLINCHED IT!"[68] Villagers and Hanford Camp residents alike were proud of their collaborative effort and doing their part to end the war. Echoing their parents' pride, the Richland High School "Beavers" changed their mascot to the "Bombers," adopting the atomic mushroom-cloud emblem in September of 1945 (Figure 7.8).[69]

Richland was ecologically, economically and demographically shaped by the events and practices surrounding B Reactor. As an EIO it contributes to Richland's place ethos. It also reminds us of

Figure 7.8 Richland High School Bombers T-shirt logo, c. 2000. Author's collection.

"marginalized voices and a spatial connection to other geographic locations, a single building that had extraordinarily far-flung historic effects."[70] The first successful nuclear reaction using plutonium occurred at the B Reactor facility.[71] To commemorate that scientific achievement, B Reactor was listed on the National Register of Historic Places in 1992 and designated as a National Historic Landmark by the federal government in 2008.[72] Tourists can visit the site on a tour bus and see the remnants of the Hanford plant.

Today, the work at Hanford primarily consists of environmental cleanup, involving about 8,000 workers employed to clean up the residue of radioactive waste.[73] B Reactor is an iconic EIO of the "'atom bustin' city of the West" and a historical marker of the nuclear-industry's scientific research that continues to be primary for Richland.[74]

Performance EIO: Atomic Frontier Days

As WWII ended, Richland opened a new chapter.[75] The city commemorated their pride in their WWII accomplishment and their new role in nuclear development of the atomic age by creating Atomic Frontier Days. The event celebrated atomic energy as they "worked together for the creation of [atomic] power, in hopes of bringing world-wide peace and benefits to humanity."[76] The 1949 Atomic Frontier Days souvenir program touted the caption "'Hard Hats' and 'Assault Masks' in the Northwest Desert ... They are clearing the Atomic Wilderness on this, our last frontier."[77] (See Figure 7.9.)

The Atomic Frontier Days celebration linked Richland's new Atomic Frontier image to a nostalgic remembrance of the American Western Frontier and highlights Richland's identification with the frontier image.[78] Historians Findlay and Hevly note, in the years following its forefront in world news and American history: "Richland imagined itself as a frontier of science and technology."[79] Reinventing

Figure 7.9 Richland's Second Annual Atomic Frontier Days Souvenir Program Cover, 1949. This is an experiential landscape EIO which gives expression to the theoretical categories of *Dwelling* as City planning and promotion; *Ritual* as Celebrating atomic heritage; and *Story* as changing personas. Scanned image courtesy of East Benton County Historical Society.

itself as "a new light on the old frontier" helped the city's residents to negotiate its "supervision" in a community that continued to be completely owned by the US government.[80]

Residents eventually sought to manage their own affairs and Richland reincorporated in 1958, when the government relinquished control. The city chose not to continue the Atomic Frontier Days celebration and constructed "atomic frontier" persona as its city-wide celebrations varied in character and theme in ensuing decades.[81] However, no celebration since the Atomic Frontier Days made such a comprehensive attempt at forging and constructing a citywide identity for Richland.[82] Perhaps this is the reason for its resurrection in 2019, commemorating the 75th anniversary of the MED's Manhattan Project at Hanford. Reminiscent of the 1950s Atomic Frontier Days context, participants can eat a "mess hall dinner," listen to music from the 1940s era, and earn "top secret security clearance…an educational activity [that] brings early culture at Hanford to life, and teaches about the history and legacy of [the] region."[83]

For many years, efforts to "clean up" the Hanford image overshadowed the local history of Richland. Richland's atomic heritage associated with a weapon of mass destruction and the resulting nuclear toxic waste was difficult to negotiate when the cultural Common Sense (see Chapter 6) was to "go green." Coupled with the recently built Hanford Reach Interpretive Center located in Richland—a $27 million museum funded by the federal government with exhibits encompassing nature, the environment and ecological responsibility[84]—as a performance EIO, the Atomic Frontier Day 2019 ushers in a new era for the city that acknowledges its past, accepts it present and once again reinvents it as "a new light on the old frontier"[85] (Figure 7.10).[86]

Figure 7.10 Atomic Frontier Day 2019: Richland once again celebrating its role as "the atom bustin' city of the West." City of Richland, WA; see credits.

Richland's Place Meaning Revealed in EIOs

Richland today has a unique place ethos linked to its days as the HEW Village and "The Atomic City," evidenced in its EIOs. The Atomic Frontier Day 2019 graphic with the atomic symbol, the newest city logo and the commemorative Manhattan Project symbol provides a composite of the city's EIOs still evident today. Once unsure of how to negotiate its controversial "Atomic City" and nuclear production roots, Richland's EIOs exhibit a constancy of place meaning. While Richland's early agriculture and farming township is mostly erased, remnants of that history remain in its newly developing vineyard industry. Similarly, the Atomic City identity constructed post WWII, once overshadowed, is now being resurrected to the advancement of nuclear energy and research. The surrounding desert landscape, perceived as a place of dust and desolation, and therefore perfect for the Manhattan Project, along with the Alphabet houses and the Hanford B Reactor, serves as a reminder of Richland's government-town persona that shaped and formed the city. The resurrection of the Atomic Frontier Days celebration, reminiscent of the city's atomic roots, reveals Richland as a contested place that the city is now willing to acknowledge. Richland as a city with a complex ethos has worked to create a new future without ignoring its controversial past. Uncovering the context based on the history of Richland's dwellings, rituals and stories brings us to a new way of viewing the city's spatial context and understanding of its place ethos (Figure 7.11).

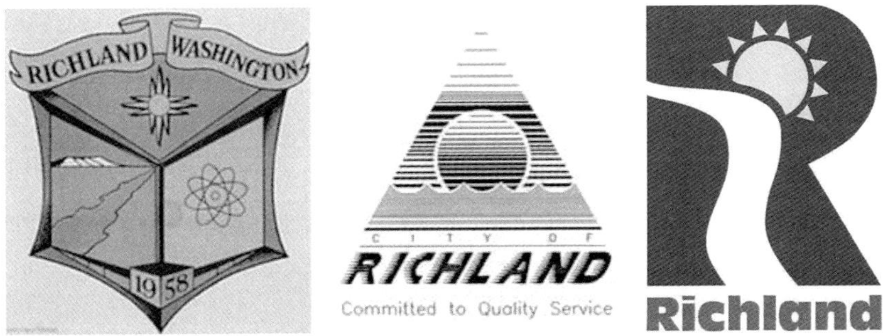

Figure 7.11 Richland's changing identity evidenced in its city logos. Left to Right: 1958, 1990, 2015. City of Richland, WA; see credits.

Conclusion: Place Meaning through EIOs

As evidenced in the EIOs of Richland, communal meanings of place are not static. The city of Richland experienced extensive changes over time. Some resulting place meanings remained constant, others were intentionally left behind and new ones, developed or fabricated from the past, reinvented Richland's place story. Understanding sociocultural context in design settings uncovers meanings behind the façade of the built environment. As anthropologist Keith Basso states, "No one lives in the world in general. Everybody lives in ... the world around here."[87] In order to do anything enduring as designers, we need to understand the context and constructs of a place. Otherwise, we may fall prey to creating environments that do not resonate with communities, creating visual noise that conveys "somewhere else" to residents, rather than contributing to an existing sense of place that communicates "my city."[88]

Derived from theoretical and experiential underpinnings, EIOs provide a logical framework for analyzing the corporate "belongings" of a community. Layering Lefebvre's spatial categories with Greek meanings for word "ethos" grounds EIOs in the ancient Greek cultural preoccupation with the communal *polis.* The result are three theoretical categories of dwelling, ritual and story that shape subjective perceptions through cultural forces. These in turn inform four categories of how a sense of place flourishes in a community through the landscape, vernacular objects, iconic objects and performance.

As Dolores Hayden notes, place is "tricky" to define and "an overloaded term" that can hold different meanings in different contexts.[89] This research provides a framework for how we shape the places in which we live into places of significance and belonging through EIOs. Furthermore, EIOs provide a way to comprehend the "insideness" of a specific place and define the psychological relationship that connotes a sense of interiority. EIOs identify how a sense of place reflects individual perceptions born out of cultural forces but also the intrinsic character of a place that resonates with a community of people.

* * * *

Discussion and Exercises

Reflections about the Chapter You Just Read:

1. Please refer to the standard features of a research project explained in the introduction to the book. Then:
   a. In one sentence, identify the *research topic*. This sentence can be in the form of a question but does not have to be. In any case, write one grammatically correct sentence that captures the research topic of this chapter.
   b. Identify the *literature* related to this research project.
   c. Identify the *method* which the author used and the *data* which this method generated for analysis.
   d. Explain how this approach is *generalizable* (or not).
   e. Explain how you can have confidence (or not) of the *internal and external validity* of this author's overall approach.

2. Refer again to the Editors' Introduction to this chapter. Describe in your own words how to derive a logical framework.
3. Describe the process Vaux used to develop and validate the EIO framework. How does the process inform the research and contribute to our understanding of place meaning?
4. Consider how Vaux posits that an interior represents multiple layers manifested in EIOs.
   a. How do EIOs manifest the "culture of the occupants," the "physical location" and the "social context" of an interior?
   b. In light of Petra Perolini's definition of interiority as "a process within a person that reflects an individual's unique awareness of the world and a psychological relationship to the world that is meaningful,"[90] describe how Richland's EIOs provide insight into a unique awareness of the city's persona.
   c. The Editors' introduction stressed that logical argumentation typically brings together interdisciplinary sources. How does Vaux use linguistics and philosophy to construct her theoretical categories of dwelling, ritual and story, and then historical resources to gain her understanding of Richland's EIOs?
5. Describe in your own words how Vaux's EIO framework can apply to other settings. In what way is her logical framework generalizable to other scales such as the interior of a church or the ethos of a university campus?

Exercises/Suggestions for Further Study

1. Choose a city or town you are familiar with in an ethnographic sense—you have lived there or visited several times. Identify the landscape, the vernacular built forms, an iconic form and a public performance. Explain how these relate to the physical dwelling, the rituals or common human activities, and the stories that contribute to the uniqueness of that specific locale.
2. You work for the Chamber of Commerce in the town you investigated in exercise #1. Design a brochure for tourists who visit this town that orients them to its sense of place.
3. Read the following study: J. Kim and R. Kaplan, "Physical and psychological factors in sense of community: New urbanist Kentlands and nearby Orchard Village," *Environment and Behavior* 36, no. 3 (2004): 313–340. Examine the neighborhoods of Kentlands and Orchard Village as presented by Kim and Kaplan in this study. What EIOs can you identify? What physical dwelling is prominent? What rituals do the communities engage in? What stories animate these communities? How does identifying the EIOs help you to understand each neighborhood as unique?

Additional Connections and Information

Cronon, William. "A Place for Stories: Nature, History, and Narrative." *Journal of American History* 78, no. 4 (1992): 1347–1376.

Fortier, Anne-Marie. "Re-Membering Places and the Performance of Belonging(s)." *Theory, Culture & Society* 16 (April 1999): 41–64.

Glassberg, David. *Sense of History: The Place of the Past in American Life.* Amherst: The University of Massachusetts Press, 2001.

Hayden, Dolores. *The Power of Place: Urban Landscapes as Public History.* Cambridge, MA: London: The MIT Press, 1995.

Jiven, Gunila, and Peter Larkham, "Sense of Place, Authenticity and Character: A Commentary." *Journal of Urban Design* 8, no. 1 (2003): 67–81.

Lefebvre, Henri. *The Production of Space.* Translated by Donald Nicholson-Smith. Oxford; Cambridge, MA: Blackwell, 1991.

Lewis, Pierce F. "Axioms for Reading the Landscape." *The Interpretation of Ordinary Landscapes*, ed. D. W. Meinig, 11–32. New York & Oxford: Oxford University Press, 1979.

Marcus, Clare Cooper, "Environmental Memories." In *Place Attachment*, ed. Irwin Altman and Setha Low, 87–112. New York: Plenum Press, 1992.

Relph, Edward. *Place and Placelessness.* London: Pion Ltd, 1976.

Schneekloth, Linda H. and Robert G. Shibley. *Placemaking: The Art and Practice of Building Communities.* New York: John Wiley & Sons, Inc., 1995.

Tuan, Yi-Fu. *Space and Place: The Perspective of Experience.* Minneapolis: The University of Minnesota Press, 1977.

Upton, Dell and John Michael Vlach, eds. *Common Places: Readings in American Vernacular Architecture.* Athens; London: The University of Georgia Press, 1986.

Vaux, Dana and David Wang. "Ethos-Intensive Objects: Toward a Methodological Framework for Identifying Complex Client Cultures." *Journal of Interior Design* 41, no. 4 (2016): 13–27. DOI:10.1111/joid.12076.

Notes

1 Christopher Alexander et al., *A Pattern Language: Towns, Buildings, Construction* (New York: Oxford University Press, 1977). Rachel Kaplan and Stephen Kaplan, *The Experience of Nature: A Psychological Perspective* (Cambridge: Cambridge University Press, 1989); Ramon Oldenburg, *The Great Good Place: Cafes, Coffee Shops, Bookstores, Bars, Hair Salons and other Hangouts at the Heart of the Community* (New York: Marlowe and Company, 1989/1999).

2 Kevin Lynch, *Image of the City*, MIT Press, 1960.

3 Joseph Pine and James Gilmore, "Welcome to the Experience Economy," in *Harvard Business Review*, July-August (1998): 97-105.

4 Linda Groat and David Wang, *Architectural Research Methods*, 2nd ed. (New York: John Wiley & Sons, 2013), 207.

5 Ibid., 224, 234–241.

6 Dolores Hayden, *The Power of Place: Urban Landscapes as Public History* (Cambridge, MA: London: The MIT Press, 1995), 15.

7 Thomas Gieryn, "A Space for Place in Sociology," *Annual Review of Sociology* 26 (2000): 463–496.

8 Anne-Marie Fortier, "Re-Membering Places and the Performance of Belonging(s)." *Theory, Culture & Society* 16 (April 1999): 42.

9 Dana Vaux and David Wang, "Ethos-Intensive Objects: Toward a Methodological Framework for Identifying Complex Client Cultures," *Journal of Interior Design* 41, no. 4 (2016): 15.

10 Petra Simona Perolini, "Interior Spaces and the Layers of Meaning," *Design Principles and Practices* 5, no. 6, (2011): 170.

11 Merriam-Webster Dictionary, www.merriam-webster.com/dictionary/ethos.

12 C.J. Hewlett, "The Future of Interior Design," *Journal of Interior Design Educators and Research* 11, no. 1 (1985): 10–12.

13 Council for Interior Design Qualification. www.cidq.org/definition-of-interior-design. Accessed August 2018.

14 Hayden describes these layers are the "material, social, and imaginative" dimensions of people's attachment to place. Hayden, op. cit., 43.

15 Vaux and Wang, op. cit., 22.

16 Ibid., 15–19.

17 See Peter Katz, Vincent Joseph Scully, and Todd W. Bressi. *The New Urbanism: Toward an Architecture of Community*, Vol. 10 (New York: McGraw-Hill, 1994). New Urbanism is an example of a dwelling EIO. It proposes specific elements for city planning in order to achieve an idealized "sense of community."

18 David Glassberg, *Sense of History: The Place of the Past in American Life* (Amherst: University of Massachusetts Press, 2001), 7.

19 Chris Wilson, *The Myth of Santa Fe: Creating a Modern Regional Tradition* (Albuquerque: University of New Mexico Press, 1977), 232. Consider the city of Santa Fe, New Mexico, as an example. In his book *The Myth of Santa Fe*, Chris Wilson discusses how beginning early in the 20th century, the city of Santa Fe, New Mexico, began to craft for itself a historical image and character, a story of place. Based in factual history, but with selectively chosen elements, the city remade itself into a tourist destination depicting its version of the "Old West" and its Pueblo-Mexican past. Eventually, the fabrication reflected itself in the local vernacular, reshaping Santa Fe into a historical allegory with a cultural image of its own making.

20 Alison Isenberg, *Downtown America: A History of Place and the People Who Made It* (Chicago, IL: University of Chicago Press, 2004), 6.

21 This process was conducted with three cities over a period of many years. Dana E. Vaux, *Ethos of Place: A Historical Understanding of Place Experience through Ethos-Intensive Objects,* Unpublished Doctoral Dissertation, Washington State University, 2015.

22 William Cronon, "A place for stories: Nature, history, and narrative" in *Journal of American history* 78, no. 4 (1992):1375.

23 The Vernacular Architectural Forum; Architectural historians Dell Upton and John Michael Vlach interpret the vernacular as intertwined cultural landscapes, regionally distinctive "remnants from the past embedded in today's scene." Dell Upton and John Michael Vlach, eds. *Common Places: Readings in American Vernacular Architecture* (Athens; London: The University of Georgia Press, 1986), xxiii.

24 Vaux, op. cit., 96–148. Portions of this text are from this author's PhD dissertation and used in Part Two of this chapter with permission.

25 Mountain Bike Review, Forum, Classic Mountain Bike Forums, 29ers Bikes, "Exploring the deserts of... WASHINGTON?!" [blog] posted 6-07-2008. http//forums.mtbr.com/29er-bikes/exploring-deserts-washington-420539.html.

26 U.S. Department of the Interior, U.S. Geological Survey. http://mrdata.usgs.gov/geology/state/sgmc-unit.php?unit=IDQpg%3B0; Tri-Cities Washington Guide, [website] "Geology" page, http://tri-citiesguide.org/geology.htm; J. Eric Schuster, *Geologic Map of Washington State,* Geologic Map GM-53. Washington Division of Geology and Earth Resources, 2005.USGS, www.usgs.gov/index.htmlhttp://ngmdb.usgs.gov/Info/dmt/docs/schuster07b.pdf.

27 US Department of Energy, "Ordinance and Explosive Waste Records Search Report," January 1995. Acc. D196020536, p. 10. http://pdw.hanford.gov/arpir/pdf.cfm?accession=D196020536.

28 Hanford Reach Museum [Facebook Page]. www.facebook.com/pages/Hanford-Reach-Interpretive-Center/235544711055; U.S. Fish & Wildlife Service, Hanford Reach National Monument, Washington [website] www.fws.gov/refuge/Hanford_Reach/; John Gottberg Anderson, "Reach for the Hills," (Bend Oregon) *The Bulletin,* Sunday, 13 July 2014, Community Life, sec. C4, col. 2.

29 Leslie Groves, *Now It Can Be Told: The Story of the Manhattan Project* (New York: Harper, 1962), 75; Franklin T. Matthias, *Diary and Notes of Colonel Franklin Matthias 1942–1945.* Acc. 8113, Department of Energy Reading Room, Richland, WA, January 16 and 17, 1943; Mart Young former HEW Manager Components Engineer, Interview with Dana Vaux, Personal interview, Richland, WA, July 2013; Hill Williams, *Made in Hanford: The Bomb that Changed the World* (Pullman: Washington State University Press, 2011), 12.

30 Franklin T. Matthias, "Franklin Matthias Interview." [Audio and transcript] Interview by S.L. Sanger. *Voices of the Manhattan Project* (San Francisco, CA, 1986). www.manhattanprojectvoices.org/oral-histories/franklin-matthiass-interview; Franklin T. Matthias, Interview in Sanger, *Working on the Bomb: An Oral History of WWII Hanford* (Portland, OR: Continuing Education Press, Portland State University, 1995), 19.

31 S.L. Sanger, *Working on the Bomb: An Oral History of WWII Hanford* (Portland, OR: Continuing Education Press, Portland State University, 1995), 18; Young, Interview, op. cit.; Groves, op. cit., 84–86. This attitude is also apparent in Grove's recounting of the story.

32 Matthias, December 31, 1942 and January 2, 1943; Young, interview, op. cit.; Williams, op. cit., 10; Anderson, op. cit., C4, col. 3; US Department of Energy, "Waste Records Search Report," p. 10.

33 Matthias, Interview, op. cit., 20.

34 Groves, *Story,* 75; Matthias, January 16 and 17, 1943; Young, Interview, op. cit.

35 E.I. du Pont de Nemours and Company, Inc., "DuPont Report on Richland Government City Site." Richland Box, East Benton County Historical Society, n.d.

36 Martha Berry Parker, *Tales of Richland, White Bluffs & Hanford, 1805–1943, Before the Atomic Reserve* (Fairfield, WA: Ye Galleon Press, 1986), 354–357; Hales, op. cit., 20–22, 93.

37 June Doyle, "Little Town Lost," *The Courier: Journal of the East Benton County Historical Society* 18, no. 3 (July 1996): 11.

38 Young, interview, op. cit.; Parker, op. cit., 37; Williams, op. cit., 11; Ted Van Arsdol. *Hanford–: The Big Secret* (Richland, WA: Columbia Basin News, 1958), 10, 14.

39 Doyle, op. cit., 12.

40 Matthias, *Diary,* op. cit., March 2, 1943.

41 Vaux, op. cit., 109–120.

42 Matthias, *Diary,* March 2, 1943.

43 Jeremy Wells, "Architectural History: Richland, Washington Government Letter-Houses." East Benton County Historical Society website, n.d. www.ebchs.org/

44 Matthias, *Diary,* December 16, 1942; Groves, Interview by Groueff; Bruce Hevly and John M. Findlay, *The Atomic West* (Seattle; London: University of Washington Press, 1998), 90; E.I. du Pont, "Construction," 101–102. Later the distance requirements from the production plant were altered to accommodate the Hanford site, but DuPont did not think it "desirable from a security angle to locate living facilities [for their employees] close to the operating area."

45 E.I. du Pont, "Construction," 101–103; Matthias, *Diary,* December 16, 1942; Groves, Interview by Groueff.

46 "Richland, Washington," [website] citydata.com, www.city-data.com/city/Richland-Washington.html
47 Matthias, March 2, 1943; Young, interview, op. cit.; Carol B. Roberts, *Modern Pioneers.* Hand-typed personal memoir (1960) "Richland" Box, East Benton County Historical Society, Kennewick, WA, 2; Gary Fetterolf, Walking Tour, *Alphabet Houses of Richland Walking Tour* (Richland, WA: CREHST Museum, 2012), 1.
48 G. Albin Pehrson, *Report on the Hanford Engineer Works Village, (Richland, Washington)* (Spokane, WA: Office of G. Albin Pehrson, November 1943), 19; Fetterolf, op. cit., 1.
49 Roberts, op. cit., 1-3.; Paul P. Beardsley, *The Long Road to Self-government: The History of Richland Washington, 1943-1968,* City 25th Anniversary Booklet. Richland, WA: S.n., 1968. Author's collection, 2.
50 Roberts, op. cit., 2.
51 Pehrson, op. cit., 11; Matthias, *Diary,* June 23, 1943; Wayne Killard, Interview by author July 2013, Former Hanford employee and museum docent, CREHST Museum, Richland, WA.
52 Hope Sloan Amacker, interview in Sanger, *Hanford and the Bomb,* 105–106; Matthias, *Diary,* June 21, 1943.
53 Beardsley, op. cit., 10; Barbara J. Kubik, *Richland: Celebrating Its Heritage* (Richland, WA: City of Richland, 1994), 39; Roberts, op. cit., 3.
54 Beardsley, op. cit., 2–3; "*Atomic Frontier Days,*" Souvenir Program, op. cit., 10.
55 David W. Harvey and Kathryn H. Kraft, "Hanford Engineer Works Village: (Richland, WA): Shaping a Nuclear Community." [Paper Presented to the Society of Architectural Historians, Marion Dean Ross – Pacific NW Chapter, October 11, 1997.] On file at East Benton County Historical Society, 9.
56 "Richland, Washington." www.city-data.com/city/Richland-Washington.html.
57 Anderson, op. cit., C4, col. 2.
58 "Richland, Washington." www.city-data.com/city/Richland-Washington.html.
59 City of Richland. [website] www.ci.richland.wa.us/; William Yardley, "Making History but Leaving a Toxic Mess," *New York Times Media Group: The International Herald Tribune,* September 12, 2008, News, 1; Ralph Vartabedian, "Doubts Grow About Plan to Dispose of Hanford's Radioactive Waste," *Los Angeles Times,* November 29, 2013. www.latimes.com/nation/la-na-hanford-nuclear-risks-20131130,0,5013027.story#ixzz2mE9wWI7a.
60 Vaux, op. cit., 121–134.
61 US DOE, *Hanford* [Website], "About Us" http://www.hanford.gov/page.cfm/HanfordOverviewandHistory
62 Hope Sloan Amacker interview in S.L. Sanger, and Robert W. Mull, *Hanford and the Bomb: An Oral History of World War II* (Seattle, WA: Living History Press, 1989), 105; Helen Ruth Gale Smith, "A Summer Job at Hanford," *The Courier: Journal of the East Benton County Historical Society* 18, no. 3 (July 1996): 4; Carol Krogness, and Gary Gesell, eds., *Great Memories: Early Hanford and the Tri-Cities* (Richland, WA: S.n., April 1994), 2, 36, 46.
63 Veterans of Foreign Wars of the United States, *Pictorial History of the Second World War: A Photographic Record of all Theaters of Action Chronologically Arranged,* Vol. 4 (n.p.: Wm. H. Wise & Co., Inc., 1946), 2019. No mention of any foreign scientists in the effort (including Fermi and Oppenheimer who were key contributors), only as "a joint effort of British, Canadian, and American scientists and workers, but America was the site of the two billion dollar project." Pride in the *American* accomplishment was primary.
64 Matthias, *Diary,* February 26, March 2 and 8, 1943; Groves, op. cit., 74–75; Doyle, op. cit., 10; Pehrson, op. cit., 5; Van Arsdol, op. cit., 14–15, 18.
65 Doyle, op. cit., 12.
66 Ibid.; "It's Atomic Bombs." *Pasco Herald,* Extra, August 6, 1945, vol. 43, no. 34-A, p 1, col. 3-5. Manuscripts, Archives and Special Collections, Washington State University Libraries.
67 Ibid.
68 *The Villager,* Hanford Engineer Works, August 14, 1945, Headline, 1, MASC, WSU.
69 Keith Maupin, *The Bomber—The Myth.* Personal letter with accompanying research paper addressed to Historical Society. 2000. East Benton County Historical Society. "Richland" Box, EBCHS.
70 Williams, op. cit., 1-18.
71 Mathhias in Sanger, *Working on the Bomb,* 19–20.
72 Joann Wardrip and Chris Paolino, "DOI Designates B Reactor at DOE's Hanford Site as a National Historic Landmark," *Health Physics* 95, no. 5 (2008): 688–689; Patricia Leigh Brown, "Preserving the Birthplaces of the Atom Bomb," *New York Times,* 7 April 2001, sec. A, p. 1; Yardley, op. cit., 1; "Hanford" [website] www.hanford.gov/page.cfm/BReactor
73 Vartabedian, op. cit.; Hanford.gov, "About Hanford Cleanup," [website] www.hanford.gov/page.cfm/AboutHanfordCleanup
74 *Richland Day: Souvenir Program, September 1, 1947: Richland, Washington, the Atom Bustin' Village of the West. Richland, WA: Chamber, 1947,* Cover page. Benton County Historical Society.
75 "Richland Day Committee is Hard at Work." *Villager (Richland, WA),* vol. 1, no. 24A (August 9, 1945), Manuscripts, Archives, and Special Collections, Washington State University Libraries; Beardsley, op. cit., 9; *Alive!: Richland and the Hanford Project,* 25th anniversary program (Richland, WA: Advance Advertising, 1983), 9.
76 *Atomic Frontier Days Souvenir Program,* September 4-5-6, 1948, 31. Benton County Historical Society.
77 Ibid, cover page.
78 Hevly and Findlay, op. cit., 91; Vaux, op. cit., 135–144.
79 John M. Findlay, and Bruce Hevly. *Atomic Frontier Days: Hanford and the American West.* Seattle; London: University of Washington Press, 2011, 103.
80 *Atomic Frontier Days, 2nd Annual: August 12–14, 1949:* 8.
81 Beardsley, op. cit., 36. The last recorded Atomic Frontier Days celebration in Beardsley's detailed timeline of Richland from 1943 to 1968 is in 1959, its first year as an independent city.

82 Amy Adamczyk, "On Thanksgiving and Collective Memory: Constructing the American Tradition," *Journal of Historical Sociology* 15, no. 3 (September 2002), 343–365. Adamczyk argues that civic forms of commemoration and celebration do not necessarily contain a connection to an initial occasion, but instead are socially constructed.

83 City of Richland [website] op. cit., "Atomic Frontier Day" Facebook page, www.facebook.com/events/howard-amon-park/atomic-frontier-day/505640273306386/

84 Sara Schilling, "Ag Hall of Fame, Hanford Reach to Collaborate," 22 February 2014, Local News section. *Tri-City Herald*, Pasco, WA; Anderson, op. cit., C4 col. 2; Robin Wojtanik, "Hanford Reach Interpretive Center Moving Forward," June 29, 2011, KEPR-TV.com, CBS affiliate, Pasco, WA. www.keprtv.com/news/local/124723159.html.

85 *Atomic Frontier Days, 1949,* op. cit., 8.

86 *Atomic Frontier Days, 1949,* op. cit., 8.

87 Keith H. Basso, *Wisdom sits in places: Landscape and language among the Western Apache*. UNM Press, (1996), 262.

88 Vaux, op.cit., 225.

89 Hayden, op. cit., 15; See also, Clare Cooper Marcus, "Environmental Memories," in *Place Attachment*, eds. Irwin Altman and Setha Low (New York: Plenum Press, 1992), 87–112.

90 Petra Simona Perolini, "Interior Spaces and the Layers of Meaning," *Design Principles and Practices* 5, no. 6 (2011), 170.

Chapter 8

Mixed Methods

Editors' Introduction by Dana E. Vaux and David Wang

The term "mixed methods" indicates that understanding complex human and environmental dynamics in real-life settings may require more than just one textbook research method. In writing about her research on environments for the homeless, Jill Pable says in this chapter, "Because these are human beings responding to crises in real time, determining 'what is going on' with homeless people in these settings by using singular research methods might be limiting." For Pable, using a mixture of research methods allowed her and her colleagues to gain deeper empathy for those experiencing homelessness. This in turn informed their design interventions for this population.

In their text on architectural research, Groat and Wang identify several ways to combine research methodologies.[1] One is to use different research methods sequentially over time in studying one topic. Another approach combines a dominant research method with a secondary one in support. The third way is to use a variety of methods of equal weight. Of these, Pable's mixed-methods research on environments for the homeless is primarily sequential, and this chapter summarizes her work in six research projects conducted over a nine-year period. These studies began with qualitative observations of participants in two resident bedroom designs. But through the sequence of studies, due to the outcomes of the first five, the sixth study made use of inferential statistics to clarify earlier findings.

Within the research design of each of the six studies, we see a mixture of methods as well. For example, while the first study is dominantly qualitative, Pable also used research tactics from quantitative research, such as a control group. The control group is used in experimental research for purposes of comparison. In her first study, one of the two resident bedrooms received 18 design interventions, while the second bedroom did not receive the interventions. The qualitative data collected from both rooms allow for comparison of the differences in resident responses. Note that similar participants occupied each room, consisting of a mother and her two children. This is a requirement in using a control group because it assures that the observed results are due to the interventions and not to some other preexisting differences between the subjects. The first study also used pre- and post-test surveys. This is a quantitative research tactic as well. The subjects reported their observations prior to the interventions and then reported their observations afterward. This tells the researchers the impact of the interventions. Pable's use of a control group and pre- and post-test surveys is called "quasi-experimental." This is because it involves participants who were at hand; they were not randomly selected from a larger population to represent a statistically significant sample of that population. Design research using control groups are often quasi-experimental. For further discussion about experimental research in general, see the editorial comments both front and back of Chapter 11.

The second study "broadened the inquiry." Here, Pable and her colleagues used tactics in qualitative research to dive deeply into interview responses from a larger population. These tactics involved various *coding* techniques. A researcher sorts data after he or she has collected a large amount of interview responses: the aim is to look for general themes (open coding); relationships between themes (axial coding) and drawing out thematic threads to frame larger conclusions (selective coding). Pable also mentions microanalysis, in which the researcher examines details, sometimes line for line, of transcripts of the interviews.

The table in Figure 8.1 provides a snapshot of the sequence of methods Pable used over nine years but also of the combinations of methods used in each of her six studies. It would be helpful to refer to this table for an overview of the research topics, and the mixture of methods Pable used to address them, prior to reading the chapter. As you read this chapter:

1. Note the advantages Pable lists for research conducted in sequence, particularly how one stage informs the next.
2. An important point of new knowledge coming out of this sequential series is the psychological constructs pattern (PCP). As you read, keep track of how this pattern emerges from the findings of each study. Notice how the PCP is *generalizable* beyond the cases of Pable study.
3. Using a mixture of methods also calls for becoming familiar with a mixture of types of literature to inform the studies. Note how Pable relates the social science and psychology literatures to the design literature, and how this interdisciplinary mix led her to new results.

Often in matters related to research methodology, one comes across the term "longitudinal study." This usually means observational studies of a designated group of people over a sustained period of time, measuring how a specific factor or factors change in this sample population. Longitudinal studies are commonly used in social science or medical research. For instance, here is an example from the Institute for Work and Health:

> we might choose to look at the change in cholesterol levels among women over 40 who walk daily for a period of 20 years. The longitudinal study design would account for cholesterol levels at the onset of a walking regime and as the walking behavior continued over time.[2]

Longitudinal studies of this nature are usually not feasible for design research. As Pable notes, each of her studies over nine years sampled different people. Pable says, "It is better to describe these studies as a series of repeated inquiries into homelessness over nine years." So here, the domain (environments for the homeless) remained the same, but the subjects involved in each study were different.

Interiority

As noted in the Introduction to this book, interiority as an experienced reality can either be explicitly mentioned in these chapters or only be present implicitly. Here, Pable does not address interiority specifically. But if we recall Petra Perolini's description of interiority as "a process *within* a person that reflects an individual's unique awareness of the world and a psychological relationship to the world that is meaningful,"[3] this chapter precisely aligns with the larger theme of interiority that weaves throughout this book. With this in mind:

1. Consider Pable's six studies as telling a story about the gradual emergence of understanding, on the researchers' part, on the relationships between psychological perceptions (what Pable calls "constructs") of the residents, on the one hand, and environmental factors, on the other. In short, consider how the PCP is itself a kind of map of the felt interiority of the residents.
2. Pable mentions terms including *security, stress management, sense of community, sense of personal control* and *feels like home*. Note how these terms can all come under the umbrella of felt interiority because of the PCP. Consider how this PCP can in turn be used for understanding the felt interiority of other demographic groups as they interact with their non-home environments. For example: inpatients in hospitals; refugees; immigrant groups (see Chapter 1); prisoners in detention facilities, and the like.

Put another way, the PCP relates comfortably to Perolini's definition for interiority. Pable's PCP captures "an individual's unique awareness of the world" in a definable pattern of six constructs. This is a valuable outcome of her work in this field over nine years.

One last editorial note about this chapter. To make the flow of the chapter more readable, Pable often uses endnotes to further elaborate on points she makes; please read them for a deeper understanding of her work.

* * * *

Validating "Feeling at Home": Developing a Psychological Constructs Pattern to Aid in the Design of Environments for the Homeless

Jill Pable

This chapter summarizes six research studies conducted over nine years; the goal was to understand the psychological and environmental needs of people experiencing homelessness. These studies used both qualitative and quantitative research strategies. Together, these studies clarified and confirmed a series of psychological constructs valued by the homeless, shedding light on how design interventions can help them feel more comfortable and at peace. Specifically, understanding the psychological needs of the homeless can help us design interiors that promote an increased sense of protection while also supporting a sense of dignity for the occupants.

Homelessness is a growing challenge. With over 10,000 community housing and homeless shelters operating in the United States alone, and over 553,000 people homeless on any given night, it is important to consider the effects of interior environments on a demographic that is arguably among the neediest.[4] Facilities that serve the homelessness are often beset by low budgets and rushed schedules. Many facilities serving the homeless are repurposed buildings, making intentionally planned spaces difficult. Often, the look and feel of these buildings are austere because they were designed primarily for durability and ease of maintenance. In sum, thoughtful design research can inform the design of interior environments that can better serve this demographic.

Interactions between people and built environments are always important to understand for designers. How mind, body and place interrelate is complicated for anyone, but it may be especially so for a person experiencing homelessness. The quality of a physical environment can either support or challenge that person's sense of well-being during a time of great need. The psychological crisis for someone having just lost his or her home can easily alter perceptions and hamper ability to make clear choices.[5]

Because these are human beings responding to crises in real time, determining "what is going on" with homeless people in these settings by using singular research methods might be limiting.[6] For this reason, my colleagues and I have used mixed-methods research in the six studies described here. Taken together, these studies embrace both traditional research and design as a form of research inquiry. These studies do not constitute a longitudinal study, as they did not track the same individuals over the entire course of the six studies.[7] It is better to describe these studies as a series of repeated inquiries into homelessness over nine years. Repeated inquiries of the same focused topic offer certain advantages.[8] First, they permit the ability to collect a breadth and depth of data that a single study does not provide. Second, each round of data collection queries a population sample at that point in time, yielding a series of cross-sectional estimates that can gauge perceptions over time. Third, new participants in settings that are similar can help maintain a *current* sample of a population. But perhaps the most important reason for a sequential study in this setting is that the homeless population is by definition transient, which would make a traditional longitudinal study difficult to operationalize. In sum, repeated sampling can generate a pattern of perceptions, produce a hypothesis pattern over time and permit testing the findings for purposes of verification. These six studies are outlined by the table in Figure 8.1.

Numbered one through six in Figure 8.1, these studies used multiple research tactics. Two of the studies (#1 Dormitory case study and #6 Psychological constructs study) involved collecting both quantitative and qualitative data. Quantitative data helps to define numerical factors, but numerical approaches are not ideal for revealing the lived experiences of a homeless individual. Thus, we used qualitative data to "bring quantitative data to life."[9] The quantitative and qualitative aspects of this research moved between what the editors in the Introduction of this book call "what-is-the-case" research, and "what-to-do" interventions that embrace design solutions. The design opportunity came by way of collaboration with a government organization for pro bono design consultation on the design of a homeless shelter (studies 2 and 5). The cycles of research findings informing design decisions recall Donald Schön's ideas on design as reflective practice. Schön's insight is that iterative loops consisting of a proposed solution, reflective assessment of that solution, and proposing a stronger solution based upon the reflective assessment[10] are particularly apropos for testing emerging findings on the design of environments for the homeless.

Also, through reflective cycles over the course of the studies, we were able to fill in some gaps in the extant literature on homelessness.[11] More specifically, links between what the literature calls psychological constructs, on the one hand, and simple environmental factors such as locks on

Year	Author(s)	Title	Strategies & Tactics	Geographic Location	Publication/ Dissemination
2011	Pable	1. **Dormitory case study. The transitional homeless shelter family experience: a case study examining the potential effects of physical living conditions on perceptions of crowding, control, helplessness and related issues**	A comparative case study using a pre, post structure with altered bedroom as the treatment. Interview, standardized survey instruments, photo documentation, interview of 3 stakeholder groups.	HOPE Transitional Shelter. Big Bend Homeless Coalition. Tallahassee, Florida.	J. Pable, "The homeless shelter family experience: examining the influence of physical living conditions on perceptions of internal control, crowding, privacy, and related issues," *Journal of Interior Design 37,* no. 4 (2012): 9-37.
2011	Pable, Waxman & McBain	2. **Housing report.** Invited report for the Florida Housing Finance Corporation: **Recommendations for design and construction standards for transitional and permanent supportive housing.**	Interview and photo-documentation. Microanalysis, open coding, axial coding and selective coding.	Locations throughout northern and central Florida including Tallahassee, Lake City, Jacksonville, and Tampa.	J. Pable, L. Waxman, and M. McBain, "Low income housing: resident well-being as policy," *Environmental Design Research Association Annual Conference Proceedings* (McLean, VA: EDRA, 2011): 333.
2014	Pable & Fishburne	3. **POE study. A Case Study in Support of Multiple Post Mortem Assessments**	Interview, photo-documentation, survey	Locations throughout northern and central Florida including Tallahassee, Lake City, Jacksonville, and Sarasota.	J. Pable and K. Fishburne, "A case study in support of multiple post mortem assessments," *Journal of Systemics, Cybernetics and Informatics 13,* no. 1 (2015). Accessed July 1, 2019, http://www.iiisci.org/journal/sci/FullText.asp?var=&id=JR527FM15.
2016	Pable & Fishburne	4. **Shelter design project.** Pro-bono design consultation for Kearney Comprehensive Emergency Services Center.	Design programming regarding concept selection and design and specification of lighting, signage, color palette, finishes and furnishings.	Tallahassee, FL	K. Fishburne and J. Pable, "With empowerment and dignity in mind: a new multi-service emergency shelter for homeless men and women." *Interior Design Educators Council National Conference Proceedings* (Chicago: Interior Design Educators Council, 2016), 73-82.
2016-2018	Pable	5. **Case studies. *Design Resources for Homelessness* Case Study Collection**: five distinct reports on homeless shelters and supportive housing developments.	Interview of three stakeholder groups, photo documentation analyzed in six human needs constructs.	Los Angeles, Seattle, Austin, New York City and Southampton, United Kingdom.	The five reports are at http://designresourcesforhomelessness.org/foundation-information/
2018-2019	Pable & Gomory	6. **Psychological constructs study. Identification and validation of psychological construct pattern set for persons experiencing homelessness.**	Interview, surveys, cognitive mapping; culminates in quantitative survey that permits inferential statistical analysis.	Phase 1: populations in Florida and San Francisco. Phase 2: electronic survey engaging populations from multiple locations across the United States.	To be determined.

Figure 8.1 Research studies and related activities undertaken from 2011 to 2019.

doors and curtains for privacy, on the other, became so evident that my colleagues and I began to itemize the findings as the studies progressed.[12] One might say that using curtains for privacy might be obvious, but through literature review, we saw that only limited research findings exist on what such a simple intervention has upon a sense of restfulness for residents, particularly studies with an architectural focus.[13]

The cycles of learning in these studies enabled us to make a targeted inventory of environmental factors in relation to psychological constructs. Informed by Schön's framework for reflection-in-action,[14] what the research cycles taught us was that psychological constructs in relation to environmental factors—as embodied experiences—express themselves in *patterns*.[15] For example, building on the

Explanation building iteration	Study in the series	Contribution to the emerging psychological constructs pattern
Make an initial theoretical statement	Study 1: Dorm case study	Encountered ideas from first participants that there may be fundamental psychological needs connected to housing for persons experiencing homelessness.
Compare the findings of an *initial case* against such a statement	Study 2: Housing Report	Included more participants asking them about the psychological constructs that emerged from Study 1; created a first draft list of 13 psychological construct and related ideas.
Explore further context	Study 3: POE	Expanded the inquiry to administrators and case managers; noted that resident constructs were often in tension with administrators and case workers' priorities like budget and cleaning/maintenance.
Compare other details of the case against the revision	Study 4: Design of the Kearney Center	Applied select psychological constructs to the design of an actual interior environment. Demonstrated the applicability of the constructs to design decisions.
Compare the revision to the findings from further cases	Study 5: Shelter and supportive housing design case studies	Continued literature review resulted in a reduced and revised list of six total psychological constructs. Used the constructs as the critical framework for five case studies, further confirming their applicability through survey and interview data from new participants.
Repeat this process as many times as is needed	Study 6: Psychological constructs study	New participants contributed photos of home objects and settings that expressed the six psychological constructs, identifying those objects and places most commonly associated with the constructs. This collective of individual perspectives served to validate the construct pattern. The study's two phases permitted repeated evaluation and revision of both the pattern's six categories and the objects/places participants associated with each.

Figure 8.2 Explanation building activities within each study and their contribution to the development of the Psychological Constructs Pattern, or PCP.

idea that "security" is a psychological construct, we looked further for a pattern of constructs that captured the entirety of what people value in feeling "at home." To develop an understanding of pattern in this sense, findings in the earlier studies (1, 2 and 3) were held in abeyance; we regarded them as "maybe" findings. We needed the later studies to confirm to us (or to alter) the strength of the earlier results. In this way, we also increased confidence that the ultimate findings were generalizable. These latter findings enabled us to formulate the Psychological Constructs Pattern, or PCP (see below).

As well, the social science literature offers *explanation-building* as a research tactic to help researchers working in this vein to establish validity for their findings.[16] For these studies, explanation-building helped to clarify patterns of what William Trochim calls "good fits" between "a theoretical pattern and an operational one."[17] The steps for explanation-building in the left column of Figure 8.2 describe the process of developing a pattern, comparing it to what is observed, revising the pattern and comparing it again.[18] The right column enumerates how these observations contributed to the framing of the PCP.

What follows is a summary of our research over the six projects, highlighting the iterative nature of our information gathering, how we formed the PCP, and checking and rechecking the ideas based on new information.

Moving between Research, Design and Validation: Summary of the Six Studies

Study 1. Dormitory Case Study: Initial Exploration

The research question for this initial study was: *What difference can the design of an interior environment make for someone's state of mind when homeless?* We examined participants' experiences of a transitional shelter bedroom design, specifically two families each comprising a mother and two children. Each family was assigned a bedroom space, with one bedroom kept as-is and the second altered by 18 targeted improvements.[19] The experiences of the parents were documented through photographs, interviews and observations for approximately three months (Figure 8.3).

While this approach was primarily qualitative in nature, it has a quasi-quantitative aspect in the use of a control. This study also used standardized numerical surveys authored by other researchers; these surveys examined perceptions of crowding and sense of helplessness. The surveys were administered in pre- and post-test queries 11 weeks apart; they helped us to understand changes in the mothers' opinions about their bedroom surroundings.[20]

In summary, privacy was an issue of high importance to each of the parents in the study, and the ability to organize possessions was similarly prized. The parent in the altered room felt a heightened sense of personal control, and this family voluntarily spent more time in the room. Not surprisingly, the parent occupying the unaltered bedroom felt more crowded, and her children either avoided or defaced the bedroom more than the children in the altered bedroom. Other results came to light as well.[21] For instance, environmental features may impact the children's perceptions of the parent; this because the altered bedroom allowed for such interactions as "time-outs" using the bed curtains or the parent granting privileges for writing on the marker boards. In general, expressions

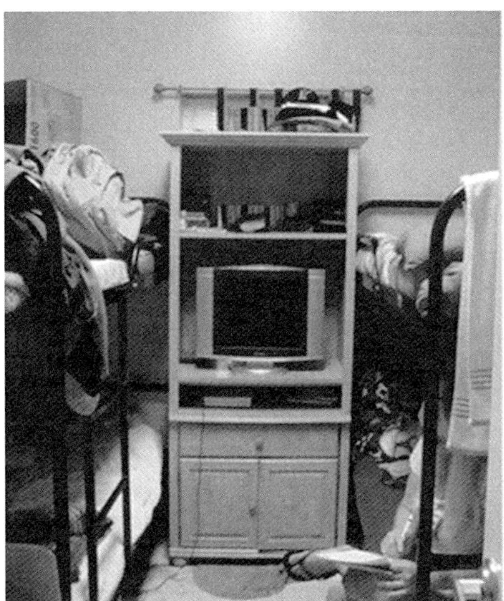

Figure 8.3 Study 1 dormitory site showing the built environment before renovation on the left and after renovation on the right. See credits.

of territoriality and personalization occurred more in the altered bedroom, suggesting deeper bonds being developed between room and occupants. These "maybe" findings were the first indications of the relationship between psychological constructs and environmental settings. These findings were the beginnings of what resulted as our PCP.

Study 2. Housing Report: Broadening the Inquiry

The first study led to an invitation from the Florida Housing Finance Corporation (FHFC), charged with distributing federal housing grants to private developers of low-income housing. Interested in increasing the livability of newly built supportive housing and shelters, FHFC asked me, along with my colleague Dr. Lisa Waxman and graduate research assistant Marsha McBain, to examine the current outstanding needs of low-income resident groups of housing developments not yet addressed by FHFC loan requirements.

One benefit of this collaboration was new access to state-wide respondents who already had a relationship with FHFC; these included shelter administrators, developers, on-site case workers and housing and shelter residents. It exposed us to the needs and perceptions of more diverse resident groups including veterans, frail elders, adolescents in the foster care system and victims of domestic violence. In total, we conducted 27 interviews and visited and photographed 12 shelters and supportive housing venues throughout Florida, asking questions about participants' experiences. The questions included: "Tell me how you feel about safety and security for you and your family?" and "How important is it to you that you have a network of friends?" This qualitative data was analyzed using microanalysis as outlined by Strauss and Corbin, involving open coding, axial coding and selective coding.[22] This process allowed us to eventually identify a list of 13 categories that included psychological and physical health constructs as well as one budget/financial category (Figure 8.4).

These formed the first pattern of "what was going on" in our series of studies. Further, we tapped our knowledge from previous design practice and derived 103 specific, actionable design recommendations that address these categories so that housing developers could include them in their designs. This study underlined the multidimensionality of human needs and compelled us to examine related factors in human health, safety and welfare, including how cost of living and sense of community impact residents (Figure 8.5).

Privacy
Security and safety
Sense of community
Identity and territoriality
Self esteem
Place attachment and sense of place
Sense of space/crowding
Cost of living, including the cost of maintenance and utilities
Physical health
Dignity
Respect
Delight
Discovery

Figure 8.4 A list of 13 needs categories describing psychological and physical health constructs as well as one budget/financial category that emerged from Study 2.

Grocery shelf ✓✓

The sequence of entering a residence is often hampered by having things in hand such as groceries, a coat, a purse or other items. These have to be managed while keys are surface next to the outside of the door that is at least 12" wide and deep adjacent to the doorknob side (Center for Universal Design, 2004). Ideally, if the surface is small it has raised sides 2 to 4" tall to contain unstable items such as a shopping bag while locating one's keys.

Intentional walk-off mats ✓✓✓

The approach to a residence may or may not be well protected from walked-in dirt from foot traffic. Floors are likely the first surface in a residence to get dirty, and among the finishes that landlords must replace most frequently. Therefore, residents can be assisted in keeping their unit clean if walk-off mats are planned for within new construction or significant renovation projects. Ideally, plan for walk-off mats that are recessed so that they are flush with the outside entrance ground level of the residence, and have a removable grate (offered in a variety of materials such as rubber)

Figure 8.5 Two of the 103 actionable design recommendations in the Study 2 report that housing developers could reference when planning their projects.

Study 3. A Post-occupancy Evaluation

Through interviews of such diverse stakeholders, Study 2 highlighted the real complexity of human needs regarding shelter. This, along with findings from the first study, spurred us to conduct a post-occupancy evaluation (POE). Different from the pre- and post-test tactic from Study 1, in which the post-test looked for the impact of targeted interventions, a POE looks to appraise more general conditions after a design is in place.[23] We wanted to capture contrasts in the needs of different stakeholders, defined for the study as residents, case workers and staff directors. We hoped for a more comprehensive understanding of factors that can influence successful designs of supportive interiors. For example, cleaning requirements favored by administrators might result in environments that feel sterile to residents. Similarly, locking down furniture, storage bins and other elements to prevent theft makes it more difficult for residents to feel at home.

In 2013, Kenan Fishburne and I visited five regional homeless shelters and surveyed/interviewed 22 shelter residents, case managers and shelter directors with a view to gather "user" and "operational" perceptions of (1) their own facilities and (2) their thoughts about the Study 1 bedroom features. We toured each facility and took photographs. Participant perceptions varied by stakeholder role. For example, residents highly valued personal ventilation fans, wall mirrors and seating cubes. In contrast, shelter directors found that these features were not positive additions, generally due to issues of durability and maintenance. Fans and mirrors break, and seating cubes can be stolen. Given these differences in stakeholder priorities, we determined from this study that administering more than one POE could lead to better understanding of multiple stakeholder priorities. The first would be a user POE capturing residents' needs. The second would be an operational POE capturing administrative priorities such as budget and funding, or "security" understood in anti-theft terms primarily. If administered to the two groups in a project, this POE set could better inform design decisions for these projects.[24]

The multiple POEs also brought to light new information about patterns of psychological constructs such as security, personal control and beauty from more diverse participants and more locations than we had access to before. We gained a deeper appreciation of the complexity of requirements a designer will confront if she or he were to honestly search for answers for the needs of such a diverse range of stakeholders. It led us to more mindfully choose products and finishes in Study 4, described below, and to ultimately concentrate on only those constructs that residents most value (rather than the constructs, say, of directors and case workers) for the sake of clarity in Studies 5 and 6.

Study 4. Applying Patterns of Human Needs in a Large Design Project

Two years after the conclusion of Study 3, my colleague Kenan Fishburne and I offered pro-bono design consultation services to a new, large homeless shelter in Tallahassee, Florida. This study further clarified what would become our PCP. We volunteered our services believing that our previous studies and our "maybe" findings regarding PCPs might offer context to this 300-bed project's design decision-making. This was our opportunity, as Schön describes, to "think of intelligent practice as an *application* of knowledge to instrumental decisions."[25] We found that giving attention to psychological constructs in specific relation to environmental factors kept human well-being "center-stage" in our design decisions. Working alongside the project's architect and interior designer for the Kearney

Comprehensive Emergency Services Center, we helped guide the project's concept, custom art, lighting, signage and furnishings specifications, prioritizing the psychological constructs' support of resident and staff perceptions of dignity, security, beauty and other needs as we currently understood them at the time (see Figure 8.4). Our presentation for the project justified many of its recommendations by referencing the psychological constructs. For example, a "welcome mat" carpet insert was suggested at each case worker's office door to support residents' self-esteem (Figure 8.6). Similarly, we recommended a new suspended art mobile in a key interior intersection to bring an element of beauty and visual interest to the space (Figure 8.7).

Figure 8.6 The corridor to the dining room in the Comprehensive Emergency Services Center project is a place where clients queue. A "welcome mat" carpet insert was included at each case worker's office door to support residents' self-esteem and encourage engagement with support services. See credits.

Figure 8.7 A suspended art mobile in a key interior intersection within the Comprehensive Emergency Services Center lends beauty, assists with wayfinding and sends a message of respect to clients. See credits.

Figure 8.8 Aids to wayfinding is an important part of clearly designed interior spaces for the homeless. This signage is additionally helped by uplighting.

This was the first time we actively referenced the emerging list of 13 psychological constructs as a framework for thinking through our design decisions. We used these constructs as logical justifications for our recommendations as we presented to the clients. We found that this approach resonated well because administrators were, after all, sensitive to the well-being of their residents and staff. In this way, the constructs helped us tie architectural recommendations to positive psychological outcomes for users. For example, having seen the impact of visual chaos that results in places that do not provide adequate storage or the means to organize objects and possessions, Kenan Fishburne specified swivel chairs at computer stations that self-right themselves after someone finishes sitting there. (Visual chaos, in our analysis, relates to the PCP category of beauty.) It was in this project that we also had the opportunity to experiment with research findings from other fields, such as situated cognition theory that led us to design illuminated wayfinding signage that uses uplighting, a technique that cognitive psychologists suggest infers a sense of optimism in an environment.[26] Engagement with this project provided us further assurance that the collection of human needs that previous studies began to reveal could be expressed with positive effect in a new architectural setting (Figure 8.8).

Study 5. Multiple Case Studies: Broadening Understanding of the Psychological Constructs[27]

While we were providing design services to the Kearney Center, I launched a non-profit organization called *Design Resources for Homelessness* (DRH). This is a website offering research-curated information helping to inform architectural and interior design decision-making for homeless shelters, day centers, supportive housing and similar venues. DRH was inspired by the lack of a centralized source on this topic coupled with the potential value in approaching this challenge from a human wellness perspective.[28] In support of human experience and well-being, the mission and informational research summaries, reports, project databases and case studies of DRH are directly tied to the PCP.[29] My work with the external authors who created the reports on the DRH site, as well as the many designers and architects I interviewed, strengthened my conclusion that the emerging pattern of psychological constructs could function well as a means to define the priorities of lived experience, and as such could bring definition to abstract, experiential ideas to which architecture and interior architecture could respond. For example, with the understanding of security as a critically important psychological need, on-the-ground interior design features such as door locks,[30] workable ways to secure one's possessions from theft and visual privacy for one's children often become high-priority items to be addressed in homeless shelter design. Similarly, knowing that a sense of community can combat the isolation many homeless persons feel, designing for gathering spaces with clear sightlines becomes imperative.[31]

In the course of my literature review undertaken to launch DRH, I found several influential social work and psychology frameworks that aligned with the human-centered design approach of Studies 1 through 4. Trauma-informed care is an approach to therapy for persons experiencing homelessness; it seeks to preserve dignity, grow sense of empowerment and foster a sense of control that is much needed to graduate from the homeless condition.[32] Other helpful literature included a series of studies from environmental psychology and social work identifying the "key qualities of home" that confirmed the psychological constructs elements in these studies: security, privacy, identity and community.[33]

Exposure to this literature led to a framework for the PCP developed through logical argumentation.[34] As a result, the earlier 13 elements were reduced to six. This was not a matter of deletion as much as it was one of consolidation, in which some constructs became subcategories to other primary ones. For example, "privacy" was one of the 13 constructs coming out of Studies 1, 2 and 3. It now seemed logical that privacy could be a sub-topic under a larger construct that grouped privacy with security and personal space. "Delight" and "discovery" could find a home under "beauty and meaning" and so on. The hope was that this shorter list can be more comprehensible for applied use by those outside the design fields.[35] All told, these are the six elements of the PCP at the conclusion of this fifth study:

Dignity and self-esteem
Empowerment and personal control
Security, privacy and personal space
Stress management
Sense of community
Beauty and meaning

Among the DRH information is a series of five case studies that examine existing shelters and permanent supportive housing through the evaluative framework of lived human experience.[36] It asks the question, "How are current shelters and supportive housing projects attending to human needs?" To date, case studies have been completed for projects across the United States and the United Kingdom. These were informed by videos and interviews of a total of 25 residents, social workers, directors and the architects of these projects as well as site visits and on-site photography. The six psychological constructs form the lived experience framework of inquiry for these case studies, shaping the interview and survey questions and the resulting format of the reports.[37] Comments and advice from these participants have largely shown that the six psychological constructs describe residents' needs for their shelter and housing environments, while also providing examples of how these needs can be addressed through architecturally designed features (Figure 8.9).

Figure 8.9 The Design Resources for Homelessness case study identified that the psychological constructs of empowerment, sense of community and presence of beauty were at play in the café located in the Booth Centre, a Salvation Army supportive housing facility in Southampton, United Kingdom. See credits.

Study 6: Confirming and Validating the Psychological Constructs Pattern

The last study sought to confirm that each of the six elements in the PCP is necessarily important and irreducible to persons experiencing homelessness. The validating of these constructs was undertaken with co-principal Tomi Gomory of the College of Social Work at Florida State University. Methodologically, this study used both in-person cognitive mapping and an online quantitative and qualitative survey. We wanted to determine if the six constructs were accurate for a broader sample of people than Studies 1 through 5 permitted. These are discussed in further detail below.

This study had two aims. First, we explored the "fit" of the PCP with the reality of what people perceived, asking questions such as "are the six current categories a comprehensive and assistive description of psychological needs for persons who experience homelessness?" Secondly, we were interested in perceptual *differences* between persons experiencing homelessness and other "housed" groups such as designers, social workers and laypersons. Examining these groups' perceptions would reveal similarities and differences in priorities and perspectives that might serve to point out, for example, how designers' perceptions of what matters differ from someone who has experienced homelessness. This could identify ways designers can increase their empathy for homeless persons as they design for their needs. The results can also reveal how perspectives in a general population differ from people who have lost their homes.

We were aware that ideas like "security" and "sense of community" outlined in the PCP might come across as abstract. Wanting to make this as straightforward as possible for participants, we worked from the assumption that everyone has a personal and unique sense of what, in an environmental sense, "feels like home." We therefore asked participants to identify physical objects and places within a home that speak to the ideas such as "sense of personal control" and "stress management." In short, we framed the PCP in terms that are generally understandable. We used a cognitive mapping tactic called the 3CM process in which participants contribute their own photographs that capture these ideas.[38] In this personalized fashion, an evolving set of images helped us access the psychological constructs in a concrete and less abstract manner (Figure 8.10).

Figure 8.10 In the cognitive mapping process used in Study 6, participants grouped self-selected photos of home into the psychological construct categories with the option to create other categories as they saw fit.

The first phase of the study built the collections of photos to be used in the second phase. Participant groups in the resident, designer, social worker and general public categories took photographs of their homes or selected photos from other sources they felt pertained to each of the six constructs. Participants were also invited to add constructs they perceived were missing. Each participant also ranked the importance of each construct for him or her. The resulting consensus set of photos brought to light new connections between places and objects and the feeling of home to which the constructs contributed. In some instances, preferred choices were specific to a participant group, hinting at fundamental differences in perspective. For example, homeless persons were more likely to choose photos showing a refrigerator full of food. This relates to a sense of security in a more pronounced fashion than exhibited by the choices of the other housed groups.[39] In total, 31 participants representing the four groups (residents, designers, social workers and laypersons) provided their photographs in Phase 1 to shape the consensus photo set. Analysis of the phase one qualitative data suggested that the six psychological constructs in the pattern were acceptable to all the participant groups.[40]

The second phase of this study examined the choices of photos and their frequency from the first phase, noting those photo categories most frequently selected by group. We then developed an online survey, specifically including photos that represented both the most frequent choices from each of the four groups and a series of choice contrasts in the data that might describe differences between the groups.[41] The survey itself reached more people—a total of 249 participants—to assure a meaningful sample for inferential statistical analysis. The survey was administered using Qualtrics online software to participants from across the United States; the participants were sorted into the same four groups as used in the first phase.

To answer the research question "is the current construct pattern a comprehensive, assistive description of what is necessary to feel 'at home'? the frequencies of participants' responses to this survey question were tallied. A total of 72 of the 77 persons (95%) who experienced homelessness (the "resident" group) answered that the list was accurate and complete as-is. For the designer, layperson and social worker groups, 80% or more of all participants in each group (85%, 80% and 95%, respectively) also indicated that the six constructs were comprehensive in their current state. To determine if the results identified group differences, a 4-sample test for equality of proportions without continuity was run indicating there was a strong, statistically significant difference between at least one or more of the groups ($X^2 = 27.263$, df = 3, $p < 0.001$). A follow-up 2×4 chi-square test for independence confirmed these group differences ($X^2 = 27.263$, df = 3, $p < 0.001$). To determine specific between-group differences, further 2×4 chi-square tests showed that differences were statistically confirmed between the resident and designer groups ($X^2 = 24.751$, df = 1, $p < 0.001$), the resident and layperson groups ($X^2 = 20.939$, df = 1, $p < 0.001$) and the resident and designer groups ($X^2 = 24.751$, df = 1, $p < 0.001$). Collectively, these results showed that the homeless resident group was more consistently sure that the six constructs accurately captured how they felt than the other groups (however, all groups indicated 80% agreement or higher).

Survey results also revealed which of the provided photos participants associated most strongly with each of the constructs. Based on an analysis of response frequencies, sometimes one photo was chosen most frequently by all groups, such as associating security with a photo of a front door with a deadbolt. However, choices differed between groups as well. For example, the homeless resident group was the only one to choose a car as their most important indicator of a sense of dignity, whereas the other three groups most frequently chose a photo of a residential bathroom. These results at times indicate how conceptions of physical space and their associations with psychological constructs can differ, which may be influenced by degree of scarcity or degree of plenty (or what is "taken for granted") in a person's lived experience.[42] At the time of this writing, this study is concluding its analysis of findings and we intend to seek publication of the full results in the near future.

Conclusions and Observations

These six studies constitute a search for knowledge that began as "maybe" findings. Through inquiries of diverse sets of stakeholders, and also applied design projects informed by the empirical research, the studies gradually focused the findings. Mixed methods both within individual studies and across the collection of studies helped capture the lived experience of participants, and also verified a broader generalizability of those experiences and perceptions with quantitative analyses such as inferential statistics. Throughout, the studies used an explanation-building process that led to the emergence of the PCP. Also, these studies harnessed Schön's reflection-in-action in a particular way, by drawing from the results of one study to inform the research design of the next in an iterative fashion. Study 6 concluded with findings verifying that the PCP may be especially valid for persons who have experienced homelessness. It also suggested that people's ideas and needs for their home may vary depending on demographics and personal histories. It shows that for those who have experienced homelessness, the differences in perception and values, and how these are expressed in prioritizing physical attributes of environments, can be significant.

Multiple studies conducted over time can permit the exploration and confirmation of important, complex topics such as what we need to experience "sense of home." The need to understand the complexity of "a sense of home," and how it relates to constructs of psychological well-being, can inform the designer's role in helping a person to graduate from homelessness with more dignity. If we are to make progress with successfully connecting the intricacies of human perception to well-suited interior spaces, research methods that confront these complexities effectively take time and planning, iteratively responding to lessons learned earlier, so that actions taken later in the process can best inform our designs of built forms and interiors.

* * * *

Discussion and Exercises

Reflections about the Chapter You Just Read:

1. Please refer to the standard features of a research project explained in the Introduction. Then:
    a. In one sentence, identify the *research topic*. This sentence can be in the form of a question but does not have to be. In any case, write one grammatically correct sentence that captures the research topic of this chapter.
    b. Identify the *literature* related to this research project.
    c. Identify the *method* which the author used and also the *data* which this method generated for analysis.
    d. Explain how this approach is *generalizable* (or not).
    e. Explain how you can have confidence (or not) of the *internal and external validity* of this author's overall approach.
2. Refer to the table in Figure 8.1 as a guide.
    a. Make a list of *all* of the research tactics Pable used in these studies. A research tactic is something the researcher *does*. Within qualitative research strategy, there are many tactics that we do: conducting interviews, performing post occupancy evaluations (POE) and so on.
    b. For each study, remove one of the research tactics mentioned, and discuss how the absence of that tactic would prevent (or alter) Pable from collecting her data.
3. In regard to literature:
    a. Discuss what literature Pable had on hand at the beginning, and what literature she found during the nine-year process. This chapter is an excellent example of the fact that "literature review" is not just something done at the beginning of research but an activity that spans throughout the research project, whether that is one project or six.
    b. How did Pable use literature from non-design disciplines to fuel her ongoing research? How many different disciplinary sources did Pable use? Discuss how these sources helped shape Pable's research topics through the course of the six studies.

Exercises/Suggestions for Further Study

1. Familiarize yourself with a tiny home community for the homeless; there are an increasing number of these in the United States. If one is not local to you, here is a link that describes ten such communities: https://www.curbed.com/maps/tiny-houses-for-the-homeless-villages (accessed August 3, 2019). Drawing from Pable's research, how would you implement a research study to discover how residents' psychological needs relate to design factors in their tiny homes and/or in their community?
2. Go to "Design for Recovery" on the Design Resources for Homelessness mentioned by Pable. http://designresourcesforhomelessness.org/people-1/education/. Download the document *A Review of Research* and read through page 36. Write down ideas for further research to conduct the study in #1 above.

3. The rest of *A Review of Research* is a long section titled "A Select Annotated Bibliography" (pp. 37–75).
   a. Carefully note the structure of each entry, consisting of (a) a complete reference of the source and (b) a short paragraph summarizing the key features of the publication.
   b. Note also how the annotated bibliography is divided into subsections, each addressing a particular theme, for example: "Homelessness – General" on page 37; "Children and Youth," on page 40; and so on. Make a list on one sheet of paper of these subsections. This will give you an overview of the issues related to homelessness.
4. Write an annotated bibliography entry for *A Review of Research* (pages 1–36). Your entry will consist of: (1) a full citation for the reference; (2) a one-paragraph summary of the contents of this publication. And then, additionally, (3) assuming you are developing a research topic for the tiny home community mentioned in the first exercise above, write a paragraph or two about how *A Review of Research* gives you ideas about a specific research topic.
5. Finally, reflect on how your anticipated findings will help you design a tiny home community for the homeless.

Additional Connections and Information

Pable's work is very much related to social justice and equality. Often, these themes fall under the moniker "critical theory." Critical theory came out of The Frankfurt School, active in Germany in the early decades of the 20th century (between the two World Wars). Critical theory introduced the idea that new knowledge need not only be of the "objective" kind in which a scientist studies his or her subject matter in a removed and dispassionate way. Instead, a critical theorist situates *inside* the social situation under study, for the purposes of bringing about change. Max Horkheimer, one of the leading members of the Frankfurt School, captures this intention, "If … the theoretician and his specific object are seen as forming a dynamic unity with the oppressed class, so that his presentation of societal contradictions is not merely an expression of the concrete historical situation but also a force within it to stimulate change, then his real function emerges."[43] Pable's research certainly rings true to this description. The following literature provides further information about critical theory; several of these sources are in context of mixed-methods research. (Please also refer to the many resources listed in the endnotes of this chapter.)

Abbas Tashakori and Charles Eddlie (eds.). *The Handbook of Mixed Methods in Social & Behavioral Research* (Thousand Oaks, CA: Sage, 2003).

Bohman, James. "Critical Theory." *The Stanford Encyclopedia of Philosophy* (Fall 2016 Edition), ed. Edward N. Zalta https://plato.stanford.edu/cgi-bin/encyclopedia/archinfo.cgi?entry=critical-theory.

Denzin, Norman and Yvonna Lincoln. *Collecting and Interpreting Qualitative Materials* (Los Angeles, CA: Sage, 2008).

Mertens, Donna. *Research Methods in Education and Psychology: Integrating Diversity with Quantitative and Qualitative Approaches* (Thousand Oaks, CA: Sage, 2009).

Notes

1 Linda Groat and David Wang, *Architectural Research Methods*, 2nd ed. (Hoboken, NJ: John Wiley & Sons), 441–449.
2 "Cross-sectional vs. longitudinal studies," In Institute for Work & Health, August, 2015. www.iwh.on.ca/what-researchers-mean-by/cross-sectional-vs-longitudinal-studies. Accessed May 20, 2019.
3 Petra Simona Perolini, "Interior Spaces and the Layers of Meaning," *Design Principles and Practices* 5, no. 6 (2011): 170.
4 IbisWorld, "Community Housing & Homeless Shelters in the US," *Ibisworld*, May 1, 2019. www.ibisworld.com/industry-statistics/number-of-businesses/community-housing-homeless-shelters-united-states; U.S. Department of Housing and Urban Development, "HUD Exchange," *The 2018 annual homeless assessment report (AHAR) to Congress*, 2018. Accessed May 21, 2019. Also: Reporting at the 2007 Symposium on Homelessness Research convened by the U.S. Department of Housing and the Department of Health and Human Services, Rog & Buckner described that "specifically the need exists to refine the question from *whether* homelessness has an effect to what *aspects* of homelessness are prone to creating problems in what age groups and in what domains…" www.hudexchange.info/resources/documents/2018-AHAR-Part-1.pdf. Accessed May 21, 2019. See also: D. Rog and J. Buckner, "Homeless Families and Children," *Toward Understanding Homelessness: The 2007 National Symposium on Homelessness Research* (Washington, DC: Department of Health and Human Services and U.S. Department of Housing and Urban Development, 2007), 5–22.
5 S. Mullinaithan and E. Shafir, *Scarcity: Why Having Too Little Means So Much* (New York: Henry Holt, 2007).
6 This is particularly true for research seeking to understand people in crisis situations, in part because they may have many reasons to adapt their answers is such ways that minimize their perceptions of vulnerability. For example, a person may say that a shelter bedroom is superbly designed because he or she fears that revealing true feelings might lead to eviction from the only place that offers a refuge. For example, using interviews in a stand-alone fashion may be counterproductive because they do not speak to how *many* people may feel a certain way. Qualitative methods of research have not always been viewed as legitimate in the research academy, and owe at least some of their elevated standing to the rise of alternative ways of thinking in the late 20th century. Critical theory in particular has elevated qualitative methods as a means to shine a spotlight on the value and variety of people's lived experience. See J. Neale, "Theorizing Homelessness," in *Homelessness and Social Policy*, eds. Roger Burrows, Nicholas Pleace and Deborah Quilgars (New York: Routledge, 1997), 40–49.
7 Querying the same people throughout the entire period of the studies in a longitudinal study does have certain advantages, like tracking people's changing perceptions through time (such as during or after a homelessness crisis for a person). However, collecting continuous data on persons experiencing homelessness is notoriously difficult, as such persons may not have a consistent address and can depart a shelter at any time without leaving a forwarding address.
8 G. Duncan, "Panel Surveys: Uses and Applications," *International Encyclopedia of the Social & Behavioral Sciences*, 2015, pp. 462–467. www.sciencedirect.com/science/article/pii/B9780080970868440407. Accessed May 22, 2019.
9 Center for Innovation in Research and Teaching, *Overview of Mixed Methods*, n.d., https://cirt.gcu.edu/research/developmentresources/research_ready/mixed_methods/overview. Accessed May 22, 2019.
10 Schon explains that a back-and-forth movement between testing an idea and applying it is a dynamic way of moving discovery forward, harnessing the benefits of both When someone reflects-in-action, … he does not keep means and ends separate, but defines them interactively as he frames a problematic situation. He does not separate thinking from doing, ratiocinating his way to a decision which he must later convert to action. Because his experimenting is a kind of action, implementation is built into his inquiry. Thus reflection-in-action can proceed, even in situations of uncertainty or uniqueness. D. Schon, The Reflective Practitioner: How Professionals Think in Action (New York: Basic Books, 1983), 68–69.
11 Research about built environments in the closely related area of behavioral health is still in the early developmental stages. See M. Shepley and S. Pasha, "Center for Health Design," *Design Research and Behavioral Health Facilities*, July 28, 2013. www.healthdesign.org/system/files/chd428_researchreport_behavioralhealth_1013-_final_0.pdf. Accessed May 23, 2019.
12 For example, many interviewees remarked on their intense need for privacy when they lived in shelters and their desire for dignity. Other ideas that emerged were having personal control over a room's features and needing to be expressive or be in the presence of beauty. Beauty and the ability to be expressive might seem frivolous in the larger context of homelessness. However, this series of studies consistently showed us how residents would seek to surround themselves with symbols of self-determination and hope, such as a plant in a Styrofoam cup on a dresser or a quotation displayed in a picture frame. Residents' needs for and expression of beauty were demonstrated in a variety of ways in these studies including posting their children's artwork on the wall, displaying collections, or children's dress-up behaviors. The control of visual clutter, a significant issue in design of shelters, also proved to be an aspect of beauty for these studies. My experience with these studies' sites and participants showed me that presenting a person with the opportunity to experience something they find aesthetically interesting is a gift perceived subtly but consistently by the recipient—who can interpret this as a bestowal of dignity and empowerment by the organization that made the environment possible.
13 Other researchers have examined the psychological constructs of what produces a feeling of being "at home" for people in general who have not experienced homelessness. See E. Diener, S. Oishi, and L. Tay, *Handbook of Well-being* (Salt Lake City, UT: DEF Publishers, 2018). However, there is less literature on the needs of people who have lost their home, and very little that examines this issue with an eye toward constructing built environments that can respond to these needs. See D. Padgett, "There's No Place Like (a) Home: Ontological Security among Persons with Serious Mental Illness in the United States," in *Social Science & Medicine* 64, no. 9 (2007): 1925–1936. See also M. Bird, H. Rhoades,

J. Lahey, J. Cederbaum, and S. Wenzel, "Life Goals and Gender Differences among Chronically Homeless Individuals Entering Permanent Supportive Housing," *Journal of Social Distress and the Homeless* 26, no. 1 (2017): 9–15; and L. Rivlin and J. Moore, "Home-making: Supports and Barriers to the Process of Home," *Journal of Social Distress and the Homeless* 10, no. 4 (2001): 323–336. There may be a very good reason to consider the potential of "feeling of home" for persons in crisis, however. Literature has suggested that there is an important link between feeling "at home" and the establishment and maintenance of self-esteem. This sense of grounding, in turn, can help people to take steps toward their future such as maintaining a job and stable housing. See S. Burn, "Loss of Control, Attributions, and Helplessness in the Homeless," *Journal of Applied Social Psychology* 22, no. 15 (1992): 1161–1174.

14 Schon notes that there is some puzzling, or troubling, or interesting phenomenon with which the individual is trying to deal. As he tries to make sense of it, he also reflects on the understandings which have been implicit in his action, understandings which he surfaces, criticizes, restructures and embodies in further action. Schon, op. cit., 50.

15 See P. Price, R. Jhangiani, and I. Chiang, "Understanding Psychological Measurement," *Research Methods in Psychology*, 2013. https://opentextbc.ca/researchmethods/chapter/understanding-psychological-measurement/. Accessed May 24, 2019.

16 R. Yin, *Case Study Research: Design and Methods* (Los Angeles, CA: Sage, 2014).

17 W. Trochim, "Outcome Pattern Matching and Program Theory," *Evaluation and Program Planning* 12 (1989): 355–366. Also note this from Schon: when a designer finds himself stuck in a problematic situation which he cannot readily convert to a manageable problem, he may construct a new way of setting the problem—a new frame which, in what I shall call a 'frame experiment,' he tries to impose on the situation. Schon, op. cit., 63.

18 Adapted from Yin (2014).

19 These included bed privacy curtains, lighting for reading, enhanced storage for possessions, a combination lockbox for valuables, an attached wall cushion to use a bed as a sofa and bulletin and marker boards for self-expression.

20 For example, Duttweiler's Internal Control Index measure (P. Duttweiler, "The Internal Control Index: A Newly Developed Measure of Locus of Control," *Educational and Psychological Measurement* 44 (1984): 209–221) was administered as both a pre- and post-measure to both mothers to examine their perceptions of how helpless they felt about their life situation. This test measures their cognitive processing, autonomy, resistance to influence by others and self-confidence, and yields a numerical score identifying the change in score from the pre- to the post-test administrations, and therefore an opportunity to compare the degree of change between the two scores. The mother who inhabited the altered room indicated a 10% positive change, whereas the mother who inhabited the control room showed only a 2% positive change. While the implications of numerical test scores when administered to only two people should be and was regarded with significant caution in the reported results, the degree of difference between the two participants was an intriguing result that deserves further attention.

21 The study's findings also brought to light the needs of parents to engage with their children and the role environmental features may play in children's perceptions of the parent as an authority figure (through the parent being able to grant or withhold privileges such writing on the marker boards and "time-outs" using the bed curtains). The altered room also enhanced young children's ability to engage in imaginative play, lending comfort to the mother because her children were safe and positively engaged. Expanded expressions of territoriality and personalization were also observed in this family, suggesting that they established a deeper bond with the altered room, and that it possibly served as a more sufficient reflection of their identity as a result.

22 Strauss and Corbin (*Basics of Qualitative Research: Techniques and Procedures for Developing Grounded Theory* (New York: Sage, 1998) identify a process of (1) microanalysis that generates initial categories and discovers relationships through a line-by-line analysis of phrases from interviews; (2) open coding whereby categories of phenomena are named; (3) axial coding that relates categories to subcategories of content. Mind mapping analysis software also helped us with this stage; and (4) selective coding where we integrated and refined the categories to form a larger theory scheme. For further details see J. Pable, L. Waxman, and M. McBain, "Low Income Housing: Resident Well-being as Policy," *Environmental Design Research Association Annual Conference Proceedings* (McLean, VA: EDRA, 2011), 333.

23 My colleague Kenan Fishburne and I had an experience that further interested us in this topic. We returned to the Study 1 altered bedroom nine months after it was installed, and after several other families had occupied the room. To our surprise and dismay, we discovered that at least 75% of the 18 room alterations we had made were significantly altered. Storage bins were missing due to theft, the room had been repainted in a different color by well-meaning charity volunteers and the attached backrests (seemingly permanent) had been removed. Clearly there were forces that I had not anticipated when designing the bedroom that should have been detected and folded into the design process. It was a difficult but valuable lesson that understanding the challenge of designing for human well-being in this situation was best informed by multiple stakeholders' perspectives so that a project might be functional on both "ribbon-cutting day" and beyond.

24 Another way to put this is that a single POE can appraise different populations' responses to the same setting (editors).

25 Schon, op, cit., 50.

26 B.P. Meier and M.D. Robinson, "Why the Sunny Side is Up: Associations between Affect and Vertical Position," *Psychological Science* 15 (2004): 243–247.

27 Further information related to this study: J. Pable, "Through the Lens of Lived Human Experience: US Case Studies of Supportive Housing," *Government & Housing in a Time of Crisis: Policy, Planning, Design and Delivery. Architecture: Media, Politics, Society International Conference Proceedings* (Liverpool: Architecture: Media, Politics, Society, 2016), n.p.

28 As a part of my due diligence in confirming the need for a centralized information center on this topic, I surveyed 34 researchers, designers, social workers and advocacy organization administrators from across the United States on the need for such a resource. Approximately 70% felt it was "very important" to develop it. Further results of this survey can be found at http://designresourcesforhomelessness.org/about-us-1/.

29 The belief statement of *Design Resources for Homelessness* directly references several of the psychological constructs, describing that "dignity, empowerment, safety, function and economic efficiency can be supported by physical architecture." See http://designresourcesforhomelessness.org/.

30 While door locks may seem an obvious and ubiquitous feature in a sleeping space, many shelters do not permit residents to lock their doors because it makes bed checks difficult. This tension between safety procedure and sense of personal security is among the most frequent issues I encounter in my consultations with homeless shelters.

31 At the time of this writing, interior design researcher Dr. Yelena McLane and I are engaged in a study that compares the architectural design of resident community spaces in two supportive housing projects in the United States and the United Kingdom to examine their effectiveness from resident and staffs' points of view. Resident isolation is no minor matter as it is a common affliction among people experiencing homelessness and can lead to depression and even suicide. See R. Calati, C. Ferrari, M. Brittner, O. Oasi, E. Olié, A. Carvalho, and P. Courtet, "Suicidal Thoughts and Behaviors and Social Isolation: A Narrative Review of the Literature," *Journal of Affective Disorders* 245 (2019): 653–667.

32 For a review of five trauma-informed care frameworks see E. Hopper, E. Bassuk, and J. Olivet, "Shelter from the Storm: Trauma-informed Care in Homelessness Services Settings," *The Open Health Services and Policy Journal 3* (2010): 80–100.

33 See L. Rivlin, "The Significance of Home and Homelessness," *Marriage & Family Review* 15, no. 1–2 (1990): 39–56; L. Rivlin and J. Moore, "Home-Making: Supports and Barriers to the Process of Home", *Journal of Social Distress and the Homeless* 10, no. 4 (2001): 323–336; and D. Padgett and B. Henwood, "Qualitative Research for and in Practice: Findings from Studies with Homeless Adults Who Have Serious Mental Illness and Co-occurring Substance Abuse," *Clinical Social Work Journal* 40, no. 2 (2012): 187–193. While these works addressed built environment design only tangentially, their focus on user lived experience had clear implications for the design of built space, and the articles' points were often specifically related to the experience of persons experiencing homelessness. For example, Rivlin notes, we must question the kinds of memories that shelters, welfare hostels, transitional housing and the street are creating and their contributions to people's identities. They are not the ingredients of strong, positive feelings and a healthy sense of self. They are not likely to foster connections to places that contribute in positive ways to a person's identify. If anything they communicate a message of unworthiness that is threatening rather than supportive. (p. 49)

34 Logical argumentation is defined as engaging in reasoned consideration of a topic and drawing conclusions from evidence. Logical argumentation can use inductive reasoning by gathering a series of examples from others' works and arguing that the presence of these examples justifies a new conclusion that is bolstered by this related evidence. See University of New Orleans Learning Resource Center, "Making logical arguments," Writing Center, n.d., accessed July 2, 2019, www.uno.edu/lrc/writingcenter/documents/MAKING-LOGICAL-ARGUMENTS.pdf for a helpful summary.

35 Similarly, succinct frameworks were observed from Bird, 2017; Rivlin, 1990; Rivlin and Moore, 2001; and C. Despres, "The Meaning of Home: Literature Review and Directions for Future Research and Theoretical Development," *Journal of Architectural and Planning Research* 8, no. 2 (1991): 96–115.

36 Available at Design Resources for the Homeless. http://designresourcesforhomelessness.org/.

37 Within the case studies, the constructs influenced the decision that on-site photos would not be 'staged' or rooms altered or cleaned up before photos were taken so as to capture the full 'lived experience' of inhabiting the space.

38 A. Kearney and S. Kaplan, "Toward a Methodology for the Measurement of Knowledge Structures of Ordinary People the Conceptual Content Cognitive Map (3CM)," *Environment and Behavior* 29, no. 5 (1997): 579–617.

39 Some individual responses were striking. One homeless participant chose a mirror as an expression of self-esteem, stating, "A mirror shows that I 'exist' still because I can get lost in all the shuffling of being homeless." Another homeless participant pointed in the importance of sensory perceptions in a shelter by choosing a photo of a small room with two lounge chairs and an ottoman as a representation of stress management. She remarked that "this quiet setting makes me feel peaceful. Quiet conversation is favored over shouting in crowded rooms."

40 Eleven participants also proposed a further category such as "love," "thankfulness," "comfort," "humor" or "connection to nature." These will be taken into consideration for the development of sub-categories under the six main psychological constructs headings as a part of the study's analysis.

41 For example, phase one data suggested that people who have experienced homelessness may be more likely to choose a photo of a desk with a Wi-Fi-enabled computer than other groups for the stress reduction category. Perhaps this might reveal that homeless persons would choose this because the presence of a computer is less of a sure thing in their daily experience than the housed persons, or perhaps the internet represents needed escape from daily stress for someone experiencing homelessness.

42 Given the diversity of experiences persons who have lost their homes may have, this study should be replicated, potentially exploring sub-groups of people. For example, people who have been homeless for more than five years may have different perspectives than those who have been homeless for only a few months. There are many other groups that deserve inquiry too, such as adolescents aging out of the foster care system, veterans and victims of domestic violence.

43 Max Horkheimer, "Traditional and Critical Theory," in *Critical Theory, Selected Essays* (New York: Continuum Publishing, 2002), 215.

Chapter 9

Correlation

Editors' Introduction by Dana E. Vaux and David Wang

Correlation is a research strategy that uses statistical measures to describe a relationship between two variables. In correlational studies, the researcher examines what is naturally occurring in an environment, rather than attempting to control or manipulate variables. This makes correlation studies well suited for quantitative measures in interior design research, which, in general, seeks to understand the human–environment relationships in their natural settings. One challenge of correlating two variables in these natural settings is isolating them from other variables that might also be present. This chapter illustrates some of these challenges.

Gravetter and Wallnau in their text, *Statistics for Behavioral Sciences*, provide a simple example of correlation regarding the consumption of hot and cold beverages relative to temperature at a concession stand during an outdoor sporting event. When temperatures are warm, beer sales go up; when temperatures are cold, coffee sales go up. A direct correlation exists between the choice of beverage and the environmental temperature.[1]

A value of correlation research is its ability to establish predictive relationships between variables.[2] The predictive relationship is established by statistical significance, which is the *probability* that the relationship did not occur by chance. The *value* of one variable predicts the *value* of the other: when X changes, Y changes. Again, consider the example of beer and coffee sales mentioned above. When temperatures are warm, beer sales go up, so the vendor can expect to sell more beer. When temperatures are cold, coffee sales go up, so the vendor can expect to sell more coffee. However, while correlation describes the relationship between two variables, it does not provide proof of cause and effect. For example, even if coffee sales go up during cold days, we cannot know for certain that a particular person will purchase a cup of coffee rather than a bottle of beer; so cold weather cannot be said to *cause* purchases of cups of coffee.

Consider also Oscar Newman's study on crime in publicly funded low-income housing projects.[3] Newman found a *relationship* between the rate of crime and the height of an apartment building: the higher the building, the higher the crime rate. This relationship is established by statistical data. However, Newman's study does not establish that high-rise apartment buildings *cause* crime. Additionally, it does not establish a relationship between other factors and crime. Higher buildings may have more apartments and more tenants, but the study does not inform us whether these variables contribute to more crime, only that as building stories increase rate of crime increases.

Experts in correlation research suggest important points to consider in a correlational study that are evident in this chapter. First is this issue of cause-and-effect. Gravetter and Wallnau state that correlation "should not and cannot be interpreted as proof of a cause-and-effect relationship between two variables."[4] Linda Groat concurs, noting that correlation studies can "establish predictive relationships," but not causality.[5] Similarly, in this chapter Alana Pulay establishes a positive relationship between teacher satisfaction with classroom lighting, on the one hand, and teacher productivity, on the other. When teacher satisfaction with classroom lighting increases, their self-reported productivity increases. Pulay's study indicates a relationship between these two variables; but it does not prove that teacher satisfaction with classroom lighting *causes* increased teacher productivity. Establishing causality requires a researcher to purposely manipulate and isolate the variables under study while controlling for other variables (as one might do in an experimental study—see the Additional Connections and Information in Chapter 11) so that they do not influence the outcomes.[6]

Second, a correlational study measures two or more *specific* variables. Unlike qualitative methods of real-world settings in which variables emerge during observation, correlation studies can clarify and describe relationships among *predetermined* variables. Data is collected in the natural setting without manipulation.[7] This chapter illustrates how difficult it is for a researcher to isolate two variables in real-time classrooms where so many other factors are active. This is especially true when studying interior lighting due to the complexity of the contributing components that are likely to be present, such as varied luminaire and lamp types, the presence of exterior windows and views, as well as daylight. Correlational studies are most useful when the researcher seeks to clarify broad patterns, as Pulay does in this chapter.

Third, generalizations must be within a statistical range of data—the range of the data collected impacts the outcome and the possible validity of a correlation.[8] The range of data that Pulay collected—the high number of responses from teachers in school districts across the state of Oklahoma—strengthens the correlational relationship in her study. As an example, Pulay notes that other studies have correlated *student* productivity and satisfaction with classroom lighting. However, Pulay's range of data does not include students. Therefore, her findings are limited to the relationship between teacher satisfaction with lighting and teacher productivity and are not directly generalizable to student populations.

Fourth, "A correlation means … one variable *partially* predicts the other" as a percentage of the total variance.[9] For example, a correlation of 1:1 means that when X happens, Y happens 100% of the time. But a correlation of 0.5:1 does not predict a 50% occurrence. In correlation research, relationships between two variables under study are determined by *squaring* the variance. Hence, a 0.5:1 relationship indicates a 0.25 variability, or 25% likelihood of chance occurrence. According to Groat and Wang, "Typically, researchers consider the .05 level of significance (i.e. 5% likelihood of correlation) to be the minimum standard for generalization to a larger population."[10] Pulay's findings establish a 0.014 (or 1.4%) level of relationship between teacher productivity and lighting satisfaction. While this is a very small correlation that will require further validation for generalizability, we use this study to illustrate how two variables are established in a correlational study and, more specifically, to encourage future studies on these two variables.

In addition to establishing a relationship between variables, correlation research adds credibility to a study in other ways. Establishing a statistically significant correlation illustrates that the relationship between two variables is not due to chance. As Pulay notes in her conclusion, the value of this study is indicating that a relationship exists. While there is a great deal of literature on the impact of lighting satisfaction in other settings, no studies to date have established a relationship between teacher productivity and satisfaction with classroom lighting. Hence, the opportunity for future research on these variables. Remember again that this chapter found a very small statistical relationship between the two variables. The usefulness of this chapter is its clarity in illustrating how to identify, analyze, and correlate two variables.

Remember these important points for understanding correlation research while reading this chapter. (Please note that a glossary of statistical terms is provided by Pulay in the Additional Connections and Information section at the end of this chapter.)

1. A correlation describes a significant statistical relationship between variables but does not provide proof of cause and effect.
2. Consider how Pulay works to isolate perceptions of classroom lighting and perceptions of teacher productivity from other variables in a real-world setting. Critically think through the many scales Pulay uses in trying to clarify this correlation.
3. Outliers: responses that are outside the normal range can affect the value of the correlation. Notice in the analysis section of the chapter how Pulay accounts for this by ensuring the responses fall within a normal distribution.
4. A statistical correlation is proportional, suggests the strength of a relationship and demonstrates how much of the variance is explained by the relationship. In other words, a correlation can tell us about how likely one variable can effectively predict another variable.

Interiority

The Introduction to this book cites several commentators' definitions of "interiority." This book has cited Petra Perolini many times on this point.[11] Cathy Ganoe casts interiority as "internal values regarding social and personal awareness."[12] While Perolini's and Ganoe's insights are qualitative, design researchers ought not to think that interiority is only reachable by qualitative methods.

1. Quantitative methods, such as the statistics used in this chapter, offer numerical measures to assess an individual's sense of "insideness."
2. Pulay's work seeks a correlation between a teacher's *perceived* receptions of light quality in the classroom with how he or she productively performs work. This is accessing a teacher's "internal values regarding social and personal awareness."

* * * *

Chapter 9

Correlating Interior Lighting with Teacher Productivity Levels in the Public Pre-K–12 Classroom

Alana Pulay

Multiple studies, both experimental and non-experimental, have been performed on public K-12 classroom lighting in relation to student academic performance.[13] From these studies, we know that interior classroom lighting can influence student success. This study uses correlational research to study the relationship between teachers' perceptions of their classroom interior lighting with teachers' productivity levels. The research question is this: does a correlation exist between teacher satisfaction with classroom interior lighting and self-reported teacher productivity?

Literature

The literature tells us that interior lighting affects occupants' ability to view stimuli, impacts their mental state and also affects their overall comfort level within the space.[14] Interior lighting also impacts visual acuity.[15] However, no studies to date correlate public K-12 classrooms' interior lighting to teacher productivity. Therefore, to study this relationship, this chapter builds on previous studies that examine the impact of interior lighting on worker productivity in an office environment. Many office environment studies suggest that interior lighting influences worker productivity levels,[16] concentration, mood, cognition,[17] alertness levels,[18] depression and stress.[19] For these reasons, interior lighting is an important variable in office space design.[20]

Well-designed office lighting impacts visual comfort, defined as appropriate lighting levels to see objects and details clearly.[21] Good visual comfort results when colors appear the same inside as they would outside under the sun.[22] Good visual comfort also calls for uniform and balanced brightness, so that the interior environment has the same or similar illumination levels throughout. This reduces visual fatigue.[23] The literature also shows that interior lighting with equal proportions of direct and indirect lighting positively impacts occupant comfort. This means light is coming from multiple directions and not only from direct overhead lighting, thus reducing shadows.[24] And finally, spaces providing visual comfort tend to be free from glare, which occurs when brightness from a light source obscures a person's view.[25] Workplaces offering good visual comfort increase workers' mental states by decreasing visual fatigue. Low visual comfort results in possible negative health outcomes of burning, tired eyes and headaches, which negatively influence productivity levels.[26]

Workplace visual comfort includes not only the items mentioned above but also windows and views. Studies suggest that office workers are more productive when they have a desk located near a window and have access to sunlight and views to the exterior. This provides them with a connection to nature that keeps stress levels down and allows them to focus on the task at hand.[27] Another component to visual comfort is having personal control over the lighting level. Since employees perform different tasks and have different personal preferences, they prefer having control over their own desk light illumination levels.[28] Workplace studies suggest that when employees are satisfied with the workplace interior lighting due to good visual comfort, their productivity increases.[29]

Since the classroom is a teacher's workplace, literature for workplace settings can also apply to the teaching environment. Workers in many fields multitask, but this is particularly true for teachers who continually transition throughout the day from large-scale visual tasks (such as lecturing and using the white board) to small-scale visual tasks (such as working one-on-one with students at their desks or computers).[30] Visual fatigue is often an outcome of these types of transitions. Increasing visual comfort in the classroom with appropriate lighting design could help to reduce visual fatigue and contribute to increased teacher productivity.[31]

Methodology

An online survey was administered to public school teachers within the state of Oklahoma. The survey gathered information on two variables: (1) teachers' satisfaction with their classroom lighting, and (2) self-reported productivity levels. The aim was to see if a correlation existed between those two variables.

After obtaining IRB approval, a pilot test was first administered to a convenience sample of Oklahoma Family and Consumer Sciences teachers at a regional conference. In the pilot test, a paper survey was distributed for an expected higher response rate, which turned out to be 98% (n = 127).[32] One reason to conduct the pilot test was to confirm that the survey instrument captured sufficient data, and in the correct format, to answer the research question. The pilot test indicated no changes to the survey instrument were necessary for the current research.

Following the pilot test, the survey was administered using Qualtrics online software.[33] The survey was administered by email to all public school principals within the state of Oklahoma. One school district out of the 512 did not participate due to administrative guidelines that restricted participation. The email asked each principal to distribute the survey link to teachers at his or her school. The principal email listserv was obtained from the Oklahoma Department of Education website. The survey remained open for four weeks. Reminder emails were sent at the end of week 2, and then again with three days remaining. The email with the survey link was sent to 1,045 principals. This approach led to a total of 535 participants completing the online survey. Eighty-four percent of those were female and 14% were male, while ten participants preferred not to identify gender. Ninety-five percent of the participants (n = 508) worked full-time as a teacher. The majority of participants taught English (24%) or math (24%), and 40% of respondents taught in a high school setting. The survey instrument contained four sections:

Section 1: Demographic Information (Figures 9.1 and 9.2. This instrument was used to provide background information for the study subjects.)

Section 2: Cognitive Load Scale (Figure 9.3.This instrument was used to determine one of the two variables to be correlated: teacher productivity.)

Section 3: Classroom Lighting Scale (Figure 9.4. This instrument was used to determine the other variable to be correlated: teacher satisfaction with classroom lighting.)

Section 4: Classroom Interior Variables (Figure 9.5. This instrument was used to identify other variables that need to be ruled out as factors.)

Section 1: Demographic Information

This section used questions that were derived from the Teacher Questionnaire: Schools and Staffing Survey (SASS), which is a national survey of teachers. The SASS documents a teacher's background,

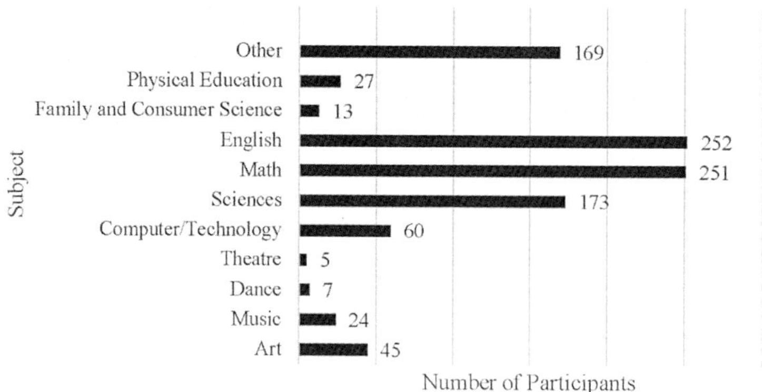

Figure 9.1 Subjects taught by study participants.

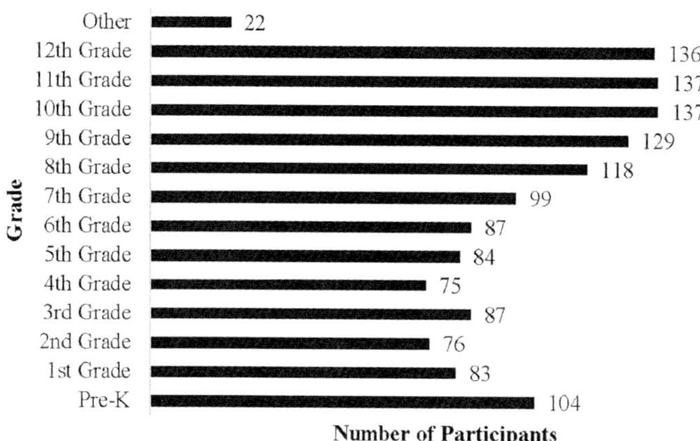

Figure 9.2 Grades taught by study participants.

work environment, professional development and teaching philosophy.[34] The current study only took questions from the background and work environment sections and collected information such as participant gender and age, years of teaching experience and grade levels and subjects taught. See Figures 9.1 and 9.2 for the results on subjects and grades taught.

Section 2: Cognitive Load Scale

This study used the Cognitive Load Scale since Oklahoma's Department of Education does not collect data on teacher productivity levels (Figure 9.3).[35] The Cognitive Load Scale is a valid method to gain productivity levels based upon previous studies performed by Hadie and Yusoff[36] and Pignatiello, Tsivitse and Hickman.[37] Pignatiello and colleagues define the cognitive load as "a multidimensional construct representing the load that performing a particular task imposes."[38]

The Cognitive Load Scale consists of five categories impacting productivity: mental demand, physical demand, time pressure, frustration level and effort level. In this study, each item measures

Cognitive Load Scale Items that participants responded to based on the five categories. Participants ranked each item on a 10 point scale, with 1 being Low and 10 being High.

Rate how much mental activity is required to teach
Rate how much physical activity is required to teach
How much pressure do you feel about the rate (or time) at which you are required to teach
Rate how hard do you have to work (mentally and physically) to accomplish your level of productivity in teaching
Rate how discouraged, irritated, stressed and annoyed you feel while teaching

Figure 9.3 Cognitive Load Scale.

the amount of demand required during teaching on a 10-point Likert scale, with 1 = low and 10 = high (refer to Figure 9.3 for questions). Participants were asked to respond to five questions relative to cognitive load. The responses are tabulated to find the mean, which defines the overall productivity score per participant. For example, if a participant responds 10 for mental demand, 3 for physical demand, 9 for time pressure, 6 for frustration and 8 for effort, the Cognitive Load Scale mean is 7.2. This was done for each participant and used in the analysis as the variable of teacher productivity level. (See Figure 9.3.)

Additionally, a Cronbach's alpha[39] was performed, in order to check the internal consistency to ensure that all of the questions in the Cognitive Load Scale were closely related to accurately measure cognitive load. Cronbach's alpha is a statistical test measuring whether a scale (in this case, the Cognitive Load Scale) is reliable. The Cronbach's alpha helps to ensure that all of the different, but related, questions on a given scale measure the same thing. Cronbach's alpha is considered acceptable if it is above 0.70. It is considered good from 0.80 to 0.89, and anything above 0.90 is considered excellent in determining the internal reliability of a scale. The Cognitive Load Scale questions came together as an internally consistent scale with an acceptable Cronbach's alpha of α = 0.70, which validates the reliability.[40]

Section 3: Classroom Lighting Scale

To collect data on the visual comfort of the classroom lighting, Section 3 of the survey instrument employed the Classroom Lighting Scale, which used questions from Eklund and Boyce's Office Lighting Survey.[41] This survey was developed in 1995 to document workers' opinions of office lighting conditions and lighting comfort levels and has been used for various workplace lighting studies.[42] Each question consists of a 5-point Likert scale ranging from (1) "Not at all Satisfied" to (5) "Extremely Satisfied." The items came together as an internally consistent scale with a good Cronbach's alpha of α = 0.81 (see Figure 9.4 for a list of questions).

In addition to the questions adapted from Eklund and Boyces' survey, the last question in Section 3 provided examples of six typical classroom luminaires and asked participants to select the image that best matched the overhead interior lighting in their classroom. These images represented the most common luminaires installed in public pre-K to 12th-grade school classrooms across the nation.[43] All of the luminaires were assumed to have fluorescent lamps. This information was gathered to identify which classroom interior lighting type exists. It helps to determine if there is a connection between classroom lighting type and teacher productivity. The six luminaire images included recessed 2×4, recessed can, pendant, surface mount, recessed 2×2 and troffer 2×2. Participants were also offered the option "none of the above."

Overall Satisfaction with Classroom Lighting Scale Items. Participants responded by ranking these on a 5-point Likert Scale.

Appropriate amount of interior lighting
Appropriate amount of windows to the exterior
Windows provide good views to the exterior
Distracting glare is present in my classroom from the windows
Windows provide good natural light into the classroom
All of the classroom lighting comes from the ceiling
Classroom lighting level is adjustable to accommodate various classroom activities
Overall classroom interior lighting

Figure 9.4 Classroom lighting scale. See credits.

Overall Satisfaction with Classroom Interior Variables. Participants responded by rating these items on a 5 point Likert Scale.

Overall functionality of classroom (size & function)
The classroom temperature is appropriate
There is distracting noise that impedes teaching
My desk storage space is adequate
There is adequate wall space to display personal and work material
Classroom wall paint color does not distract from displaying student work
The classroom flooring material makes it hard to teach
The classroom provides easy access to electrical outlets and ports
The classroom has the appropriate amount of electrical outlets and ports

Figure 9.5 Classroom Interior Variables.

Section 4: Classroom Interior Variables

Because of the many variables present within a classroom space, Section 4 obtained comprehensive data on teachers' perceptions of these other variables. These other variables were used as a control to identify if any variables outside of interior lighting contribute toward teacher productivity. The Classroom Interior Variables scale (Figure 9.5) was based upon the Learning Environment and Working Conditions Survey which has been used to document learning environments and working conditions.[44] These items were based upon a 5-point Likert scale ranging from (1) "Not at all Satisfied" to (5) "Extremely Satisfied." The items came together as an internally consistent scale with a good Cronbach's alpha of $\alpha = 0.82$. See Figure 9.5 for the variables included in this scale.

Analysis

Data was imported into the statistical software program SPSS, or "Statistical Package for Social Sciences." To ensure that all of the data was complete, accurate and imported correctly into SPSS, data cleaning was implemented. Cleaning the data requires consistency checks for any importing (copying and pasting) errors and addresses any missing data.[45] For this study, the participants who did not fully complete the survey were deleted ($n = 490$). Because the most common statistical tests rely on the normality of the sample, it is often useful to test whether the distribution is normally distributed. A normal distribution is when the data forms a symmetrical bell curve.[46] This can be checked graphically

Table 4

Skewness and Kurtosis of Variables Used in Analysis

Variable	Skewness	Kurtosis
Satisfaction with Lighting	-0.85	-0.68
Cognitive Load Scale	-0.96	1.65

Figure 9.6 Skewness and kurtosis.

by a histogram or by checking skewness and kurtosis through SPSS. Skew involves the symmetry of the distribution while kurtosis is a measure of whether the data is skewed too much to the left or to the right. Skew should fall between −1,1 and kurtosis should be between −2,2.[47] For the variables used in this analysis, there were no outliers present, and skew and kurtosis values were within the normal range. (Figure 9.6 shows that variables fall within accepted distributions.)

After ensuring the data was normally distributed, descriptive statistics were used to describe participant demographics and determine the average satisfaction with classroom lighting. A Pearson correlational analysis was conducted to analyze teachers' satisfaction with classroom lighting and self-reported productivity from the Cognitive Load Scale. Pearson correlation assesses the linear relationship between two continuous variables. A linear relationship is when a change in one variable is associated with a proportional change in the other variable. Pearson correlation is a number between −1 and 1, where 1 implies all data points lie on a line that increases and −1 implies that all data points lie on a line which decreases. A value of 0 implies there is no linear relationship.[48]

To identify if lighting type is associated with teacher productivity, a one-way ANOVA was performed between the results of the lighting types from Section 3 of the survey and teachers self-reported productivity from the Cognitive Load Scale. A one-way ANOVA determines if there is any statistically significant differences between the means of two or more groups.[49] The groups were based upon the six types of luminaires mentioned in Section 3 of the survey. Since no teachers reported having recessed can lighting, the result was six groups, which are: 1. 2×4 (n = 18), 2. pendant (n = 14), 3. surface mount (n = 53), 4. 2×2 (n = 306), 5. trouffered 2×2 (n = 74), and 6. none of the above (n = 16).

Finally, a step-wise regression analysis was performed to identify if the other Classroom Interior Variables from Figure 9.5 are predictors of teacher productivity. Regression analysis is a statistical test used to identify potential relationships between two or more variables and often used in studies to control for outside variables.[50] In this case, regression can determine if the other Classroom Interior Variables from Table 3 contributed towards teacher productivity. For step 1 of this study, all of the Classroom Interior Variables were put into a regression model to determine if any were statistically significant with teacher productivity. Then, for step 2, satisfaction with interior lighting was added to the regression model. The percent of variance explained by each model was then compared to indicate the proportion of variation that occurs from the Classroom Interior Variables on teacher productivity compared to the model that included satisfaction with interior lighting.[51]

Results

Descriptive statistics performed on lighting satisfaction indicate that, on average, participants reported their level of overall classroom lighting as satisfied. Refer to Figure 9.7 for all descriptive statistics results. Seventy-eight percent of participants (n = 387) rated their overall classroom lighting as "Satisfied," "Somewhat Extremely Satisfied" and "Extremely Satisfied." Almost half, 49%, of participants (n = 241) indicated that they are "Not at all Satisfied" or "Somewhat Not Satisfied" with the adjustability or control over their classroom lighting.

Descriptive statistics within the Cognitive Load Scale indicate that participants reported their productivity levels as high (M = 7.26, SD = 1.58 on a 10-point scale). Teacher productivity levels were statistically significant, and positively related to their satisfaction of the classroom lighting ($r = 0.12$, $p = 0.007$). The positive correlation between the two variables was statistically significant ($p < 0.01$).

A one-way ANOVA was conducted to determine if teachers' self-reported productivity level was different based upon lighting of their classroom. The luminaires were classified into six different groups, as noted above. There were no statistically significant differences in teacher productivity levels based on luminaire types as determined by one-way ANOVA ($F(5, 475) = 0.64$, $p < 0.67$). This may be in part due to the fact that results indicated that 70% of teachers reported having 2×2 luminaires recessed into acoustical ceiling tiles in their classroom.

A step-wise multiple regression was conducted to evaluate whether the other variables from the classroom Interior Variables scale (referenced in Figure 9.5) influenced teacher productivity levels. At step 1 of the analysis, all variables from the Classroom Interior Variable scale were entered into the regression equation and was not significantly related to teacher productivity levels ($F(9, 459) = 1.059$, $p > 0.05$). The multiple correlation coefficient was 0.020, indicating approximately 2% of the variance of teacher productivity could be accounted for by these other classroom variables. Satisfaction with lighting was entered into the equation at step 2 of the analysis. Satisfaction with classroom lighting is a positive significant predictor of teacher productivity levels $F(10, 458) = 1.65$, $p < 0.05$). The multiple correlation coefficient was 0.034, indicating an increase of 1.4% variance of teacher productivity when lighting is added into the equation. See Figure 9.8.

Findings of the study support the hypothesis that satisfaction with classroom interior lighting is positively correlated to teacher productivity as indicated in the Pearson Correlation. Results from the one-way ANOVA showed no statistical relationship between classroom lighting and teacher productivity. While controlling for other interior classroom variables in the regression analysis, satisfaction with classroom lighting explains only around 1.4% of the variance in teacher productivity. The regression analysis indicated that when other interior classroom variables are accounted for, they contribute 2% toward teacher productivity. When satisfaction with lighting is added to these other classroom variables, together they contribute 3.4% toward teacher productivity.

Descriptive Statistics from Classroom Lighting Scale using a 5-point Likert Scale (n = 490)

Item	Mean	Standard Deviation	Variance
Appropriate amount of interior lighting	3.95	1.09	1.18
Appropriate amount of windows to the exterior	3.35	1.41	2.00
Windows provide good views to the exterior	3.02	1.44	2.07
Distracting glare is present in my classroom from the windows	3.05	1.29	1.68
Windows provide good natural light into the classroom	3.19	1.41	1.99
All of the classroom lighting comes from the ceiling	3.19	1.26	1.6
Classroom lighting level is adjustable to accommodate various classroom activities	2.63	1.38	1.91
Overall classroom interior lighting	3.34	1.12	1.25

Figure 9.7 Descriptive statistics.

Overall Satisfaction with Classroom Interior Variables on a 5-point Likert Scale (n=477)

Item	Mean	Standard Deviation	Variance
Overall functionality of classroom (size & function)	2.70	1.22	1.49
The classroom temperature is appropriate.	2.65	1.28	1.63
There is a distracting noise that impedes teaching	2.99	1.21	1.47
My desk storage space is adequate.	2.81	1.28	1.64
There is adequate wall space to display personal and work material.	2.65	1.28	1.63
Classroom wall paint color does not distract from displaying student work.	2.23	1.14	1.30
The classroom flooring material makes it hard to teach.	2.92	1.24	1.54
The classroom provides easy access to electrical outlets and ports.	3.22	1.33	1.78
The classroom has the appropriate amount of electrical outlets and ports.	3.12	1.31	1.71

Figure 9.8 Classroom Interior Variable Scale.

While interior lighting is 1.4% of influence on teacher productivity, which is a very small amount, given that it was statistically significant (i.e. above 0), independently and in addition to other classroom variables, it is enough evidence to support additional studies on this topic.

Discussion and Future Considerations

A strength of this study was the number of participants and the diverse sample of Oklahoma public school teachers, including participants from across the state, school buildings of varied type and vintage, as well as different budgets. The sample also represented participants from all grades (K-12) and various subjects in addition to multiple years of teaching experience.

This study demonstrated the complexity of variables that need to be accounted for in the built environment. One of the interior lighting variables that needed to be accounted for was the lighting type in each classroom. The study hoped to discover whether teachers might have different responses to different luminaires. Results indicated that the majority of classroom lighting is 2' × 2' recessed luminaires installed in acoustical ceiling tiles and that none of the classrooms in the study had recessed can-lights. While it was beneficial to identify this information to understand the lighting in each classroom, the current study did not benefit from this question because the result of the finding was not statistically significant. Future studies identifying differences in classroom lighting type could help to inform the specification of appropriate classroom lighting in design projects. This information might also justify a shift in budgetary funds toward improving classroom lighting.

In future studies, a different instrument to gather this data or a different research method could uncover the link between lighting type and teacher productivity. For example, the researcher might ask participants to upload a digital photograph of their classroom luminaires rather than choose from a selection of images provided. This would help in analyzing the state of the current classroom lighting based on the current classroom lighting type.

Conclusion

The overall goal of this correlational study was to determine if a relationship exists between teacher productivity and classroom lighting. While study findings revealed lighting to have a low percentage of influence (1.4%) on productivity, the results show a correlation and therefore warrant additional research on this topic. Furthermore, since no studies have examined pre-K–12 public school teachers regarding their classroom interior environment, future studies with more precise instruments could yield better and more accurate results. The results of this study should be used as a foundation for future research focusing on the relationship between public school classroom interior lighting and teacher productivity.

* * * *

Discussion and Exercises

Reflections about the Chapter You Just Read:

1. Please refer to the standard features of a research project explained in the Introduction. Then:
   a. In one sentence, identify the *research topic.* This sentence can be in the form of a question but does not have to be. In any case, write one grammatically correct sentence that captures the research topic of this chapter.
   b. Identify the *literature* related to this research project.
   c. Identify the *method* which the author used and also the *data* which this method generated for analysis.
   d. Explain how this approach is *generalizable* (or not).
   e. Explain how you can have confidence (or not) of the *internal and external validity* of this author's overall approach.
2. Although the statistical relationship is small, Pulay's study indicates a positive correlation between teacher productivity and teacher satisfaction with classroom lighting. When teacher satisfaction with lighting goes up, teacher self-reported productivity goes up. How can this information be useful for lighting design in classrooms? For lighting design in general? What additional information or variables might a design researcher need to uncover in order to explain that relationship? Provide specific examples.
3. Discuss the limitations of determining both variables (satisfaction with classroom light and teacher productivity) by self-reporting.
4. Consider that this study measures teacher productivity based on a survey distributed by school principals who *evaluate* teacher performance. How might this influence teachers' self-reporting?
5. Pulay's respondents consist of teachers from all grades K-12. This is an enormous difference in student age and maturity. How might this factor impact the validity of Pulay's findings?

Exercises/Suggestions for Further Study:

1. Conduct a study on non-design students' satisfaction with lighting and classroom seating (Please clear with your IRB as needed.).
   a. Create and conduct a survey by modifying the questions in Figure 9.4, *Satisfaction with Classroom Lighting Scale*, for students.

b. Calculate the means of the results to indicate student level of satisfaction with lighting. (To do this, add the numbers for each respondent's total score and then divide the total by the number of questions; the sum divided by the count.)
c. Map the location of the students' desks and compare it with the level of satisfaction. Use a graph to compare location of seating to light level. (See William Whyte's study *The Social Life of Small Urban Spaces* for an example of a seating placement and preference. A short video version is available at: https://www.metalocus.es/en/news/social-life-small-urban-spaces.)
d. Do your findings suggest any correlation between the location of students' desks and satisfaction with classroom lighting?

2. Pulay uses surveys to collect her data in this chapter. In *Architectural Research Methods*, Groat and Wang refer to additional tactics useful for collecting data in correlational studies.[52] These include observation, mapping, sorting, and archives. Design a research study using some of the tactics suggested by Groat to correlate two variables. Next, suggest how you might study the same two variables using an alternative tactic.
3. Read the following additional studies that measure different aspects of electric lighting and human response. Evaluate the similarities and differences between these studies and Pulay's study. Are these methods interchangeable? Are there reasons why certain methods might be more useful to a specific environment?

Day, Julia, Judy Theodorson, and Kevin Van Den Wymelenberg. "Understanding controls, behaviors and satisfaction in the daylit perimeter office: a daylight design case study." *Journal of Interior Design* 37, no. 1 (2012): 17–34.

Hegde, Asha L., and Jesse McCoy Rogers. "Effects of Light, Illuminance and Color on Subjective Impression Rankings." Design Principles & Practice: An International Journal 6, no. 1 (2012): 33-44.

Theodorson, Judy. "Architectural Vocabularies: exploring the analogous relationship between light and water." Retrievable from archives-ouvertes.fr. (2016).

Additional Connections and Information

1. Glossary. Pulay references many technical terms in this chapter common to quantitative research. She provides definitions of these terms in the following list:

ANOVA stands for *analysis of variance*, which is a statistical method that compares the means from two or more unrelated groups. A one-way ANOVA has one independent variable, whereas a two-way ANOVA has two independent variables.

Continuous variables are numbers that are consecutive such as 1 to 7. In this research study, Likert scale data is the sum of multiple items and thus treated as continuous. They are often used in survey research to ask participants their opinions of a statement. The overall satisfaction with lighting scale used in this study is an example of a Likert scale. This scale asked participants to rate their satisfaction of classroom lighting in one of five categories. The categories were arranged in order from "Strongly Agree" to "Strongly Disagree."

Convenience sample is when participants are selected based upon how easy it is to find them or if they are readily available.

Correlation: explains the relationship between two variables. It is a number on a scale between –1 and +1, which indicates if the correlation is a positive relationship or negative relationship. The closer to 1 or –1, the stronger the positive or negative relationship. A value of 0 means no relationship exists.

Descriptive statistics are used to describe, show or summarize the data. This can include mean, standard deviation or variance, minimum and maximum values, kurtosis and skewness.

Histogram is a graphical representation of the data using bars of varying height. Each bar contains a range of numbers; the higher the bar, the more data in that range of numbers.

Homogeneity of variance is a statistical assumption when performing ANOVAs in which the population distribution between two samples is equal.

Internal consistency: how closely a set of items in a group is related.

Kurtosis and skewness: Skew involves the symmetry of the distribution, while kurtosis is a measure of whether the data is long tailed or light tailed relative to the normal distribution.[53] Data sets with higher kurtosis tend to have outliers, or data that is outside of the bell curve, which makes the bell curve asymmetrical, thus indicating the sample is not normally distributed.

Normal distribution describes how variables are distributed. A normal distribution will ensure there are no outliers that will influence the results.

Normality means that the data fits a symmetrical bell curve shape. Normality is needed before performing certain statistical tests.

Pearson correlation is a number on the scale between –1 and 1 that assesses the *linear* relationship of two variables. A positive number (above 0) implies that most data points lie on a line that increases. A negative number (below 0) implies that most data points lie on a line that decreases. A value of 0 implies there is no linear relationship.[54]

Pilot test: a preliminary research study that tests the validity of the tactics.

Reliability: means the results are consistent when tested numerous times.

Response rate: defined as the number of people who completed the survey divided by the number of people who make up the total sample group. For example, if 129 people were given a pilot test survey and 127 completed the survey, one would divide 127 by 129 for a survey response rate of 98%.

Sample size described as a sample of a population. For instance, teachers were used in this study. They don't represent all teachers (population), but researchers use a sample (sample) in order to make inferences for the population, since it's unrealistic to study the entire population.[55]

Statistical significance indicates that the relationship between two variables is occurring not purely by chance.

Step-wise regression analysis: a set of regression models that give details about how the variables vary with each other. The results are the variables that best explain the distribution.

Validity means that the findings truly represent what you are claiming to measure.

2. A *Scatter plot* is a graphical way to display two variables of data. Each data point is a representation of the value of one variable on the horizontal (x) axis while the other variable value is represented as a position on the vertical (y) axis. A scatter plot displays the relationship and distribution of the data. Below (see Figure 9.8) is a scatter plot based on Pulay's findings. The scatter plot can help us understand the Pearson correlation in several ways:

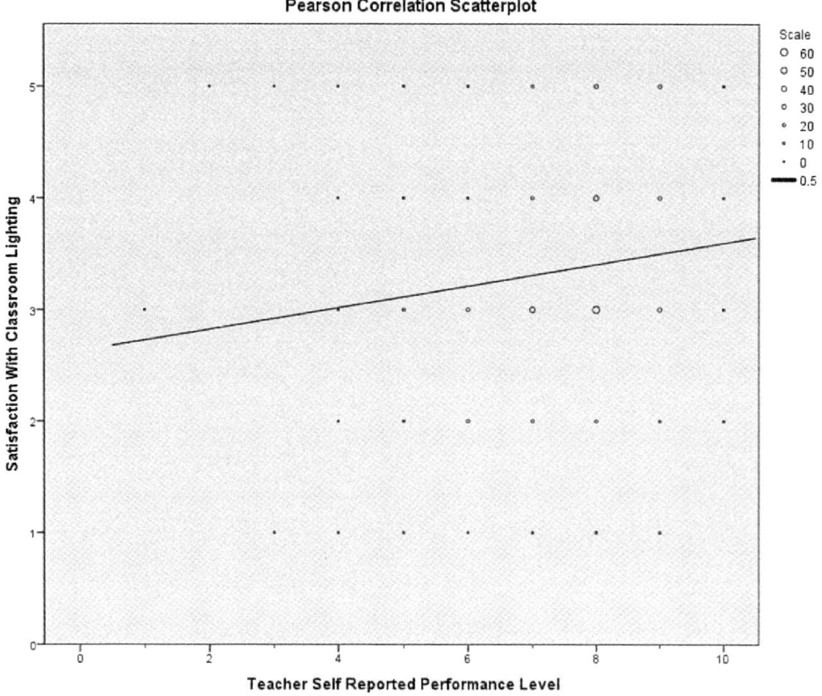

Figure 9.9 Scatter plot.

a. The direction of the correlation, whether positive or negative, is shown on the plot. Notice how the scatter plot from this study conveys the general trend in these data as a positive linear relationship between the information on the x axis (teacher self-reported performance) and the information on the y axis (satisfaction with classroom lighting): as numerical values of (y) satisfaction with classroom lighting increase, the numerical values of (x) teacher self-reported performance increase. Teachers who are satisfied with the lighting in their classroom tend to report higher levels of productivity. (If it were a negative relationship, the linear expression would go the other direction, indicating that as one variable increases the other decreases.)
b. In the scatter plot, the points tend to form a straight line if the measure is consistent. Notice how these data points from Pulay's study increase in size as the value of each variable increases (as noted in the scale, the largest circle equal to 60, the smallest equal to 0). This line indicates the consistency and predictability of the correlation. If the data points were scattered randomly with no clear trend of relationship between increases and decreases in values, it would indicate no consistency or correlational relationship (Figure 9.9).

3. Additional literature related to correlation research and lighting:

Biswas, Dipayan, Courtney Szocs, Roger Chacko, and Brian Wansink. "Shining light on atmospherics: How ambient light influences food choices." *Journal of Marketing Research* 54, no. 1 (2017): 111–123.

Frederick J. Gravetter and Larry B. Wallnau. *Statistics for the Behavioral Sciences*, 8th ed., Belmont, CA: Wadsworth, Cengage Learning, 2009, 519–561.

Hegde, Asha. "Understanding sensory processing disorder and their considerations in the built environment." *Lighting Design and Application* 45, no.1 (2015): 56–60.

Al Horr, Y., M. Arif, A. Kaushik, A. Mazroei, M. Katafygiotou, and E. Elsarrag. "Occupant productivity and office indoor environment quality: A review of the literature." *Building and Environment* 105 (2016): 369–389.

Oscar Newman, *Defensible Space: Crime Prevention through Urban Design*. New York: Macmillan, 1972.

Scott, Jennifer, and Judy Theodorson. "Psychological, physiological, and phenomenological effects of colored light." *SHS Web of Conferences*, vol. 64, p. 01001. EDP Sciences, 2019.

Notes

1 Frederick J. Gravetter and Larry B. Wallnau, *Statistics for the Behavioral Sciences*, 8th ed. (Belmont, CA: Wadsworth, Cengage Learning, 2009), 522.

2 Ibid., 534; Linda Groat and David Wang, *Architectural Research Methods*, 2nd ed. (New York: Wiley, 2002), 309.

3 Oscar Newman, *Defensible Space* (New York: Macmillan, 1972).

4 Gravetter and Wallnau, op. cit., 531.

5 Ibid.

6 Groat and Wang, op. cit., 309.

7 Ibid. This characteristic means that it is particularly appropriate in circumstances when variables either *can't* be manipulated for practical reasons or *shouldn't* be manipulated for ethical reasons ... one of the strategy's great advantages is its potential for studying the range and extent of multiple variables. However, its consequent disadvantage is that a robust and deep understanding of that circumstance may not be revealed.

8 Ibid.

9 Groat and Wang, op. cit., 309.

10 Perolini, op. cit., 170.

11 Cathy J. Ganoe, "Design as Narrative: A Theory of Inhabiting Interior Space," *Journal of Interior Design* 25, no. 2 (1999): 1.

12 Peter Barrett et al., "The Holistic Impact of Classroom Spaces on Learning in Specific Subjects," *Environment and Behavior* 49, no. 4 (May 2017): 425–451. https://doi.org/10.1177/0013916516648735; Sapna Cheryan et al., "Designing Classrooms to Maximize Student Achievement," ed. Susan T. Fiske, *Policy Insights from the Behavioral and Brain Sciences* 1, no. 1 (October 2014): 4–12. https://doi.org/10.1177/2372732214548677; Valeria De Giuli, Osvaldo Da Pos, and Michele De Carli, "Indoor Environmental Quality and Pupil Perception in Italian Primary Schools," *Building and Environment* 56 (October 2012): 335–345. https://doi.org/10.1016/j.buildenv.2012.03.024; Melissa A. Milkie and Catharine H. Warner, "Classroom Learning Environments and the Mental Health of First Grade Children," *Journal of Health and Social Behavior* 52, no. 1 (2011): 4–22. http://www.jstor.org/stable/23033160; Alana Pulay and Amy Williamson, "A Case Study Comparing the Influence of LED and Fluorescent Lighting on Early Childhood Student Engagement in a Classroom Setting," *Learning Environments Research* 22, no. 1 (April 2019): 13–24. https://doi.org/10.1007/s10984-018-9263-3; Sanaz Ahmadpoor Samani and Soodeh Ahmadpoor Samani, "The Impact of Indoor Lighting on Students' Learning Performance in Learning Environments: A Knowledge Internalization Perspective," *International Journal of Business and Social Science* 3, no. 24 (2012): 11; Cynthia L. Uline et al., "Improving the Physical and Social Environment of School: A Question of Equity," *Journal of School Leadership* 20, no. 5 (September 2010): 597–632. https://doi.org/10.1177/105268461002000504.

13 Yousef Al horr and others, "Impact of Indoor Environmental Quality on Occupant Well-Being and Comfort: A Review of the Literature," *International Journal of Sustainable Built Environment* 5, no. 1 (June 2016): 1–11. https://doi.org/10.1016/j.ijsbe.2016.03.006; Peter Boyce and Christopher Cuttle, "Effect of Correlated Colour Temperature on the Perception of Interiors and Colour Discrimination Performance," *Lighting Research & Technology* 22, no. 1 (March 1990): 19–36. https://doi.org/10.1177/096032719002200102; Breanne K. Hawes et al., "Effects of Four Workplace Lighting Technologies on Perception, Cognition and Affective State," *International Journal of Industrial Ergonomics* 42, no. 1 (January 2012): 122–128. https://doi.org/10.1016/j.ergon.2011.09.004; Judith Heerwagen and Dean Heerwagen, "Lighting and Psychological Comfort," *W+A* 16, no. 4 (1986): 47–51.

14 Geun Young Yun et al., "A Field Survey of Visual Comfort and Lighting Energy Consumption in Open Plan Offices," *Energy and Buildings* 46 (March 2012): 146–151. https://doi.org/10.1016/j.enbuild.2011.10.035.

15 Igor Knez and Christina Kers, "Effects of Indoor Lighting, Gender, and Age on Mood and Cognitive Performance," *Environment and Behavior* 32, no. 6 (November 2000): 817–831. https://doi.org/10.1177/0013916500326005.

16 Pubuduni Anuradha Meegahapola and Ranga Prabodanie, "Impact of Environmental Conditions on Workers' Productivity and Health," *International Journal of Workplace Health Management* 11, no. 2 (April 3, 2018): 74–84. https://doi.org/10.1108/IJWHM-10-2017-0082.

17 Jacqueline Vischer, "The Effects of the Physical Environment on Job Performance: Towards a Theoretical Model of Workspace Stress," *Stress and Health* 23, no. 3 (2007): 175–184.
18 Meegahapola and Prabodanie, op. cit., 74–84.
19 Yousef Al Horr and others, "Occupant Productivity and Office Indoor Environment Quality: A Review of the Literature," *Building and Environment* 105 (August 2016): 369–389. https://doi.org/10.1016/j.buildenv.2016.06.001; Philomena Bluyssen, Sabine Janssen, and Fons Van De Vijver, "Assessment of Wellbeing in an Indoor Office Environment," *Building and Environment* 14, no. 12 (2011): 2632–2640; Heerwagen and Heerwagen, "Lighting and Psychological Comfort"; Knez and Kers, op. cit., 817–831; Veronika Kretschmer, Karl-Heinz Schmidt, and Barbara Griefahn, "Bright Light Effects on Working Memory, Sustained Attention and Concentration of Elderly Night Shift Workers," *Lighting Research & Technology* 44, no. 3 (September 2012): 316–333. https://doi.org/10.1177/1477153511418769; Vischer, "Effects," op. cit., 175–184; Nastaran Shishegar and Mohamed Boubekri, "Natural Light and Productivity: Analyzing the Impacts of Daylighting on Students' and Workers' Health and Alertness," *International Journal of Advances in Chemical Engineering and Biological Sciences* 3, no. 1 (May 21, 2016). https://doi.org/10.15242/IJACEBS.AE0416104.
20 Jennifer A. Veitch, "Psychological Processes Influencing Lighting Quality," *Journal of the Illuminating Engineering Society* 30, no. 1 (January 2001): 124–140. https://doi.org/10.1080/00994480.2001.10748341.
21 Boyce and Cuttle, op. cit., 19–36.
22 Ibid., 19.
23 Kretschmer, Schmidt, and Griefahn, op. cit., 316–333.
24 Anna Steidle and Lioba Werth, "In the Spotlight: Brightness Increases Self-Awareness and Reflective Self-Regulation," *Journal of Environmental Psychology* 39 (September 2014): 40–50. https://doi.org/10.1016/j.jenvp.2013.12.007.
25 Heerwagen and Heerwagen, op. cit., 47–52; Kretschmer, Schmidt, and Griefahn, op. cit., 316–333.
26 Al Horr and others, op. cit., 5–11.
27 So Young Lee and Jay L. Brand, "Effects of Control over Office Workspace on Perceptions of the Work Environment and Work Outcomes," *Journal of Environmental Psychology* 25, no. 3 (September 2005): 323–333. https://doi.org/10.1016/j.jenvp.2005.08.001.
28 Al Horr and others, op. cit., 5–11. Vischer, "Effects," op. cit., 175–184; Lee and Brand, op. cit., 323–333.
29 Illuminating Engineering Society, "American National Standard Practice on Lighting for Educational Facilities." (Illuminating Engineering Society of North America, 2014).
30 Ibid.
31 The nomenclature "*n*" indicates the number of respondents.
32 Qualtrics is a common survey instrument and has been used as an instrument for the current study to administer, manage and collect data for online surveys. Qualtrics. www.Qualtrics.com.
33 National Center for Education Statistics, "Teacher Questionnaire School and Staffing Survey" (U.S. Department of Education, 201–2011). https://nces.ed.gov/surveys/sass/pdf/1112/SASS4A.pdf.
34 Fred Paas, Alexander Renkl, and John Sweller, "Cognitive Load Theory and Instructional Design: Recent Developments," *Educational Psychologist* 38, no. 1 (March 2003): 1–4. https://doi.org/10.1207/S15326985EP3801_1; Tilanka Chandrasekera and So-Teon Yoon, "The Effect of Tangible User Interfaces on Cognitive Load in the Creative Design Process," *IEEE International Symposium on Mixed and Augmented Reality – Media, Art, Social Science, Humanities and Design* (Washington, DC: IEEE Computer Society, 2015), xiv–xvi. https://doi.org/10.1109/ISMAR-MASH'D.2015.18.
35 Siti Nurma Hanim Hadie and Muhamad Saiful Bahri Yusoff, "Assessing the Validity of the Cognitive Load Scale in Problem-Based Learning Setting," *Journal of Taibah University Medical Sciences* 11, no. 3 (2016): 194–202.
36 Grant Pignatiello, Emily Tsivitse, and Ronald Hickman, "A Preliminary Psychometric Evaluation of the Eight-Item Cognitive Load Scale," *Applied Nursing Research* 40 (2018): 99–105.
37 Ibid., 100.
38 Mohsen Tavakol and Reg Dennick, "Making Sense of Cronbach's Alpha," *International Journal of Medical Education* 2 (2011): 53–55. Cronbach's alpha is a statistical test measuring whether a scale (in this case, the Cognitive Load Scale) is reliable.
39 Jose M. Cortina, "What Is Coefficient Alpha? An Examination of Theory and Applications," *What Is Coefficient Alpha? An Examination of Theory and Applications* 78, no. 1 (1993): 98.
40 Neil H. Eklund and Peter R. Boyce, "The Development of a Reliable, Valid, and Simple Office Lighting Survey," *Journal of the Illuminating Engineering Society* 25, no. 2 (1996): 25–40.
41 Al Horr and others, op. cit., 6; Bluyssen, Janssen, and Van De Vijver, op. cit., 2630–2640; Boyce and Cuttle, op. cit., 19–36; Knez and Kers, op. cit., 817–831; Lee and Brand, op. cit., 323.
42 For typical images see Illuminating Engineering Society, "American National Standard Practice on Lighting for Educational Facilities."
43 Peter Barrett and others, "The Holistic Impact of Classroom Spaces on Learning in Specific Subjects," *Environment and Behavior* 49, no. 4 (May 2017): 425–451. https://doi.org/10.1177/0013916516648735.
44 William Neuman, *Social Research Methods: Qualitative and Quantitative Approaches*, 7th ed. (Boston, MA: Pearson, 2010).
45 David J. Sheskin, *Handbook of Parametric and Nonparametric Statistical Procedures*, 5th ed. (Boca Raton, FL: Chapman & Hall, 2011), 500–619.
46 Edward R. Mansfield and Billy P. Helms, "Detecting Multicollinearit," *The American Statistician* 36, no. 3a (n.d.): 158–160. https://doi.org/10.1080/00031305.1982.10482818; Peter H. Westfall, "Kurtosis as Peakedness; 1905–2014. R.I.P," *The American Statistician* 68 (2014): 191–195; E. Mansfield and B. Helms, "Detecting Multicollinearit," *The American Statistician* 36, no. 3a (n.d.): 158–160. https://doi.org/10.1080/00031305.1982.10482818.
47 Laerd Statistics, "One-Way ANOVA; SPSS Statistics," n.d., https://statistics.laerd.com/premium/spss/owa/one-way-anova-in-spss.php.

48 Quirk, "Excel 2010 for Social Science Statistics: A Guide to Solving Practical Problems."
49 Groat and Wang, op. cit., 309.
50 Westfall, op. cit., 158–160.
51 Gravetter and Wallnau, op. cit., 526.
52 Ibid, op. cit., 4.

Chapter 10

Scale Creation

Editors' Introduction by Dana E. Vaux and David Wang

Third places are widely studied in interior design. In fact, at the time of this writing, Lisa Waxman's article on coffee shops and third places is the most cited article in the *Journal of Interior Design*.[1] However, as Langlais and Vaux point out in this chapter, individuals now socially gather as frequently in cyberspace as they do in "real" space. In response to this phenomenon, Langlais and Vaux created a scale to measure whether social networking sites (SNS)—specifically Facebook, Snapchat, Instagram and Twitter—can also be third places.

Researchers often utilize different types of scales as tools for comparison, coalescing data, and to make qualitative (open-ended) data measurable. In the previous chapter, Pulay uses research-informed scales that have been validated in previous studies to establish a correlation between two factors: classroom lighting and teacher productivity. In this chapter, Langlais and Vaux critically analyze relevant literature to *create* a scale.

After creating the scale, the authors then use it to test if Facebook, Snapchat, Instagram and Twitter qualify as third places. As a follow-up, they also conduct analyses to examine differences between all four of these SNS in the context of how well they meet third place criteria and answer the question: does one network meet characteristics of third places more than the others? In order to conduct this analysis, the means (or the averages) for the third place characteristics for each social media network are compared to determine if they are significantly different from one another. The typical way to compare means is by conducting independent sample *t*-tests, which are statistical tests that compare the averages of data between two independent groups, such as men and women. However, this approach is only effective when comparing two groups. If you are comparing more than two groups (such as the four social media in this study), analysis of variances (ANOVAs) are conducted. This approach tests whether different groups are statistically different from each other, taking into consideration the sample size (number of participants in the study) and standard deviation (amount of deviation from the mean) in order to determine if two means are different or not. A benefit of using these approaches is that you can potentially rank by mean the compared variables from lowest to highest, or vice versa, based on the results. In the case of this chapter, Langlais and Vaux organize the social media by how much they align with third place characteristics.

As you read the chapter, notice the process Langlais and Vaux use to conduct their study:

1. They review literature on virtual and physical third places.
2. They create a scale based on findings from previous studies.
3. They use the scale to test the "thirdplaceness" of four social networking sites.

Interiority

Throughout this textbook, a common theme emerges that interior design is not limited to physical spaces enclosed within four walls. We use the technical term *interiority* to explain how subjective experiences of "feeling inside" range from personal perceptions which constitute an "interior" and impact one's outlook, to entire neighborhoods as interior places. In this chapter, the authors expand the context of interiority to digital spaces without physical attributes. Individuals develop and maintain relationships in cyberspace, wholly separate from physical space. These relations take place within a digital interior that is not only interior to a person but also have extension in some sort of spatial sense. However, an individual must be somewhere in "real" space in order to access Facebook. As technology merges physical and virtual reality in individuals' everyday lives as they work, live and socialize, understanding space as a digital environment as well as a physical one can impact design decisions.[2]

The theoretical value of Langlais and Vaux's chapter is expanding the concept of third place to include the *union* of these two realities into a new dimension of what "interior" can mean. Additionally, their research contributes a quantitative approach to the third place literature. As you read:

1. Notice how each of the four social media are distinctly different but also similar to a sense of "thirdplaceness" in physical third places.
2. In their conclusions, notice the questions Langlais and Vaux raise on issues regarding the interface of physical and virtual space and the potential multi-level experience of being in two "places" at the same time.

* * * *

Measuring the "Thirdplaceness" of Social Media

Michael R. Langlais and Dana E. Vaux

Third places offer and promote social experiences associated with benefits for building interpersonal relationships.[3] As informal gathering venues away from home and work, third places provide spontaneous opportunities for socializing without worry of membership or performance.[4] Traditionally defined as physical environments, recent research illustrates that internet-based settings, such as massively multiplayer online games (MMOGs) and Twitter chats, can also be third places.[5] This chapter asks whether the social networking sites (SNS) Facebook, Snapchat, Instagram, and Twitter can also be third places.

Including virtual environments as third places requires an update of third place characteristics that reflect socializing trends in the 21st century.[6] The benefit of updating and extending the definition of third places to encompass virtual environments is that the new characteristics can then be used to measure other virtual environments, which may include various SNS. Currently, there is no approach to test the "thirdplaceness" of a virtual environment with quantitative data that can be counted, measured and expressed using numbers. Creating a quantitative measure would increase the consistency in which researchers study third places. This process can help identify whether non-physical environments represent third places based on updated third place characteristics.

In order to achieve the goals of this study, the authors first reviewed third places as defined by Ray Oldenburg and extended by Memarovic and colleagues.[7] Next, they used empirical and qualitative research to review how each characteristic represented current socializing trends on SNS to justify updated third place terminology. Based on this information, they created a scale to quantitatively measure contemporary third place characteristics. Subsequently, they used this scale to determine the degree to which different virtual environments (i.e., social networking sites) qualify as third places.

Overview of Third Place Theory

Oldenburg and Brissett initially identified third places as a solution to an apparent loss of sense of community in American culture, contending that these physical environments away from work and home provided important opportunities for additional social relationships beyond work colleagues and family.[8] Oldenburg's definition of third places consists of eight characteristics that contribute to the sociability of a third place environment.[9] These characteristics are the following:[10]

Neutral: Third places are relaxed settings that primarily serve to enhance relationships among people.
Levelers: Third places do not require membership or exude a sense of exclusivity.
Conversation: Conversation is the main activity in a third place.
Accessibility and Accommodation: Third places are often convenient locations between work and home.
Regulars: A consistent, predictable group of people frequent third places.
Low Profile: Third places are common, vernacular places.
Playful Mood: Third places offer light and playful banter that encourages relational connection.
Home Away from Home: Third places are comfortable environments with characteristics of "homeness."

These characteristics proffered by Oldenburg identify third places in physical environments, but recent studies suggest that virtual environments echo these traits. For example, McArthur and White have introduced how conversations on Twitter represent a third place, and Ducheneaut and Moore discuss how MMOGs represent third places. Both studies use Oldenburg's eight characteristics as a measure of "thirdplaceness."[11] Recently, researchers have argued that Oldenburg's traditional third place characteristics are not representative of virtual environments. Memarovic and colleagues have developed three new characteristics based on recent socializing trends:

Discovering third places in advance: accessing virtual third places from any physical location.
Declaring type of supported social activity: promoting social engagement through SNS.
Extending engagement with/within a third place: sharing social experiences through SNS.[12]

Although Memarovic and colleagues' characteristics expand Oldenburg's definition, their study highlights the fact that traditional third place characteristics do not encompass the current use of social media as third places.

Establishing Evolving Third Place Characteristics

In a previous article by Vaux and Langlais, Oldenburg's third place characteristics were analyzed by thoroughly examining literature on third places and Facebook.[13] The critical analysis of the literature reveals a need to update Oldenburg's third place characteristics to embrace traits of emerging third places. Two of Oldenburg's eight original characteristics remained consistent amid societal changes, while six required redefining and one additional characteristic needed to be added. Subsequently, the updated characteristics were then checked and verified by a survey to ensure that they were both representative of third place characteristics established in the literature and representative of current socializing trends. The study findings verified nine *evolving* characteristics, termed as such because socializing on SNS is a newer development and will most likely continue to develop and adapt with socializing trends. These evolving characteristics and their definitions are summarized in Figure 10.1.[14]

The new scale created by Vaux and Langlais consists of the following nine evolving characteristics that update third place theory: #1 Relationship Initiation and Maintenance, #2 Equalizer, #3 Conversation Main Activity, #4 Active and Passive Engagement, #5 Reciprocity, #6 People over Place, #7 Playful Mood, #8 Cognitive Separation and Reprieve, and #9 Third Place within a Third Place.[15] In what follows, we describe the evolution from Oldenburg's and Memarovic's characteristics to the new elements of the scale.

From "Neutral" to #1 Relationship Initiation and Maintenance

Oldenburg's definition of third places describes them as *neutral* environments where no one is "required to play host, and in which all feel at home and comfortable." The primary element of this characteristic is the "freewheeling" socializing made possible by third place environments.[16] In evolving third places such as Facebook and other SNS, individuals engage in social relationships with close friends as well as strangers.[17] The result is an expansion of possibilities for both maintaining and initiating relationships by cultivating new friendships that are less likely to occur in person. As a result, *#1 Relationship Initiation and Maintenance* is a more accurate definition of Oldenburg's "neutral" category.[18]

	Traditional Characteristics		New Evolving Third Place Characteristics	Updated Definition
	Oldenburg and Memarovic		Vaux and Langlais	Encompasses traditional characteristics and new findings
1	Neutral	1	Relationship Initiation and Maintenance	The environment promotes social relationships by providing opportunities to maintain existing relationships and/or establish new ones
2	Leveler	2	Equalizer	Individuals have equivocal opportunities to socialize with others in an environment
3	Conversation Main Activity	3	Communication Main Activity	Conversation is the primary activity and the means to form social relationships in an environment
4	Accessibility/Accommodation	4	Active and Passive Engagement	Individuals can be active participants in an environment or be passively engaged through observations
5	Regulars	5	Reciprocity	An expected responsiveness between individuals exists in a third place environment
6	Low Profile	6	People Over Place	Individuals focus more on social connection than the specific attributes of the environment
7	Playful Mood	7	Playful Mood	Individuals seek wit and humor when socializing with others
8	Home Away from Home	8	Cognitive Separation and Reprieve	Individuals can disconnect from a stressful environment and connect to another environment in a for respite from routine, monotony, or isolation
9	Discover in Advance, Declaring Type of Supported Social Activity, Extending engagement with/within a third place	9	Third Place Within a Third Place	Individuals can access a virtual third place while being in a physical third place environment

Figure 10.1 Summary of evolving third place characteristics.

From "Leveler" to #2 Equalizer

A third place is an inclusive, yet public, environment (i.e., *leveler*) where anyone is accepted and "worldly status claims [are] checked at the door in order that all within may be equals."[19] Evolving third places expand *leveler* to overcome geographic limitations and allows individuals to socialize with others despite differences, perhaps even without initial awareness of differences. While Oldenburg's term "leveler" refers to social stratification, the new term emphasizes evolving third places are also spatial *equalizers*. SNS are not bound by geographic location and allows individuals to create relationships with others worldwide.[20] To represent evolving third places, *#2 Equalizer* advances this aspect, identifying how individuals have equivalent access to social networking sites and equal opportunities to virtually communicate with almost anyone, almost anywhere.

Conversation Remains the Same for #3 Conversation as Main Activity

While the main activity of a third place remains *conversation*, the types of conversation (i.e. "lol") and the ubiquity of opportunities for conversation have evolved. In virtual environments, the conversation can take place anytime, anywhere, with anyone (as mentioned above) through 24 hour access providing an ever-present opportunity for asynchronous conversations. Individuals also choose to supplement face-to-face communication with interactions in virtual environments, which augments the number of conversations and connections between individuals.[21] Since the settings that promote the primary purpose of a third place continue to be environments where conversation is the main activity, #3 *Conversation as Main Activity*, remains a characteristic for evolving third places.

From "Accessible and Accommodating" to #4 Active and Passive Engagement

Physical third places are *accessible* physical environments between work and home, without the responsibilities that encumber those environments. They also *accommodate* the socializing needs of individuals or groups.[22] This is also true of virtual third places. As mentioned earlier, individuals can log in or check SNS from anywhere, whenever it is convenient. In virtual third places, participants can also passively view content, as well as engage in active conversations with others. For instance, individuals can passively view others' pictures on Facebook and Instagram, or they can choose to actively comment on an image or status. Individuals may also "people watch" and experience a social environment without actively engaging.[23] Given these societal changes represented in both physical and virtual third places, *#4 Active and Passive Engagement* is a more representative term for this characteristic.

From "Regulars" to #5 Reciprocity

Regulars are a trademark of third places.[24] This characteristic is also evident in virtual third places. For example, checking Facebook is part of many individuals' daily routines.[25] This highlights the change in third place characteristics from daily visits in physical environments to a continual connection in virtual third place environments. Additionally, it would be unusual for someone to not respond to another individual who initiated a conversation through SNS. Oldenburg's original term, *regulars*, indicates consistent involvement in third places, but engagement in virtual third places can be continual with the expectation of reciprocal responses. As a result, *#5 Reciprocity* updates the category.

From "Low Profile" to #6 People over Place

In physical third places, people often meet in vernacular settings having a *low profile* —people might meet at a gas station as easily as at a coffee shop. Oldenburg has noted that third places are "typically plain ... third places are unimpressive for the most part."[26] Oldenburg's term *low profile* already privileges people interaction over the physical quality of the space. Virtual third places further this point, by eliminating physical locales altogether.[27] Thus, this category is updated to *#6 People over Place* as individuals are concerned more with connecting with others than the specific attributes of the environment. "Thirdplaceness" is independent of the physical place per Oldenburg but all the more so in SNS—it's the people that make a third place, not the physical attributes.

"Playful Mood" Remains the Same for #7 Playful Mood

Third places are known for creating a playful mood that supports emotional expressiveness and encourages "vitality and interest" through conversations with wit and humor, offering reprieve from the everyday stressors.[28] This characteristic is true of virtual third places as well, as individuals often converse using humorous expressions, such as "haha," and "lol".[29] Because individuals typically use virtual and physical third places to form or flirt with playful banter and display their relationships, the term *#7 Playful Mood* remains a logical descriptor for this third place characteristic.

From "Home Away from Home" to #8 Cognitive Separation and Reprieve

Third places are comfortable environments with characteristics of "homeness." Oldenburg defines this as *Home Away from Home,* where individuals are free to act and behave in a way that reflects who they are.[30]

> Studies show that evolving third places extend the "away" aspect of third places by offering opportunities to cognitively separate individuals from the context of their present environment. This occurs through social disengagement in a physical environment or physical disengagement through a virtual environment.[31]

Interactions that occur online provide additional reprieve from the physical environment regardless of the location and provide individuals with a mentally relaxing diversion, even while at work or home.[32] Consequently, *#8 Cognitive Separation and Reprieve* is more representative of thirdplaceness.

Figure 10.2 Individuals can access a virtual third place while in a physical third place, essentially being in two third places at the same time (#9 *Third Place within a Third Place*).

From "Contemporary Characteristics" to #9 Third Place within a Third Place

As noted earlier, Memarovic and colleagues added three specific characteristics to virtual third places to be included with traditional third place characteristics.[33] These three reflect how individuals can access a third place on their smartphone or tablet, "like" or "share" content in a virtual environment, and engage with a virtual third place remotely. Similarly, on Facebook individuals often spend time viewing what others are doing in physical third places through the Newsfeed.[34] Individuals can also create events, invite peers to activities at physical third places or observe communication pertaining to events without being at the physical location. These activities can be summarized into #9 *Third Place within a Third Place*, which illustrates that someone can access a physical third place through virtual third places and vice versa; someone can access a virtual third place while in a physical third place. (Figure 10.2).

The Current Study

Given this information, individuals can experience a third place either physically or virtually. Because of the benefits of third places, the next step is to determine whether certain virtual environments qualify as third places using the evolving third place characteristics. In order to make these claims, it is practical to create a scale that can be used to see which characteristics a virtual environment exhibits in order to determine its "thirdplaceness." Therefore, the first goal of this study is to use information previously published by Vaux and Langlais[35] to create a quantitative measure that can be used to determine if and to what degree a virtual environment represents a third place. The nine new categories outlined above are the measures of the new scale. Next, quantitative analyses applying this scale is used to determine the "thirdplaceness" of four different SNS.

Method

The current investigation used two different methodological approaches to achieve the goals of this study. First, individuals were recruited via word-of-mouth from the primary investigators to complete a brief, online survey regarding their motivations for using social media. Each question on this online survey corresponded with one of the new characteristics of third places. For example, regarding the characteristic *relationship initiation and maintenance,* participants answered the question, "How often do you use the following social media to meet new friends and learn more about new friends?" with a response ranging from 1 (*never*) to 7 (*all the time*). (A copy of the questionnaire is in the "Additional Connections and Information" section of the chapter. See Figure 10.6) Participants answered each question in the survey for each of the following social media platforms: Facebook, Snapchat, Instagram and Twitter. If participants did not use a specific social media platform, they selected "N/A."

Next, we used a snowball method of recruitment by sending e-mails to friends and colleagues asking for help in completing the online survey and then requesting that they send the survey to others they know. This approach led to 354 participants completing the online survey; however, only 323 were used in the current investigation as 31 participants reported no social media use. The average age of participants in this study was 35.95 (*SD* = 17.20) and the majority of participants were white (91.9%) and from the Midwestern United States (85.1%).

The data were then analyzed to understand why individuals use social media. First, we examined the means of each social media network for all nine third place characteristics. If means were larger than the median of the scale (4.0), then this characteristic was deemed as representative of third places for that particular SNS. For example, if the mean for #1 *Relationship Initiation and Maintenance* was greater than 4.0 for Twitter and Facebook, but not Snapchat and Instagram, then Twitter and Facebook would meet this third place characteristic, while Snapchat and Instagram do not. As a second step to further quantitatively analyze these findings, an ANOVA was conducted to examine differences in motivations for using the four different SNS. This approach helped illustrate which SNS were statistically significant from each other, which allowed the authors to rank SNS by how much they aligned with the third place characteristics.

Third, an integrative literature review was used to examine whether certain SNS and texting represent these new characteristics of evolving third places. PsychINFO, JSTOR and Google Scholar were used to search for any journal articles that contained the words "Facebook," "Snapchat," "Instagram" or "Twitter" and either "third place" or "close relationships." To be included in the review, articles needed to meet the following criteria: (1) report the results of an empirical study, literature review or meta-analysis; (2) published since 2004 (the inception of the first major social media network, Facebook); and (3) discuss social media in the context of social space, such as connecting with others or forming relationships. This search resulted in a total of 134 studies. All selected articles were thoroughly analyzed for key information that was then organized into a separate file to align with the new characteristics of third places. After this file was formed, the authors designated which information corresponded to a specific characteristic of third places.

Findings

In addition to creating a scale to measure third place characteristics, the goal of this study was to examine if current social media platforms adhered to these new characteristics of third places: #1

Relationship Initiation and Maintenance, #2 Equalizer, #3 Conversation Main Activity, #4 Active and Passive Engagement, #5 Reciprocity, #6 People over Place, #7 Playful Mood, #8 Cognitive Separation and Reprieve, and #9 Third Place within a Third Place. To test this, we examined current research on Facebook, Snapchat, Instagram and Twitter, and collected quantitative data to determine if these SNS were representative of the new third place characteristics.

First, quantitative data was analyzed using ANOVAs to examine mean differences across SNS using Bonferroni post hoc analysis to view mean differences according to social media. Results of these analyses are presented in Figure 10.3. First, not all individuals indicated that they used all SNS. Of the 323 participants in the study, 313 used Facebook, 237 used Snapchat, 228 used Instagram and 227 used Twitter.

Next, the authors examined the means to see if any of the social media attributes aligned with the new characteristics of third places. For a characteristic to be aligned with a social media network, the mean reported by participants needed to be higher than 4.00, which was the median option for each question on the online survey. Means higher than the median represented that more individuals would use that SNS for that specific purpose, which would also support whether a particular SNS aligned with a third place characteristic. This information is in Figure 10.3, which presents all the means for each platform.

Through this examination, seven of the nine evolving characteristics of third places were associated with Facebook, one of the nine evloving characteristics were associated with Snapchat and Instagram, and none of the characteristics were associated with Twitter. Additionally, tests of the mean differences revealed that the primary social media platform associated with third places was Facebook, as the means for each characteristic were significantly higher than means for other SNS. On the other hand, means for each of the characteristics were significantly lower for Twitter compared to the other SNS. As for

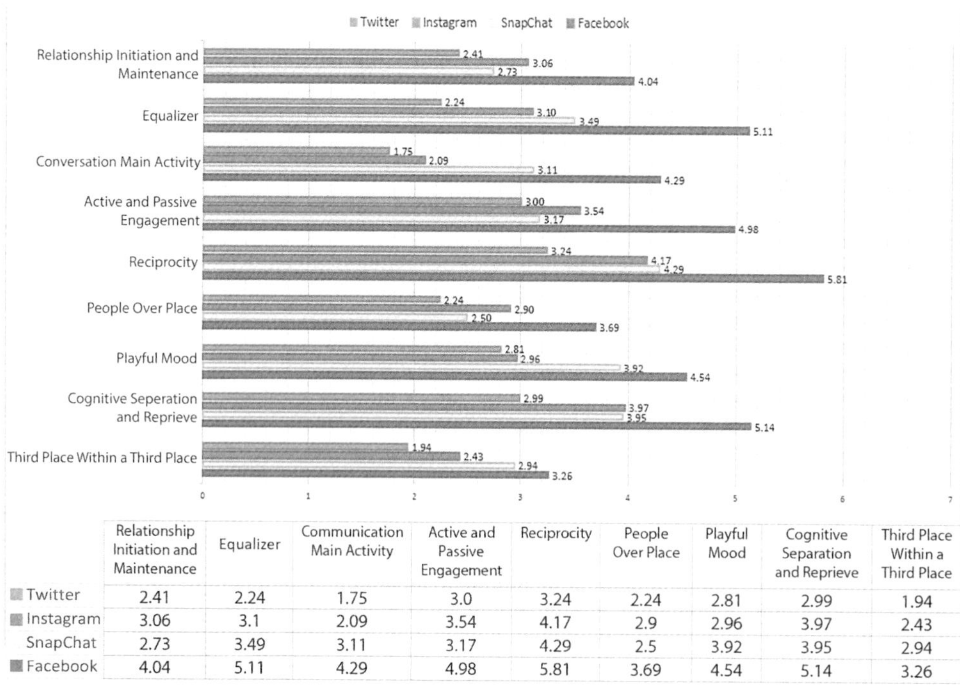

	Relationship Initiation and Maintenance	Equalizer	Communication Main Activity	Active and Passive Engagement	Reciprocity	People Over Place	Playful Mood	Cognitive Separation and Reprieve	Third Place Within a Third Place
Twitter	2.41	2.24	1.75	3.0	3.24	2.24	2.81	2.99	1.94
Instagram	3.06	3.1	2.09	3.54	4.17	2.9	2.96	3.97	2.43
SnapChat	2.73	3.49	3.11	3.17	4.29	2.5	3.92	3.95	2.94
Facebook	4.04	5.11	4.29	4.98	5.81	3.69	4.54	5.14	3.26

Figure 10.3 Means for each third place characteristic –Twitter, Instagram, SnapChat, Facebook– based on social media platform measuring thirdplaceness.

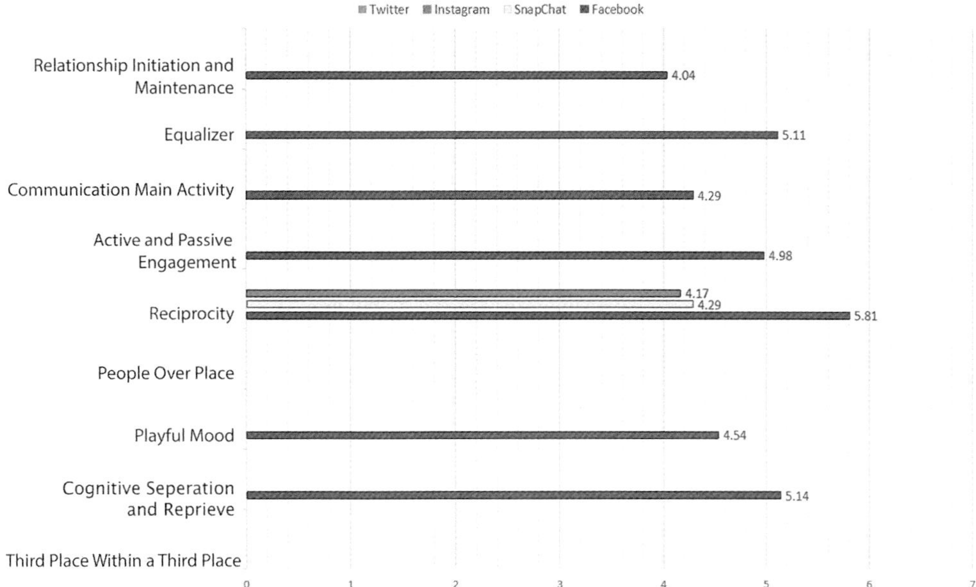

Figure 10.4 Means for each third place characteristic based on social media platform measuring thirdplaceness, altered to show only relevant data with means greater than 4, with Instagram, SnapChat, Facebook for *Reciprocity*.

Snapchat, means were significantly larger for the following characteristics when compared to Instagram and Twitter: #2 Equalizer, #3 Conversation Main Activity, #7 Playful Mood and #9 Third Place within a Third Place. For Instagram, the means were significantly higher for the following characteristics compared to Snapchat and Twitter: #1 Relationship Initiation and Maintenance, #4 Active and Passive Engagement, and #6 People over Place. Based on these analyses, there was strong support that Facebook could serve as a third place, which is consistent with past studies examining Facebook as a potential third place.[36] Additionally, there is partial support that Snapchat and Instagram adhere to some of the characteristics of third places but not all of them. Last, there is no quantitative support that relates Twitter as a third place, based on the evolving third place characteristics (Figure 10.4).

Next, to triangulate the data, we conducted an integrative literature review to see if any research studies would provide evidence that these SNS would represent the new third place characteristics. The information is presented below and organized by social media network in order of popularity (Facebook, Snapchat, Instagram and Twitter).[37] We organized the results by social media, as the research on some of these SNS is scarce. The known literature is discussed and then verified if the information supports any of the new characteristics of third places.

Facebook

Facebook has been extensively investigated in terms of the benefits offered by third places. The research presented for Facebook provides support for nearly all nine evolving characteristics of third places. First, in support of #1 *Relationship Initiation and Maintenance*, one academic study found that individuals universally cited Facebook as their primary tool for meeting new people, and another describes Facebook as a beneficial way for individuals to learn more about new friends.[38] Facebook use has also been linked to the formation and maintenance of romantic relationships.[39] Second, the mission of Facebook is "to give people the power to share and make the world more open and connected."[40] Facebook is popular not only in the United States but also in the Eastern Hemisphere, with 300 million daily active users in Asia and 233 million daily active users in Europe.[41] Studies have illustrated that Facebook is the primary social network used to interact with friends, family members, acquaintances and even strangers.[42] "Individuals have equal access to evolving third places and equivocal opportunities to socialize."[43] Facebook extends this by overcoming geographic barriers, age barriers (anyone aged 13 or older can have a Facebook account), and is actively used by 1.49 billion individuals *daily* around the world.[44] All of this information supports that Facebook represents #2 *Equalizer.*

Conversation is the main activity (#3) on Facebook. People use Facebook to stay connected with friends and family, as well as broader social spheres to discover what's going on in the world, and to share and express what matters to them through conversational posts, comments and messages both within and outside of their social circles.[45] On average, there are 55 million status updates made by 35 million people daily on Facebook.[46] According to Park and colleagues, self-disclosure on Facebook encourages communication from others.[47] Studies note a primary reason users' access Facebook is for communication. In support of #4 *Active and Passive Engagement*, individuals may passively view content by themselves or engage in active conversation with others. Passive activities can include "liking" others' information on Facebook. Some studies have shown that posting and sharing content, particularly photos, in addition to viewing other content on Facebook, promotes bridging and bonding social capital.[48] "Bridging social capital refers to tentative relationships that form between social networks ... Bonding social capital refers to exclusive relationships characterized by strongly tied individuals, such as family and close friends."[49] Moreover, users can log in to Facebook around the clock, from a computer, tablet or smartphone from any location with internet access. Also, there is partial support for #5 *Reciprocity.* When individuals send someone a message, click "like" on a post, or respond to someone else's messages, posts, or comments on Facebook, reciprocity is expected. An integral part of many individuals' lives, 50% of individuals check Facebook within 15 minutes of rising each morning.[50]

On Facebook, connecting with people is more important than the place in which it occurs. In fact, the physical attributes have little to do with the social interactions. As McArthur and White note, virtual environments are characterized by the coming together in time more than the space itself.[51] This supports #6 *People over Place* as a characteristic. Facebook also provides many opportunities for #7 *Playful Mood.* Individuals often include emojis and humorous expressions on their posts. One study found that 51.4% of expressions on Facebook contain "haha" and 1.9% of Facebook posts contain "lol," an acronym for "laugh out loud."[52] Additionally, people use Facebook to organize parties and social events.[53] Kissmetrics found that 62% of millennial users post about their activities with friends to share their own anecdotes and fun with others.[54]

Interaction on Facebook cognitively separates individuals from the context of their present physical environment. Individuals feel comfortable logging in and viewing a variety of content on Facebook, and 67% of users say the site provides them with current news and stories that are personally relevant.[55] This information demonstrates that Facebook provides #8 *Cognitive Separation and Reprieve.* Last, there is support that Facebook represents #9 *Third Place within a Third Place.* As of May 2013, there was an average of 4.5 billion "likes" on Facebook a day.[56] Individuals participate in a virtual third place, either actively or passively. Participants create events, invite friends to events or places on Facebook, or encourage friends to join groups with massive memberships, all of which are not location dependent. Generally, there is support that Facebook is representative of a majority of the evolving characteristics of third places.

Snapchat

Snapchat is slightly different from Facebook in that the material shared is ephemeral, meaning that the content disappears after it is viewed. The goal of Snapchat is to reinvent the camera "to improve the way people live and communicate."[57] Individuals use Snapchat by sending "snaps," which are pictures and videos. Each photo and video can be edited to add filters, emojis, text or other content. The content is often more personal and direct than other SNS. One study found that the majority of individuals use Snapchat to send "funny content."[58] Individuals check Snapchat multiple times a day, typically averaging 25–30 minutes a day on the social media platform.[59] Although research is limited, there is support that Snapchat, despite being ephemeral, promotes communication and provides a sense of community with a small network of individuals. Research illustrates that individuals use Snapchat to maintain relationships rather than to initiate them, and that networks on Snapchat are significantly smaller than networks on Facebook.[60] However, there is some evidence that Snapchat provides a means of self-disclosure in order to learn more about others.[61] Other studies show that not only is Snapchat used to communicate with others, both proximally and far away, the primary function for using Snapchat is for entertainment.[62] In terms of romantic relationships, Snapchat is seen as more jealousy-provoking than Facebook, hinting that its use may not promote relationship maintenance.[63] Along with the statistical data, this information provides support for #2 *Equalizer*, #3 *Conversation* and #7 *Playful Mood*, as well as some support and some opposition for #1 *Relationship Initiation and Maintenance*. Snapchat does not offer individuals their own profile but is connected to Bitmoji, another application that allows you to create a cartoon character of yourself that you can use to promote interactions with others.[64] This evidence provides some support for #6 *People over Place*.

Another feature of Snapchat is the "Story" function, which allows individuals to post snaps for their entire social network to see. However, research shows that individuals spend more time sending and receiving snaps than posting snaps to their story. Participants primarily send snaps of themselves (i.e., selfies), but the pictures are less tempered (in the sense that they are spontaneous) than on other social media platforms. Individuals are most likely to send and receive snaps from a close friend and spend the bulk of their time communicating on Snapchat while they are at home.[65] Based on this additional information, Snapchat appears to also reflect #5 *Reciprocity*, #8 *Cognitive Separation and Reprieve* and #9 *Third Place within a Third Place*. There is not much support for #4 *Active and Passive Engagement* on Snapchat. Snapchat information for the other characteristics of third places is limited, given the lack of research on this SNS to date.

Instagram

Instagram is a photo-sharing application that allows individuals to privately or publicly share pictures with one's social circle. Individuals can also message other users through Instagram. The creators of Instagram wanted to solve three problems via their application: lack of quality photos for online posting, the inability to share photos on multiple platforms and the inefficiency of uploading photos.[66] Although the application has been around since 2010, there is little research on Instagram in context of third places. However, we discuss studies that provide evidence that Instagram may meet some of the new characteristics of third places below.

Instagram has been linked to bridging social capital but not as much to bonding social capital.[67] Motivations for using Instagram have been associated with social interaction, archiving, self-expression, escapism and peeking. Also, studies illustrate that individuals engage in behaviors on Instagram to seek "likes" from one's social network rather than form or maintain relationships.[68]

Based on the available literature, there is support that Instagram meets some of the criteria of third places but not all of them. Given that the goal of Instagram is to post and share pictures, it is very common for participants to passively view content, which is representative of #4 *Active and Passive Engagement*. However, passive content viewing can have detrimental effects, which is likely to oppose other third place characteristics, such as #1 *Relationship Initiation and Maintenance*, #2 *Equalizer* and #5 *Reciprocity*. Few studies illustrate that individuals use Instagram to communicate with others despite this feature being available on Instagram. For these reasons, Instagram appears to moderately meet evolving characteristics on the scale.

Twitter

Twitter has also been examined in the context of third places. The most well-known study was performed by McArthur and White, who used textual analysis to find support that conversations on Twitter were representative of third places based on Oldenburg's characteristics.[69] Essentially, these authors found that Twitter chats predominantly adhered to traditional third place characteristics. This current study expands on the discussion to see if Twitter would qualify as a third place using the evolving third place characteristics and focusing on multiple features on Twitter. The focus on Twitter chats may be overemphasized as Twitter conversations are not a predominant behavior on Twitter. Instead, individuals often use Twitter to communicate with a general audience, without expectation of reciprocity, by posting "tweets," which are posts that are limited to 140 characters and can be seen by a private or public audience. Individuals commonly tweet about various live events, with an example being Super Bowl XLIX, which was the most tweeted event between 2014 and 2015. In regard to communication on Twitter, 26% tweet to a general audience (public or private), 6% retweet another individual's tweet and 68% reply to a tweet on Twitter.[70] Another study found that individuals primarily use Twitter to read other peoples' tweets, with only 37% reporting that they post information or communicate with others regularly on Twitter. Nearly 80% of Twitter users report using Twitter on their phones, meaning they can access the social media network wherever they have their phones. Additionally, many users say that they use Twitter to keep up with the news, as opposed to communicating with others, and to learn more about celebrities, athletes, politicians and other famous or popular individuals.[71]

Research on Twitter links the SNS to bonding social capital but is otherwise unrelated to forming or maintaining relationships.[72] Clayton found that excessive Twitter use is detrimental for romantic relationships and marriages, as it is likely to produce Twitter-related conflict.[73] However, other studies have found that the use of Twitter in educational contexts can boost academic outcomes.[74] Twitter is also used by various organizations to promote their business, event, organization or policy.[75] Individuals can respond to organizational tweets, as well as the tweets of celebrities, but are rarely responded to.[76] Information posted by organizations or celebrities on Twitter pages is considered appealing to Twitter users but does not result in increased socialization.[77]

Based on findings from this study, there is generally little support that Twitter adheres to the evolving characteristics of third places. Twitter appears to meet the characteristics of #4 *Active*

Figure 10.5 Past investigations have measured third places based on characteristics developed for the physical environment when it is evident that certain virtual environments challenge these theories to accommodate current societal and technological shifts.

and Passive Engagement and #6 *People over Place* but does not meet the characteristics of #1 *Relationship Maintenance*, #2 *Equalizer*, #3 *Conversation* #5 *Reciprocity* and #7 *Playful Mood*. Additionally, based on this information, there is some initial support for #8 *Cognitive Separation and Reprieve* and #9 *Third Place within a Third Place*, but more research is needed to support this claim.

Discussion

This study had two goals. First, this study created a scale to measure of evolving third place characteristics that can be used with virtual environments (Figure 10.5). Second, the study used this measure to determine the "thirdplaceness" of four different SNS. Past investigations have measured third places based on characteristics developed for the physical environment when it is evident that certain virtual environments challenge these theories to accommodate current societal and technological shifts. In this context, identifying *evolving* third place characteristics relevant to virtual environments may more accurately reflect current social behaviors.

Regarding each SNS, results of this study demonstrate that Facebook consistently adheres to evolving third place characteristics. This finding is consistent with past studies examining this association and other studies that make connections between Facebook third place characteristics and benefits.[78] Individuals appear likely to socialize with others actively and passively on Facebook, which is the primary aim of third places. Individuals can access Facebook anywhere, which allows individuals to cognitively separate from current tasks. Individuals can, and often do, access Facebook from home or work, meaning that Facebook appears to be a third place, within a third place.

Subsequently, Snapchat and Instagram were moderately associated with "thirdplaceness," whereas Twitter was inconsistently associated with evolving third place characteristics. Individuals may use Twitter more to observe others passively rather than communicate directly with others. Although passive engagement is associated with third places, more emphasis is placed on the benefits of socializing with others in third places. McArthur and White found that conversations on Twitter are representative of third places, however these types of conversations do not appear to be particularly common with the current study sample. Results did reflect that Instagram and

Snapchat were slightly representative of third places. On these platforms, individuals engage in a variety of behaviors that are reflective of third places. However, they were not consistent in their "thirdplaceness." These SNS may be used less often or in shorter time periods, which likely limits the socializing benefits compared to Facebook.

Limitations and Conclusions

Although this research advances knowledge on third places and SNS, this study is not without its limitations. First, data was self-reported from a sample that was not diverse in terms of gender, ethnicity or location. Details about their social media use were also not collected. Additionally, only single items were used when establishing the scale used in this study (i.e., one question per third place measure). Future investigations should incorporate more items in order to create a more precise measure of "thirdplaceness." By creating more items, this scale can be tested for precision and validity.

Oldenburg and Brissett offered the third place as a solution to changing 20th-century socializing trends.[79] As digital and physical space interface in human socializing practices, the findings of this study provide insights into understanding how, why and where individuals seek relationships. As evidenced in this study, third places may not equate to a specific physical location since certain virtual environments, specifically SNS, are representative of the ways that individuals currently socialize. The data from this study provides initial evidence that various SNS provide some degree of "thirdplaceness."

* * * *

Discussion and Exercises

Reflections about the Chapter You Just Read:

1. Please refer to the standard features of a research project explained in the Introduction. Then:
    a. In one sentence, identify the *research topic.* This sentence can be in the form of a question but does not have to be. In any case, write one grammatically correct sentence that captures the research topic of this chapter.
    b. Identify the *literature* related to this research project.
    c. Identify the *method* which the author used and the *data* which this method generated for analysis.
    d. Explain how this approach is *generalizable* (or not).
    e. Explain how you can have confidence (or not) of the *internal and external validity* of this author's overall approach.
2. Describe the characteristics of a third place in your own words. Identify a physical location that meets these third place characteristics for you. Explain why you consider this location a third place.

3. Given the results of the study, describe how someone can engage in a third place within a third place (see page 196 in the chapter).
4. If you were to conduct a follow-up study, describe what virtual environments you would analyze as potential third places, such as (1) gaming environments (such as MMOGs), (2) Zoom, (3) TikTok and (4) WeChat. How might information from this follow-up study impact the design of physical spaces?

Exercises/Suggestions for Further Study:

1. Sign into a social networking platform in which you participate regularly. Create a matrix to track your behavior and the behavior of others on the site (i.e., monitoring others' content, posting pictures, "liking" content, etc.). Decide whether the behaviors you observe are similar to those of a physical third place. What are the similarities and what are the differences? Based on your findings, determine if the virtual venue meets the evolving third place characteristics outlined in this chapter.
2. Read the article by McArthur & White, 2016, "Twitter Chats as Third Places: Conceptualizing a Digital Gathering Site" (see full citation in Additional Resources and Information). Based on the information presented in the article, decide whether Twitter can be a third place. Create two teams and stage a debate between those who defend Twitter as a third place and those who defend that Twitter is not a third place.
3. Visit a local physical third place. Through non-participant observation, notice how, or if, virtual space is integrating with physical space. How are individuals using technology to socially connect virtually while in the physical location (for example by texting on cell phones, using hand devices—iPads, iPhones, etc.—to access virtual social networks)? Does the venue use SNS (such as Facebook or Twitter) to advertise or build a social community? In your opinion, does the virtual venue augment the physical third place? Why or why not?
4. Propose a design for a physical third place environment that incorporates virtual third places. Consider the concept the authors of this chapter propose of a "third place within a third place." What are important considerations of designing for the integration of virtual socializing with physical settings?

Additional Connections and Information

1. See Figure 10.6 on page 206 for the survey used in this study.
2. Additional literature on third places and virtual third places:

Ducheneat, Nicolas, and Richard Moore, "Virtual 'Third Places': A Case Study of Sociability in Massively Multiplayer Games." *Journal of Collaborative Computing* 16 (2007): 129–166.

Ellison, Nicolem, Charles Steinfield, and Cliff Lampe, "The Benefits of Facebook 'Friends:' Social Capital and College Students' Use of Online Social Network Sites." *Journal of Computer-Mediated Communication* 12 (2007): 1143–1168.

Memarovic, Nemanja, Sidney Fels, Junia Anacleto, Roberto Calderon, Federico Gobbo, and John Carroll, "Rethinking Third Places: Contemporary Design with Technology." *The Journal of Community Informatics* 10, no. 3 (2014): 8.

The goal of this survey is to understand general reasons for using social media, which includes Facebook, Twitter, SnapChat, and Instagram. Please answer each of the following questions as they pertain to your social media use.

1. How often do you use the following social media to meet new friends and learn more about new friends? Responses: 1: Never 4: Sometimes 7: All the time
   a) Facebook ____ b) SnapChat ____ c) Instagram _____ d) Twitter _____

2. How often do you use the following social media to connect with someone who you cannot meet in person due to geographical constraints (i.e., they don't live near you)? Responses: 1: Never 4: Sometimes 7: All the time
   a) Facebook ____ b) SnapChat ____ c) Instagram _____ d) Twitter _____

3. How often do you use the following social media to supplement face-to-face communication or arrange a face-to-face encounter? Responses: 1: Never 4: Sometimes 7: All the time
   a) Facebook ____ b) SnapChat ____ c) Instagram _____ d) Twitter _____

4. How often do you use the following social media to observe others' conversations and activities? Responses: 1: Never 4: Sometimes 7: All the time
   a) Facebook ____ b) SnapChat ____ c) Instagram _____ d) Twitter _____

5. How often do you check the following social media? Responses: 1: Never 4: Sometimes 7: All the time
   a) Facebook ____ b) SnapChat ____ c) Instagram _____ d) Twitter _____

6. How often do you personalize your profile on the following social media? Responses: 1: Never 4: Sometimes 7: All the time
   a) Facebook ____ b) SnapChat ____ c) Instagram _____ d) Twitter _____

7. How often do you use the following social media to express or share humor with others? Responses: 1: Never 4: Sometimes 7: All the time
   a) Facebook ____ b) SnapChat ____ c) Instagram _____ d) Twitter _____

8. How often do you use the following social media to relax or take a break? Responses: 1: Never 4: Sometimes 7: All the time
   a) Facebook ____ b) SnapChat ____ c) Instagram _____ d) Twitter _____

9. How often do you use the following social media in an environment where you can meet others face-to-face? Responses: 1: Never 4: Sometimes 7: All the time
   a) Facebook ____ b) SnapChat ____ c) Instagram _____ d) Twitter _____

The following questions ask general demographic information and will be used to organize and compare social media usage.

1. What is your current age?
   a) 18-24
   b) 25-29
   c) 30-34
   d) 35-39
   e) 40-44
   f) 45-49
   g) 50-54
   h) 55-59
   i) 60+
   j) Prefer not to say
2. What best describes your cultural background? Check all that apply
   a) White
   b) Black/African-American
   c) East Asian or Pacific Islander
   d) Other Asian
   e) Latino or Hispanic
   f) American Indian
   g) Middle Eastern
   h) Other – please specify
   i) Prefer not to say
3. What is your gender?
   a) Male
   b) Female
   c) Prefer not to say
4. What best describes your current location?
   a) West
   b) Southwest
   c) Midwest
   d) Southeast
   e) Northeast

Figure 10.6 Study survey.

McArthur, John A., and Ashleigh F. White, "Twitter Chats as Third Places: Conceptualizing a Digital Gathering Site." *Social Media + Society* 2 (2016): 1–9.

Oldenburg, Ramon, and Dennis Brissett. "The Third Place." *Qualitative Sociology* 5, no. 4 (1982): 265–284.

Oldenburg, Ray. *The Great Good Place: Cafes, Coffee Shops, Bookstores, Bars, Hair Salons and Other Hangouts at the Heart of the Community* (New York: Marlowe &Company, 1999), 14–15.

Soukup, Charles. "Computer-Mediated Communication as a Virtual Third Place: Building Oldenburg's Great Good Places on the World Wide Web." *New Media & Society* 8, no. 3 (2006): 432.

Steinkuhler, Constance, and Dmitri Williams. "Where Everybody Knows Your (Screen) Name: Online Games as 'Third Places'" *Journal of Computer-Mediated Communication* 11, no. 4 (2006).

Waxman, Lisa. "The Coffee Shop: Social and Physical Factors Influencing Place Attachment." *Journal of Interior Design* 31, no. 3 (2006): 35–53.

Notes

1 Lisa Waxman, "The Coffee Shop: Social and Physical Factors Influencing Place Attachment," in *Journal of Interior Design* 31, no. 3 (2006): 35–53; Information provided by the *Journal of Interior Design* regarding most cited articles [website]. https://onlinelibrary.wiley.com/page/journal/19391668/homepage/productinformation.html

2 John A. McArthur, *Digital Proxemics: How Technology Shapes the Ways We Move* (New York: Peter Lang Publishing, Inc., 2016), 12–14.

3 Ramon Oldenburg and Dennis Brissett, "The Third Place," *Qualitative Sociology* 5, no. 4 (1982): 265–284; Kennon Sheldon, Neetu Abad, and Christian Hinsch, "A Two-process View of Facebook Use and Relatedness Need-Satisfaction: Disconnection Drives Use, and Connection Rewards It," *Journal of Personality and Social Relationships* 1 (2011): 770.

4 Ray Oldenburg, *The Great Good Place: Cafes, Coffee Shops, Bookstores, Bars, Hair Salons and other Hangouts at the Heart of the Community* (New York: Marlowe and Company, 1989/1999), 22–23; Alex Lambert, "Intimacy and Social Capital on Facebook," *New Media and Society* 14, no. 7 (2016): 2562.

5 John A. McArthur and Ashleigh F. White, "Twitter Chats as Third Places: Conceptualizing a Digital Gathering Site," *Social Media + Society* 2 (2016): 3. Cuihua Shen and Wenhong Chen, "Gamers' Confidants: Massively Multiplayer Online Game Participation and Core Networks in China," *Social Networks* 40 (2015): 211. Scott Wright, "From "Third Place" to "Third Space": Everyday Political Talk in Non-Political Online Spaces," *Javnost – The Public* 19, no. 3 (2012): 42.

6 Charles Soukup, "Computer-mediated Communication as a Virtual Third Place: Building Oldenburg's Great Good Places on the World Wide Web," *New Media and Society* 8, no. 3 (2006): 438; Dana E. Vaux and Michael R. Langlais, "An Update of Third Place Theory: Evolving Third Place Characteristics Represented in Facebook," *International Journal of Technology and Human Interaction* 17, no. 4 (in press): n.p.

7 Nemanja Memarovic, Sidney Fels, Junia Anacleto, Roberto Calderon, Federico Gobbo, and John Carroll, "Rethinking Third Places: Contemporary Design with Technology," *The Journal of Community Informatics* 10, no. 3 (2014): 8.

8 Ramon Oldenburg, and Dennis Brissett, "The Third Place," *Qualitative Sociology* 5, no. 4 (1982): 265–284.

9 Ray Oldenburg, *The Great Good Place: Cafes, Coffee Shops, Bookstores, Bars, Hair Salons and Other Hangouts at the Heart of the Community* (New York: Marlowe &Company, 1999), 14–15.

10 Dana Vaux, "Interior People Places: The Impact of the Built Environment on the Third Place Experience," in *Handbook for Interior Design*, eds. Jo Ann Thompson and Nancy Blossom (New York: Wiley-Blackwell, 2014), 347–365; Lisa Waxman, "The Coffee Shop: Social and Physical factors Influencing Place Attachment," *Journal of Interior Design* 31, no. 3 (2006): 48.

11 John A. McArthur and Ashleigh Faley White, "Twitter Chats as Third Places: Conceptualizing a Digital Gathering Place," *Social Media + Society* 2, no. 3 (2016): 7; Ducheneaut, Robert J. Moore, and Eric Nickell, "Virtual 'Third Places': A Case Study of Sociability in Massively Multiplayer Games," *Computer Supported Cooperative Work* 16 (2007): 144. doi: 10.1007/s10606-007-9041-8.

12 Memarovic and others, op. cit., 8; Vaux and Langlais, op. cit., n.p.

13 Vaux and Langlais, op. cit., n.p.

14 Ibid., n.p.

15 Ibid., n.p.

16 Oldenburg, op. cit., 22.

17 Nicole Ellison, Charles Steinfield, and Cliff Lampe, "The Benefits of Facebook 'Friends:' Social Capital and College Students' Use of Online Social Network Sites," *Journal of Computer-Mediated Communication* 12, no. 4 (2007): 1151.
18 Vaux and Langlais, op. cit., n.p.
19 Oldenburg, op. cit., 25.
20 Facebook, "Stats." http://newsroom.fb.com/company-info/
21 Tara Sinclair and Rachel Grieve, "Facebook as a Source of Social Connectedness in Older Adults," *Computers in Human Behavior* 66 (2017): 365.
22 Oldenburg, op. cit., 32–33.
23 Waxman, op. cit., 48.
24 Oldenburg, op. cit., 20.
25 Amanda Lenhart, "Teens, Social Media, and Technology Overview 2015." http://www.pewinternet.org/2015/04/09/teens-social-media-technology-2015/
26 Oldenburg, op. cit., 36.
27 Ducheneaut and others, op. cit., 131; McArthur and White, op. cit., 7.
28 Oldenburg and Brissett, op. cit., 270–271.
29 Kevin Smith, "Marketing: 47 Facebook Statistics for 2016." www.brandwatch.com/blog/47-facebook-statistics-2016/
30 Oldenburg, op. cit., 39.
31 Vaux and Langlais, op. cit., n.p.; Smith, op. cit.
32 Ducheneaut, op. cit., 163.
33 Memarovic and others, op. cit. As noted these characteristics are "discovering third places in advance" (accessing virtual third places from any physical location), "declaring type of supported social activity" (promoting social engagement through SNS) and "extending engagement with/within a third place" (sharing social experiences through SNS).
34 Facebook, op. cit.; Smith, op. cit.
35 Vaux and Langlais, op. cit., n.p.
36 Ibid., n.p.
37 Lenhart, op. cit.
38 Jesse Fox, Katie Warber, and Dana Makstaller, "The Role of Facebook in Romantic Relationship Development: An Exploration of Knapp's Relational Stage Model," *Journal of Social and Personal Relationships* 30, no. 4 (2013): 1150; Chiung-Wen Hsu, Ching-Chan Wang, and Yi-Ting Tai, "The Closer the Relationship, the More the Interaction on Facebook? Investigating the Case of Taiwan Users," *Cyberpsychology, Behavior, and Social Networking* 14, no. 7–8 (2011): 474.
39 Fox and others, op. cit., 1150; Leah LeFebvre, Kate Blackburn, and Nicholas Brody, "Navigating Romantic Relationships on Facebook: Extending the Relationship Dissolution Model to Social Networking Environments," *Journal of Social and Personal Relationships* 32, no. 1 (2015): 82.
40 Facebook, op. cit.
41 Smith, op. cit.
42 Cherrie Billedo, Peter Kerkhof, and Catrin Finkenauer, "The Use of Social Networking Sites for Relationship Maintenance in Long-distance and Geographically Close Romantic Relationships," *Cyberpsychology, Behavior, and Social Networking* 18, no. 3 (2015): 154; Tara Sinclair and Rachel Grieve, "Facebook as a Source of Social Connectedness in Older Adults," *Computers in Human Behavior* 66 (2017): 365.
43 Vaux and Langlais, op. cit., n.p.
44 Facebook, op. cit.
45 Ibid.
46 Kissmetrics, "Facebook Statistics." https://blog.kissmetrics.com/facebook-statistics/
47 Namkee Park, Borae Jin, and Seung-A Jin, "Effects of Self-disclosure on Relational Intimacy in Facebook," *Computers in Human Behavior* 27, no. 5 (2011): 1979.
48 Joe Phua, Seunga Venus Jin, and Jihoon Kim, "Uses and Gratifications of Social Networking Sites for Bridging and Bonding Social Capital: A Comparison of Facebook, Twitter, Instagram, and Snapchat," *Computers in Human Behavior* 72 (2017): 119.
49 Vaux and Langlais, op. cit., n.p. Vaux and Langlais are summarizing work done by Robert Putman in *Bowling Alone: The Collapse and Revival of American Community* (New York: Simon & Schuster, 2000), 22–24.
50 Amanda Lenhart, "Teens, Social Media, and Technology Overview 2015." http://www.pewinternet.org/2015/04/09/teens-social-media-technology-2015/
51 McArthur and White, op. cit., 4.
52 Smith, op. cit.
53 Kennon Sheldon, Neetu Abad, and Christian Hinsch, "A Two-process View of Facebook Use and Relatedness Need-satisfaction: Disconnection Drives Use, and Connection Rewards It," *Journal of Personality and Social Relationships* 1 (2011): 770.
54 Kissmetrics, op. cit. This data does not account for the fact that not all banter on Facebook is playful, as social media is also associated with cyberbullying, particularly in the adolescent and young adult context. See R. Dredge, J. Gleeson, and X. de la Piedad Garcia, "Presentation on Facebook and Risk of Cyberbullying Victimization," *Computers in Human Behavior* 40 (2014): 16–22.
55 Smith, op. cit.
56 Zephoria Digital Marketing, "The Top 20 Valuable Facebook Statistics." https://zephoria.com/top-15-valuable-facebook-statistics/
57 Snapchat. "Snap Inc." www.snap.com/en-US/.

58 Bianca Bosker, "Study Shows How People Use Snapchat – And it's Not Sexting." www.huffingtonpost.com/2014/07/14/Snapchat-sexting-study_n_5574642.html
59 Biz Carson, "Snapchat Users Now Spend 25 to 30 Minutes Every Day on the App, and it's Trying to Attract the TV Money Because of It." www.businessinsider.com/how-much-time-people-spend-on-Snapchat-2016-3
60 J. Mitchell Vaterlaus, Kathryn Barnett, Cesia Roche, and Jimmy Young, "Snapchat is More Personal: An Exploratory Study on Snapchat Behaviors and Young Adult Interpersonal Relationships," *Computers in Human Behavior* 62 (2016): 596.
61 Phua, Jin, and Kim, op. cit., 119.
62 Narissra Punyanunt-Carter, J.J. De La Cruz, and Jason Wrench, "Investigating the Relationships among College Students' Satisfaction, Addictions, Needs, Communication Apprehension, Motives, and Uses & Gratifications with Snapchat," *Computers in Human Behavior* 75 (2017): 872.
63 S. Utz, N. Muscanell, and C. Khalid, "Snapchat Elicits More Jealousy than Facebook: A Comparison of Snapchat and Facebook Use," *Cyberpsychology, Behavior, and Social Networking* 18 (2015): 141–146.
64 Casey Newton, "Snapchat's Bitmoji Avatars are Now Three-dimensional and Animated." www.theverge.com/2017/9/14/16303504/Snapchat-bitmoji-world-lenses-animation-gabsee.
65 Lukasz Piwek and Adam Joinson, "What Do they Snapchat About? Patterns of Use in Time-limited Instant Messaging Service," *Computers in Human Behavior* 72 (2016): 352.
66 Bad Chen, "What is Instagram's Mission and Vision Statement?" www.quora.com/What-is-Instagrams-mission-and-vision-statement
67 Phua, Jin, and Kim, op. cit., 119.
68 Tara Dumas, Matthew Maxwell-Smith, Jordan Davis, and Paul Giulietti, "Lying or Longing for Likes? Narcissism, Peer Belonging, Loneliness and Normative Versus Deceptive Like-seeking on Instagram in Emerging Adulthood," *Computers in Human Behavior* 71 (2017): 6.
69 McArthur and White, op. cit., 1–9.
70 Katherine Boyarsky, "How Do People Use Twitter? [Infographic]." https://blog.hubspot.com/marketing/twitter-usage-stats
71 Tom Rosenstiel, Jeff Sonderman, Kevin Loker, Maria Ivancin, and Nina Kjarval, "How People Use Twitter in General." www.americanpressinstitute.org/publications/reports/survey-research/how-people-use-twitter-in-general/.
72 Phua, Jin, and Kim, op. cit., 119.
73 Russell B. Clayton, "The Third Wheel: The Impact of Twitter Use on Relationship Infidelity and Divorce," *Cyberpsychology, Behavior, and Social Networking* 17, no. 7 (2014): 427–428. doi:10.1089/cyber.2013.0570.
74 Heather K. Evans, Victoria Cordova, and Savannah Sipole, "Twitter Style: An Analysis of How House Candidates Used Twitter in Their 2012 Campaigns," *Political Science and Politics* 47, no. 2 (2014): 455 doi:10.1017/S1049096514000389; Reynol Junco, C. Michael Elavsky, and Greg Heiberger, "Putting Twitter to the Test: Assessing Outcomes for Student Collaboration, Engagement and Success," *British Journal of Educational Technology* 44, no. 2 (2012): 276. doi: 10.1111/j.1467-8535.2012.01284.x
75 Hyojung Park, Bryan H. Reber, and Myoung-Gi Chon, "Tweeting as Health Communication: Health Organizations' Use of Twitter for Health Promotion and Public Engagement," *Journal of Health Communications* 21, no. 2 (2016): 192–193.
76 Xia Liu, Alvin C. Burns, and Yingjian Hou, "An Investigation of Brand-Related User-Generated Content on Twitter," *Journal of Advertising* 46, no. 2, (2017): 237.
77 Lemi Baruh and Zeynep Cemalcilar, "Rubbernecking Effect of Twitter: When Getting Attention Works Against Interpersonal Attraction," *Cyberosychology, Behavior, and Social Networking* 18, no. 9 (2015): 510–511 doi:10.1089/cyber.2015.0099
78 See Vaux and Langlais, op. cit., (in press); Fox, and others, op. cit., 1150.
79 Oldenburg and Brissett, op. cit., 267.

Chapter 11

Virtual Simulation

Editors' Introduction by Dana E. Vaux and David Wang

Virtual reality (VR) is increasingly prominent in our computer-enabled global information culture. Interior design education is right in step with this development. The 2018 Council for Interior Design Accreditation Report identified VR as an important emerging technology.[1] Also in 2018, CIDA awarded an Excellence Award to Jason Maneely for his work in using VR to put his students "into the shoes of others." His students experienced virtual spaces from a wheelchair, and through the eyes of someone with low vision stemming from diseases such as cataracts or macular degeneration. Maneely also developed virtual tours of "cutting-edge" spaces, which his students experience while he lectures about them in real time. These virtual site tours are just one example of how VR technology contributes to design education.[2]

The importance of VR for research lies in its power to simulate real-world conditions. Accurate simulations allow us to gain new knowledge while steering clear of other limitations. For instance, simulating an earthquake teaches us how structures respond without actual harm to lives and infrastructure. Flight simulators crash airplanes but pilots walk away better prepared. There are many examples. In this chapter, Saleh Kalantari outlines a method to conduct post-occupancy evaluations of interior spaces *before they are built*. Usually, post-occupancy evaluations, or POEs, are conducted *after* a project is built. POEs assess occupant response, and building systems performance, in accord with design intentions. But Kalantari's way of assessing a design before it is built helps to avoid not only construction costs but also serve as an invaluable tool in the design process itself.

Because the goal of simulation research is to recreate a real-world condition as accurately as possible, recent developments in VR technology exponentially increase our ability to model actual conditions. But this benefit also presents important challenges for the VR researcher. How is he or she confident that the simulation model actually reflects the real-world condition?

In this chapter, Saleh Kalantari uses a variety of research tools to increase confidence of accuracy. Be on the lookout for these "clusters" of research tactics Kalantari uses to assure accuracy. As you read:

1. Note how Kalantari confines his research to what is usually called a *unit of test*, a term mentioned elsewhere in this book. Creating a clear unit of test assures that factors extraneous to the conditions under study are not impacting the results in unintentional ways. Refer to Figure 11.1 in this chapter. It shows an isolated participant within an environment where only what she sees in the VR headset impacts her; and her responses are measured by a pre-arranged array of sensors. Kalantari takes great care in not allowing any other factors to influence this participant.
2. Another way to assure accuracy is setting up a step-by-step process. Note how Kalantari sets up four stages in his research: (1) A preparation stage in which a participant learns to use the virtual equipment but is not told what the experiment will entail; (2) A second stage in which physical classrooms are used to measure a participant's responses in the actual real world and (3) The third stage is the actual VR simulation, shown in Figure 11.1. This is followed up with (4) An exit survey comprising the fourth stage. All of these stages ensure that the unit of test is accurate.

The term "unit of test" is a primary feature of experimental research. This book does not have a specific chapter featuring experimental research because, even though it is an important research typology in the physical and applied sciences (and also in some areas of social science research), designers infrequently use strict experimental methods. Please see the backmatter to this chapter for additional connections to experimental research. Simulation research is similar to experimental research in setting up units of test, because both kinds of research aim to get at real-world conditions by isolating factors impacting those sets of conditions. *But this is also the big difference between experimental versus simulation research.* While experimental research reduces a unit of test to just the relevant variables, the goal of units of test in simulation research is to *include* as many real-world variables as possible, and these variables can be innumerable. In reading this chapter, look for the tension between isolating a unit of test and capturing as many real world variables as possible in the virtual simulations.

Interiority

While some of the chapters in this book directly refer to interiority, this chapter does not explicitly mention this term but still exemplifies a way to understand it. Interiority in its various theoretical manifestations all share one trait in common. It concerns subjective dimensions of place identity in which individual or communal responses to an external environment evoke an existentially felt sense of belonging (or not) on the part of the participant that extends beyond merely measurable physical features. In this chapter:

1. Note how interiority can be understood as a level of comfort, or a sense of assurance for performance, that participants feel when in a classroom setting.
2. Note how, for interiority in this chapter, the power of VR technology can put quantifiable measures to subjective feelings. So:
3. Consider how VR research is one means to comprehend the qualitative aspects of interiority through quantitative terms. Also, consider how this approach differs from the statistical approaches featured in Chapters 9 and 10.

* * * *

Chapter 11

Biometric Data and Virtual Response Testing in a Classroom Design

Saleh Kalantari

Evidence-based design and human-centered design encourage researchers to document the positive and negative effects of the built environment for human well-being. Rigorous post-occupancy studies are an important part of this process. The rigor of post-occupancy studies is important to the design fields since built environments can have significant impact on human health and well-being. Interior design variables ranging from window placements to wall textures to overall spatial arrangements have been strongly correlated with human factors such as health outcomes, emotional mood, stress levels and productivity.[3] However, the effectiveness of post-occupancy studies in evaluating these human outcomes has some important limitations. Due to the tremendous financial investment required by construction, it can be costly to experiment with new architectural designs to test innovations that might help improve environmental impacts on human health. This limits our ability to collect reliable data on alternative design possibilities. In addition, the uniqueness of each building and architectural setting presents challenges for isolating design variables and rigorously comparing them against other possible designs.

To address these challenges, our team has developed a toolset to conduct in-depth virtual testing of human responses *before* the designs are physically constructed. We created a prototype testing platform that monitors study participants' physical and conscious responses as they carry out various activities within a virtual environment. The system collects biological measurements, including head motions, brain activity, heart rate and galvanic skin response, and correlates them in real time with the participants' activities as they explore the virtual environment. These measurements can also be correlated with the participants' subjective, self-reported responses. Using this approach allows us to rigorously examine changes in human responses and capabilities, such as anxiety and concentration, when specific design variables are digitally altered. The process allows designers to gain important feedback on their work—to help resolve problems or justify the human benefits of a design—prior to investment in physical construction. After developing and calibrating this human-response testing equipment, we created a general research protocol for its use and applied it by conducting a pilot study on classroom design. This chapter describes our testing equipment and research protocol and reports the results of the pilot study.

Advantages in Using This Approach

Numerous studies have demonstrated that an evidence-based approach to design can successfully improve the perceived human qualities of architectural environments, as well as measurements of building performance.[4] Evidence-based design has become particularly influential in healthcare settings, where it has been associated with improvements in the quality of care, greater patient satisfaction and a decrease in the number of medical errors.[5] Despite these demonstrated benefits, however, there are also challenges and limitations that have led to skepticism and slow adoption in many sectors of the design industry. Aside from the up-front construction costs already noted, another issue is that generalizability of research findings from one design project to another remains tenuous. Finding past human-response studies that provide evidence relevant to a new design can be difficult, and the site-specific nature of design studies often leads to complex and sometimes contradictory conclusions.

Another limitation in the existing human-response literature is that most of these studies rely on subjective evaluations such as surveys and interviews, which are often limited in persuasive force when compared to more empirical behavioral measurements.

Currently, research into human responses to design is beginning to take more of a neurological and experimental turn, in which researchers not only gather broad behavioral data but also seek to describe the underlying brain mechanisms that mediate human responses to architectural features.[6] Unfortunately, even in this area, data from neurological assessments often suffer from a lack of consistent research protocols and limited study designs. For example, the majority of existing neurological studies measure participants' brain responses while they view two-dimensional pictures of architectural designs. These studies may not really capture brain responses associated with moving fluidly through an immersive, three-dimensional environment. While virtual reality experiences may also have limits in their ability to mimic fully embodied engagements with architecture, they do allow a much richer sense of surroundings and are thus more likely to capture accurate measures of neurological responses.

Our solution immerses volunteer participants in virtual environments to comparatively measure their responses to design variables using both biometric data and self-reported data. This approach allows for more precise isolations of the design variables under study, since the virtual environments can be constructed to be identical apart from specific design alterations the researcher wants to evaluate. Meanwhile, the collection of biometric data provides empirically robust measurements of human responses, more so than in conventional Post Occupancy Evaluations (POE) studies. Most importantly, this research can be carried out at a fraction of the cost associated with constructing new designs and *then* learning about their successes and flaws retrospectively. As well, the precision of the research allows for standardized protocols that can enhance experimental replication and thus allows for better comparisons and data-sharing among commensurate studies. We believe virtual testing during design development can greatly enhance the success of new designs and help spur responsible and data-driven innovation in the field.

Equipment and Research Protocol

An important goal in this research was to create a testing platform with broad potential for use in multiple design-testing studies. The first task was to develop a virtual environment that can enable the easy and intuitive presentation of various architectural design features. For this purpose, we used Epic Games' Unreal Engine (www.epicgames.com), a sophisticated virtual reality simulation program. The Unreal Engine uses blueprint scripting, which allows for a quick learning-curve on the part of researchers and designers, making the construction and modification of new virtual reality architectural models a relatively easy process. The virtual modeling can be performed using Autodesk Maya, a familiar program to most designers, and surface textures can be added either procedurally through Substance Designer or manually through Photoshop.

The virtual experience was presented to research participants using Oculus Rift and HTC Vive head-mounted displays. These headsets are lightweight, comfortable for the user, and have a strong market share with ongoing development. For an even greater immersive experience, a treadmill device called Virtuix Omni gave participants a real sense of walking through the virtual environment using physical leg motions on the treadmill. The treadmill yields important data such as participants' gait speed and length of pauses. Accelerometers were included to measure motions of the head and torso.

Another technology incorporated into the testing platform is electroencephalography (EEG), a powerful tool for quantitatively measuring brain responses. By fitting participants with an EEG cap, we can collect a wide range of data about cognition, perception, emotion and mental activity in complex environments.[7] These measurements can be synchronized in real time with other data, including conscious feedback from participants and recording their activities within the virtual space. The EEG device and associated software used in the platform accommodate a range of head motions without physically binding the user while still providing robust data outputs. The capability to allow free head movements is relatively new in EEG technology, enabling better measurements of brain activity during physical activities.[8] The relevant components include a 64-channel Brain Products actiCAP, along with the Brain Amp DC amplifier, the wireless MOVE system and BrainVision software. The overall data-collection system is further supplemented with electrooculography (EOG) sensors to record eye motions, electrocardiogram sensors (EKG) to record heart rates and a galvanic sensor response (GSR) unit to record skin conductance (Figure 11.1).[9]

After selecting and optimizing the virtual reality technology and the biological measurement equipment, we developed a general protocol for using our platform under research conditions. The intent is for this protocol to allow future researchers to easily replicate findings and conduct additional experiments mutually compatible with past outcomes while minimizing confounding variables.

We divided the overall research protocol into four stages: (1) participant preparation, (2) real environment, (3) virtual environment and (4) exit interview. During the initial preparation stage, the participants were given an introduction to the study and allowed five minutes to try out the equipment. They were informed about the general purpose of the study but were not made aware of any of the particular hypotheses or design variables being tested. The participants were assured they could stop the testing at any time and for any reason if they felt uncomfortable. They were then asked to fill out a brief demographic questionnaire (age, gender, ethnicity, education, occupation, alcohol/caffeine/substance use, and any known neurological conditions). No personally identifiable information was collected. The reason for asking about drug use and neurological conditions is to help identify physical factors that may affect the biometric data. The time of day in which the experiment took place was

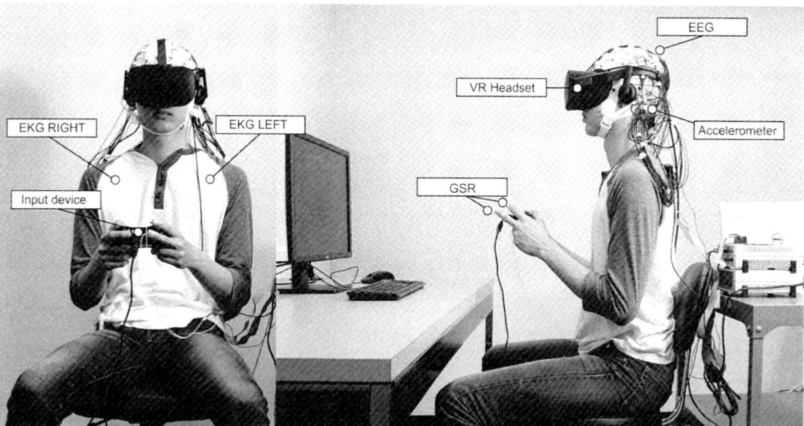

Figure 11.1 EEG, EOG, GSR, and EKG sensors, VR headset, and accelerometer to measure motions of the head and torso, as worn by a study participant. The Virtuix Omni treadmill device is not shown in this image.

also recorded on the demographic form, as this can affect the biophysical measurements. After this, the research team carefully fitted each participant with an EEG cap and other measurement devices.

During stage two of the experiment, participants were asked to perform various tasks and activities in an actual interior environment without the use of virtual immersion. This establishes a baseline of biometric data, allowing us to compare participants' responses in real environments against their responses in virtual environments. This further helps validate the toolset by determining if the experience of virtuality itself has an effect on the biometric data.

After collecting data on these baseline states, the experiment proceeded to stage three, when the participants put on their virtual reality headsets and were exposed to the virtual architectural settings. Specific design factors that can be tested using this approach are almost limitless, but our pilot study focused on adjusting minor design elements of a classroom, such as the ceiling height and the placement of windows. Participants remained active in each virtual environment for about ten minutes before taking a two-minute break, and then entering a new version of the classroom. The order in which the designs were presented varied randomly for each participant to help eliminate familiarization and fatigue effects. While in these environments, participants were asked to engage in a variety of tasks, ranging from free exploration to specific learning exercises and games based on well-known neuropsychological tests. They were also asked to share their subjective responses and opinions about the environments.

Finally, during stage four of the experiment, each participant completed a short exit survey, which allowed them to comment on the overall experience and to make comparative subjective evaluations of the designs.

Implementing the Classroom Design Study

Again, responses to healthcare designs, educational designs, residential environments, retail stores, public spaces such as parks and museums, overall urban environments and landscape designs, just to name a few, are all amenable to rigorous investigation using this approach. Researchers may choose to study environmental effects on anxiety, wayfinding, learning performance, productivity or a host of other human factors. To test and calibrate our method we conducted a pilot study focused on the interior design of a classroom environment. We investigated the effects of design changes in educational settings for the human factors of attention, stress and visual memory.

Previous research indicates that student performance may be significantly affected by physical design factors. Poor-quality learning environments may create barriers such as impaired concentration, boredom or claustrophobia. Higher-quality physical design of learning environments, in contrast, has been correlated with higher levels of student engagement.[10] Despite these tentative links between learning environments and student outcomes in the research literature, the specific design elements within the environments that affect students have not been rigorously broken down and empirically investigated. The educational researcher Paul Temple observed, "Where connections between the built environment and educational activities are made, the basis for doing so tends to be casual observation and anecdotes rather than firm evidence."[11]

Previous work in this area suggests some general themes in the optimal design of learning spaces. Perhaps the most dominant theme in the recent research literature is that educational spaces need to be flexible, both pedagogically and physically, so that they can be adjusted to reflect the nuances of teaching different knowledge areas, learning styles and educational technologies.[12]

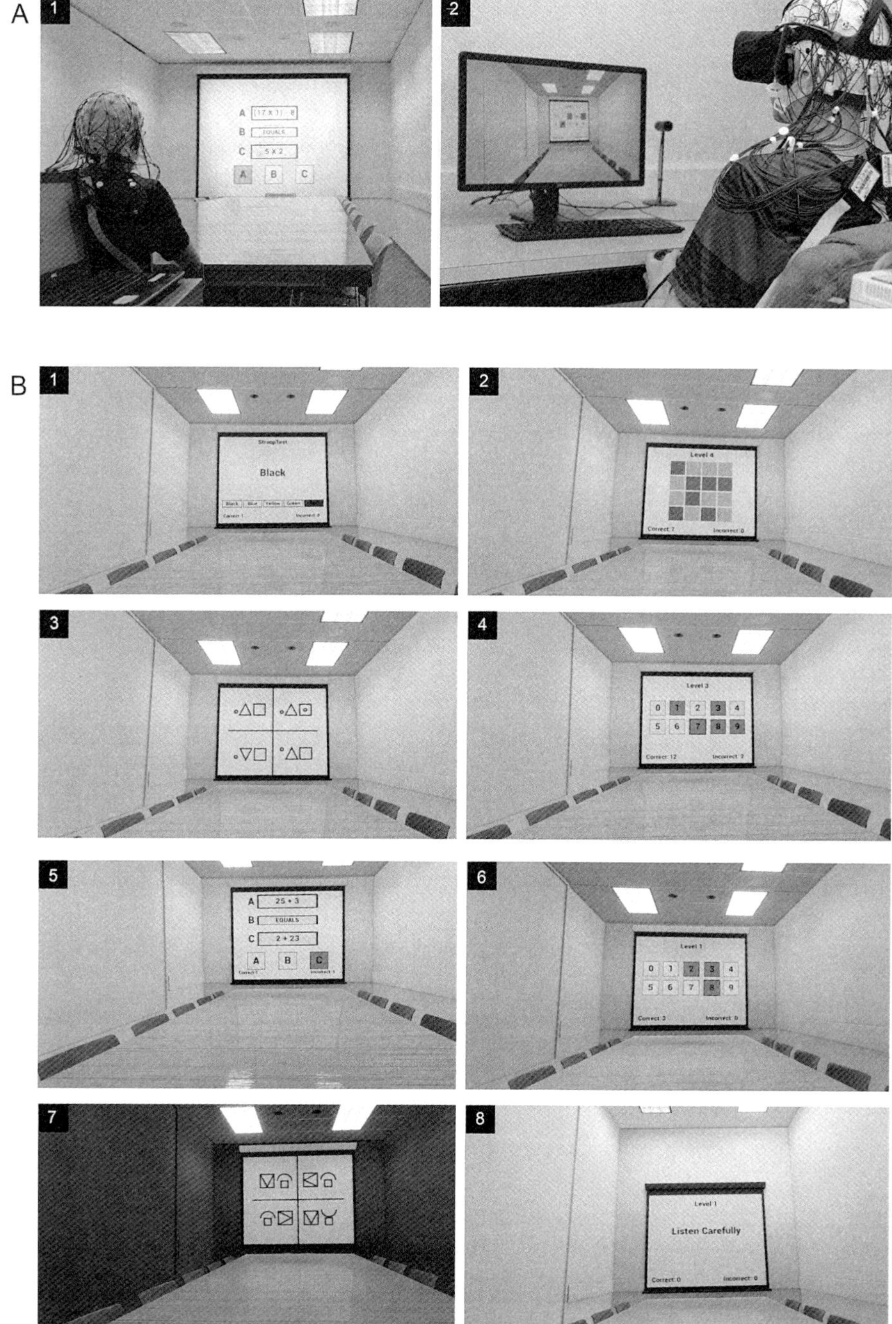

Figure 11.2 Study participants engaged in memory and attention tasks in (A1) an actual classroom and (A2) a virtual rendering of the classroom. The tasks included: (B1) the Stroop attention test, (B2) a visual memory test, (B3) the Benton retention test, (B4) the Digit Span Task and (B5) a mathematical puzzle. Alterations in the virtual environment included different color schemes (B6, B7) as well as changes to the room's width and height (B8), and the addition of windows and various furniture designs.

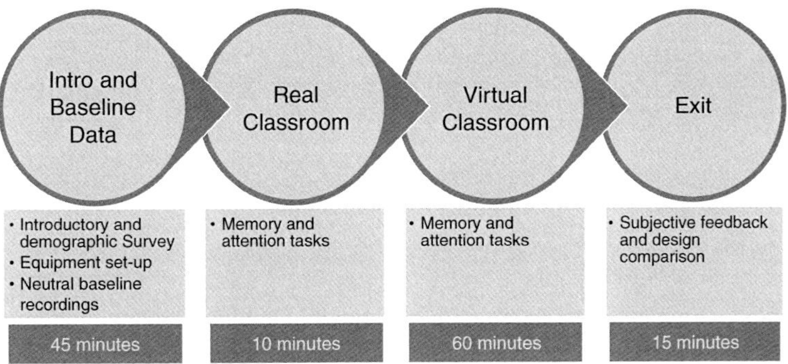

Figure 11.3 Timeline of the pilot study.

Other general design factors that have been associated with better student performance include "naturalness" (in light, sound, temperature, air quality and links to nature) and environments that provide greater stimulation and sensory impact.[13] The detailed investigation of these factors remains a relatively new and undeveloped area in the design literature, and nearly all of the existing research reports express a hope that future investigators can adopt more rigorous empirical methods.

For our pilot study, 30 student and educator participants were presented with an interior classroom view (using a real-world classroom as a base template), with various modifications to the room's height, width, window locations, furniture design, lighting and color. The choice of design variables to modify was based on a literature review of previous educational design research.[14] While the virtual immersion time-period is too brief to measure actual substantial learning outcomes, the pilot study was able to determine provisional measures for the participants' concentration, task accomplishment and stress levels. These are factors that have been previously shown to contribute to student learning outcomes over the long run.[15]

Following the research protocol described in the previous section, participants were asked to answer questions and engage in learning tasks, first within the real classroom, then within an identical virtual rendering of the classroom (using the same lighting, color, furniture, room dimensions, etc.), and finally within different virtual variations of the classroom (with specific alterations in the design features). The tasks that the participants engaged in were based on standard memory and attention tests, including the Benton Test, Visual Memory Test, Stroop Task, Digit Span Task and a mathematical puzzle (Figures 11.2 and 11.3). The Benton Test involves participants reproducing shapes from memory after seeing them on a screen; the Visual Memory Test involves recalling the location of highlighted items within a grid pattern; and the Stroop Task focuses on quickly naming a color when encountering conflicting visual information (for example, if the word "blue" is printed in red ink). The Digit Span Task involves correctly remembering a series of numbers, while our mathematical puzzle was based on a qualitative comparison of two different equations.

Data Analysis and Results

Three of the pilot study participants were university faculty members, while the other 27 were undergraduate and graduate students. All of the participants were associated with the University of Houston, representing the Departments of Electrical Engineering, Computer Science, Physics,

Architecture, Biomedical Engineering, English, Industrial Design, Civil Engineering and Finance. Their age range was from 18 to 55, with an average age of 26.06 years. Twelve were female and eighteen were male. The participants had a variety of ethnic backgrounds: eighteen reported as Asian, one as Latino, one as Middle Eastern and ten as White. These study participants also represented a wide variety of national backgrounds, with the United States (12), India (8) and China (3) being the most common places of birth. The participants were asked to report their sleep patterns and rate their fatigue level at the time of the experiment. Thirty-six percent reported getting more than seven hours of sleep the previous night, 40% reported between six and seven hours of sleep, and 24% reported less than six hours of sleep. The average reported fatigue level was 3.92 on a Likert scale ranging from 1 to 10.

In the first part of the data analysis we compared the results of the participants' task accomplishment (Benton Test, Visual Memory Test, Stroop Task, Digit Span Task and Mathematical Puzzle) between the identically designed virtual and real classrooms, as well as among the different design variations of the virtual classroom. In these analyses we used the C/T ratio as measure of task success. This simply refers to the number of correct responses (C) divided by the total number of questions attempted by the participant (T). Thus, a C/T ratio of 1.00 would mean that the participant correctly answered every attempted question, while a C/T ratio of 0.00 would indicate that the participant did not correctly answer any of the attempted questions. (In future studies additional performance metrics may be considered.)

When comparing the real classroom against an identical virtual classroom, the participants had extremely similar C/T performances. The average C/T score for the Digit Span Task was 0.69 in the real classroom and 0.65 in the virtual classroom. This pattern of closely similar task success rates was repeated in the Mathematical Puzzle (0.65 for real vs. 0.60 for virtual), the Benton Test (0.87 for real vs. 0.93 for virtual), the Stroop Task (0.97 for real vs. 0.98 for virtual) and the Visual Memory Test (0.95 for real vs. 0.93 for virtual). For the Digit Span Task, the Mathematical Puzzle and the Visual Memory Test, the participants fared slightly better in the real classroom. However, for the Benton Test and the Stroop Task, their performance was slightly improved in the context of virtual immersion. Overall, the differences in these average scores were minimal (Figure 11.4a). This finding helps to support the view that virtual environments can be reasonable proxies for testing human responses to designs before they are physically constructed.

When the average task accomplishment scores were compared among different design variations of the virtual classroom, a much larger range of results was found. Ten different iterations of the classroom design were tested, including versions of the room with a higher ceiling, a longer width, added windows in different locations (some windows on the front wall with direct views to nature, others that were on the side wall and no direct view), as well as adjustments to seating arrangements, and wall color. The full results for the C/T scores in these different room variations are presented in Figure 11.4b. While these room redesigns were associated with significant variations in average C/T scores (as much as 15% to 20% score variation, for the Stroop Task and Digit Span Task, respectively), there was a great deal of inconsistency in these initial pilot study results. For example, in the Mathematical Puzzle results, the design variation of the classroom with more rounded edges was associated with a marked decrease in the participants' performance. However, this result does not hold up for the other tests, where the room with more rounded edges was associated with equal or greater performance. Similarly, views to nature were associated with a large performance increase in the Digit Span Task, particularly compared against the other versions of the classroom that had windows too on the side walls. However, this advantage of natural views as seen in the

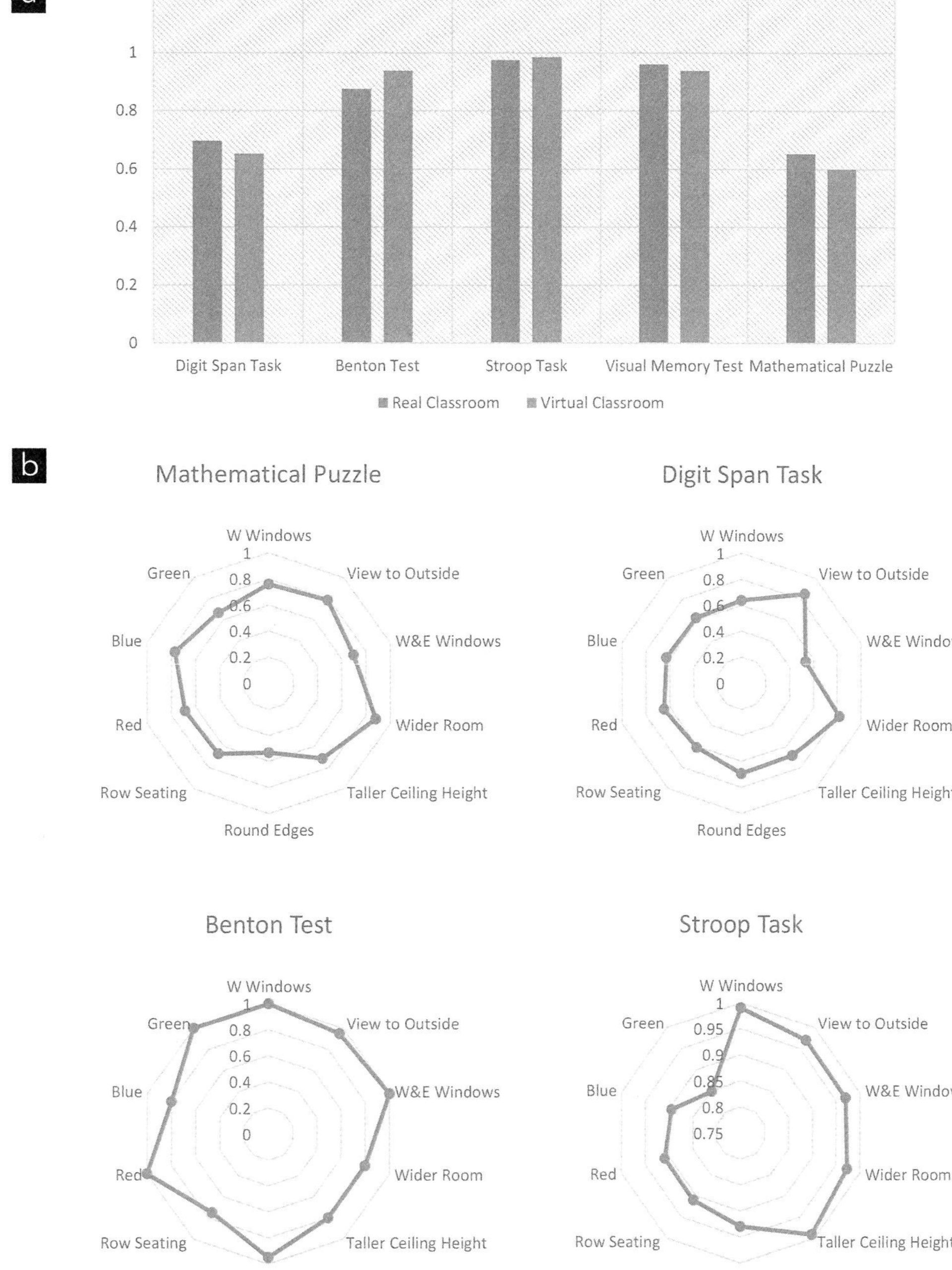

Figure 11.4 Pilot study results for task accomplishment scores. (a) Comparing the C/T Ratio in the real classroom vs. an identical virtual classroom; (b) Comparing the C/T ratio in ten different design variations of the virtual classroom. "W Windows" refers to a design alteration with added windows high on the western classroom wall (with no views to nature), while "W&E Windows" refers to windows placed high on both the western and eastern classroom walls. "Round Edges" refers to the classroom with curved edge and no corner, while "Green," "Blue" and "Red" refer to the wall colors.

Digit Span Task did not hold up in the results of the Stroop Task and Benton Test (Figure 11.4b). While much of the task performance data was inconclusive, a statistical analysis (*t*-test) of the combined performance for all tasks does indicate a moderate but significant advantage for the virtual classroom design with expanded width. This finding is intuitively reasonable given that the original classroom was somewhat horizontally constricted (as can be seen in Figure 11.2a).

In the second part of the analysis, we examined the biometric data and subjective feedback that was collected from the study participants. For the biometric data, signal processing was carried out using the open-source EEGLAB software and other MATLAB functions. The H-∞ filtering program was used for initial pre-processing. This filter helps to stabilize the EEG and EOG signals and reduces artifacts caused by eye movements. The data was subsequently pre-processed using a modified PREP pipeline and band-pass filtered between 0.1 and 100 Hz, then processed using independent component analysis and dipole fitting. This step helps to ensure that the data is comparable among participants with slightly different head shapes. Each additional biometric signal was individually band-pass or high-pass filtered to further reduce "noise" and signal variations. From there, values such as heart rate, heart rate variability, average GSR power and average magnitude of acceleration were calculated.[16]

An example of the biometric data collected from one study participant is shown in Figure 11.5, including data collected while the participant was sitting quietly with eyes open, sitting quietly with eyes closed, conducting tasks in a real classroom, conducting tasks in an identical virtual classroom and conducting tasks in a virtual classroom with added windows. Although the full statistical analysis of this data is still ongoing, an initial overview has provided promising results. Most notably, the readouts collected while participants were performing tasks in the real classroom and the identical virtual classroom (the third and fourth columns in Figure 11.5) were remarkably similar, as compared against baseline non-active states and against task completion in the virtually adjusted classroom designs. Similarities between the real classroom and its identical virtual representation affirm the results discussed above and lend credence to the hypothesis that virtual response testing can be used as a reliable proxy for evaluating human responses in actual constructed buildings.

In examining the biometric data for the virtual design variations, an initial analysis indicated that the addition of windows to the classroom helped to reduce stress levels and improve attention. The data recorded in the classroom variations with windows consistently indicated fewer stress and distraction signals in comparison to the classroom variations with plain white walls, green walls, blue walls or red walls. This benefit did not seem to be tied to whether or not the windows provided a view to nature; even the windows placed on the side wall, which did not provide a scenic external view, still provided similar benefits in stress reduction. In regard to adjustments in the classroom's width, the biometric data indicated lower levels of stress and distraction for the wider classroom variations. This confirms the similar finding in the task success measurements as described above, which also indicate a benefit from the wider classroom designs. We did not find any significant effects in the biometric data for the tested variations in ceiling height or row seating.

In regard to the participants' subjective feedback, one notable finding was that only mild stress responses were reported intrinsic to the use of VR and to wearing biometric sensors. This factor is likely to vary by population, and it is almost certainly affected by the manner in which the researchers presented the equipment and the study to the participants. The initial "play" period and familiarization with the equipment, along with explanations of the study's purpose, are an important part of the research protocol and are intended to help reduce these intrinsic stress responses. This approach seems to have worked, as very little equipment-related stress was reported. The respondents were

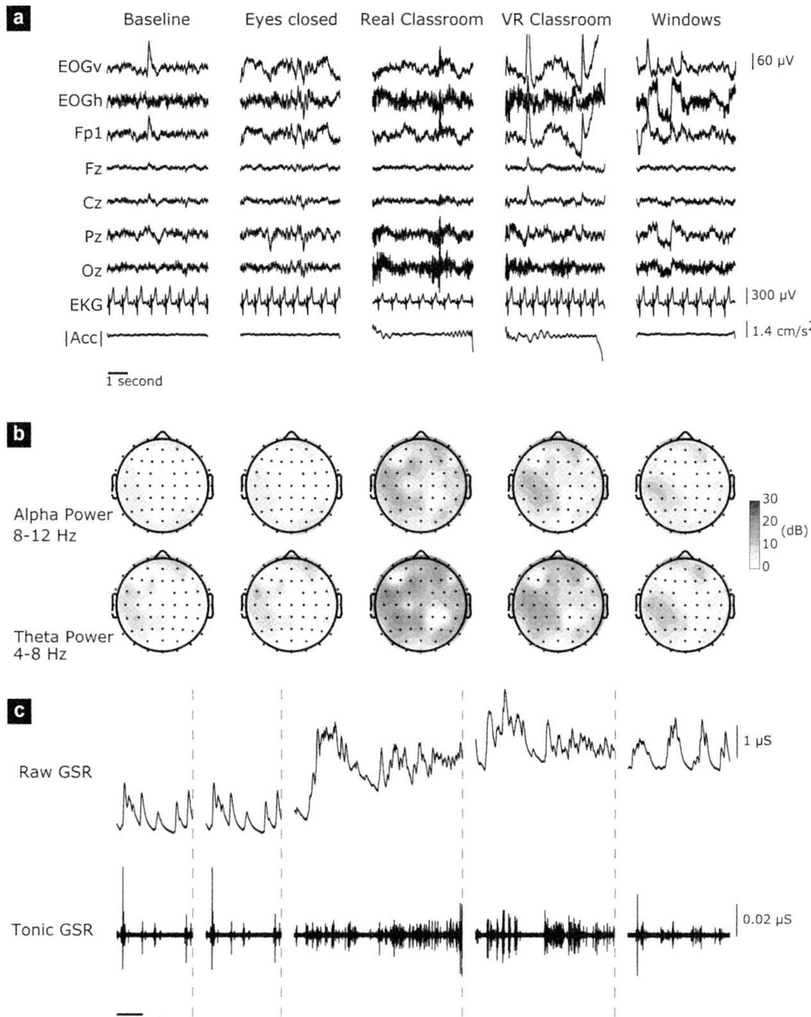

Figure 11.5 Pilot study biometric data for five environmental conditions (indicated in columns): baseline eyes open, baseline eyes closed, task completion in the real classroom, task completion in an identical virtual classroom and task completion in the virtual classroom with added windows. The figure rows show (a) the initial 5s of data from selected EEG, EOG, EKG and head-acceleration channels; (b) total alpha (8–12 Hz) and theta (4–8 Hz) power in all EEG channels, and (c) raw and tonic GSR (skin conductivity) signals.

also asked to rate how similar they felt the VR classroom experience was compared to being in a real classroom. The average response to this question was 6.22, on a Likert scale ranging from 1 to 10. The participants did not provide further details about what made the two environments similar or different. The subjective feedback given by the participants regarding their opinions of the different classroom designs was also limited and did not yield any consistent results. However, when asked if the virtual reality experiment helped to enhance their awareness of architectural design and its effects, 75% of the participants replied in the positive.

Discussion

One of the most important findings from this pilot study was the similarity of the data collected in the real classroom environment compared to the identical virtual rendering of the classroom. When the real classroom design and arrangements were compared to an identical virtual replica, the participants exhibited extremely similar stress metrics. Along with the subjective feedback from the study participants, this finding suggests that virtual design-testing has the potential to be an effective process with results that will extend to the success of actual constructed environments. Of course, much more extensive testing is needed to confirm this, and to analyze the specific places where virtual results and real results might differ. As an initial proof-of-concept, however, the findings of the current study are extremely positive. The experiment demonstrated that biometric data collection can be an effective technique for design-testing, with clear differences in stress and attention responses noted between baseline passive states and different architectural environments. Again, however, the effectiveness of these measurement tools needs much more extensive testing, calibration and comparison against other forms of data before it can be considered conclusive.

Regarding the specific pilot study findings for classroom design, there are a few notable provisional results. The most robust design conclusion supported by this study is that classrooms can be too narrow in their horizontal dimensions, and that expanding their width (presumably in proportion to their height) can help to reduce student stress and improve attention and memory performance. This conclusion was supported both by the task-accomplishment data and by the biometric response data. In addition, the biometric data supported the value of windows in classrooms for helping to reduce stress and improve concentration, though this result was not clearly reflected in the task-accomplishment scores. As this research continues to develop, it will be possible to carry out more expansive studies with larger populations and more detailed variable increments in order to confirm these findings and more rigorously analyze classroom design factors.

Conclusion and Future Research

This pilot study demonstrates the potential of a new paradigm of virtual human-response testing in architectural design. The next step in our research, in addition to carrying out broader studies using this approach, will be to streamline the data recording and analysis procedures into a convenient, open-source plug-and-play software tool, so that other designers and researchers can readily adopt our method. We want the equipment set-up and data-gathering process to be as simple and streamlined as possible, so that even designers and researchers without a great deal of experience in this area can readily learn how to conduct virtual response-testing for their design ideas. This will help raise interest in, and broader adoption of, the method. Eventually, our aim is to establish standardized virtual reality testing as a source of "big data" for the design industry. We will incorporate into our software plug-in tool an option for design firms and research labs to validate their results, and then upload the validated results to an open-access online database. This database will aggregate rigorous evidence from across the globe and systematically tag, categorize and compare the findings based on the type of project (e.g., "healthcare"), the design detail (e.g., "nurse station"), demographic details (e.g., "elderly populations," "Singapore") and the human factor being investigated (e.g., "stress").

Our hope is that the existence of such a database will help to promote the greater adoption of evidence-based design standards throughout the industry. In an academic sense, the research has a great potential to assist design researchers, educators, sociologists, psychologists and neuroscientists who are seeking to understand the relationship between architectural form and human experience. All of this is in addition to how this platform can help designers create better-quality human environments. The ability to gain robust feedback on design ideas prior to physical construction will allow designers to take more risks, identify potential problems sooner and inexpensively develop a body of evidence to justify the value of a design concept. So, while intellectually rigorous, this testing method does not lead to a mechanical one-size-fits-all design approach. By including demographic variables in the data analysis, designers can become more aware of the variability in human responses to design, especially those of minority populations whose needs and perspectives have been historically overlooked in the field. In addition, the reduced cost of our approach will make it more feasible for researchers to carry out human response testing on an international scale. This is significant because most existing post-occupancy studies have been conducted in a small number of developed countries, with results that may not be fully generalizable to the global population.[17] Perhaps most importantly, the virtual response–testing method can encourage more active participation of the greater public in shaping design outcomes. By looking to the public to provide feedback and participate in design evaluations, our method helps designers to ensure that they are truly serving the needs of the community.

* * * *

Discussion and Exercises

Reflections about the Chapter You Just Read:

1. Please refer to the standard features of a research project explained in the Introduction. Then:
    a. In one sentence, identify the *research topic*. This sentence can be in the form of a question but does not have to be. In any case, write one grammatically correct sentence that captures the research topic of this chapter.
    b. Identify the *literature* related to this research project.
    c. Identify the *method* which the author used and also the *data* which this method generated for analysis.
    d. Explain how this approach is *generalizable* (or not).
    e. Explain how you can have confidence (or not) of the *internal and external validity* of this author's overall approach.
2. List the four stages of Kalantari's research. Why are the four stages necessary? What does each stage contribute to the logic of the overall research plan? Itemize the various tactics each stage required in order to obtain his data.
3. The chapter notes the inconsistency in data in the impact of classrooms with rounded versus square corners, and exactly how views of nature relate to user responses. How might these inconsistencies be further tested to gain clarity about these issues in future experiments?
4. Besides classroom design, Kalantari lists these other design typologies that can make use of this method: residential environments, retail stores, public spaces such as parks and museums,

overall urban environments and landscape designs. Select one of these typologies and describe what specific data this kind of approach would generate for that typology? (For example: what would designers look for in simulations of retail spaces or public parks?)

Exercises/Suggestions for Further Study

1. As a way to assess the relationship between human behavior and environmental factors use a Semantic Differential (SD) scale to measure individuals' attitudes toward a specific environment. An SD scale records experiential perceptions such as comfortable vs. uncomfortable, pleasant vs. unpleasant, bright vs. dull. Refer to this study for an example of an SD scale and how to use it: Judy Theodorson, "Daylit Classrooms at 47N, 117W: Insights from occupation." *PLEA2009*, 26th Conference on Passive and Low Energy Architecture, Quebec City, Canada, 22–24 June 2009. https://www.academia.edu/6665889/Daylit_Classrooms_at_47N_117W_Insights_from_occupation.
2. Input one of your projects into a VR-compatible platform (such as REVIT) to conduct a post-occupancy study. Use Kalantari's process for setting up a study with live participants:
    a. Inform them about the general purpose of the study but not the particular hypotheses or design variables being tested.
    b. Ask them to fill out a brief demographic questionnaire (age, gender, ethnicity, education, occupation, alcohol/caffeine/substance use, and any known neurological conditions).
    c. Introduce participants to the study and allow them to try out the equipment for five minutes, assuring them that they can stop the testing at any time and for any reason if they feel uncomfortable.
    d. Have participants virtually move through the space.
    e. Record their responses. (Please keep this to a classroom exercise with the information not to be shared beyond the class and clear with the university's IRB if needed.)
    f. Compare the success of the space to the design intent.
3. Set up a comparative study testing the accessibility of an environment to understand how environmental factors impact human health and safety.
    a. Outline the process of conducting an assessment of an environment by having students engage in it while confined to a wheelchair. Can they easily navigate the space? Can they appropriately reach counters, products and so on? Do they have direct access to paths or are they required to extensively circumnavigate to get to it an entrance?
    b. Create a digital model of the same space and have classmates navigate it virtually.
    c. Compare: variables, outcomes and so on between real and virtual.
4. Read the following studies that also use VR but measure different aspects of the human-environment interface. Evaluate the similarities and differences between these studies and Kalantari's study. Are the tactics interchangeable? Are there reasons why certain tactics might be more useful to a specific environment?
    a. Ahmed Alawadhi and So-Yeon Yoon, "Shopping behavioral intentions contributed by store layout and perceived crowding: an exploratory study using computer walk-through simulation." *Journal of Interior Design* 35, no. 3 (2010): 34–50.
    b. So-Yeon Yoon, Hyunjoo Oh, and Ji Young Cho, "Understanding furniture design choices using a 3D virtual showroom." *Journal of Interior Design* 41, no. 4 (2010): 29–46.

5. Refer to the term "thick description" as defined in Chapter 2. Even though Kalantari doesn't mention thick description, summarize how his research plan realized thick description, and why thick description is helpful. Compare and contrast this use of thick description to how this same term is used in Chapter 12.

Additional Connections and Information

1. Reference was made to experimental research in the Introduction to this chapter. Experimental research is the methodological expression of "scientific method." This entails the following. Scientific knowledge assumes that a given reality can be described by numerical quantities, so it uses experimental research to identify those quantities, and to discover relationships between those quantities in mathematically precise ways. Therefore, experimental researchers often use equations, or inferential statistics, toward these ends. Specific cases vary, but the key characteristics of experimental research are listed below. (Let us use as an example a new window unit being developed by a window manufacturer before the unit can be put on the market. The manufacturer wants to know the window's insulating qualities. This is done by determining the U-value of the window design. U-values provide quantitative measures of heat transfer. The lower the U-value, the higher the insulating performance.) Experimental research on this window will entail the following features. How does each feature figure into Kalantari's pilot study?
    a. *Unit of test.* To conduct an experiment measuring for U-value, the window is isolated in a setting in which only factors related to measuring for U-value are present, and can be measured. Care is taken to exclude any "hidden factors" interfering with the experiment because they will nullify the accuracy of the result.
    b. *Independent variable.* This is the variable the experimenter can manipulate. It is the active variable impacting the unit of test external to the features of the unit of test itself. For instance, the researcher can increase thermal conditions on the exterior of the window, to see how much heat is transmitted through the window.
    c. *Dependent variable.* This is the resulting measure(s) that are caused by the independent variable. By increasing external thermal conditions (the independent variable), the experimental researcher measures the U-value properties of the window unit in response to the new external conditions.
    d. *Instruments.* Experimental research, then, often requires measuring instruments to ascertain the independent and dependent variables in quantifiable terms (by weight, force, length, width, scales of measure such as temperature, distance, magnification).
    e. *Cause.* Experimental research seeks to identify *causality.* In our example, the experimenter must be confident that the U-value measures were caused by the manipulated thermal condition (the independent variable) and not any other factors.
    f. *Control.* To assure the accuracy of causal measures, experimental research often uses a control, which is a duplicate of the unit of test in every way—except this control unit does not receive the independent variable. In our window test, the control can be quite simple: just the same window set-up which does not have the thermal condition altered. Controls become more important when testing for human responses. For example, in

pharmacological studies that measure the impact of a drug on behavior, we want to have a control group of participants who do not receive the drug, to compare their responses to those participants in the active unit of test, who do receive the drug (as the independent variable).

   g. O_1-X-O_2. You will often see this kind of nomenclature related to experimental research. The O_1 denotes the initial condition of the unit of test. The X is the imposition of the independent variable, and the O_2 denotes the resulting condition of the unit of test.

2. In correspondence with the editors, Kalantari had these additional points to make (these are his words, but adjusted for this publication):
   a. VR has been used in the last 20 years in design research, and maybe Immersive VR has been used in the last five years. The combination of VR and biometric sensors is the new knowledge represented by this design research tool. The platform has not been implemented in the field of interior design as yet.
   b. My research brands this line of inquiry as *computational neuroarchitecture*. In some of these new studies, I am using AR (augmented reality) or just EEG alone in real environments.
   c. I am running a new set of experiments in different contexts that might be helpful for better defining future studies using this research tool. In retail design, we are evaluating emotional arousal and attractiveness comparing different store layouts and storefront design. In consumer behavior, we are evaluating purchase intentions comparing the presence of digital review on products. In healthcare design, we are collaborating with an architecture firm evaluating their wayfinding strategies for a real hospital project. We are also running an experiment with nurses, evaluating nurse–patient interaction in different healthcare settings. All of these types of experiments are based on the VR + EEG platform.
3. Additional literature related to post-occupancy evaluation (POE):
   a. Dennis, Samuel F. Jr., and Alexandra Wells, and Candace Bishop. "A post-occupancy study of nature-based outdoor classrooms in early childhood education." *Children, Youth and Environments* 24, no. 2 (2014): 35–52.
   b. Marley Jenifer, MaryEllen C. Nobe, Caroline M. Clevenger, and James H. Banning, "Participatory post-occupancy evaluation (PPOE): A method to include students in evaluating health-promoting attributes of a green school." *Children, Youth and Environments* 25, no. 1 (2015): 4–28.
   c. Preiser, Wolfgang F.E. "Post-occupancy evaluation: how to make buildings work better." *Facilities* 13, no. 11 (1995): 19–28.
   d. Sherman, Sandra A., James W. Varnis, and Roger S. Ulrich. "Post-occupancy evaluation of healing gardens in a pediatric cancer center." *Landscape and Urban Planning* 73, no. 2–3 (15 October 2005): 167–183.
4. Additional literature related to VR + EEG, or VR and other types of biometric sensors:
   a. Banaei, M., J. Hatami, A. Yazdanfar, and K. Gramann. "Walking through architectural spaces: the impact of interior forms on human brain dynamics." *Frontiers in Human Neuroscience* 11 (2017): 477.
   b. Jang, J. Y., E. Baek, S. Y. Yoon, and H. J. Choo. "Store design: Visual complexity and consumer responses." *International Journal of Design* 12, no. 2 (2018): 105–118.
   c. Jelić, A., G. Tieri, F. De Matteis, F. Babiloni, and G. Vecchiato. "The enactive approach to architectural experience: A neurophysiological perspective on embodiment, motivation, and affordances." *Frontiers in Psychology* 7 (2016): 481.

d. Shemesh, A., R. Talmon, O. Karp, I. Amir, M. Bar, and Y. J. Grobman. "Affective response to architecture–investigating human reaction to spaces with different geometry." *Architectural Science Review* 60, no. 2 (2017): 116–125.

e. Shin, Y.-B., S.-H. Woo, D.-H. Kim, J. Kim, J.-J. Kim and J. Y. Park. "The effect on emotions and brain activity by the direct/indirect lighting in the residential environment." *Neuroscience Letters* 584 (2014): 28–32.

f. Vartanian, O., G. Navarrete, A. Chatterjee, L. B. Fich, H. Leder, C. Modroño, et al. "Impact of contour on aesthetic judgments and approach-avoidance decisions in architecture." *Proceedings of the National Academy of Sciences* 110, no. 2 (2013): 10446–10453.

Notes

1 Council for Interior Design Accreditation, "Emerging Technologies: Big Picture Trends," *2018 Summit Report: A Strategic View to the Future*. https://accredit-id.org/wp-content/uploads/2018/07/Final_CIDA_Summit_Report.pdf. Accessed October 23, 2019.

2 Jason Maneely, *Finding Virtue in the Virtual: A Values Driven Approach for VR in Design Education*. https://vimeo.com/292331644. Accessed May 2, 2019.

3 A few representative studies in this area include: Rikard Küller et al., "Color, Arousal, and Performance: A Comparison of Three Experiments," *Color Research and Application* 34 (2009): 141–152; Oshin Vartanian et al., "Impact of Contour on Aesthetic Judgments and Approach–Avoidance Decisions in Architecture," *Proceedings of the National Academy of Sciences* 110, supplement 2 (2013): 10446–10453; Heeyoung Choo et al., "Neural Codes of Seeing Architectural Styles," *Scientific Reports*, January 10, 2017, n.p.; and Y. B. Shin et al., "The Effect on Emotions and Brain Activity by Direct/Indirect Lighting in the Residential Environment," *Neuroscience Letters* 584 (2014): 28–32.

4 Some of this evidence in diverse design areas is summarized in D. Kirk Hamilton and David H. Watkins, *Evidence-based Design for Multiple Building Types* (Hoboken, NJ: Wiley, 2009); and Kerstin Sailer et al., "Evidence-based Design: Theoretical and Practical Reflections of an Emerging Approach in Office Architecture," in *Undisciplined! Proceedings of the Design Research Society Conference* (Sheffield: Sheffield University Press, 2009).

5 See Rosalyn Cama, *Evidence-based Healthcare Design* (Hoboken, NJ: Wiley, 2009); Roger S. Ulrich, "Effects of Healthcare Environmental Design on Medical Outcomes," *Design and Health: Proceedings of the Second International Conference on Health and Design* (Stockholm, Sweden: Springer, 2001), 49–59; and Roger S. Ulrich et al., "A Review of the Research Literature on Evidence-based Healthcare Design," *Health Environments Research and Design Journal* 1, no. 3 (2008): 61–125.

6 Several important "neuroarchitectural" studies have emerged in recent years. Oshin Vartanian and colleagues have carried out systematic investigations of how brain-effects are correlated with variations in contour (Vartanian et al., "Impact of Contour," op. cit.) and variations in ceiling height (Vartanian et al., "Architectural Design and the Brain: Effects of Ceiling Height and Perceived Enclosure on Beauty Judgements and Approach–Avoidance Decisions," *Journal of Environmental Psychology* 41 [2015]: 10–18). Heeyoung Choo and colleagues ("Neural Codes of Seeing," op. cit.) studied the neural representation of different architectural style in the human brain. Jenny J. Roe and colleagues ("Engaging the Brain: The Impact of Natural Versus Urban Scenes Using Novel EEG Methods in an Experimental Setting," *Environmental Science* 1 [2013]: 93–104) studied older people's neural activation in response to a changing urban environment while walking. Rikard Küller and colleagues ("Color, Arousal, and Performance," op. cit.) investigated the psychological and physiological effects of colored room interiors, and similarly, Y. B. Shin and colleagues ("The Effect on Emotions and Brain," op. cit.) analyzed how variations in lighting affected emotions and brain oscillations. Finally, Maryam Banaei and colleagues ("Walking through Architectural Spaces: The Impact of Interior Forms on Human Brain Dynamics," *Frontiers in Human Neuroscience*, September 27, 2017, n.p.) investigated the impact of different interior forms on the perceivers' affective state and the accompanying brain activity.

7 Klaus Gramann et al., "Imaging Natural Cognition in Action," *International Journal of Psychophysiology* 91 (2014): 22–29; Klaus Gramann et al., "Toward a New Cognitive Neuroscience: Modeling Natural Brain Dynamics," *Frontiers in Human Neuroscience*, June 19, 2014, n.p.

8 Trieu Phat Luu et al., "Real-time EEG-based Brain-computer Interface to a Virtual Avatar Enhances Cortical Involvement in Human Treadmill Walking," *Scientific Reports*, August 21, 2017, n.p.

9 For more information about these various types of biometric sensors, see N. Sharma and T. Gedeon, "Objective Measures, Sensors, and Computational Techniques for Stress Recognition and Classification: A Survey," *Computer Methods and Programs in Biomedicine* 108, no. 3 (2012): 1287–1301; and George I. Christopoulos et al., "The Body and the Brain: Measuring Skin Conductance Responses to Understand the Emotional Experience," *Organizational Research Methods*, December 8, 2016, n.p.

10 T. C. Chan and M. D. Richardson, *Ins and Outs of School Facility Management: More than Bricks and Mortar* (Lanham, MD: Scarecrow Education, 2005); Jose L. Martín, "Determining Eligibility Under Section 405: Fundamentals and New Challenge Areas," Council of Educators for Students with Disabilities, 2010,http://www.504idea.org/Council_Of_Educators/Resources_files/Modern%20504%20Eligibility.pdf.

11 Paul Temple, *Learning Spaces for the 21st Century* (London: Centre for Higher Education Studies, 2007), 4. See also P. Woolner et al., "A Sound Foundation? What We Know About the Impact of Environments on Learning," *Oxford Review of Education* 33, no. 1 (2007): 47–70; and M. L. Kaup, H. C. Kim, and M. Dudek, "Planning to Learn: The Role of Interior Design in Educational Settings," *International Journal of Designs for Learning* 4, no. 2 (2013): 41–55.

12 R. Brooks, A. Fuller, and J. L. Waters, *Changing Spaces of Education: New Perspectives on the Nature of Learning* (New York: Routledge, 2012); D. Butin, *Multipurpose Spaces* (Washington, DC: National Clearinghouse for Educational Facilities, 2000).

13 For the value of "naturalness" in educational settings, see J. Daisey, W. Angell, and M. Apte, "Indoor Air Quality, Ventilation, and Health Symptoms in Schools," *Indoor Air* 13 (2003): 53–64; and P. Wargocki and D. P. Wyon, "The Effects of Moderately Raised Classroom Temperature and Classroom Ventilation Rate on the Performance of Schoolwork by Children," *HVAC&R Research* 13, no. 2 (2007): 193–220. For the value of stimulation and sensory impact, see R. Küller, B. Mikellides, and J. Janssens, "Color, Arousal, and Performance," *Color Research and Application* 34, no. 2 (2009): 141–152; and A. Fisher, K. Godwin, and H. Seltman, "Visual Environment, Attention Allocation, and Learning in Young Children," *Psychological Science* 25, no. 7 (2014): 1362–1370.

14 A full literature review of educational design studies cannot be replicated here due to space limitations. However, representative analyses include the discussion of ceiling heights in Gary T. Moore et al., *Recommendations for Child Care Centers* (Milwaukee, WI: Center for Architecture and Urban Planning Research, 1979); the examination of window placements in Dongying Li and William C. Sullivan, "Impact of Views to School Landscapes on Recovery from Stress and Mental Fatigue," *Landscape and Urban Planning* 148 (2016): 149–158; and the investigation of surface textures in C. Kenneth Tanner and Ann Langford, "The Importance of Interior Design Elements as They Relate to Student Outcomes," Carpet and Rug Institute. https://files.eric.ed.gov/fulltext/ED478177.pdf. As can be seen from these examples, the literature on classroom design elements is frequently based on anecdotal evidence and extremely limited study designs; thus a more rigorous analysis of the relevant design variables is sorely needed.

15 See Mart van Dinther, Filip Dochy, and Mien Segers, "Factors Affecting Students' Self-efficacy in Higher Education," *Educational Research Review* 6, no. 2 (2011): 95–108.

16 For more information on these EEG data-processing techniques, see A. Delorme and S. Makeig, "EEGLAB: An Open Source Toolbox for Analysis of Single-trial EEG Dynamics," *Journal of Neuroscience Methods* 134 (2004): 9–21; Atilla Kilicarslan, Robert G. Grossman, and Jose Luis Contreras-Vidal, "A Robust Adaptive De-noising Framework for Real-time Artifact Removal in Scalp EEG Measurements," *Journal of Neural Engineering* 13, no. 2: n.p.; and N. Bigdely-Shamlo, T. Mullen, C. Kothe, K. M. Su, and K. A. Robbins, "The PREP Pipeline: Standardized Preprocessing for Large-scale EEG Analysis," *Frontiers in Neuroinformatics* 9 (2015): 16.

17 See Saleh Kalantari et al., "Designing for Operational Efficiency: Facility Managers' Perspectives on How Their Knowledge Can Be Better Incorporated During Design," *Architectural Engineering and Design Management* 13, no. 6 (2017): 457–478.

Chapter 12

Creative Scholarship

Editors' Introduction by Dana E. Vaux and David Wang

This chapter is based on conversations with Andrew Kudless, along with information drawn from many available sources about his work. Computational design is an important emerging domain in design education and practice, so we regard this chapter not as a conclusion to this book but rather as a launching point for new inquiries about design computation from a research perspective.

Kudless's work is also an excellent example of creative scholarship in general. Creative scholarship is vital in design academia, regardless of whether the research is in computational design or in design more broadly (or traditionally) considered. This chapter can therefore serve as a reference to students or faculty seeking to frame their creative design projects through a research lens.

Andrew Kudless describes the work of his office, Matsys, as "a design studio that explores the emergent relationships between architecture, engineering, biology, and computation."[1] This mission statement is further processed through three particular research themes: (1) organic performance, (2) craft in the age of computation and (3) the meaning of "drawing." Kudless says: "These three themes are my interest, and there are certain designers who can integrate these really well. I would say ... the pre-eminent model is from biology, in that we see growth and formation without any externally intentional factors."[2]

As you read this chapter, note how these three themes constantly recur:

1. *Organic performance.* Any designed object can be evaluated in terms of its performance. "There is a wide spectrum of kinds of performance: financial performance, structural performance, environmental performance, artistic performance, political performance ... so I think we need to think how a design process captures all this from within."[3] In mimicking natural processes of generation, how can all of these dimensions of "performance" inform design thinking without privileging one or another?

2. *Craft in the age of computation*. Kudless says, "I believe craft in the age of computation is simply having a level of mastery over the tools and materials where you push them to their limits and the result is unknown from the start." He notes that this view resonates with David Pye's definition of workmanship: "using any kind of technique or apparatus, in which the quality of the result is not predetermined, but depends on the judgment, dexterity and care which the maker exercises as he works."[4] In this chapter, note how this organic play between crafting materials to their limit while not predicting outcomes expresses itself in Kudless's works.
3. *What is drawing? Code, cypher, script, constraint*. A theoretical question of Kudless and his colleagues in the computational design world is this: What is the status of "drawing" in design thinking and practices now increasingly informed by computation? "Among my peers there are a number of people who talk about design to production as this workflow where you go directly from the digital model ... to code that runs the machines, to robots that assemble it for you. In that case the drawings just disappear entirely."[5] Kudless's question regarding the status of "drawing" in design thinking has been a topic interior designers have grappled with for decades as the design development process has shifted from hand drawing and drafting to computer drafting, modeling and rendering.

This chapter features three Kudless projects. Each is a snapshot of how "we see growth and formation without any externally intentional factors." All three are well documented in the literature: the Pavilion in Confluence Park, the P-Wall projects (there are several) and the Walled City project. Our aim here is to showcase how these projects exemplify *research* in creative scholarship. For this purpose, then, we consider each project through four aspects common to all research methodologies: (A) research topic/research question, (B) literature, (C) research tactics and (D) validity and generalizability. These four aspects, overlaid on Kudless's three research themes, produce an analytical matrix for the organization of this chapter.

Each project foregrounds one of Kudless's three research themes, but it is very important to note that all three are always present in Kudless's design thinking for *every* project (Figure 12.1). In a recent symposium on design research at Penn State University, Kudless challenged the idea that a "research method" must be a fixed system. For Kudless, research is a continuous process of discovery.[6] This view is itself in step with a semblance of biological generation. For a book on research methods, however, the real value lies in the fact that through conversations with Kudless and reviews of his published statements, standard research themes emerge.

	1. Organic performance	2. Craft in the age of computation	3. The meaning of "drawing"
A. Topic / research question			
B. Literature			
C. Research tactics			
D. Validity/ Generalizability			

Figure 12.1 Analytical matrix for this chapter: Kudless's three research themes assessed by standard elements of research.

Interiority

Kudless's work takes on dimensions of organic flow in design productions. Interiority here is regarded as something like a life-force that operates from within the production process itself, freed from intentional agency from external sources while including those external factors. As you read this chapter look for the logic of internal growth in each of the three Kudless projects.

1. Note how the "organic" internal logic ultimately expresses itself in physical form(s).
2. Note also the methodological steps taken to mimic this organic spontaneity of growth, as if it comes from "within."

* * * *

Computational Design: Organic Growth and Research Tactics

Interview with Andrew Kudless by David Wang and Dana E. Vaux

Linkages between natural processes and human design have fascinated thinkers for a long time.[7] Productions of nature seem spontaneous, while human productions require intentional design and construction. Andrew Kudless devotes his teaching and practice to the following question: How can human design processes echo the spontaneity of natural productions?

There are external and internal challenges to answering this question. Externally, design and construction take place within social contexts like professional offices, construction schedules, cultural trends, functional needs and material limitations; the list is long. In these complicated venues, to produce a workable design, designers usually privilege certain priorities over others. Says Kudless: "the concept comes first and then they have to kind of layer on the pragmatics; it's always like a negotiation and a compromise that things are being torn away from the concept, while you struggle to maintain that concept."[8] The resulting design is an imprint of prioritized external factors, often working against the initial concept. But if a project is to echo a natural process of formation, this entails *internal* workings of organic growth. "What if a project can be grown from within, like how an apple grows?" Kudless asks.[9] He has in mind Michael Pollan's *Botany of Desire*, noting the symbiotic relationships between humans and nature (e.g., apples, tulips, weeds like the cannabis plant) that shape our cultural world. Kudless's research asks how design processes can also be symbiotic in like manner. What follows is an analysis of three of his projects through a research lens.

Organic Performance: Pavilion at Confluence Park

Kudless's Pavilion is located in Confluence Park (Figure 12.2), a 3.5-acre site along the San Antonio River. Formerly a parking area for trucks, Confluence Park is now an educational/recreational site emphasizing low-impact development. The overall project was a collaboration between Kudless's

Figure 12.2 The Pavilion at Confluence Park.

firm, Matsys, with Lake Flato Architects, Rialto Studio and Architectural Engineers Collaborative. Kudless says:

> One feature of my work is the integration of form, growth and behavior inspired by the ideas of D'Arcy Thompson, but on architectural terms. When form, fabrication, and performance are taken into account as organic growth, what does something look like, or what shape does it have? How does that shape come into being, in terms of its physical attributes, as part of a generative design process? How is it made?[10]

D'Arcy Thompson (1860–1948) was a Scottish biologist famous for his book *On Growth and Form*. Thompson demonstrates that the structures and sizes of natural forms, from molecules to plants to animals large and small, conform to uniform natural forces such as gravity, volumetric pressure, surface tension and equilibrium. For Thompson, natural forms do not come about willy-nilly but are the outcomes of an organic logic *in* the forms themselves. Here is Thompson's description of a leaf:

> The form, then, of any portion of matter, whether it be living or dead, and the changes of form which are apparent in its movements and in its growth, may in all cases alike be described as due to the action of force. In short, the form of an object is a diagram of forces.[11]

The generation of form is always in conformance to these forces from within the form.

In like fashion, Kudless's Pavilion consists of 22 concrete "petals." At the base, a petal is 16–18.5" thick, but as it ascends to 30 feet, the tip of each petal is 4" thick. The petals are then connected with pins such that continuous seams of natural light undulate and intersect across the upper reaches of the "leaf" canopy. To negotiate the curving contours of the petals, Kudless used a parametric algorithm based on the logic of *Cairo tiling* (Figure 12.3), a complex pattern similar to that of beehives. According to Kudless's website:

> The design uses the Cairo tile, an irregular pentagon, as the underlying base grid in order to resolve the tension between cost-effective modularity and the desire for spatial richness.

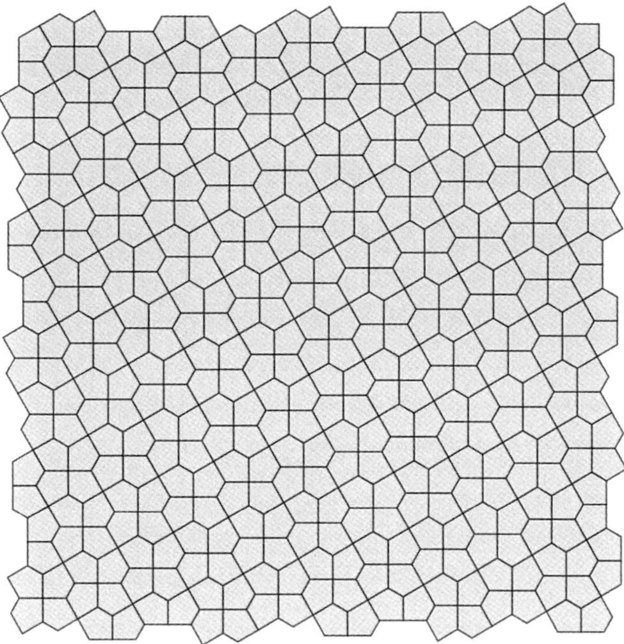

Figure 12.3 A standard Cairo tile pattern. WIKI commons; see credits.

> The pentagon is subdivided into 5 triangles in a way that results in only three unique modules: two asymmetrical triangles that are mirrors of each other and one equilateral triangle. From this irregular triangular base grid, a parametric model was used to create the three-dimensional solids of each petal.[12]

In this way, the Pavilion achieves a biomimetic rigor not imposed externally (i.e., simply making a shape look plantlike) but generates the plantlike form from an interior logic. The logic of the double curve making up the upper and under sides of each petal collects rainwater, directing this flow into the underground cistern below. This is where craft comes to the foreground in Kudless's approach. Three machines were used to mill the formwork for the concrete petals: two different five-axis CNC machines[13] and a six-axis robot with an external rotary table (so seven axes in total).

> After milling the foam forms, a 2 inch thick composite structure composed of inner and outer layers of fiberglass composite with a central core of balsa wood was applied. The formwork was then shipped to the site to be cast as a modified tilt-up wall construction ... the bottom is cast against the smooth fiberglass while the top is broom-finished with the broom strokes aligning with the direction of the water flow.[14]

To ensure optimal performance, Kudless tested his design with water flow analysis using particle simulations. To do all of this, the development of new codes "situates craft as part of the internal organic growth, staying in step with how the design-as-organism internally unfolds itself. This is the excitement in writing original code that behaves in this way."[15] We now consider Kudless's Pavilion project through the four methodological aspects noted in Figure 12.1.

The Pavilion: Methodology

A. Research Topic and Question

A clear research topic always comes out of a clear research question; the two go together. Joseph Maxwell has noted that "all other components" of a research project links to the research question.[16] Often in a written research project, the title of the project is in a way an answer to its research question. This is why titles to written research projects tend to be long; they need to capture the specificity of the topic. Groat and Wang give this example of a research title: *Dwelling Well: An Application of Christopher Alexander's Theory of Wholeness to Investigate Affective Responses to Homes Incorporating Renewable Natural Resources.*[17] This is a very precise topic, and it takes a lot of work on the part of the researcher to get the title of the inquiry to this level of clarity. The embedded research question, then, is something like this: How do people living in off-grid homes emotionally relate to their residential environments?

One might say that creative projects such as this pavilion *seem* to have an advantage over written research projects because the design is almost always a single built form or environment: interiors for a hospital, a residential interior, a pavilion in a park, and so on. In this sense, the design project itself is the topic of research. But how to proceed so as to assure that the design activity is creative *scholarship*? Here is a key: for both written and design research, *the work should clearly interact with a body of theory.* Once the theory is clear, both the research question and research topic become clearer. Note that the example above makes use of a theoretical framework from Christopher Alexander. In the case of Kudless's Pavilion, the link to theories of biological processes is also clear; as noted, Kudless looks to the theory of D'Arcy Thompson. From Thompson, Kudless can ask: "How does a physical form come into being through a generative process *within* the physical manifestation of it? How is it made?"[18] In short, "What processes go into the design of a Pavilion that comes closest to organic self-generation?" A clear question (or a clear set of related questions) drawn from a body of theory energizes research because the question tells the researcher how to think, what to ask, where to look and what to do. This applies to both written and design research.

B. Literature

If anything comes across in Kudless's work, it is the *excitement* that drives his search for answers. Put another way, for either written research or design projects, if there is no *love* for one's topic, it is very difficult to follow through to good results. A characteristic of all prominent designers is that they know a vast amount of "literature" related to their designs: in terms of history; in terms of theory; in terms of exemplars; in terms of current affairs; in terms of relevant and emerging materials and construction techniques. In short, if there *is* excitement and love for the project, then "literature" is simply the many resources and references the researcher interacts with to inform his or her research. Again, D'Arcy Thompson's *On Growth and Form* was an inspiration for the Pavilion at Confluence Park. But there is also the Cairo tile. Frank Morgan, Atwell Professor of Mathematics Emeritus at Williams College, describes this pattern as follows: "The ... Cairo tile, long popular in Cairo, Egypt, has two right angles and three angles of 120 degrees, circumscribed around a circle. The 120-degree angles meet happily in threes; the right angles meet happily in fours."[19] The mathematical literature, then, contains knowledge that is unavoidable in questions related to Kudless's theme of organic performance. Thompson's *On Growth and Form* is filled with equations. In Kudless's Pavilion, biology and mathematics are harnessed to serve *design* thinking and praxis; this is the interdisciplinary value of Kudless's approach. Moreover, there is the base expertise in computational design and Kudless's commitment to develop original code as a digital craft. This exploration also requires knowledge of the computational literature that biologists would not know, nor mathematicians necessarily. It is yet another body of literature at Kudless's disposal. Together, these sources are the "literature" that Kudless draws from for this project.

C. Research Tactics

In research, "tactics" denote the actions a researcher takes in order to obtain his or her results. For example, a scientist doesn't just sit in the lab and think about an experiment; the experiment has to be set up, the results measured or weighed. To write a history of Dorothy Draper's career, a historian must visit the archives; projects must be documented; important people related to Draper must be interviewed. These *actions* are called research tactics. Similarly, the list of tactics employed for a design project is almost endless. Kudless did not simply "come up" with the petals of the Pavilion. Many design iterations had to be modeled. He conducted water flow analyses using particle simulations. The forms for the concrete petals had to be carefully assembled.

D. Validity and Generalizability

As noted in the Introduction to this book, internal validity relates to the logical coherence of a research project itself. External validity relates to whether the findings can be replicated by others using the same internal logic of the project, under similar conditions.[20] Here, the site of Confluence Park itself, once a parking lot for trucks, becomes the unit of test. Causality becomes agency, understood as the human intentionality that changes a given "structure," understood as a status quo set of social circumstances.[21] In relation to the Pavilion, the independent variable relates to the sources that inspired Kudless's actions: biological generation, organic performance as a function of craft, biomimicry and so on. And the dependent variable is the resultant change brought on by the Pavilion, and Confluence Park as a whole, a pleasant restoration of natural conditions to an underused site, but also as an educational resource for low-impact development. All of these can be regarded as the coherence of validity.

Craft in the Age of Computation: P-Wall

In a keynote lecture titled "Bodies of Formation" at the University of Virginia, Kudless noted that he conceives of his creative research in terms of "morphotypes." The familiar theme of organic biological formation is clear in all these types: shells, cells, fields, eggs, stacks, strands, pneus and totems.[22] For Kudless, these morphotypes are "research areas." In all categories, the focus is a process relating concepts to forms and then to fabrication techniques, with the overarching question

Figure 12.4 The P-Wall at SFMOMA.

of how an object *per*forms, understood as its organism-like behavior. For any specific object, the intersection of these priorities creates a space of tension between computer and human craft. For Kudless, craft pays attention to the production of unique objects in which the craftsperson works with intimate knowledge of the material, perhaps stretching it to its maximum capacities, one object at a time.[23] On the other hand, computation programs can generate products quickly and in great quantities. When computation intersects craft, this can entail writing custom codes for unique problems the designer wants to solve. And in the case of the P-Wall, craft understood as hand work also plays an integral part of the creative scholarship (Figure 12.4).

The name "P-Wall" comes from Kudless's desire to avoid standard names associated with architecture. "When I was working on this project, it looked like a voluptuous kind of cloudy landscape. People would say, 'Oh, it looks like a pregnant belly.' A brain surgeon once came to the studio and she said, 'It looks like the brain.' So I just kind of follow the practice of titling a Japanese house, where you would have H-House, or M-House."[24] "P-Wall" simply falls under Kudless's category

Figure 12.5 The form used to fabricate P-Wall sections for SFMOMA.

Figure 12.6 Poured sections of the P-Wall.

of pneumatic structures (pneus). The word "pneumatic" concerns how a substance responds to pressure impinging upon it; the pressure could be a gas or liquid. In this case, Kudless applied the pressure of poured plaster (in later P-Wall projects it is concrete) to a mesh held in place by a wooden frame either rectangular in shape or hexagonal (Figures 12.5 and 12.6). In turn, the cured pours form sections that are placed together to assemble the wall. There are currently several installed P-Walls: a commissioned work in 2006 for an installation at the Knowlton School of Architecture at the Ohio State University[25]; a much larger 2009 commission for SFMOMA; and the 2013 commission for the FRAC Centre in France, designed by Jacob + MacFarlane. The SFMOMA wall was 45 feet long in a passageway 8 feet wide.[26] In what follows, we consider the P-Wall in terms of the methodological research terms, topic/question, literature, tactics, validity and generalizability.

P-Wall: Methodology

A. Research Topic and Question

"So, when I began this research ... it was either simply a joy to do ...; like there's something really pleasurable about making (the thing) in some way. *Or* it's about a problem; it's something *not* a joy, but more like a grit of sand that's really annoying you." Kudless said this in relation to his P-Wall research but noted that it applies to all of his projects.[27] This goes to an earlier point: creative scholarship (like all scholarship) calls for deep emotional commitments on the part of the artist or researcher. It is this commitment that spurs the researcher on, through joys, or (more often) through perplexing challenges to solve. The P-Wall project is a good illustration of how a question is formed. In 2005, while giving a seminar at Yale University, Kudless was struck by the form of a column on the architecture building designed by Paul Rudolph (Figure 12.7). The organic contours of the form stirred in Kudless the question: how would a mesh respond if it received a cementitious pour? From this question Kudless wrote a simple script using the computer modeling software, Rhino, for the image of a mesh of 18" × 36" in which various points are mapped to represent supports to hold the mesh during the pour. Along with the Rhino script, Kudless performed trial-and-error pours (what he calls "iterative testing"), from which he learned that supports 2 inches apart result in a very shallow "sag,"

Figure 12.7 This detail at the Yale Art and Architecture Building first stirred the ideas that resulted in the P-Wall projects.

but if placed at 8 inches apart, the mesh brakes and "you are left with plaster on the floor." He then embedded this information in his script.

All of Kudless's P-Wall projects ask the same question about how a mesh pneumatically responds to the pressure of a cementitious material poured onto it. But even though the primary question remained the same, each project stirred new tactics and generated new knowledge. In this sense, each of the projects can be regarded as iterations of what Donald Schon terms *reflection in action* in which, for each iteration, the designer gains new perspectives to inform the next creative iteration.[28] For instance, Kudless wanted to lessen the visual presence of the seams between each poured section of the 2006 wall. For the SFMOMA project in 2009, Kudless experimented with, and decided upon, hexagonal frames for his pours, and worked with the supports such that deep and shallow areas of each section altered in ways to minimize the visual seams. For its part, because the SFMOMA wall is 45 feet long, the client's initial request to Kudless was simply to make additional sections of the wall he had previously designed. But this would of course not be creative scholarship; it would just be some sort of mass production. Kudless obviously rejected this idea because the new commission offered new opportunities to develop tactics in fabricating the sections.

With the P-Wall at the FRAC center came another set of new research questions from both the client and Kudless. The client wanted to know what the FRAC P-Wall would look like. To this, Kudless responded that the very nature of his P-Wall is that it makes its own "look" as it is poured. But upon the client's continued insistence, Kudless developed computer simulations of what the FRAC Center P-Wall *can* look like, and he notes that developing code for this helped him think through ideas for future projects of this nature. On Kudless's part, an important theoretical question emerged by the time of the FRAC Center commission: is the P-Wall art, or is it architecture? At SFMOMA, a guard watched the P-Wall *as a work of art* to keep visitors from touching the plaster. ("A Rothko is right around the corner and if we let people touch your piece, they'll touch the Rothko too; we can't set a precedent for touching art.") But the FRAC Center regarded the P-Wall to be architecture, so it can be touched just as visitors touch other parts of a building. In response to this, Kudless began to develop the P-Wall in sections of thin-shell concrete for a more durable material. This led to tactics such as consulting with concrete fabricators, making rubber molds of the sections and then filling the molds with fiber reinforced concrete. Through writing a code for these sections, Kudless developed five sections that can be arranged in different ways. In sum: the guiding question for this research remained the same, but additional questions related to each iteration had to be identified and answered by both computer coding and handcraft.

B. Literature: Examplars

In Kudless's presentations and certainly in our interview, he repeatedly mentions people who in some way impacted his thinking. Particularly in creative scholarship, an *exemplar*—a person or object that serves as a model or an example—is itself a category of literature and literature review. Early in his University of Virginia lecture, Kudless identified the German architect and structural engineer Frei Otto (1925–2015), the Swiss engineer Heinz Isler (1926–2009) and the Spanish Mexican architect Felix Candela (1910–1997) as *theoretical* exemplars who spurred him to wonder how their work in strong and lightweight structures can be extended as precedents into the digital realm.[29] For the P-Wall, Kudless specifically cites the work of Miguel Fisac (1913–2006) as a forerunner who explored concrete pours into mesh forms to create inexpensive but very innovative walls that embed deep aesthetic values right into the fabrication process.

> Soon after starting the project, I discovered the work of Miguel Fisac in Spain. He had practiced there from the 1940s – 1980s. So, when I began the research, I had some questions about literature review and things like that. (And) I'd say this is how most of my research begins.[30]

Kudless also acknowledges Mark West, founding director of CAST, the Center for Architectural Structures and Technology.

> At CAST, he focuses on flexible casting into canvas. It is similar I would say to Fisac when he started in the 40s. The construction of the wooden formwork is more expensive, and wasteful; you throw it away; it gets soaked with the water. So, he began to think about how he could get rid of using wood in the formwork, or minimizing the use of wood and using canvas instead, because you could wash it and reuse it; so it was cheap. This was in the 40's, so it wasn't about sustainability yet, it was about efficiency and budget.[31]

Unlike drawing inspiration from D'Arcy Thompson for the Pavilion at Confluence Park, in creative scholarship, "literature" can also include built work, and those who designed them, as existing information. Importantly, using prominent designers as a literature source must entail more than just pictures of their work. Understanding these individuals and their work as design exemplars will necessarily lead to research of *standard* literature: the historical background, the theoretical background, how the work (or the designer) fits into the currents of his or her time, the important critical commentaries about the exemplar and, most importantly, how this exemplar impacts the creative scholarship at hand specifically. Kudless speaks of these aspects of his exemplars effortlessly—such as linking Fisac's work with West's—precisely because he has tracked them deeply.

C. Research Tactics

Kudless recalls his first foray into pouring plaster into a mesh.

> I had an idea about what I wanted it to look like. And I kept on trying to cast it again and again and again, and it never looked like that; it looked really ugly. I was embarrassed because it looked like this belly button or something. It was supposed to look like this beautiful sculpture that's at the Art and Architecture building at Yale ... a kind of mathematical surface that's cast and standing outside the building. So, I had this idea of how I could make it, and the process of making completely resisted the form that I had in my head. So, after a couple of months (of trying), this realization came to me that maybe I needed to give up an imposed view of what I *wanted* it to be, and simply begin to work with what the materials wanted to be.

The unexpected result that initially embarrassed Kudless led to the insight that *not* being able to totally control the outcome was a key aspect of the performative nature of this creative activity. Note that "performative" here denotes what the *object* does in coming to be; not necessarily what Kudless does. This insight came out of the tactical action of making the forms and mesh and pouring plaster into them; it did not come from theoretical thinking. These trial-and-error experiments led to the 2- to 8-inch intervals that became part of the generating script. Indeed, in his lecture at the University of Virginia, Kudless still maintained that he would not know how to write code to predict how a finished P-Wall might look.

For SFMOMA, a creative desire was to reduce the visual impact of the tile seams. At a length of 45 feet along a passageway of only 8 feet in width, site conditions informed Kudless's thinking for this particular location. Given the eight feet viewing space, the wall will mostly be seen obliquely. Kudless wrote code to vary recesses and projections for each section of the wall with this in view. There was also the decision to cast hexagonal sections rather than the rectangular ones; this also required trial castings.

What becomes apparent in both the SFMOMA wall and the one at the FRAC Centre is that, aside from each site being unique, client input also played an important role in the tactics Kudless used. It is remarkable that the P-Wall is a work of art in one case but "just architecture" in the other. (So, we again see how theory intimately informs creative scholarship.) If the P-Wall at the FRAC can be touched just like any other part of the architecture, a concrete wall makes more sense than a plaster one. This raised issues of the weight of the material and the structural support required for it. It called for a new method of production. Thin-shell concrete significantly reduces the weight; these had to be poured into rubber molds and improves ease of installation. These were all tactical considerations resulting from field inputs.

D. Validity and Generalizability

For a unique work of creative scholarship, broad acclamation of the work plays a key role in the assessment of its validity. Commissions from SFMOMA and the FRAC Center, in addition to a wide variety of publications online about the P-Wall, demonstrate the external validity of Kudless's work in this ongoing research area that he terms pneus. In their 2008 publication *Scholarship in Public: Knowledge Creation and Tenure Policy in the Engaged University*, Ellison and Eatman cite the following under the heading of "A Continuum of Scholarship."

> "I'm doing work that might be useful to the public" to, "I will interpret my work in order that others may understand its value," or "I know things the public ought to know and I will teach it to them," to a very different approach that builds upon a deep collaboration with people in the broader community. I think it is a continuous movement toward, "I will work with the public to generate the kind of knowledge that will be useful to all of us."[32]

For any endeavor of public scholarship—and in the P-Wall project as in all of Kudless's creative research, public engagement is foremost—validity comes by way of a recognizable and ever-growing line of work. On the part of the creative researcher, the evolving line of thinking Kudless reports in his iterations of the P-Wall is itself a kind of internal validity that has been affirmed externally.

Drawing as Digital Craft. *Walled City: Ten Mile Version*

As noted in the Introduction to this chapter, a theoretical concern of Kudless and his colleagues is the status of "drawing" in an age of design computation:

> We've evolved as architects for hundreds of years to use drawings as the primary generative medium of our profession. We're at this point with digital technology where we've kind of evolved away from that ... it's almost like (hand) drawing may not be needed anymore in some people's minds based on the way that machines and algorithms are facilitating design. One of my research interests is trying to find the answer to this question: is there a reason to still draw?[33]

The way Kudless answers this question is another example of research as a process of creative discovery. Similar to the projects above, a disciplined set of practices guide the open-ended nature of the research. Before considering Kudless's own answer to "is there a reason to still draw?" we first consider the methodological nature of what he and his co-curator Adam Marcus devised for obtaining a *composite* answer. They asked 24 architects to each submit a 25" × 25" two-dimensional drawing that foregrounds at least one of these four terms: *code*, *cypher*, *script* and *constraint*. All of the drawings must address the intersection of digital technology with traditional drawing, each emerging as a manifestation of drawing as digital craft. Kudless says:

> The invited architects were asked to conform to a set of strict rules: consistent dimension, black & white medium, and limiting the drawing to orthographic projection. The intent is for

> this consistency to emphasize the wide range of approaches to questions of technology, design, and representation.[34]

As of this writing, Kudless and Marcus have mounted two "Volumes" of exhibitions each displaying 24 curated drawings. Each of the first two Volumes consists of four exhibitions. These exhibitions were (or are scheduled to be) held in venues across the United States.[35] The overall title of these exhibitions is *Drawing Codes*. The intent is to have four Volumes, consisting of 96 drawings. While the contributors were given rigorous formatting requirements, they had broad latitude to creatively define what "drawing codes" mean within the given parameters. For instance, Amy Campos's "Dots, Figures, Cuts" (Figure 12.8) is one contribution in the *Volume I* exhibitions. Her written description of the piece, essentially her answer to the question, is the caption to Figure 12.8.

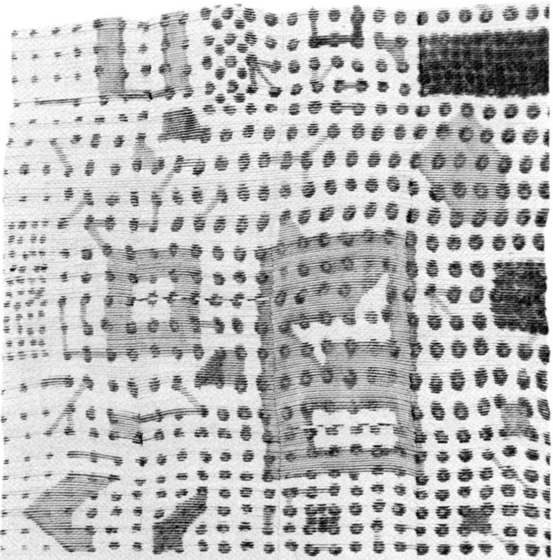

Figure 12.8 "Dots, Figures, Cuts" by Amy Campos. From the exhibit: *DRAWING CODES: Experimental Protocols of Architectural Representation, Volume 1*. Curated by Andrew Kudless and Adam Marcus. "This drawing assemblage reveals a lapse between material performance and architectural intention. Architectural drawing traditionally indicates an ideal, and often impossible, material situation. Inspired by the working processes of Sol LeWitt, Agnes Martin, and Tara Donovan, this drawing undermines intention. An ink drop is absorbed in an atypical way (asymmetrically, the viscosity of the ink changes drop by drop, it drops too soon on the wrong location, it splashes, etc) and produces imperfections. Cutting and stacking the paper reveals the material interaction between paper and ink and relates an ideal plan-based intention with a sectional material outcome. The nature of the material being somewhat out of control means that errors compound and the outcome of the assemblage is unexpected. The assembled drawing swells and deforms. By treating the paper as having sectional thickness, the assemblage falls somewhere between a drawing and a construction. Materials: black and pearlescent black liquid acrylic ink, 2.5 cm thick cotton blotting and wicking paper." http://digitalcraft.cca.edu/research/drawing-codes#vol1

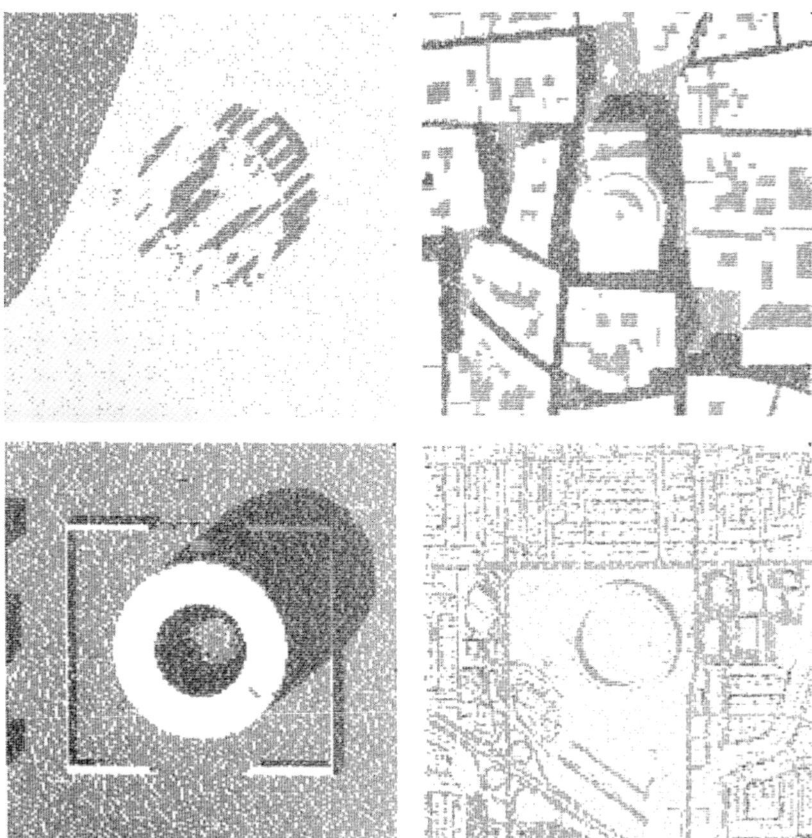

Figure 12.9 "Theory of Forms, nos. 1, 3, 4, AND 7," by Kathryn Moll and Nicholas de Monchaux. From the exhibit: *DRAWING CODES: Experimental Protocols of Architectural Representation, Volume II*. Curated by Andrew Kudless & Adam Marcus. Text—codes, standards, and specifications—shape the form of contemporary buildings in a measure far greater than lines. We depict the public realm of several historical examples—Stonehenge, the Pantheon, the Hirshhorn Museum and Apple Park—using the text of the written regulations governing their construction and use. In the buildings' shadows, we reveal another kind of text, expressing the buildings' physical affinity outside of time and circumstance: the mathematical constant pi. Made from mechanical impressions by a typewriter, the drawings are precise, but at a very poor resolution; they question our increasing assumptions about the detail and precision that we use to describe our environment, and the truthfulness and quality of the depiction that results.

Figure 12.9 shows Kathryn Moll and Nicholas de Monchaux's "Theory of Forms, nos. 1, 3, 4, AND 7," from *Volume II*. Their description of the project is also the caption.

From a methodological standpoint, we note that both Kudless and Marcus's approach itself is a research tactic: rather than a predetermined answer, a large number of sources contribute to what amounts to a composite answer. In its own way, this is obtaining a *thick description*—Clifford Geertz's famous term for collecting multiple perspectives to comprehend a single social event[36]—in the digital age and for creative scholarship. As well, Kudless and Marcus's approach is a *crowdsourcing* tactic: "the practice of obtaining needed services, ideas, or content by soliciting contributions from a large group of people and especially from the online community."[37] In this case, the sources were not online but from a targeted collection of informed individuals. All told, their approach is an example of creative scholarly research that gives teeth to the all-too-often vague term of *collaboration*. In their *Harvard Business Review* article "What kind of collaboration is right for you?", Gary Pisano and Roberto Verganti report several cases of successful design collaboration using multiple sources: the T-Shirt retailer Threadless is "an innovation mall where 600,000 members submit proposals for about 800 new designs weekly." Or: "Alessi, an Italian company famous for the postmodern design of its home products ... invited 200-plus collaborators from that domain to propose product designs."[38] Our point is that, for both thick description and crowdsourcing in this case, a rigorous set of parameters distributed to a large number of contributors resulted in ongoing composite "answers" for the conundrum of digital craft's relationship to traditional drawing. Kudless:

> within this considerable diversity of medium, aesthetic sensibility, and content, several common qualities emerge. First is the unsure link between code and outcome: glitches, bugs, accidents, anomalies, but also loopholes, deviations, variances, and departures that open up new potentials for architectural design and representation. Second is a mature embrace of technology not as a fetishized end game, but as an instrument employed

Figure 12.10 "Walled City, 10 Mile Version". Andrew Kudless.

> synthetically in concert with other architectural "tools of the trade." And finally, these drawings demonstrate how conventions of architectural representation remain fertile territory for invention and speculation.[39]

For this collaboration, Kudless's own scholarship in answer to drawing as a digital craft comes in the form of his Walled City. We assess it now for research topic, tactics and literature (considered here under one heading), and validity (Figure 12.10).

Walled City: Methodology

A. Research Topic and Question

Kudless's own words best describe how this project first took shape in his mind:

> This project began between Trump's election and his inauguration. There was just so much talk of the wall, the wall, the wall. I began thinking of walls within architecture, and the medieval walled city, and thinking about how Trump was proposing a kind of a walled country, right? It would be an enlarged nation state, but it's essentially still a medieval concept in a way. There's us, and there's them. And we're going to prevent them from being inside our space. And so, I tried to think of other ways ... Instead of getting rid of the wall, what if the wall actually consumed the city in a way? And enfolded and widened to the point where the entire interior of that wall, or of that city ... all of the program of that city was now inside or on top of that wall. And even the notion of sidedness is difficult, right? When you have a wall that's like a big circle around the city, it's very easy to understand inside and outside. But when the wall begins to fold on itself so much where you get ... I mean ... this is outside, and that's inside, and that's outside and inside ... and so forth, that you have parts in the dead center of the city that are technically on the boarder.[40]

We note that Kudless's topics and questions begin with some external input that fascinates him. ("It's something that's not a joy; it's more like ... a grit and the sand in the Vaseline ... that is just annoying you, and begins as this thing that you don't think on a rational conscious level you know why you're doing it."[41]) In the Pavilion at Confluence Park, it was the performance of organic forms. The P-Wall projects began with a happenstance encounter with a sculptural form at the Yale Architecture building. With the Walled City, political developments—"the wall"—morphed into thoughts about walls as definers of space, of community and as political lines of demarcation. All of these "grits of sand" are processed through issues raised by digital technology and, more specifically, by the boundaries at which computation is not so much a predetermined predictive tool but rather one that mimes behaviors in the simultaneity of real time that cannot be coded or scripted.

B. Literature and C. Research Tactics

Tactically, Kudless wrote a program in which a wall of a certain width grows within a given frame without crossing itself nor abutting against itself. Specifically, Kudless's "Instructions for a Walled

City" are as follows: (1) On a site of any size, create a closed wall at the site edge; (2) Gradually increase the perimeter of the wall while making sure the wall never intersects itself or the site edge; (3) Continue increasing the wall perimeter until all available land within the site is full; (4) Increase the wall thickness by some amount so that it can contain program; and (5) Divide the wall into smaller sections.[42] The result is a *drawing* but understood as one produced digitally. It has many, if not all, of the features of traditional drawing: varieties and depths of line weight, shading and so on. But, says Kudless,

> I would never have been able to draw this in any other way. It would take years to try to draw this in a digital version *or* a physical version. Or if I had to use CAD to do this. But creating an algorithm allows me to kind of understand a different conception of a city …
>
> So, some people are using robots to do drawings. Mine was plotted normally. There's nothing interesting about it from the standpoint of the physical drawing, but the entire drawing is created algorithmically so I didn't draw one thing. Everything was coded. Every tree and person … everything. I was just trying to push myself as far as I can with this … How much of a return back to hand drawing (do we need) in order to make the generative process easier for architects? … Maybe we've gone too far in privileging the digital.[43]

Kudless is referring to the participatory aspect of his own involvement in the production of this drawing. Even though the drawing is captivating, when he says that "there's nothing interesting … about the physical drawing," what he means is that the rendering seems like standard hand-drawn graphics. But *this* drawing overcomes the limitations of time (and perhaps human technique) even while the product has the appearance of a humanly crafted work. The code Kudless wrote, then, is a kind of intermediary between anonymous computing power and the human element of craft. This leads to the literature aspect of this research.

While D'Arcy Thompson's *On Growth and Form* impacted the design of the Pavilion, and the P-Wall projects drew from a variety of exemplars, the Walled City illustrates another way we can regard "literature" in creative scholarship. There is a sixth step in Kudless's "Instructions for a Walled City." Namely:

> 6) Go to www.google.com and in the search box enter the word "rooftop" followed by a space and, sequentially, each letter of the alphabet. From the list of auto-completed suggestions for each phrase, choose one phrase that suggests a possible program for the Walled City and record it. If typing only one letter after "rooftop" does not produce any interesting suggestions, type an additional letter starting from letter "a" and iterate through the alphabet again until a better suggestion appears. For this iteration of The Walled City, the following program suggestions were used: Rooftop Antenna, Rooftop Bar, Rooftop Café, Rooftop Deck, Rooftop Exhaust, Rooftop Film, Rooftop Garden… etc.[44]

Does this amount to literature? We regard it as a tactically clear engagement with external references within the guidelines of a strict protocol not only to produce a new creative work but also to exemplify a tactic for data collection in the digital age. "The Google Search Suggestions are based on commonly searched terms so the terms that come up the most frequently are literally sourced from the crowd (of every search ever made)."[45] It was a way to query the global mind's understanding of what happens on a rooftop. Often in student work, a hazard of using the internet for "literature review" is undisciplined citations from any number of non-peer-reviewed sources. Listing any URL seems to suffice. We are of course not promoting this. But this is not what Kudless does. His use of Google informs newer ways of using online resources for design scholarship.

D. Validity and Generalizability

As with the earlier examples, the internal validity of Kudless's work expresses as a coherent methodology involving both human craft and computation aligning for *generative* productions of creative objects. The logic of the processes always unfolds though the praxis, so that while they are not prescribed beforehand, the end results reflect coherent methodological approaches entailing specifiable tactics and actions. In each, the unit of test is clear, in part because of the clarity of the designed object itself but also because of the components of what constitutes each unit of test methodologically. As for independent and dependent variables, in each case the external manipulations by the researcher (the independent variables) are distinguishable from the outcomes (the dependent variables)—always with the point of creativity located at the seam between what is predictable by human planning versus what is organically unpredictable; and hence the uniqueness of the created object. As we see in this as well as Kudless's other projects for external validity, his logic for each of his projects is repeatable; they provide a pattern by which other design investigators can produce their own (distinct) works.

Conclusion

The projects summarized here highlight a trait of creative scholarship, namely, that new productions by others are not replications of the initial "experiment," as perhaps laboratory-based research demands. But new creative work based upon Kudless's methods will bear a "family resemblance" to his ideas. In this way creative scholarship might be impactful in the sense of bringing about "schools" or "lineages" of design thinking. But again, in creative scholarship, external affirmation of a designer's work is no doubt the primary sign of external validity. And we have noted above that the one trait of Kudless's works is that they are cited nationally and internationally; they result in repeat commissions for him (which speaks to *generalizability*) and are well documented by commentaries, articles and book chapters such as this one. Lastly, Elison and Eatman's points about public scholarship are germane to Kudless's work, and we suggest that creative scholarship in general provides many linkages to the public research arena.

* * * *

Discussion and Exercises

Reflections about the Chapter You Just Read:

Editors' note: In previous chapters, the first question of this section asks the reader to reflect on aspects of research in the chapter just read. Since the framework of this chapter organizes around the aspects of research for the three Kudless projects, there is no need to do that here.

1. The Introduction to this book stated that methodology is the "engine" that drives research.
   a. In this vein, discuss how the methodological framework for each of Kudless's projects—outlined in four categories related to (A) Topic, (B) Literature, (C) Research tactics and (D) Validity and Generalizability—*drove* his creative research.
   b. Relatedly, discuss how *theory* informed methodology in Kudless's thinking and actions for each project.
2. In your own words, describe how *each* of Kudless's three projects exemplifies:
   a. an organic performance
   b. computation understood as a craft
   c. "drawing" in a digital age
3. Recount how each of Kudless's three projects required human, as opposed to computerized, actions. Be specific in itemizing these for each project.

Exercises/Suggestions for Further Study

1. For each of Kudless's projects, some external input stirred his creative design research: the organicism of plants, a sculpture outside of a building, a charged political term ("wall"). Consider *your* most recent design project. What external input inspired you to give form to your design? Are you able to trace the impact of this external input throughout the design decisions you made for your project? Having read this chapter, think of ways you can use external points of inspiration to motivate your next design project. Be specific with regard to theory and method.
2. What designers act as *exemplars* from which you take inspiration?
   a. Identify who these people are.
   b. State specifically how their works, or other aspects of their life and times, inform your design thinking.
   c. To help you think through 2(b) above, the chapter said this about exemplars: "A characteristic of all prominent designers is that they know a vast amount of 'literature' related to their designs: in terms of history; in terms of theory; in terms of exemplars; in terms of current affairs; in terms of relevant and emerging materials and construction techniques."
3. In order to populate his Walled City, Kudless used a Google search technique to populate the project. Use the same Google search technique Kudless used in step 6 of his Walled City project (outlined on page 246) to generate 20 initial programming ideas for your current (or next) design project.

Additional Connections and Information

1. References for creative scholarship:

Chu, Karl. "Metaphysics of Genetic Architecture and Computation." *Perspecta* 35 (2004): 74–97.

Dollens, Dennis. "Architecture as Nature: A Biodigital Hypothesis." *Leonardo* 42, no. 5 (2009): 412–420.

Preston, Julieanna. "Elocutions, Elaborations, and Expositions of Interior Design Creative Scholarship." *Journal of Interior Design* 43, no. 1 (2018): 5–8.

Schumacher, Patrik. "Design Parameters to Parametric Design." In Mitra Kanaani and Dak Kopec, editors, *The Routledge Companion for Architecture Design and Practice* (Routledge, 2016), 3–20.

Vriesendorp, Madelon, Matthew Austin, Gavin Perin, et al. "Augmentations." In Laura Allen and Luke Caspar Pearson, editors, *Drawing Futures: Speculations in Contemporary Drawing for Art and Architecture* (UCL Press, 2016), 1–68.

2. References for public scholarship:

Ellison, Julie and Timothy K. Eatman, Scholarship in Public: Knowledge Creation and Tenure Policy in the Engaged University (Syracuse, NY: Imagining America, 2008).

Kotsiopulos, Antigone and Craig Birdsong, "The Citation Gap: Documenting Creative Scholarship" (Focus Report) Journal of Interior Design 26, no. 1 (2000): 48–55.

Pable, Jill. "Interior Design Identity in the Crossfire: A Call for Renewed Balance in Subjective and Objective Ways of Knowing," (Perspective) Journal of Interior Design 34, no. 2 (2009): v–xx.

Pedersen, Elaine L., and Kathryn L. Burton, "A Concept Analysis of Creativity: Uses of Creativity in Selected Design Journals." Journal of Interior Design 35, no. 1 (2009): 15–32.

3. Indeed, designers (and their works) can be part of "the literature" in creative scholarship. But this still requires concerted work in standard literature review. In traditional research (and we maintain this is required for good creative scholarship as well):

    a. A *literature review* usually means that part of a research document in which a researcher summarizes the key sources that informed his or her thinking. To keep track of the (usually) voluminous literature that informs any robust research project, and more importantly to *process* that information for relevance, the researcher maintains throughout his or her research.

    b. An *annotated bibliography*. This is a document that itemizes, in alphabetical order by authors' last names, all of the references that informed the researcher for his or her project. So, the annotated bibliography usually enumerates more references (sometimes much more) than what actually appears in a published literature review. In other words, while the literature review is for the benefit of the reader, the annotated bibliography is an overall summary by the researcher of all the works that impacted the research in some way. Refer also to comments about annotated bibliography on page 167 at the end of Chapter 8.

Notes

1 Tommy Kuhl and Jon Meyer, "Andrew Kudless: P-Wall" https://modularvariations.files.wordpress.com/2013/02/andrew-kudless-p-wall.pdf. Accessed August 14, 2019

2 David Wang's interview with Andrew Kudless at the California College of the Arts, Oakland, California, December 7–8, 2018.

3 Interview, Ibid.

4 David Pye, *The Nature and Art of Workmanship* (New York: Bloomsbury Publishing, 1995): 20.

5 Interview, op. cit.

6 Andrew Kudless, "Recent Work" (Lecture), Graduate Research and Innovative Design Association, Stuckeman School, Department of Architecture, Penn State University, April 19, 2018.

7 For example, Aristotle once said that if nature can produce a house, it would produce it in the way that art would. *Physics* 199a 12–19.

8 Interview, op. cit.

9 Interview, ibid.

10 Interview, ibid.
11 D'Arcy Wentworth Thompson, *On Growth and Form* (New York: Cambridge University Press, 1961), 11. Note this is from the 1961 edition.
12 Matsys, "Confluence Park," https://www.matsys.design/confluence-park, 2018. Accessed August 15, 2019.
13 "One small (4'×8'×4') and one very large (70'×20'×8')". Kudless email to editors, October 30, 2019.
14 Ibid.
15 Interview, op. cit.
16 Joseph A. Maxwell, *Qualitative Research Design* (Thousand Oaks, CA: Sage, 2005), 65–67. This point is noted in Groat and Wang, op. cit., 145.
17 Linda Groat and David Wang, *Architectural Research Methods* (John Wiley & Sons, 2013), 148. The title is from Cherie Peacock, Master of Science in Architecture Thesis, Washington State University, 2005.
18 Interview, op. cit.
19 Frank Morgan, "Can Math Survive Without the Bees?" *Huffington Post*, December 6, 2017. https://www.huffpost.com/entry/bees-honeycomb-mathematics_b_1318258. Accessed August 28, 2019. Note: Cairo tiling characterizes street paving in some parts of that city.
20 For an overall framework for how design can be seen through the lens of research, see David Wang, "A Continuum of Measures of Validity for Research in the Making Fields." *FormAkademisk*. 11, no. 1 (2018): Art.1, 1–17. https://pdfs.semanticscholar.org/1698/1b3603d94a1173f7ce6c11d0235611b11878.pdf. Accessed September 3, 2019. This article provides a chart for assessing research validity for creative projects. The chart takes standard measures of validity in experimental research—unit of test, cause/prediction, independent and dependent variables, and control—and "extrude" them across a continuum that embraces design practice and making.
21 Sharon Hays, "Structure and Agency and the Sticky Problem of Culture," *Sociological Theory* 12, no. 1 (1994): 57–72.
22 Andrew Kudless, "Bodies of Formation" (Lecture), University of Virginia School of Architecture. Published September 27, 2017. https://www.youtube.com/watch?v=PGE87Jt7qTc. Accessed September 12, 2019.
23 Interview, op. cit.
24 Interview, ibid.
25 After Kudless moved to San Francisco in 2007, it was purchased by a collector and installed in a private home in San Francisco.
26 This later wall had to be adjusted for height restrictions, so in this sense it is in effect another wall.
27 Interview, op. cit.
28 Donald Schon, *The Reflective Practitioner: How Professionals Think in Action* (New York: Basic Books, 1983)
29 University of Virginia lecture, op. cit.
30 Interview, op. cit.
31 Interview, ibid.
32 Julie Ellison and Timothy K. Eatman, *Scholarship in Public: Knowledge Creation and Tenure Policy in the Engaged University* (Syracuse, NY: Imagining America, 2008). The citation if from Judith Ramaley, President if Winona College.
33 Interview, op. cit.
34 Interview, ibid.
35 Between January 2017 and March, 2018, the following venues hosted the first Volume: California College of the Arts, the WUHO Gallery in Los Angeles, the Banvard Gallery at Ohio State's Knowlton School of Architecture, and at the Taubman College of Architecture and Urban Planning at the University of Michigan. Exhibitions of the second volume have been held at the Arthur A. Houghton, Jr. Gallery at Cooper Union, the University of Virginia School of Architecture, and will be held at the University of Miami (Florida) School of Architecture and the California School of the Arts.
36 Clifford Geertz, *The Interpretation of Cultures* (New York: Basic Books, 1973).
37 "Crowdsourcing," Merriam Webster Dictionary. https://www.merriam-webster.com/dictionary/crowdsourcing. Accessed September 22, 2019.
38 G.P. Pisano and R. Verganti, "What Kind of Collaboration is Right for You?" *Harvard Business Review*. December 2008 issue. https://hbr.org/2008/12/which-kind-of-collaboration-is-right-for-you. Accessed September 23, 2019.
39 EXHIBITION: Drawing Codes. Andrew Kudless and Adam Marcus, curators. California College of the Arts. http://digitalcraft.cca.edu/research/drawing-codes. Accessed September 22, 2019.
40 Interview, ibid.
41 Interview, op. cit.
42 The Walled City (10-Mile Version). Matsys, 2017. https://www.matsys.design/the-walled-city-10-mile-version. Accessed September 23, 2019.
43 Interview, op. cit.
44 Ibid.
45 Email correspondence between the editors and Kudless on October 31, 2019.

Credits

Book Cover: Design by Lois Corey. Used with permission. Photo by Rebecca Hermance.

3.1 Box 226, Folder 15, Visiting Nurse Service of New York Records. Archives and Special Collections at the Augustus C. Long Health Sciences Library of Columbia University. Permission Visiting Nurse Service of New York.

3.2 Box 230, Folder 25, Visiting Nurse Service of New York Records. Archives and Special Collections at the Augustus C. Long Health Sciences Library of Columbia University. Photo courtesy the Visiting Nurse Service of New York.

3.3 Box 227, Folder 19, Visiting Nurse Service of New York Records. Archives and Special Collections at the Augustus C. Long Health Sciences Library at Columbia University. Photo courtesy the Visiting Nurse Service of New York.

3.4 Box 227, Folder 22, Visiting Nurse Service of New York Records. Archives and Special Collections at the Augustus C. Long Health Sciences Library of Columbia University. Photo courtesy the Visiting Nurse Service of New York.

3.5 Box 20, Folder 25, Visiting Nurse Service of New York Records. Archives and Special Collections at the Augustus C. Long Health Sciences Library of Columbia University. Photo courtesy the Visiting Nurse Service of New York.

4.11 https://www.nps.gov/tps/standards/treatment-guidelines-2017.pdf accessed 11/12/18. Anne E. Grimmer, *The Secretary of the Interior's Standards for the Treatment of Historic Properties with Guidelines for Preserving, Rehabilitating, Restoring and Reconstructing Historic Buildings*. Washington DC: US Department of the Interior National Park Service Technical Preservation Services: 1995 (revised 2017). Public domain.

6.2 https://commons.wikimedia.org/w/index.php?search=robie+house+floor+plan&title=Special%3ASearch&go=Go&ns0=1&ns6=1&ns12=1&ns14=1&ns100=1&ns106=1#/media/File:Frederick_C._Robie_House, _5757_Woodlawn_Avenue, _Chicago, _Cook_County, _IL_HABS_ILL, 16-CHIG, 33-_(sheet_1_of_10).tif "This image or media file contains material based on a work of a National Park Service employee, created as part of that person's official duties. As a work of the U.S. federal government, such work is in the public domain in the United States."

6.5 https://commons.wikimedia.org/wiki/File:Par_05.jpg
"This work is in the public domain in its country of origin and other countries and areas where the copyright term is the author's life plus 70 years or fewer."

6.6 Permission of Nicole Clements

6.9 https://commons.wikimedia.org/wiki/File:19th_century_Victorian_living_room, _Auckland_-_0816.jpg. Jorge Royan / http://www.royan.com.ar / CC BY-SA 3.0

6.10 https://commons.wikimedia.org/wiki/File:The_Ladies%27_home_journal_(1948)_(14766257224).jpg
This image was taken from Flickr's The Commons. "The copyright is in the public domain because it has expired"

6.11 https://commons.wikimedia.org/wiki/File:William_Holman_Hunt_-_The_Awakening_Conscience_-_Google_Art_Project.jpg
"This work is in the public domain in its country of origin and other countries and areas where the copyright term is the author's life plus 100 years or fewer."

6.12 https://commons.wikimedia.org/wiki/File:CENTRAL_BATHROOM_ON_SECOND_FLOOR_-_Chateau-sur-Mer, _Bellevue_Avenue, _Newport, _Newport_County, _RI_HABS_RI, 3-NEWP, 59-32.tif
"This image or media file contains material based on a work of a National Park Service employee, created as part of that person's official duties. As a work of the U.S. federal government, such work is in the public domain in the United States. See the NPS website and NPS copyright policy for more information."

7.4 Photo by J Brew (originally posted to Flickr as Almost to West Bar) [CC BY-SA 2.0 http://creativecommons.org/licenses/by-sa/2.0)], via Wikimedia Creative Commons http://commons.wikimedia.org/wiki/File:Desert_like_conditions_of_Eastern_Washington.jpg

7.5 Public Domain, USGov-DOE (work of the U.S. federal government) - Image #N1D0060216 at http://www5.hanford.gov/ddrs/index.cfm.

7.6 Permission of East Benton County Historical Society. Wells, Jeremy. "Architectural History: Richland, Washington Government Letter-Houses." East Benton County Historical Society. n.d. http://www.ebchs.org/.

7.7 Ryan Adams / CC BY-SA (https://creativecommons.org/licenses/by-sa/3.0), Wikimedia Commons. https://commons.wikimedia.org/wiki/File:Exterior_of_B_Reactor.JPG

7.9 Permission of East Benton County Historical Society.

7.10 Permission City of Richland. https://www.ci.richland.wa.us/

7.11 Permission City of Richland. https://www.ci.richland.wa.us/

8.3 Photos by the author. Reprinted with permission from Wiley and the Interior Design Educators Council. From Jill Pable, "The Homeless Shelter Family Experience: Examining the Influence of Physical Living Conditions on Perceptions of Internal Control, Crowding, Privacy, and Related Issues," *Journal of Interior Design*.

8.6 Photo by the author. Reprinted with permission from the Interior Design Educators Council.

8.7 Photo by the author. Reprinted with permission from the Interior Design Educators Council.

8.9 Photo by the author. Reprinted with permission from Design Resources for Homelessness, designresourcesforhomelessness.org.

9.4 Permission by Taylor and Francis Group. "Permission is granted for non-exclusive one-time world English language rights print and eBook usage only, permission must be sought for any further use."

10.2 https://commons.wikimedia.org/wiki/File:Instagram_promotional_sign, _Station_Groningen_(2019)_01.jpg#p-search
Photo by Donald Trung Quoc Don, Wikimedia Commons - © CC BY-SA 4.0 International.
"This file is licensed under the Creative Commons Attribution-Share Alike 4.0 International license."

10.5 https://commons.wikimedia.org/wiki/File:Social_Media_Marketing_Strategy.jpg#p-search
This file is licensed under the Creative Commons Attribution-Share Alike 4.0 International"

12.3 https://commons.wikimedia.org/wiki/File:1-uniform_9_dual.svg
This file is licensed under the Creative Commons Attribution-Share Alike 4.0 International license.

12.8 Permission by Amy Campos.
http://digitalcraft.cca.edu/research/drawing-codes#vol1

12.9 Permission by Nicholas de Monchaux
http://digitalcraft.cca.edu/research/drawing-codes#vol2

NOTE All other images in Chapter 12 are by permission of Andrew Kudless.

Index

Note: Page numbers followed by "n" denote endnotes.